P9-BXX-874

Also by Aram Goudsouzian

King of the Court: Bill Russell and the Basketball Revolution

Sidney Poitier: Man, Actor, Icon

The Hurricane of 1938

DOWN

◆ TO THE ◆

CROSSROADS

DOWN

◆ TO THE ◆

CROSSROADS

CIVIL RIGHTS, BLACK POWER,
AND THE MEREDITH MARCH
AGAINST FEAR

ARAM GOUDSOUZIAN

FARRAR, STRAUS AND GIROUX ◆ NEW YORK

Farrar, Straus and Giroux
18 West 18th Street, New York 10011

Copyright © 2014 by Aram Goudsouzian
Map copyright © 2014 by Jeffrey L. Ward
All rights reserved
Printed in the United States of America
First edition, 2014

Library of Congress Cataloging-in-Publication Data
Goudsouzian, Aram.
    Down to the crossroads : civil rights, Black power, and the Meredith
march against fear / Aram Goudsouzian.
        pages   cm
    Includes bibliographical references and index.
    ISBN 978-0-374-19220-4 (hardback) — ISBN 978-0-374-71076-7 (ebook)
    1. Meredith, James, 1933–   2. Civil rights demonstrations—Mississippi—
History—20th century.   3. Voter registration—Mississippi—History—
20th century.   4. Racism—Mississippi—History—20th century.
5. African American civil rights workers—Mississippi—Biography.
6. Civil rights workers—Mississippi—Biography.   7. African American
college students—Mississippi—Biography.   8. African Americans—Civil
rights—Mississippi—History—20th century.   9. Black power—Mississippi—
History—20th century.   10. Mississippi—Race relations—History—
20th century.   I. Title.

E185.93.M6 G68 2014
323.1196'07307620904—dc23

                                                         2013033911

Designed by Abby Kagan

Farrar, Straus and Giroux books may be purchased for educational, business, or
promotional use. For information on bulk purchases, please contact the Macmillan
Corporate and Premium Sales Department at 1-800-221-7945, extension 5442, or write to
specialmarkets@macmillan.com.

www.fsgbooks.com
www.twitter.com/fsgbooks • www.facebook.com/fsgbooks

1   3   5   7   9   10   8   6   4   2

FOR CHRYSTAL

CONTENTS

TENNESSEE

Memphis
Florence

Hernando
Coldwater
Senatobia
Como
Sardis
Oxford
Pope
Batesville
Tupelo
Enid
Charleston
Oakland

ARKANSAS

Mississippi River

Cleveland
Holcomb
Grenada

Itta Bena
Indianola
Greenwood
Winona
Columbus
Greenville
Belzoni
Lexington
Tuscaloosa

Louise
Kosciusko
Benton
Yazoo City
Philadelphia
ALABAMA
Canton
Tougaloo
Meridian
Vicksburg
Jackson

MISSISSIPPI

THE MEREDITH
MARCH AGAINST FEAR

JUNE 1966

Fayette

Natchez

0   Miles   100
0   Kilometers   100

McComb

LOUISIANA

Mobile

Baton Rouge

Biloxi

Mississippi River

Gulf of Mexico

© 2014 Jeffrey L. Ward
New Orleans

DOWN

◆ TO THE ◆

CROSSROADS

PROLOGUE: A NEW DAY
Washington, D.C.
JUNE 1–2, 1966

Roy Wilkins was in his element. At the beginning of June 1966, 2,400 delegates gathered at the Sheraton Park Hotel in Washington, D.C., to attend the White House Conference on Civil Rights. Called "To Fulfill These Rights," the conference brought together representatives of business, government, education, labor, foundations, churches, and the civil rights movement to consider ambitious proposals to promote racial equality.

As executive director of the NAACP, Wilkins appreciated the opportunity to build alliances with influential power brokers. Soft-spoken, confident, patient, and practical, he had won friends at the highest levels. Just weeks before the conference, presidential aide Harry McPherson wrote to Lyndon Johnson that "if ever a man deserved the Medal of Freedom, it is Roy Wilkins." His lobbying had helped pass the Civil Rights Act of 1964 and the Voting Rights Act of 1965, which together promised to end racial segregation and ensure black political participation, ushering in a new age of genuine citizenship.[1]

Wilkins now sought to capitalize on the White House conference's atmosphere of goodwill. President Johnson had already presented to Congress the Civil Rights Bill of 1966, which included provisions for protecting civil rights workers, speeding school integration, and removing discrimination in jury selection and housing. Wilkins helped lead the charge for this bill. Through the conference's planning council, moreover, he was now proposing a massive federal investment in Black America— color-conscious programs for jobs, education, housing, and law enforcement that might cost $100 billion.[2]

After two days of panels and speeches, Wilkins delivered the conference's closing remarks. He spoke at a moment when the civil rights movement was already transforming the nation: the caste system of the South had begun to crumble, and many African Americans were expressing new pride and experiencing new possibilities. Yet the past year had also witnessed a destructive race riot in the Los Angeles district of Watts, which reflected an emerging hopelessness and hostility. Some civil rights leaders were slamming the federal government for its inattention, even as others aired concerns about an emerging white backlash. Wilkins still believed in pursuing remedial legislation, crafted through patient lobbying and moral suasion.[3]

"It has been held in some quarters that conferences such as this are nothing but talk," he asserted. Yes, the conference *was* a lot of talking. "But so, too, was the Sermon on the Mount . . . So were the Lincoln-Douglas debates." What were the Hebrew Lamentations, asked Wilkins, if not pleas of hope? "What, indeed, were the spirituals of the slaves of our own South but talk set to the chants for a new day of freedom and dignity?"[4]

Floyd McKissick was stirring up trouble. The new national director of the Congress of Racial Equality (CORE) led an organization with a base in northern cities. Its increasingly black membership was frustrated with the persistent poverty of the inner city. It resented the White House, which seemed more concerned with appeasing southern politicians and fighting the Vietnam War than with fostering genuine racial equality. Upon arrival in Washington, D.C., McKissick announced to reporters: "There's a prevailing sentiment that the conference has been rigged by the Administration."[5]

The conference's planning council had organized each session to feature presentations by experts, followed by audience discussion. But delegates could not vote on any resolutions. When McKissick objected that the White House was manufacturing fake consensus, conference chairman Ben Heineman, a Chicago railroad executive, invited him to a late-night policy meeting, and they crafted a last-minute compromise that allowed votes on resolutions at the final meetings of the two-day conference. McKissick then submitted a resolution for the United States "to make equal opportunities for its minority citizens the No. 1 priority" and to "cease its involvement in Vietnam."[6]

President Johnson's forces mobilized against the resolution. Whitney Young, executive director of the National Urban League and a close ally of Roy Wilkins, dismissed the relevance of the Vietnam War to the battle against black poverty. "I don't want to put that albatross around the civil rights movement," said Howard University president James Nabrit. Arthur Goldberg, the ambassador to the United Nations, toured various sessions and lobbied against the resolution. Delegates either voted it down or ruled it out of order.[7]

By defeating McKissick's militant challenge, the Johnson administration preserved the conference's image of unity. But that consensus came at a price. Many of the grass-roots activists who served as delegates grumbled about the conference's elitist approach, and they blamed the federal government for its gradualism. Outside the Sheraton Park Hotel, picketers led by Harlem activist Jesse Gray chanted, "Uncle Tom go home!" and "Watts—yes, Johnson—no!"[8]

Stokely Carmichael was nowhere in sight. The Student Nonviolent Coordinating Committee (SNCC) was boycotting "To Fulfill These Rights." In its official statement, SNCC called the White House conference "absolutely unnecessary." The organization objected that the federal government blamed black people for their own oppression, ignored the abuses of racist state and local officials, and exploited people of color throughout the world, as evidenced by the war in Vietnam. The president, moreover, bore no commitment to ensuring the rights of black citizens. SNCC stated that it "rejects its invitation to participate in this useless endeavor."[9]

SNCC's boycott elicited angst among liberals. "The SNCC leaders who are advocating this hostile, Negroes-must-go-it-alone program are doing more talking than thinking," wrote columnist Carl Rowan. The press characterized the stance as one of hostility, despair, futility, extremism, and "racism in reverse." An editorial in *The Atlanta Constitution* tut-tutted that "SNCC has finally done for itself what the White Citizens Councils tried and failed to do. It has isolated itself and abandoned the civil rights movement."[10]

Carmichael personified the movement's emerging militancy. A few weeks earlier, he had won a controversial election to become SNCC chairman. When he defeated the incumbent John Lewis, the media portrayed

it as a coup. The tall, slim, and charismatic Carmichael—fresh off organizing an all-black third party in Lowndes County, Alabama—started
to articulate SNCC's evolving emphasis on independent politics, black
pride, and global human rights. He countered the dominant perception
that blacks sought to fold into predominantly white institutions. He
insisted that, in fact, black people wanted to lift themselves up, to elect
leaders who served them, to win power. "Integration," said Carmichael,
"is irrelevant."[11]

Martin Luther King, Jr., was moping. The leader of the Southern Christian Leadership Conference (SCLC) spent the second day of the White
House conference in his hotel room, away from delegates and reporters.
The Washington Post noted that he was "conspicuously missing" from
the photograph sessions that morning. Citing illness, he also planned
to skip the closing dinner. He ultimately attended it, but only because
conference organizers outmaneuvered him by asking his wife, Coretta,
to sing the national anthem.[12]

Militants had grown frustrated with King's abiding principles of nonviolence and integration, as well as his continued willingness to work
with the federal government. The previous day, the picketers outside the
Sheraton Park Hotel had jeered King as "Black Jesus."[13]

Yet King was out of favor with the Johnson administration. While
Thurgood Marshall and Roy Wilkins delivered the prestigious banquet
speeches, King spoke briefly at just one daytime session. The Vietnam
War, especially, was carving a rift between him and the White House.
During a recent appearance on *Face the Nation*, King had urged the
United States to cease bombing North Vietnam and pursue peace negotiations. At a subsequent press conference in Chicago, he and the pacifist monk Thich Nhat Hanh called for internationally supervised free
elections in Vietnam.[14]

King was still the great personal force within the civil rights movement: revered by many African Americans, admired by liberals, detested
by conservatives. Even if he had lost some moral sway over the public,
his words inspired people, and his presence almost inevitably compelled
attention from civil rights advocates, the media, and law enforcement.
Yet he spent the conference in a state of limbo, stuck between the radicals and the establishment. He kept a low profile, avoiding the Vietnam

issue out of political consideration—he, too, wanted more laws and pro-grams to promote racial equality.[15]

It particularly galled King that Thurgood Marshall's conference speech ignored the role of mass protest in the civil rights movement. The solici-tor general of the United States boiled African American progress down to court challenges and new laws. But King had learned lessons from the Montgomery Bus Boycott of 1955–56, from the Birmingham Campaign of 1963, from the Selma-to-Montgomery march of 1965. Again and again, he had led nonviolent protesters in public demonstrations. They had faced the brutality of racists. They had stimulated the conscience of the nation. They had exerted pressure upon the federal government. For King, civil rights laws resulted from demonstrators laying their bodies on the line, sacrificing body and soul, rising to a higher moral plane. They had to compel the nation and inspire themselves. Meaningful change arrived only after the impassioned sermons, the beautiful free-dom songs, and the steady drumbeat of marching feet.[16]

James Meredith was holding a press conference. He had burst into the national consciousness in 1962, when his enrollment at the University of Mississippi spawned a political crisis and bloody riots. But now, in the elaborate press room in the basement of the Sheraton Park Hotel, few paid him much attention. When Roy Wilkins and Senator Edward Kennedy swept by, reporters gravitated to them. Only a handful of jour-nalists heard Meredith discuss his unusual plan: on Sunday, June 5, he would start walking from Memphis, Tennessee, to Jackson, Mississippi.[17]

Meredith had first announced his intentions just before "To Fulfill These Rights." He identified two main goals. First, he would "challenge that all pervasive fear that dominates the day to day life of the Negro in the United States, especially in the South, and particularly in Missis-sippi." Second, he would "encourage the 450,000 unregistered Negroes in Mississippi to go to the polls and register."[18]

It was not a typical civil rights march. "*I* plan to go by myself," said Meredith, "but of course a number of people have gotten in touch with me and indicated they wanted to go along." He allowed others to join him, but only if they were independent men. He refused to lead a mass march that imposed upon local people for food and shelter. If men wanted to participate, they should organize into groups of three to five, and each group should maintain an automobile. "Absolutely NO WOMEN OR CHILDREN should be allowed," he added. "I am sick and tired of Negro Men hiding behind their women and children."[19]

Amid the scale, order, and polish of the White House conference, Meredith's quixotic walk seemed like a bizarre afterthought. He was both courageous and strange. White supremacists despised him for the integration of the University of Mississippi, yet he had not requested aid from the federal government or any civil rights organization. One wise guy tacked a sign on a bulletin board advertising a march sponsored by "The World Committee for the Preservation of James Meredith."[20]

When quizzed on the subject, Attorney General Nicholas Katzenbach assured reporters that Justice Department officials would monitor the walk from Memphis to Jackson. But he was not particularly concerned about it. "I don't think it's going to amount to much," he said.[21]

1

THE BIBLE AND THE GUN
Memphis to Hernando
JUNE 5–6, 1966

It is sometimes said that the Mississippi Delta begins in the lobby of the Peabody Hotel in Memphis, Tennessee. For generations, the rich whites who owned the dark soil straddled by the Mississippi and Yazoo Rivers came to Memphis, twelve miles north of the state border. Here men traded cotton, secured loans, and indulged in sumptuous feasts, high-stakes poker, and fleshly pleasures. Their wives visited department stores and beauty parlors, and their children caught trains to boarding schools and elite colleges. The hub of this social world was the Peabody lobby, with its elegant splendors: stately columns, a lavish mezzanine, ornate moldings on the ceiling. In the center stood a travertine marble fountain, holding a classical sculpture festooned with flowers. Ducks waddled in the fountain pool. The hotel epitomized a particular kind of southern grace, the kind that excluded someone like James Meredith.[1]

At 1:45 p.m. on Sunday, June 5, Meredith stood outside the hotel, ready to launch what he called his "second assault on Mississippi." He was a small, slightly built black man with a thin mustache. He wore a short-sleeved checkered shirt, sunglasses, and a yellow pith helmet. In one hand he brandished an ebony walking stick with an ivory head, a gift from an African village chief. In the other he held a Bible.[2]

His walk was scheduled to begin at two o'clock, but his publicity man Sherwood Ross figured that whoever was coming was already there. So Meredith started walking. Four people accompanied him. Two were black, the New York record executive Claude Sterrett and the Memphis businessman Joseph Crittenden. The two whites were Ross and a minister from New York, Robert Weeks. It was an unusual spectacle. A few television cameras recorded footage. *The New York Times* and major wire services sent reporters, but *The Commercial Appeal* of Memphis did not. A handful of whites watched with curiosity. At first, a man behind them waved a small Confederate flag, but after two policemen requested that he desist, he left.[3]

Meredith led his cadre across Beale Street, the heart of Memphis blues, where Delta migrants such as Robert Johnson, B.B. King, and Howlin' Wolf had strummed and picked and moaned and wailed. Proving Ross wrong, some members of the Memphis NAACP arrived just after the marchers left the Peabody, including Maxine and Vasco Smith, the branch's executive director and vice president. They soon caught up to Meredith. As they weaved through the densely packed black neighborhoods south of Beale, some women and children walked alongside them, enjoying the hullabaloo. Others spilled onto porches and sidewalks, extending good wishes.[4]

Meredith puzzled Weeks. Meredith dodged deep questions by steering conversations toward trivialities, yet he possessed a spiritual calm. Weeks likened him to Joan of Arc, "a militaristic mystic." He seemed unfazed by any harassment—when reporters mentioned the man waving the Confederate flag, he just praised General Stonewall Jackson. It bothered him more that only women and children had joined the walk through Memphis. "Negro men are afraid to be men down here," he grumbled.[5]

As they walked through South Memphis, they crossed neighborhoods where much of the city's black population was concentrated. They passed near Stax Records, where Otis Redding and Rufus Thomas were popularizing the funky, soulful, modern Memphis sound. By late afternoon, about eight miles south of downtown in rural Whitehaven, they walked past a white colonial mansion, set back about a hundred yards from Highway 51, bounded by fourteen rural acres. It was Graceland, the home of Elvis Presley.[6]

As the surroundings got rural, the mood got hostile. Whites drove up and down the highway, snapping photos and yelling insults. Cars whizzed so close to the marchers that the wind whipped their pant legs. "Hurry up, nigger, you're gonna get killed in Mississippi," jeered one man. Weeks's clerical collar branded him a special race traitor. "Hey preacher!" said an old man, leaning out of his car, his face promising violent mischief. "Where are you staying tonight?" Other hecklers waved Confederate battle flags, and in the early evening, two men rode back and forth on horseback, wearing ten-gallon hats and wielding massive flags, whooping the rebel yell.[7]

A little after 6:30, Meredith's party stopped a quarter mile north of the state line. About thirty cars filled with whites had gathered to block them, but Tennessee state policemen dispersed the troublemakers before the marchers arrived. Anyway, Meredith had decided that Mississippi could wait until the next morning. Before catching a ride back to Memphis, he shrugged off the possibility of danger. He had seen worse.[8]

Ross, by contrast, had never tasted such venom. As a radio reporter, he had covered civil rights stories in northern cities, but nothing prepared him for the anger, and even distress, of their detractors along Highway 51. These young whites, he surmised, viewed Meredith as the symbol of a changing order, one that weakened their own status. He feared what would happen in Mississippi, the most notoriously racist state in the Union. They needed federal men, he figured. Ross called Whitney Young, the executive director of the National Urban League.

"Get us some protection, please," he urged. "We're going to get shot tomorrow."[9]

James Meredith had long considered himself the sole architect of his special destiny. When he was about seven years old, he accompanied his father, Moses "Cap" Meredith, to the home of a white farmer. Cap owned cows that had been grazing on the farmer's property, and he needed to pay the white man. He called out his presence from the front walkway. After a long, long silence, the white man told Cap to go to the back porch, per racial custom. But Cap refused to budge. For three hours, he sat on his mule wagon. He would not even let his squirming son urinate in the woods. Finally, the white man walked outside to conduct their business. The child learned his first lesson about manhood.[10]

Christened J.H. and known as "J," the oldest son of Cap and Roxie Meredith was born during the Great Depression in the hardscrabble Hill Country of central Mississippi, surrounded by the institutions and customs of white supremacy. But his parents provided a model of conservative self-reliance. Cap had registered to vote in 1919, and his family owned an eighty-four-acre farm north of Kosciusko, the seat of Attala County.

The children chopped cotton and slopped hogs. They learned to save money, study hard, and avoid kowtowing to whites. Whenever possible, Cap kept them on his property, away from white people's homes.[11]

From a young age, "J" saw himself as set apart, special. His family claimed ancestors that included a white chief justice of Mississippi and the leader of the Choctaw Nation—a multicultural heritage of elites that separated them from the bulk of Attala County blacks, who lived in shotgun shacks and obeyed codes of white dominance. Abiding by the ideals of frugality, order, education, and respectability, Meredith developed faith in his own potential. For his senior year of high school, he lived with an uncle in St. Petersburg, Florida. He won an essay contest sponsored by the American Legion on the subject "Why I Am Proud to Be an American."[12]

In 1951 he enlisted in the United States Air Force under the name James Howard Meredith. The military reinforced his respect for personal discipline and chain-of-command leadership. In 1957 the air force stationed him in Japan. Living without America's racial baggage was liberating—but also frustrating. He yearned to fight Jim Crow, but he could not do so while in the military. Those limits exacerbated his tendency to boil over with nervous tension, to explode with emotional exhaustion. "Patient is extremely concerned with racial problems, and his symptoms are intensified whenever there is heightened tempo in the racial problems in the United States and Africa," noted a military psychiatrist. "He loses his temper at times over minor incidents both at home and elsewhere."[13]

Meredith returned to Mississippi in 1960. While continuing his education at all-black Jackson State College, he applied for transfer to the all-white University of Mississippi, known to all as Ole Miss. It took a federal court case, elaborate negotiations between Governor Ross Barnett and Attorney General Robert F. Kennedy, multiple attempts to register for classes, the enlistment of U.S. marshals, and the activation of the National Guard, but Meredith finally enrolled at Ole Miss. When he arrived on campus, an angry horde tossed bottles, bricks, and Molotov cocktails while laying siege to the marshals. Two innocent onlookers died during the chaos. On the morning of October 1, 1962, Meredith awoke to attend his first class. He saw ravaged grounds and smelled tear gas. Because of his single-minded resolve, the federal government had enforced his constitutional right to attend the university of his choice.[14]

The crisis turned Meredith into a civil rights hero. Stoic and coura-geous, he projected the image of a loyal American citizen seeking educational opportunity. Throughout the academic year, marshals and soldiers monitored him as he encountered racist slurs, cruel pranks, hate mail, and social isolation. He refused to be a passive victim: he criticized the segregation of army units during the riot, threatened to leave the university unless conditions improved, and dismissed concerns about his personal safety. "It was an ordeal that tested not only his moral char-acter, but his mental fiber as well," lauded *The Chicago Defender* upon his August 1963 graduation. "American education, in all its turbulent history, has not had a comparable stalwart example."[15]

The Ole Miss crisis served as a flashpoint for the civil rights move-ment, dramatizing racial injustice to the entire world, just like the stu-dent sit-ins of 1960 and the Freedom Rides of 1961. But Meredith felt alienated from political organizations. He rejected any place within a mass movement. The trials of Ole Miss had scarred him—he was more of a loner than ever before. Yet the ordeal also deepened his faith in his own singular mission.

His independent streak ruffled the feathers of the black establish-ment. At the annual NAACP convention in July 1963, Meredith dispar-aged the upcoming March on Washington, complaining to a banquet room of youth leaders about "the very low quality of leadership present among our young Negroes, and the childish nature of their activities." He also called them "burrheads." In response, delegates cheered a speech that rebuked him, while black leaders and columnists ripped him. The backlash sparked Meredith's unpredictable temper. "My makeup cannot endure this kind of intolerance," he seethed, shedding tears of rage and shame.[16]

Meredith also criticized nonviolence, the movement's preeminent (and media-friendly) tactic. He disparaged the 1963 Birmingham Cam-paign, which exposed black women and children to snapping police dogs, crushing blasts from fire hoses, and violent police officers. Meredith's father had slept near a loaded shotgun. Meredith himself had served nine years in the military. Nonviolence, in his mind, crippled black manhood. A man possessed basic rights, including the right to defend himself.[17]

Yet Meredith longed for influence within the civil rights movement. In 1964 he wrote to Martin Luther King, chastising him for never returning his phone calls or letters. "I have a great need to know what is going on that will have a future bearing on my people," wrote Meredith. "I think I should know what is going on behind the scenes as well as what is going on publicly."[18]

After Ole Miss, he established the James Meredith Educational Fund for scholarship and job placement programs, but soon dropped the effort. He moved to Washington, D.C., and considered running for Congress, but in the summer of 1964 he accepted a three-year postgraduate fellowship from the University of Ibadan. He moved to Nigeria because he saw connections between the plights of black Americans and black Africans, but also because he was dissatisfied with the civil rights leadership. "It was really simply a question of whether I should destroy certain elements of our struggle, or to give it time to let it destroy itself," he reflected.[19]

Although Meredith enjoyed traveling with his wife and young son through Africa, Europe, and the Middle East, he also complained that Nigerian officials ignored his presence and delayed his funding. Within a year he abandoned his fellowship. His prestige was fading. A July 1965 headline in the *New York Amsterdam News* asked: "Whatever Happened to James Meredith?"[20]

Meredith had long plotted a march from Memphis to Jackson. In Nigeria, he announced plans for a worldwide lecture tour on race relations, culminating with the walk down Highway 51. He never did the speaking tour, and through most of 1965 the march remained a rumor, bigger in the minds of enemies than allies. After journalist Louis Lomax mentioned it during a lecture at Kentucky State University, the Federal Bureau of Investigation pressed its informants for more information, to no avail. A race-baiting Mississippi columnist named Tom Ethridge snickered that Meredith was acting out of self-interest, creating rifts among black leaders, and considering "a number of other stunts and schemes up his sleeve, to stimulate the 'revolution.'"[21]

Ironically, Meredith had inspired a similar walk in April 1963. Horrified by the Ole Miss crisis, a Baltimore postman named William Moore had started walking from Chattanooga, Tennessee, to Jackson, Mississippi, where he would deliver a message of racial compassion to Governor Ross Barnett. Like Meredith, Moore was a military veteran exercising his constitutional rights. Unlike Meredith, Moore was a white pacifist. He wore a sandwich board that proclaimed END SEGREGATION IN AMERICA and EQUAL RIGHTS FOR ALL. On the third day of his journey, near Attalla, Alabama, a Ku Klux Klansman murdered him. Five times, civil rights demonstrators and local activists tried resuming his journey, and each time police arrested them. Moore's "Freedom Walk" was never finished.[22]

In the fall of 1965, with his Mississippi march just an idea, Meredith enrolled at law school at Columbia University. He envisioned a career in politics, "the center of things where the policies are made." He joined student political clubs, sought to be a delegate at the 1967 New York State Constitutional Convention, and accepted speaking engagements around the country.[23]

He also finished writing *Three Years in Mississippi*, a memoir of his experience at Ole Miss. Published in spring 1966, it captured his contradictions. It included affecting portraits of black life in Mississippi, detached descriptions of his legal battles for admission, and grim tales of his campus ordeal. It also suggested a mystical self-assurance, one that was both profound and strange. He made repeated, matter-of-fact references to his "Divine Responsibility." Other passages implied that same sense of destiny. "My most stabilizing belief," he wrote, "is that I have never made a mistake in my life, because I never make arbitrary or predetermined decisions." Like Meredith himself, the book was sometimes lyrical and insightful, and at other times dry or bizarre.[24]

Meredith hoped that *Three Years in Mississippi* would restore him to the limelight, but he lacked the clout of major black public figures. He offered to appear on *Today*, but the NBC show declined—it had just interviewed James Baldwin, Alex Haley, and James Farmer. *The Saturday Evening Post* rebuffed his offer to write an article. *The New York Times* would not even publish his letter to the editor, which criticized press coverage of the planning session for the White House Conference on Civil Rights.[25]

Meredith conceived his Memphis-to-Jackson walk as part of a bigger crusade—one that would not only free African Americans from second-class status, but also advance his own political ambitions. "I am seriously considering running for the Democratic Nomination for Governor or Lt. Governor of Mississippi in the 1967 primary elections," he wrote to Rev. R.L.T. Smith of the Jackson NAACP. Meredith asked Smith for confidential advice about fund-raising, campaign managers, and the viability of black candidates in Mississippi. He planned to campaign while law school was out of session, and he hoped to register voters during the summer of 1966. While walking down Highway 51, he could build his political base, identifying local leaders and uniting black people under his leadership.[26]

Meredith also contacted white authorities in Mississippi, seeking the protection due any citizen. In January 1966 he wrote to Governor Paul Johnson that "I plan to go to the people where they are—in every nook and hollow in Mississippi—just the way you have done or any other Mississippian seeking to find out what the people want and how their wishes can best be served." By March, the governor had not responded, so he wrote similar letters to the sheriffs of ten counties along Highway 51. Only Madison County sheriff Jack Cauthen wrote back, assuring him that police would protect him if he acted lawfully.[27]

Perhaps most important, Meredith sought to conquer black people's fears. In July 1965, while back in Kosciusko for his father's funeral, a comment by his mother struck him. His younger brother was deploying to Vietnam. "I feel less afraid for him going to fight in Vietnam than I do to have him come home to Mississippi and have these white folks kill him," she said. Fear, thought Meredith, kept blacks on the bottom level. "I wanted to drive despair from the frustrated mind of a teenage Negro boy who had only just begun to feel the consequences of being inferior," he reflected.

> Why should he have to drop his head and restrain his fist when he is insulted and abused without cause, when his father has taught him all his life to treat everybody right? Why does he have to look the other way when a white female passes by, when every day he sees his sister approached by a white man? Who is he going to hate and vent his anger on? The white man for being so cruel, or his father for being so weak? I want that teenage boy to know himself.

By walking into Mississippi towns and encouraging voter registration, Meredith would defy this culture of racial intimidation, setting a powerful example.[28]

Robert Weeks first offered to join him. The white, forty-year-old Episcopalian minister had admired Meredith's courage at Ole Miss, and he had missed the 1965 march from Selma to Montgomery, which had drawn clergy from across the country. As chaplain for the Hampton Training School in New Hampton, New York, he tended to about two hundred troubled boys, many of whom were blacks and Hispanics from New York City. In the spring of 1966, one of the boys dismissed him as a typical white liberal. "You wouldn't shed blood for me," he said. It troubled Weeks. Was his work a calling, or was it just a career? Would he sacrifice himself for justice? When he read about Meredith's plan, he saw a chance to test his ideals.[29]

Sherwood Ross attended Meredith's press conference at the White House Conference on Civil Rights and then offered his services as a publicist. He had worked for the Urban League in Chicago and New York, but he wanted to experience the southern civil rights struggle. Though a pacifist, he had served in the air force without seeing combat, and he yearned for some sort of self-defining challenge. He also feared for Meredith's safety. If he raised the march's profile, he could surround Meredith with reporters, and then no one would attack him, except perhaps "a demented person or a fanatic." After taking a press release to the city desks of the Washington newspapers, he drove with Meredith back to New York City, where he gave the release to *The New York Times*.[30]

Ross also called the Urban League, the Southern Christian Leadership Conference, and the Congress of Racial Equality, but the big organizations told him that Meredith marched to the beat of his own drummer. No one contacted any black leaders in Memphis. Even A. W. Willis, Meredith's attorney of record during the Ole Miss lawsuit, admitted that "I don't know anything except what I read in the paper."[31]

On the plane from New York on the morning of Sunday, June 5, Meredith and Ross met Weeks. After a late breakfast at the home of his cousins, Katherine and Robert Terrell, Meredith went to the Peabody Hotel, where he saw his friend Claude Sterrett, the sharply dressed twenty-four-year-old vice president of Rojac Records. The final member of the original group, Joseph Crittenden, owned a downtown gas station and convenience store. Long active in the Memphis movement, he had also participated in the March on Washington and the Selma-to-Montgomery march. He decided to join Meredith that very day, while driving home from church.[32]

Meredith's residual notoriety from Ole Miss had stimulated some attention for his walk, but his stubborn independence prevented it from becoming a mass-marching media showcase. No one, besides Meredith himself, believed in its potential impact. To those paying attention, it simply highlighted Meredith's courage (or folly) in marching through Mississippi. An eleven-year-old girl from the Bronx named Arlene Wilder marked the occasion with a poem. It began:

> Oh God, in Heaven,
> Let James Meredith be all right.
> Let the angels watch over him,
> Day and night.[33]

But how would James Meredith watch over himself? The night before he started, he contemplated whether to carry a Bible or a gun. The choice was fraught with political symbolism. The gun reinforced his bedrock faith in self-reliant manhood—if a man was conquering fear, a man should protect himself. But Meredith also believed that an American citizen deserved the protection of the American government when exercising a basic American right. And if he wanted broad support, then he needed to appeal to the public's better instincts. Civil rights and Christian righteousness had fused in the public imagination, thanks to Martin Luther King and his kind. So Meredith made a choice that he later called "calculated propaganda." He brought the Bible.[34]

On the morning of Monday, June 6, Weeks said a prayer under a big, green WELCOME TO MISSISSIPPI sign. That sign had long evoked mixed emotions in Meredith. He adored the state's natural beauty and took pride in his family's heritage, but Mississippi also had the lowest percentage of registered black voters and the most intense history of racial violence. The ghosts of Emmett Till and Medgar Evers haunted any black person who considered challenging Jim Crow. "If only I had my fair share in the running and managing of the state of Mississippi," mused Meredith, "what a wonderful land this could be."[35]

About thirty whites glared, shouted, and gestured at the group as it passed into Mississippi. Sterrett decided to prickle the hecklers by complementing his gray suit with a tie in the Stars and Bars of the Confederacy. He carried two small flags, and across his back he draped a large silk rebel flag with the words HELL NO.[36]

As they crossed the state line, the DeSoto County sheriff and his deputies awaited. "We're here to enforce the law," said the sheriff. "Meredith can walk all the way from here to Africa if he wants to." Two cars of state highway patrolmen, sent by Mississippi governor Paul Johnson, also followed the marchers; Weeks called one officer "Ol' Stone Face" when he kept ignoring their smiles and greetings. The third law enforcement organization on hand was the FBI. Its agents followed the march to observe if state and local police protected civilians without racial discrimination.[37]

In the flat and open fields along the highway, a few black workers watched Meredith and his party, but they seemed hesitant to approach, especially if their white bosses were in sight. Occasionally a car brushed past them, or a gas station mounted a cardboard CLOSED sign, or someone yelled, "I hope to hell you die before you get there." After about eight miles, while they snacked on ham sandwiches at a small state park, Meredith admitted that he was disappointed by the black turnout.[38]

That all changed in Hernando. The seat of DeSoto County, about twelve miles south of the state line, was the first real town along the route. Passing some sagging old mansions and dozens of rickety shacks, Meredith's group looped around the courthouse and into the main square. About 150 African Americans stood waiting at the far end. They were young and old, men and women, farmhands and shopkeepers. Some men looked downward at first, but Meredith's pride buoyed them. He smiled, greeted people, and shook hands. Register and vote, he urged.[39]

Never before had a black person in Hernando so openly defied racial custom. "God bless you, James Meredith," they exclaimed, despite the group of whites leering and hooting from across the square. Local blacks treated him to a hamburger and milk at a cafe off the courthouse square, and one old farmer pressed a dollar bill into his hand. "You just keep that," he said. "You just keep that."[40]

Meredith's spirits soared. "Hernando represented to me the whole purpose of my return to Mississippi," he explained. "I had gone there to talk to Negroes, to explain that the old order was passing, that they should stand up as men with nothing to fear." Sherwood Ross had tears in his eyes. The scene reminded him of a Hollywood movie, with the hero basking in a triumphant homecoming. He bought sandwiches, apples, and orange juice for the group from a small store, and they ate a midafternoon lunch under some shady trees. If life had any meaning, he thought, it revealed itself in these beautiful moments.[41]

As they continued south, Meredith brimmed with optimism. "Did you see them?" he asked. "They were men." His party picked up a fifth marcher, Bill Massey, a twenty-one-year-old black soldier from Nesbit, Mississippi, home on furlough. Meredith had originally wanted to reach Coldwater, nine miles to the south, but decided to stop sooner. He twirled his walking stick and teased a group of reporters about getting tired.[42]

Some teenagers brandished a mocking, scribbled chalk sign decorated with Confederate flags that read, YOU'RE 197.4 MILES FROM JACKSON, JAMES, THAT'S 1,032,272 FOOTS. Meredith joked that they should join him. They laughed, and one called him a "damn fool," but in a friendly sort of way. Meredith laughed, too, and offered to shake their hands. "No," said one boy. "You're still in Mississippi."[43]

Around four o'clock, Claude Sterrett ran up, nearly breathless. He had just spoken with an elderly black man, who had warned that a gun-wielding crank was down the road. Meredith looked up from some newspaper clippings about the first day of his march. "Well," he shrugged. He knew the dangers. In Memphis, he had mentioned the possibility of an assassination by a lone sniper. Along the route, he had even pointed out suspicious characters to the police.[44]

Meredith's companions also noticed potential threats. Joseph Crittenden remembered one particular man—a stocky white fellow in dark glasses and an open white shirt, holding an unlit pipe, sizing up the scene while puttering by in his car.[45]

They passed over gently rolling hills. Thick groves of pine trees and scrub oaks lined the gray asphalt road. It had rained that morning, so even though it was hot and sunny, the air felt damp, and the red clay soil smelled earthy and alive. Cars of reporters and officers leapfrogged the marchers, sometimes disappearing behind the next hill. At about 4:15, some of the reporters and Robert Weeks ducked into a country store, where they sipped cold drinks and soothed their aching feet. A few hundred yards ahead, Meredith and three others walked down a dipping stretch of road. Some cars trailed well behind them and others were out in front.[46]

They heard a shout: "James Meredith! James Meredith!" A white man stood on the east side of the road, ahead of Meredith, in a gully lined with honeysuckle and dotted with broken pine seedlings. It was the same pipe-toting man that Crittenden had noticed. He held a shotgun in one hand. He waved people away with the other. "I only want James

Meredith!" Deliberately, even calmly, he walked closer, to about thirty feet in front of them. He paused a moment, waiting for people to clear away. The policemen hung back. The armed man had rendered everyone panicked, paralyzed. The moment was at once frenzied and in slow motion.[47]

The man raised his gun; a glint of sunshine reflected off the barrel. "James, look out!" shouted Crittenden. A shot boomed out, and Meredith screamed. Everyone scrambled away, tripping over each other. The man fired again. Meredith crawled across the road, trying to reach cover behind a car. His eyes were white with panic. His mouth gaped open. "Who, who . . ." he cried. The white man walked onto the road and fired a third shot, this time from closer range. Then he walked back into the woods.[48]

Meredith lay on his left shoulder and arm, with his right leg pulled up. Blood pooled below his right shoulder, and more blood dotted his head, neck, leg, and arm. His pith helmet had flipped off and landed upside down, while his walking stick lay on the ground, its ivory tip cracked and bloodstained. Reporters barked questions, photographers snapped away, and marchers screamed for an ambulance. Someone suggested that Weeks administer last rites. At that moment, while splayed on the gravel shoulder of Highway 51, Meredith regretted taking the Bible. He should have brought the gun.[49]

2

LEAVING EGYPT
Hernando to Coldwater
JUNE 7, 1966

The ambulance from Hernando took only a few minutes to arrive, but it felt like a lifetime. Meredith was murmuring for help, and Robert Weeks was moaning, "Oh my God, oh my God." Sherwood Ross sat in front while Weeks, Joseph Crittenden, and Mohammed Rauf of *The Washington Daily News* piled into the back with the wounded victim. No police escorted them. The young white driver started out slowly, but when Ross yelled that he would be responsible for the death of James Meredith, he flipped on the siren and accelerated to ninety miles an hour.[1]

Meredith retained consciousness throughout the twenty-five-minute ride to Memphis. He lay on his left side, with his right hand dangling over the stretcher. Most of his mutterings made little sense. Once he whispered that Rauf should call his wife. Later he mumbled the name of his insurance company. Finally they arrived at John Gaston Hospital and wheeled out the stretcher. "James Meredith has been shot!" yelled Ross, leading them into the hospital. The doctors took over and pushed the victim into a treatment room. As Rauf tried calling Mrs. Meredith in New York City, Ross stood in the waiting room, his shirt splotched with Meredith's blood. He bitterly recalled the prediction from Attorney General Nicholas Katzenbach that the march would not amount to anything.[2]

By then, the news was out: James Meredith was dead.

James Meredith was not dead. The rumor started with young journalist Ron Alford. Everyone else at the Memphis bureau of the Associated Press was either sick or on vacation, so he was alone. When Alford heard the breaking news, he hurried down the hall to the newsroom of *The Commercial Appeal*. An editor let him pick up an extension as reporter Ramon Himmel phoned in his account. Himmel said, "Meredith has been shot in the back and the head." Alford thought he heard, "Meredith has been shot dead." He sent the news to Nashville's AP office, and from there it circulated nationwide.[3]

It took the AP thirty-five minutes to correct the mistake. By then, a number of radio and television stations had picked up the original bulletin. NBC's Chet Huntley announced that Meredith had died; twenty-eight minutes later, he interrupted David Brinkley with the corrected version. Rival wire service United Press International had reported that Meredith was just wounded, highlighting the AP's blunder. Reporters snickered jokes about "Assassinated Press," and they passed along stories of AP staffers hearing the conflicting account from UPI, dropping to their knees, and pleading in half-jest, "Die, Meredith, die!"[4]

In fact, the emergency room doctor at John Gaston Hospital pronounced Meredith in "satisfactory condition with multiple superficial wounds." Meredith soon got transferred to nearby, better-equipped Bowld Hospital, where FBI agents, Memphis policemen, and telephone operators took over three adjacent rooms. The attacker had used No. 4 bird shot, so Meredith endured dozens of painful wounds in his head, neck, back, and leg. Some pellets got picked out by doctors, some oozed out slowly, and some stayed lodged inside him.[5]

June Meredith never heard the false news about her husband, but she presumed his death from the demeanor of her friends. She sobbed uncontrollably in her bedroom. Police cars rushed to their quiet street near Columbia University, and officers stood guard both within and outside their apartment. "Oh God, thank God!" she cried upon hearing that James was alive. That evening, he called her. She asked if she should come to Memphis, but he preferred that she remain in New York. He also tried calling his mother in Kosciusko, but she was under sedation— she had fallen apart after hearing of his death. Two days later, she finally learned that he was alive.[6]

In Harlem, word of the shooting spread from block to block. Transistor radios turned from music to news. The atmosphere of confusion, jumpiness, and rage recalled the mood before a race riot there in 1964. Was Meredith really dead? Livingston Wingate, executive director of the social justice organization HARYOU-ACT, sent a white friend downtown in a taxicab, just in case. A crowd gathered on the corner of Seventh Avenue and 125th Street. One man proclaimed that if white racists only understood violence, then "we have to kill one of them every time they kill one of us." Others added: "What the hell are we fighting in Vietnam for? . . . Let's get some guns and retaliate." The threat of violence dissolved only after the radio confirmed that Meredith was alive.[7]

At the White House, about fifty demonstrators, led by Marion Barry of the Free D.C. Movement, chanted, "Freedom . . . Meredith . . . Freedom . . . Meredith." The next day, some of those activists picketed outside the Justice Department. Five tried entering the office of the attorney general and had a shoving match with security guards. A man named Glenn "Freedom X" Gurley got arrested for disorderly conduct after rushing straight at the human chain of guards.[8]

"Brother I am tired of turning the other cheek," cracked a street speaker in Los Angeles. "I got four (two up and two down) and I just plumb ran out." The Long Beach, New York, branch of the NAACP wrote a threatening letter to "The People of Mississippi" care of Governor Paul Johnson, urging an end to such viciousness, because the days of peaceful protest were over. J. Franklin Bourne of the Prince George's County, Maryland, NAACP promised that from now on, "I'm going to protect myself. I've been leaning over backward, but this is ridiculous. Anybody who comes my way had better be armed because I'm going to be ready."[9]

Black Americans had watched nonviolent activists in the mold of Martin Luther King achieve the moral high ground, winning favor within some of the nation's most powerful institutions. Yet James Meredith got shot for walking down a highway. After the murder of Emmett Till, the Montgomery Bus Boycott, the integration of Central High School in Little Rock, the student sit-in movement, the Freedom Rides, the Birmingham Campaign, Mississippi's Freedom Summer, the march from Selma to Montgomery, and countless other civil rights demonstrations, how much more could black people sacrifice? For some, the Meredith shooting was a last straw. It broke their faith in nonviolence, their faith in racial brotherhood, their faith in America.

A Brooklyn man named Sidney Street heard about the shooting and grabbed his American flag. The bus driver for the New York Transit Authority was a World War II veteran and recipient of the Bronze Star. He walked out his front door and onto the sidewalk, where a small crowd gathered around him. He lit a match. "If they let that happen to Meredith, we don't need an American flag," he said. Then he burned the Stars and Stripes to ashes.[10]

That night, Meredith managed some restless sleep. When he woke up early on the morning of June 7, he saw a bouquet of flowers from Dick Gregory. The comedian had arrived at Bowld Hospital at 3:00 a.m. along with his wife, Lillian, and five associates. Others were talking about it, others were planning it, but Gregory first acted upon it: he would continue the march on behalf of James Meredith.[11]

At first, Gregory had assumed that Meredith was dead, and from his home base in Chicago he fired off a telegram to President Lyndon Johnson, which he copied to Attorney General Nicholas Katzenbach and released to the press. The United States, he wrote, now had an international reputation "for the unpunished murder of black men." He quoted from the Declaration of Independence, listed martyrs in the civil rights movement, and added a Bible passage. "How much longer will America stand for it?" he asked. "I am one American who intends to find out for myself or die standing up for it." When he and Lillian arrived at O'Hare Airport for the red-eye flight to Memphis, a throng of black people wished them good luck. But Gregory saw fear in their eyes: Would he meet the same fate as Meredith?[12]

Gregory had always defused his own fears with confidence and humor. Born poor in St. Louis, he had won a track scholarship to Southern Illinois University, and then his wit had propelled his stand-up comedy career. Avoiding the underground black circuit, he landed gigs at well-paying clubs with white customers. He achieved mainstream success by employing cool irony and mocking racists:

> Last time I was down South I walked into this restaurant, and this white waitress came up to me and said: "We don't serve colored people here."
> I said: "That's all right, I don't eat colored people. Bring me a whole fried chicken."

He also tweaked liberal guilt. Sometimes, after a laugh, he would pause: "Wouldn't it be a hell of a thing if all this was burnt cork and you people were being tolerant for nothing?"[13]

Unlike most celebrities, Gregory put himself on the movement's front lines, from Birmingham to Selma to Watts. He was fearless. If racists called him nigger, he called *them* nigger. "He called the Mississippi police everything but the child of God," said Mark Stansbury, a *Jet* photographer who covered Gregory's delivery of twenty thousand Christmas turkeys to poor black Mississippians in 1964. "I'd never seen black people talk to white people that way. Never in my life."[14]

Gregory had befriended Meredith during his battle to enter Ole Miss, hosting him in Chicago and visiting him in Mississippi. He loved Meredith's independence and pride. So when Meredith got shot, he arranged for his fellow activists to meet him in Memphis. He wanted to start marching in the dark, but the police promised protection if he waited for daylight. When he learned that civil rights leaders were planning to continue Meredith's march south, he refused to fold into the bigger demonstration, explaining that "I could only be responsible for my group." So that morning at the Lorraine Motel in Memphis, Gregory announced a "reverse walk" from Hernando to Memphis.[15]

South of Hernando, Gregory saw Meredith's dried blood on the highway. Across the road, highway patrolmen radioed that the marchers had arrived. "How you goin' to handle it?" crackled the voice through the speaker. "The same way we did before," responded the officer. Only later did Gregory realize that the Highway Patrol meant to protect him, not kill him.[16]

Black people would either get equality or begin a revolt, Gregory told reporters, peppering his pronouncements with profanity. Now, "people are scared of Negroes." He pointed at a highway patrolman. "Take that white cop over there, for example. His power is his gun. Take that away from him and put him in a Negro playground and he'd be scared to death." Gregory had donned his customary attire for southern civil rights demonstrations: a big white cowboy hat. It conveyed that he was the good guy, the hero, the fearless freedom fighter.[17]

By 12:40, Gregory was leading his group up the highway's left shoulder. They came into Hernando, where they picked up about fifteen locals. "I just wanted to get in with these folks," explained seventy-five-year-old Haywood Wilkins, who had just voted for the first time.

Fourteen-year-old Dennis Farrell had not marched the previous day, "but when Mr. Meredith got shot, it gave me a better spirit to come on out." As they defiantly belted out freedom songs, whites lined the streets, delivering icy glares and stony silence.[18]

The marchers encountered no violence, just a flash thunderstorm followed by muggy heat. All morning, Gregory had been wound into tight knots, but now he took heart from the greetings of field hands, the thanks of local people, and the mettle of his fellow marchers—especially Lillian. "I was afraid until right now," he said. "I'm not afraid now."[19]

The one-day trek ended at six o'clock, about fifteen miles north of Hernando. Gregory was sitting on a car's rear bumper, rubbing his feet, when a white preacher from Walnut, Mississippi, waved a red Bible in his face, beseeching him to "turn back before there's more violence."

Gregory's wise-guy instincts kicked in: "We can't turn back. We're already finished. Where have you been all day, preacher man? Where were you when we needed you?" Some of his companions surrounded the frazzled minister, shouting down his weak protests. After a little more mockery, Gregory hopped in a car and sped back to the Lorraine Motel.[20]

By then, the march was already bigger than the individual visions of James Meredith or Dick Gregory. As Gregory walked north, civil rights leaders headed south, determined to resume Meredith's march and enrich its significance. The movement's next great spectacle was under way.

Floyd McKissick was the first leader who vowed to continue Meredith's quest. The national director of CORE had recently moved to New York, just like Meredith, and Meredith often visited McKissick's family. On the Monday that Meredith fell, McKissick urged volunteers to walk to Jackson. As his office fielded call after call inquiring about details, he planned a trip to Meredith's bedside.[21]

McKissick had a reputation as a black nationalist, but his militancy sprung from the well of his long, broad experience in the civil rights movement. A World War II veteran with five battle stars and a Purple Heart, he had integrated the University of North Carolina Law School, crusaded to desegregate North Carolina institutions, advised the NAACP Youth Council, and represented students during the 1960 sit-in campaigns.[22]

He became CORE's national director in March 1966. Founded in 1942 to promote an interracial and pacifist agenda, CORE boomed in membership and donations with the 1961 Freedom Rides. By the mid-1960s, however, CORE's membership had become more working-class, urban, and black. Its shifting constituency opened new questions: Was nonviolent direct action still relevant? Could whites organize the black poor? Should CORE protest the Vietnam War? McKissick moved the headquarters from downtown Manhattan to a third-floor walkup in Harlem, and he announced "Phase Two" for CORE: improving the black self-image, building an economic foundation in the ghetto, and developing political power.[23]

McKissick understood that as CORE cultivated black leaders and race pride, it pushed beyond the comfort zone of white liberals. His own faith in national leaders and institutions was diminishing. Whatever laws Congress passed, blacks needed economic autonomy and psychological liberation. "For a long time in my life I didn't say this and I didn't say that," he said, intertwining his political and personal journeys. "I didn't know who I was, where I came from or where I was going. Then one day I said to myself that from this day forward I'm not going to be afraid of white people—because it inconveniences me too much."[24]

When McKissick promised to continue Meredith's march, he saw an opportunity to promote CORE's agenda on a national stage. He had two problems, though. First, CORE was broke: contributions dwindled as the organization concentrated on ghetto organization rather than dramatic civil rights campaigns. Second, CORE was based in the North: despite its grass-roots organizing in Louisiana and pockets of Mississippi, it lacked the resources to stage a mass march. McKissick needed Martin Luther King.[25]

The Monday afternoon of Meredith's shooting, King had been leading a staff meeting at SCLC's Atlanta headquarters. When they first heard that Meredith had been killed, the room hushed. Then the silence broke, replaced by exclamations of rage. Hosea Williams wanted to get on the next plane to Memphis. When Andy Young cautioned that they should formulate a plan, Williams cried that they could figure it out on the way. The two men barked at each other, nearing blows.[26]

King had plenty of reasons to avoid a march through Mississippi.

For one, SCLC had little presence there. For another, he and his staff had plans to fly to Chicago, where they were staging an ambitious campaign to tackle the knotty, sprawling issues of poverty in a huge northern city. SCLC was trying to organize gang members, create alliances with local black leaders, and engage the powerful political machine of Mayor Richard J. Daley with a summer of nonviolent protests throughout Chicago.[27]

SCLC depended on the creative tension of its inner circle: men in their thirties, mostly Protestant ministers, accustomed to authority, and driven by faith to destroy racial segregation. They all had strong personalities and big egos. Hosea Williams was brilliant and ambitious, erratic about details and ethics, forceful to the point of abrasiveness. He saw Meredith's shooting as a way to revive the drama of previous southern campaigns. Andy Young played devil's advocate, balancing a room of emotional Baptists with his rational Congregationalist style. When Williams demanded action, Young had questions about the purpose of the demonstration, its impact upon the Chicago campaign, the logistical hurdles of a long march, and the further thinning of a meager budget and staff.[28]

After calls to contacts in Memphis, they learned that Meredith had survived, but King still agreed to join the march. "Meredith had begun his lonely pilgrimage against fear," he reflected. "Wouldn't failure to continue only intensify the fears of the oppressed and deprived Negroes of Mississippi? Would this not be a setback for the whole civil rights movement and a blow to nonviolent discipline?" Different civil rights organizations had different goals, and they would have to make arrangements for tents, campsites, food, and portable toilets. But, King asserted, SCLC had "a moral obligation" to go to Mississippi.[29]

This decision had deep spiritual roots. The previous morning, from his home pulpit at Atlanta's Ebenezer Baptist Church, King had delivered a sermon called "Guidelines for a Constructive Church." The church was no social club, the minister no performer. "Monkeys are to entertain," he said, "not preachers." God had set forth principles: to help the poor, sickly, brokenhearted, and oppressed. "Some people are suffering. Some people are hungry this morning. I'm going to preach about it. I'm going to fight for them. I'll die for them if necessary."[30]

King further recognized a golden opportunity. The previous year, SCLC had staged its ideal protest campaign at Selma. It had articulated a clear objective of voting rights legislation. It had dramatized racial brutality when, on "Bloody Sunday," state troopers used tear gas and beat nonviolent demonstrators on the Edmund Pettus Bridge. It had attracted white allies: the clergy who responded to King's call for marchers, the television viewers who condemned the attack, the legislators who sped passage of the Voting Rights Act of 1965. The attack upon Meredith created the possibility of replicating Selma's success. A prolonged march through Mississippi, with a spirit both moral and martial, would keep aggravating segregationists, compelling press attention, and dramatizing the evils of a racist system.[31]

King asked James Lawson, his main liaison in Memphis, to relay news of his group's impending arrival. Lawson tried visiting Meredith at Bowld Hospital, but the hospital was surrounded by police and firefighters, as someone had called in a bomb threat. Lawson instead sent a message through Meredith's attorney, A. W. Willis. The next morning, a contingent including King, Williams, Ralph Abernathy, Bernard Lee, and Robert Green left from Atlanta. They traveled with McKissick, who had flown through Atlanta to accompany King. When the pilot noted some turbulence in the air, Williams teased that "it'll be a lot more turbulent on the ground."[32]

As Lawson picked them up from the airport, Meredith was asserting his independence. At 9:40 a.m., Willis read a handwritten statement by Meredith in a makeshift press room on the hospital's seventh floor. Meredith characterized the response in Hernando as a moment with massive implications: "Most of the Negroes in Hernando were men. The day for men being cowards is over." He also described his emotions upon getting shot: "I felt embarrassed. Embarrassed because I could have knocked off this intended killer with one shot had I been prepared, but I was not."[33]

Soon after that press conference, the Atlanta contingent arrived at Meredith's fifth-floor room. Policemen started frisking King, at least until they realized that they were searching the nation's most famous proponent of nonviolence. Upon entering the room, the civil rights leaders saw Meredith's raw pellet wounds and the shaved patch on the back of his head. King and McKissick avoided treading on his toes. They *asked* if they could continue the march, and they promised to consult him every day.[34]

Meredith was wary. In an hour-long conversation, he relayed both practical and philosophical concerns: How would they arrange food and shelter? Would a big march make life difficult for poor black Mississippians? Would women and children face danger? Would discipline and order be maintained over two hundred miles, four times the distance from Selma to Montgomery? "They did not want to continue *my* march," Meredith realized. "They wanted to continue, period." Still, they were acting out of conscience, and he could live with their plans.[35]

That day, prominent figures kept arriving at Meredith's bedside. A white candidate for Tennessee governor, John Hooker, came in the morning. In the afternoon Meredith received a delegation of seven congressmen from New York and Michigan, en route to Mississippi to observe its Democratic primary election. He accepted a visit from Assistant Attorney General John Doar, but he refused to field questions from FBI agents. That night he saw Charles Evers, field secretary for the Mississippi NAACP, and then Roy Wilkins and Whitney Young, the national leaders of the NAACP and Urban League, respectively. Meredith realized that an emerging mass protest was revolving around him, even though he possessed no authority over it.[36]

He kept reflecting on the attack, on the chilling calm of his attacker, on his own impotence in the face of danger. "I'm sorry I didn't have something to take care of that man. I'll never make that mistake again," he told a roomful of visitors, his voice soft and thoughtful. Someone chuckled that he would violate nonviolent discipline. His mood snapped. "Who the hell ever said I was nonviolent?" he growled. "I spent eight years in the military and the rest of my life in Mississippi."[37]

While talking with King and McKissick, Meredith had received another visitor: Stokely Carmichael, the new chairman of SNCC. Along with his associates, Cleveland Sellers and Stanley Wise, Carmichael shook Meredith's hand and praised his courage. Then they let Meredith rest. Outside the hospital room, Carmichael, King, and McKissick agreed that SNCC would help sponsor Meredith's march.[38]

Carmichael's group had come from Arkansas. Like CORE, SNCC was in the midst of profound transformations, and Carmichael was beginning his chairmanship by visiting project offices throughout the South. Upon hearing about the shooting, Carmichael remembered feeling cold, numb, suddenly tired. He raged that yet another black man had been martyred. Two hours later, he learned that Meredith was alive, but he still felt wrathful.[39]

Carmichael's initial response revealed his taste for independent black politics, seasoned by a deep frustration with the federal government. SNCC's statement urged the Justice Department to send monitors to every polling place for Mississippi's Democratic primary on June 7, with federal observers arresting anyone who denied voters through fraud or intimidation. Carmichael also sent a public telegram to Meredith's family. It blamed the shooting not only on Mississippi's syrup-thick racism, but also on "the knowledge of past experience that the U.S. government will do nothing." The attack reinforced "that we, the black oppressed of this country, must take the initiative and organize to control our own communities."[40]

The next morning, Carmichael, Sellers, and Wise drove to Memphis in a yellow Dodge pickup truck that they borrowed from SNCC workers in Arkansas. They debated what should come next. SNCC no longer participated in mass demonstrations. The organization had accepted no official place in the march from Selma to Montgomery, which Carmichael had considered a media show with no impact on local black people, another in a long line of "wretched, pointless marches." Moreover, Meredith was "a strange, almost eccentric brother" acting on his own terms.[41]

Yet the more the SNCC leaders talked, the more they saw possibilities. The route went through Mississippi's Second Congressional District, an area once canvassed by SNCC organizers, including all three men in the truck. They had contacts throughout the Delta, and they had helped start the Mississippi Freedom Democratic Party (MFDP), a challenge to the state's established Democratic Party. If Meredith's purpose was unclear, then Carmichael considered that "the idea's very weakness—its vague, ill-defined, amorphous quality—could be its greatest value." The march could become a massive voter registration drive, with nightly rallies led by local people, and the black community could shape and control it, unlike the Selma spectacle. By the time they reached Memphis, they grew convinced that SNCC could create a living, breathing, ever-moving national demonstration of grass-roots organizing.[42]

After visiting Meredith, the SCLC, CORE, and SNCC leaders headed to Centenary Methodist Church, the South Memphis pastorate of James Lawson. They established headquarters in a classroom and library.

Hosea Williams drove into Mississippi, checking distances and scouting campsites. King made recruiting phone calls and signed letters, especially to participants from the Selma march.[43]

They decided to resume the march immediately, so they could advertise that the demonstration would continue. They piled into four cars heading for Hernando, intentionally bypassing the stretch of Highway 51 where Dick Gregory was walking, so as to avoid overshadowing him. At 2:50 p.m., from the site of the shooting, under a warm drizzle, King led a prayer to continue "where your noble servant, James Meredith, with courage and bravery, stood up for democracy and fought for the right to vote."[44]

King, Carmichael, McKissick, and SCLC's Robert Green locked arms, leading fifteen others while singing "We Shall Overcome." They moved about two hundred yards before three highway patrolmen approached, insisting that they walk single or double file on the shoulder. "OK, let's get 'em off," barked one officer. When the policemen began shoving the marchers, King pleaded for civility. A patrolman said that they could walk to China as long as they stayed on the shoulder. "We don't want to go to China," responded King. "Just to Jackson."[45]

The face of patrolman Fred Ogg turned crimson with wrath. "Let's get 'em all," he seethed. Ogg pushed King in the chest, and as photographers snapped away, Cleveland Sellers toppled backward into the mud, King half-tripping over him.[46]

When Ogg shoved King, Carmichael's river of rage overflowed. Through countless demonstrations he had maintained nonviolent discipline. But times had changed, and so had Carmichael. He yanked his left arm free from the human chain. Ogg's hand went down to his holster. The policeman gripped his pistol, his body trembling. With some combination of fear and fury, he stared at Carmichael, his face turning ashen. Carmichael bucked and screamed, ready to attack an armed police officer with his bare hands. In a moment laden with symbolism, Martin Luther King kept his left arm locked around Carmichael's right one, reining him back. As King later quipped, "I restrained Stokely—nonviolently."[47]

Carmichael settled into a simmer. When the marchers huddled on the gravel driveway of a closed ice cream stand, he glowered back at reporters. "This is not for the press," he said. "This is for US." Although the leaders conceded to walking on the shoulder, through mud and ankle-high wet grass, the incident had inflamed the younger, more radical activists. It troubled King to hear one proclaim that he would fight back if a Mississippi authority touched him. Someone else insisted that the march should be all-black. King understood their bitterness, but to him, nonviolence and racial brotherhood were core principles—there was no justice without them.[48]

The mood was grim, the humor dark. When Charles Morgan, a white lawyer affiliated with SCLC, drove by in a station wagon, Carmichael said that he should walk, and Morgan sassed back, "I know where you'll put me in your movement, Stokely!" When Carmichael joked about the futile search for white moderates in the Deep South, he inspired a round of sour cracks. "A moderate wants a little bit of justice at a time," said James Lawson. "He hangs you with a silk rope," said someone else. Even King joined in: "He's interested more in order than in justice."[49]

As they walked, four Highway Patrol cruisers flanked them. Three carloads of DeSoto County police, two of Justice Department officials, and at least three more of FBI agents rode nearby. Another six Highway Patrol units moved up and down the highway, turning on and off dirt roads. Officers peered into bushes and culverts, looking for potential assassins. Troopers also set up a roadblock near their planned destination of Coldwater, diverting northbound cars onto nearby Interstate 55. Neither county, nor state, nor federal officials wanted a repeat of the Meredith incident.[50]

The last stretch of road north of Coldwater ran along a narrow, exposed levee. The Highway Patrol received reports that four cars with Arkansas license plates, each carrying shotgun-wielding white men, had stopped in Memphis to ask for directions to Coldwater. So they halted King before the levee, asking him to delay the march until the next morning. To their relief, King agreed.[51]

Before driving back to Memphis, the marchers once again linked arms and sang "We Shall Overcome." This civil rights anthem had long expressed ideals of faith and hope and fellowship, promising that, someday, "We shall live in peace" and "We'll walk hand in hand." It especially resonated with marching ministers such as King, Lawson, Ralph Abernathy, Bernard Lee, Ralph Jackson, Andrew White, and Kelly Miller Smith. But upon reaching the stanza that called for "black and white together," the young radicals kept quiet. Again, King got uneasy. He later asked why they muted that verse. It was a new day, they told him.

In fact, they wanted a new song. From now on, they would sing, "We Shall Overrun."[52]

That evening, King announced a national call to march through Mississippi. McKissick stated that three busloads of supporters were en route from Chicago, and Carmichael said that hundreds from New York, San Francisco, Los Angeles, Chicago, Cleveland, and Philadelphia would join them. Roy Wilkins and Whitney Young had already arrived in Memphis, and the NAACP and Urban League were ready to cosponsor the march with SCLC, SNCC, and CORE. The brutality inflicted upon James Meredith had kick-started something important. Yet each organization brought its particular personalities, its particular ideology, its particular objective to a combined mass demonstration.[53]

That night's mass meeting at Centenary Methodist Church was the first public debate over the march's meaning. More than six hundred people crammed into the church, spilling into the aisles and standing in the back. An overflow crowd gathered at nearby First Baptist Church. At Centenary, the audience stomped their feet, clapped their hands, and sang, while behind the scenes, the leaders debated who would speak first and last, the most prestigious slots. About an hour behind schedule, the master of ceremonies, Samuel "Billy" Kyles, stepped to the pulpit. He first introduced Roy Wilkins.[54]

Meredith's shooting had opened a political window; Wilkins dreaded that SNCC and CORE might slam it shut. "If you start hating all white men, you're going to waste your energies," he said. "Now you can't go home and get your gun, God forbid, but you can support the bill that is before Congress now." Whitney Young echoed Wilkins, urging black people to uphold their responsibilities as good citizens. He added that he would "publicly disassociate" from anyone urging a "segregated black nationalist society." Both Wilkins and Young won loud applause.[55]

The audience saved louder cheers, however, for the fiery rhetoric of Charles Evers, Floyd McKissick, and Stokely Carmichael. Contradicting the message of his NAACP boss, Evers thundered that if a white person attacked a black person, "we are going to hunt them until hell freezes over." McKissick called the Statue of Liberty a hypocrite: "We ought to break that young lady's leg and throw her in the Mississippi." Carmichael blasted the federal government for treating James Meredith like "a nigger in the cotton patch." If they wanted justice, they would have to seize it. "We need power!"[56]

King spoke last. He had to express both the moderates' duty and the militants' discontent, imbuing it all with his moral and spiritual code. "We *have* power," he said, "and it isn't in bricks and guns. We have another weapon—nonviolence." He recalled the police dogs and fire hoses of Birmingham, and he celebrated how they overcame that oppression with a forgiving spirit. Yet now, he admitted, "we want to put President Johnson on the spot." Black people suffered for freedom, but the government bore a responsibility to protect their citizenship: "Words can't stop bullets. We want action and we want it now!" For all their triumphs, African Americans still faced "prodigious hilltops of opposition and gigantic mountains of injustice." They had left Egypt, but they had yet to reach the Promised Land.[57]

3

BARGAINS IN BLOOD
Coldwater to Senatobia
JUNE 8, 1966

Martin Luther King sat on his bed, propped back on his elbows, dressed in an undershirt, pants, and socks, eating steak off a cafeteria tray. It was a little before midnight, and just about every major figure in the civil rights movement had gathered in King's sweaty, smoky room at the Lorraine Motel. As ideas shot back and forth, he informally presided over the debates that determined the meaning of the march.[1]

With typical bluntness, Hosea Williams insisted upon a nonviolent march. "Shut up, chubby," responded Earnest "Chilly Willy" Thomas, an original member of the Deacons for Defense and Justice, an armed self-defense organization that had formed two years earlier in Louisiana. Thomas had since opened a branch on Chicago's West Side. After the Meredith shooting, he drove a van of Deacons down to Memphis. A wide-eyed policeman spotted them spilling out of the van in the Lorraine Motel's parking lot, loaded with M-1 rifles and bandoliers. But their weapons were legal, and arrest warrant checks turned up nothing incriminating. Dick Gregory told Thomas about that night's summit in King's room.[2]

At the meeting, Thomas promised a "different march." King looked up from his steak—was Thomas planning on walking alongside them? "I don't have no intention of marching one block in Mississippi," responded Thomas. "But we're going to be up and down the highways and byways. And if somebody gets shot again, they going to have somebody to give account to for that."[3]

To SNCC and CORE, the Deacons were essential. Nonviolent CORE workers in Louisiana had worked with the Deacons, and SNCC activists had firsthand knowledge of the dangers of rural Mississippi. They generally adhered to nonviolence, but claimed the right to protect themselves from assault, just like any other man of any other race.[4]

King, by contrast, had a spiritual commitment to nonviolence. He also insisted upon it as a practical necessity: "Many Mississippi whites, from the government on down, would enjoy nothing more than for us to turn to violence in order to use this as an excuse to wipe out scores of Negroes in and out of the march." Yet he could not force another individual to abdicate his right to protect himself and his family. He also distinguished between self-defense and violent retaliation. If the Deacons only protected them, King could accept their participation.[5]

But King opposed any indication that whites were unwelcome. Stokely Carmichael and his associates wanted ordinary black people to realize their possibilities, channeling their frustrations into political organization. To that end, Carmichael lobbied for black control over the march. "SNCC was very clear here," he said. "White liberals could work with SNCC but they could not tell SNCC what to do or what to say. We were very strong about this because of the inferiority imposed upon our people through exploitation that makes it appear as if we are not capable of leading ourselves." Whites could walk with them if they wanted, but if blacks sought genuine power, they needed to lead their own movement.[6]

As King listened to Carmichael, he recalled their previous work together, fighting idealistically for a "Beloved Community." He understood Carmichael's ideological evolution, and yet the moment struck him. He pleaded for the moral choice: the march should promote interracial harmony. "I reminded them of the dedicated whites who had suffered, bled and died in the cause of racial justice, and suggested that to reject white participation would be a shameful repudiation for which they had sacrificed," he recalled. King, more than anyone else, spent the meeting trying to putty up the movement's cracks.[7]

Carmichael and Floyd McKissick found common ground with King—after all, SNCC and CORE needed SCLC's resources. They agreed that the marchers would adhere to nonviolence, as long as the Deacons protected them. They further agreed to welcome whites, as long as they focused on recruiting blacks to march and register. Yet Carmichael, in particular, wanted to chart new directions in black politics. To do that, he needed to drive out the movement's old lions.

In the room with SCLC, SNCC, and CORE, as well as Memphis leaders and Mississippi activists, were the bosses of the two most venerable black organizations: Roy Wilkins of the NAACP and Whitney Young of the National Urban League. Neither group had a reputation for mass marches, but both leaders recognized the opportunities sparked by the civil rights movement. Wilkins and Young wanted to recast the march as a lobbying effort for the Civil Rights Bill of 1966.[8]

Young was a warmhearted unity builder, one who cultivated powerful white backers for his antipoverty and job training programs while drawing broad support from African Americans. Wilkins could be pricklier. He had long fumed that dramatic protests by SCLC, SNCC, and CORE won headlines and contributions, while the NAACP—the largest, oldest civil rights organization with the most members and biggest bank account—did the legislative and organizational dirty work. It aroused his jealousy that most Americans considered Martin Luther King the premier black leader. According to a 1965 FBI report, Wilkins recognized King's importance to the movement, but "indicated he would not personally mind seeing King ruined . . . and had little respect for him."[9]

Wilkins considered SNCC a band of impudent upstarts on a dangerous drift toward black nationalism. In a recent syndicated column, he compared SNCC to the white supremacist regime in South Africa and called its policies "black group suicide." In its disdain for the Johnson administration, SNCC "buries its head in the sands of black racism."[10]

At the Lorraine Motel, Wilkins tried to set the agenda. He said that the NAACP, Urban League, SCLC, CORE, and SNCC should have one vote on key matters, and an organized march should focus on the single goal of passing the Civil Rights Bill. With Young in support, he opposed anything that deflected attention from this goal, such as voter registration campaigns or civil disobedience tactics. He objected to the participation of the Deacons, and he balked at any exclusion of whites.[11]

Carmichael drafted a manifesto for the march that painted Lyndon Johnson as an enemy, not an ally. That stance enraged the old guard. "I will not attach my signature to any statement that attacks the President personally," hissed Wilkins.[12]

Carmichael also antagonized Wilkins by playing up his own image as a wild radical. "I started acting crazy, cursing real bad," he recalled. "It was verbal abuse of the highest order." He called Wilkins and Young hired lackeys of white authorities. He accused them of diluting the march's message to appease powerful whites, and he led his SNCC comrades in blasting Wilkins as a relic who should retire from the NAACP, teach at some college, and write his memoirs. The display was in poor taste, admitted Carmichael, but "we wanted to let them know that it would be impossible to work with us."[13]

Significantly, King stayed quiet. Perhaps he figured that if the NAACP and Urban League dropped out, SCLC would control the march. In any case, his silence had profound implications. King was typically the mediator among the "Big Five" organizations. Carmichael realized that if King backed the NAACP and Urban League, then it would be "business as usual," "insider politics," "a combination of the March on Washington and Selma to Montgomery all over again." Instead, as tempers flared in the hot, smoke-filled room, King never defended Young and Wilkins, thus offering tacit support for SNCC and CORE.[14]

The debates continued until one o'clock that morning. Wilkins gathered his papers, snapped shut his briefcase, and huffed away to catch his red-eye flight to New York, since he was getting an honorary degree from Fordham University. Young followed him out. Both men had deep misgivings about SNCC and CORE. Yet upon leaving Memphis, both believed that they had managed a compromise: they would endorse a statement that called for passage of the Civil Rights Bill and refrained from attacking the president.[15]

The next morning, the NAACP's national headquarters in New York heard from Memphis that the manifesto had undergone a few changes, and that Young had already signed it. In fact, Young had not signed it. Neither would Wilkins. "We couldn't even go along with the title 'Manifesto,'" said one NAACP official, noting its association with the *Communist Manifesto*. Wilkins and Young refrained from official participation in the march.[16]

That day, June 8, the "Manifesto of the Meredith Mississippi Freedom March" was released to the press. Its opening passage stated, "This march will be a massive public indictment and protest of the failure of the American society, the government of the United States, and the state of Mississippi to 'Fulfill These Rights.'" The last phrase was a mocking echo of the White House conference.

The manifesto directly challenged the president. It called for mobile federal registrars in six hundred counties throughout the Deep South. It called for the Justice Department, FBI, and U.S. marshals to enforce civil rights laws. It called for strengthening the Civil Rights Bill's provisions to put blacks on juries and in law enforcement. Finally, it called for a massive budget, to be proposed by President Johnson and passed by Congress, "in order to bring black people of the Northern city ghettoes and Southern rural districts into the making of their own destinies."[17]

As the manifesto went public, King sent an appeal to Bayard Rustin, the architect of mass demonstrations such as the 1963 March on Washington. A master at logistics and consensus building with deep roots in the black freedom struggle, Rustin understood that the movement had entered a new phase: deeper economic and social problems, entangled with race, demanded radical changes in American politics. But Rustin argued that blacks had to foster institutional alliances with labor unions and religious organizations. Although he appreciated the frustrations of militants, he frowned upon their nihilism. With the manifesto public, Rustin lamely deflected the request to participate, claiming that he had to write an article for *Commentary*.[18]

SNCC, CORE, and SCLC had control. Now all they had to do was walk 175 miles under a hot Mississippi sun, transport and feed volunteers, arrange campsites, secure protection from government authorities, maintain media attention, defy hostile and possibly violent whites, recruit local blacks, register voters, and establish the potential of black political power in the nation's most racist setting—all in the name of James Meredith, the march's lonely martyr.

By this time, a striking image had appeared on the front page of countless newspapers: James Meredith, dragging himself across Highway 51, propped up on one elbow and screaming in agony. AP photographer Jack Thornell had heard the first gunshot while one hundred yards ahead of Meredith. After sprinting back about forty feet, he started snapping pictures with his telephoto lens. His photograph, which later won a Pulitzer Prize, not only communicated the cold brutality of the assault, but also won compassion for Meredith.[19]

Throughout the 1960s, television cameramen and news photographers had captured the savage beatings of nonviolent demonstrators, telling a powerful, straightforward story about hateful racists and heroic victims. Now Meredith became the human symbol of black suffering and redemption. He received piles of admiring telegrams and letters. "I join millions of Americans in saluting you for your courage, determination and contribution to the fight for freedom and equality of all Americans," wrote the mayor of Gary, Indiana. Admirers crafted poems that saluted his heroism. Teachers discussed his shooting to educate children about racial tolerance. People sent him contributions, planted trees in his honor, relayed disgust at southern racists, and asked him for advice about solving America's racial problems.[20]

Many whites felt compelled to present Meredith with their liberal credentials. "We have never met; but we are Brothers, indeed," wrote one man. "Please remember the color of our skin does not matter; We are all Americans under One Flag and One Constitution." A woman catalogued the assorted kindnesses of black people: a boy who stopped a dog from biting her, a man who helped her call a taxi, a security guard who found her lost daughter, a woman who brought her mother a thoughtful Christmas present. Another white woman wrote that she and her husband "are ashamed to belong to a race that considers itself superior." Meredith was a human embodiment of colorblind fellowship.[21]

"The blood stain on Meredith's back is another stain on the honor of Mississippi, another mark of revulsion that civilized people must feel at conditions that permit and encourage such cowardly acts of lawlessness," pronounced *The Philadelphia Inquirer*, capturing the prevailing mood. Newspaper profiles and columns recalled his fight to enter Ole Miss, quoted from *Three Years in Mississippi*, celebrated his courage, and analyzed his independent frame of mind. One writer concluded that African Americans considered him a folk hero, an "anti-organization man" distant from the rivalries of civil rights groups. Newspapers also printed many letters expressing despair, shame, and revulsion about the attack. One man stated that he had not felt such outrage about a public tragedy since the assassination of President John F. Kennedy.[22]

Walter Reuther of the United Auto Workers and Morton Yarmon of the American Jewish Committee denounced the injustice. Meredith's Columbia Law School professors issued a joint statement. The State Assembly in New Jersey adopted a resolution. At the U.S. Capitol, Michigan congressman John Conyers asserted that Meredith embodied African

Americans' struggle for justice "in their restraint, in their nonviolent activities and protests for full American citizenship." Ignoring the man's own statements, Conyers said that Meredith, "too, is one of those who professes to believe in the philosophy of nonviolence."[23]

In London, Billy Graham led seventeen thousand worshippers in prayer for Meredith's recovery and racism's demise. The shooting was front-page news in every major newspaper in Great Britain. *Arriba*, the Spanish organ of Francisco Franco's fascist regime, contrasted the violence with a space walk by an American astronaut: "U.S.A. Great In Space, Shamed on Earth." *Izvestia*, the official government newspaper of the Soviet Union, reported that the police and FBI gave the shooter three chances before arresting him, suggesting how Meredith's shooting illustrated the hypocrisy of American propaganda about freedom and democracy.[24]

Senator Robert F. Kennedy was visiting South Africa, where he was advancing his statesmanlike reputation by condemning apartheid. In the wake of the attack, he addressed the international dimensions of the racial struggle. The United States had seen important changes, he told South Africans, yet African Americans endured poverty, discrimination, and urban decay. The future lay in men like James Meredith. "Each time a man stands up for an ideal, or acts to improve the lot of others, or strikes out against injustice, he sends forth a tiny ripple of hope," he intoned. "These ripples build a current that can sweep down the mightiest walls of oppression and resistance."[25]

Meredith's shooting also boosted liberals in Congress. Conservatives had been objecting to the Civil Rights Bill of 1966 since its proposal in late April. As Meredith marched, Attorney General Nicholas Katzenbach appeared before a Senate subcommittee, where he listened to an hour-long harangue from North Carolina senator Sam Ervin, who called the bill an unconstitutional intrusion of federal authority.[26]

But now, Vice President Hubert Humphrey, Speaker of the House John McCormack, House Judiciary chairman Emanuel Cellar, and a host of legislators called for the bill's passage based on the shooting of James Meredith. "What James Meredith wants, and calls for, is the righting of injustices which produce such terrible tragedy," cried New York senator Jacob Javits. As the momentum shifted, the Civil Rights Commission urged the Senate to strengthen the bill. During two more days of sparring with Katzenbach in subcommittee hearings, Ervin bemoaned that it was "much more difficult to oppose legislation when the public becomes inflamed by such an outrageous act."[27]

Katzenbach had not even consulted the president when Meredith began his march. Upon the shooting, Katzenbach called Lyndon Johnson at his Texas ranch, where he had been entertaining state officials. Thirty minutes later, Johnson issued a statement condemning the attack. Soon the White House received letters calling for vigorous federal intervention in the South: signed resolutions from church conferences, objections from labor unions, demands from student leaders. One New York attorney suggested that the president himself lead civil rights marchers down Highway 51. Johnson settled for expressing his "great and grave concern" about Meredith's shooting to Mike Mansfield, while urging the Senate majority leader to speed passage of the Civil Rights Bill.[28]

"James Meredith bought life for the upcoming Civil Rights Act of 1966," stated *The Chicago Defender*. He survived the attack. His wounds would heal. It seemed a small price to pay for this legislative push. The black newspaper's headline put it simply and graphically: the shooting was "A Bargain in Blood."[29]

James Meredith did not accept the bargain. While civil rights leaders debated at the Lorraine Motel, he slept fitfully. He woke up at three in the morning, fidgety and frustrated, stuck at Bowld Hospital. The previous afternoon, King and McKissick had promised to return, but instead they had marched south from Hernando. When James Lawson had called him that evening, Meredith protested that all these organizations were acting in his name, but no one actually listened to him. Throughout the early morning, as three policemen guarded his door, he composed another press statement.[30]

Around ten that morning, King and McKissick arrived at his hospital room, along with attorney A. W. Willis. Marchers were congregating at Centenary Methodist Church in Memphis, and about fifty cars filled with reporters and marchers lined Highway 51 north of Coldwater. The leaders nevertheless delayed the start for Meredith's sake. They showed him the manifesto, which he refused to sign. He had no quibble with the statement itself, nor would he have objected to one approved by Roy Wilkins and Whitney Young. He just refused to affix his name to a doc-

ument without assuming personal responsibility for the whole operation. When they suggested that he lead that day's march by riding in a
wheelchair for a few miles, Meredith again balked.[31]

Yet Meredith was trapped in the role of victim-hero. Earlier that
morning, his attending doctor, Louis Britt, had said that he should remain hospitalized for at least one more night. Then the Bowld Hospital
staff, weary from two days of police protection and press attention, reversed course. At 10:55, administrator David Hoxie confirmed that Dr.
Britt had signed Meredith's discharge papers. The deadline to vacate
was 11:00. King, McKissick, and Willis objected to the hasty order. King
said that Meredith should be treated like the president of the United
States. After consulting his superiors, Hoxie returned to say that Dr. Britt
was unavailable, but if Meredith wanted more examination, there were
two black doctors on staff. Infuriated by the shabby treatment, Meredith demanded the discharge papers, signed them, and ordered everyone out of the room.[32]

The leaders moved up to a glass-walled lounge that was serving as
improvised press quarters. They portrayed the discharge as a civil rights
violation. "This involves my client's constitutional rights. This was tan-
tamount to an eviction," said Willis. Hoxie responded that the hospital
followed normal procedures for a recovered patient. He and his staff also
gossiped about the arguments between Meredith and others, marring
the civil rights leaders' efforts to project unity. "All I know is they got
pretty loud," said Hoxie.[33]

Before leaving for Coldwater, King insisted that Meredith was the
march leader. "We are in a supportive role," he said. But Meredith understood that his flimsy grip on the demonstration slipped with every
step King took down Highway 51. At 1:00 p.m., after the others departed,
Meredith entered the press room. He had traded his pajamas for a suit.
With a soft voice and a blank expression, he started reading a rambling
statement. Then his left hand moved up to his face. He stopped talking.
He turned toward a friend. With his face still impassive, tears rolled
down his cheeks. "Turn off the TV lights!" demanded a doctor. The
heat, the wounds, the strain, and his own tendency to collapse with
emotional fatigue conspired against him. He fainted.[34]

Doctors guided Meredith onto a chaise longue, loosening his shirt
and tie. During a brief inspection, his pulse returned to normal. At 1:37

p.m., hospital workers wheeled him to the front entrance. That evening he flew back to New York, exiting the march's center stage.[35]

The shooting of James Meredith had triggered a mystery—not over who shot him, but why. Three minutes after the assault, two Mississippi highway patrolmen found the rotund white man on a gravel side road, strolling toward his car, carrying a shotgun. He offered no resistance, though he lamely suggested that he was shooting at squirrels. After the officers turned him over to DeSoto County police, he stood at the roadside in handcuffs, his face blank, a pipe jutting from his mouth. When reporters asked why he shot Meredith, he denied the crime. Minutes later, at the jail in Hernando, he admitted his guilt. He was a forty-year-old former hardware store clerk from Memphis named Aubrey James Norvell.[36]

That night, witnesses identified Aubrey Norvell out of a police lineup. The next morning, he appeared twice before the justice of the peace: first to be charged with assault and battery, and second to be held for the DeSoto County grand jury on $25,000 bond. Norvell sat silently and sullenly throughout the proceedings. He walked out of the courthouse unshaven and sweaty, wearing dark glasses and an open white shirt. Ignoring reporters' questions, he obscured his face with a handkerchief held between his cuffed hands.[37]

Many commentators painted Norvell as a cartoon villain: a "savage," "a hate-filled white Mississippian," "an abject coward," and a "low-income, low-IQ . . . redneck." Although Norvell did not reveal a motive, Max Lerner of the *New York Post* speculated that "he was fearful of the phantoms within himself, the unreasoning terror at what would happen if the Merediths were allowed entrance into his world." Liberal southerners, such as *Atlanta Constitution* editor Ralph McGill and Alabama attorney general Richmond Flowers, blamed race-baiting southern conservatives for creating a poisonous atmosphere, spawning evildoers such as Norvell.[38]

Yet as reporters investigated Norvell, they painted a portrait quite distinct from some brutish, hate-spewing Klansman. Until June 6, 1966, he seemed somewhat respectable and entirely unremarkable. He was born in 1925 in Forrest City, Arkansas. His family moved to Memphis when he was eight. An average student, he graduated from Tech High School in 1944. During World War II he earned a Purple Heart, a Bronze Service Star, and an honorable discharge. He drove a 1965 Pontiac and lived in a five-room, ranch-style home on a three-acre lot in a subdivision on the outskirts of Memphis. He had been married for eighteen years with no children. He and his father sold their hardware store in 1963, and he had since worked as a clerk, though he was now unemployed. He liked fishing, water-skiing, and hunting birds. "I suppose the Army was the biggest thing that ever happened to him," said one neighbor, "until now."[39]

What was Norvell's motive? His parents seemed genuinely perplexed, and his wife entered a state of shock. His neighbors called him pleasant, soft-spoken, "as nice a man as I've ever met." When one neighbor went on vacation, Norvell mowed his lawn and tended his dogs, cats, and horses. He never drank alcohol, had no history of mental illness, and possessed no known ties to any white supremacy organization. "He never mentioned civil rights one way or the other," said a neighbor. According to a childhood friend, he was "the kindest man I know. He was a quiet, Christian man."[40]

Was Norvell shooting to kill? One neighbor said that Norvell hunted with No. 7½ or No. 8 shot, and Norvell attacked Meredith with the larger No. 4 shot, which penetrates the thick feathers of birds or geese. "If he had fired from 15 feet closer, Mr. Meredith would have been dead," asserted the emergency room doctor at John Gaston Hospital. Even at thirty to fifty feet, Norvell's autoloading 16-gauge shotgun packed a lethal punch. Each round discharged about 150 pellets, and Norvell shot three times. Somewhere between sixty and eighty-five pellets hit Meredith. Firearms experts thus concluded that Meredith got struck by the fringe of the shot pattern—he survived only due to Norvell's bad aim. Yet Norvell was an avid hunter and an army veteran who had earned the marksman's badge with a rifle bar. Anyway, a murderer would use bullets, not bird shot.[41]

Was Norvell acting alone? Meredith's marching companions believed that Norvell worked in concert with the Mississippi police. "As I see it, there were no two ways about it: the whole thing was planned," said Robert Weeks. Sherwood Ross described with incredulity how a DeSoto County officer just stood across the highway, failing to pursue Norvell as he sauntered back into the woods. Joseph Crittenden and Memphis photojournalist Ernest Withers maintained that deputies had plenty of time to save Meredith. Claude Sterrett recounted the various threats from passing cars, the warning from the elderly black man, the sluggish response of the police, and even how policemen and reporters kept their distance, as if they knew Norvell was coming. "This was a definite set-up," he insisted.[42]

New York Amsterdam News columnist James Hicks accepted that Norvell could have shot once from the gully. But after that, the assailant should have been "mowed down in his tracks. That is, if they were really serious about protecting the man." The NAACP Legal Defense Fund contemplated a lawsuit against Mississippi. Six congressmen demanded an investigation.[43]

Norvell's motive remained unknown, but it was highly unlikely that Mississippi officials sanctioned the attack—a mass march in the name of James Meredith caused the state exponentially more trouble than a single man's walk, and the Civil Rights Act of 1964 and the Voting Rights Act of 1965 had each won support after popular horror over racist violence. As a *Washington Post* headline frankly stated, "White Violence Aids the Negro." The columnist Richard Baker joked that the civil rights movement should erect a monument to the white southerners who had yanked public opinion toward justice. This racist Mount Rushmore would feature not only Bull Connor of Birmingham and Jim Clark of Selma, but also the "bushwhacker" Aubrey Norvell.[44]

As King and McKissick tried to appease, involve, and defend Meredith at Bowld Hospital, a crowd baked in ninety-degree heat north of Coldwater Bridge, including a gaggle of grumpy reporters. Finally, three hours after the scheduled start of 11:00 a.m., busloads of marchers arrived from Memphis, joining the locals from DeSoto and Tate Counties. After McKissick read out the manifesto and King predicted that the march would grow bigger than Selma, 120 people, including about a dozen whites, marched single file across the levee toward Coldwater.[45]

"Here he is! Here he is! Here's Dr. King!" someone shouted as the marchers approached the city limits. Dressed in a straw hat, polo shirt, and sunglasses, King shined before the waiting groups of people. He translated the manifesto into simple terms—and drew wry smiles from Carmichael—as he intoned, "We are here to put in black sheriffs! We are here to put money in your pockets! We are here for freedom!"[46]

The spirit caught some young people, who fell in behind King. But for the older generation, their fears haunted them. One black man pointed into the woods: "They're down there watching for us. I don't know if there's going to be any violence. Can't hear what a man's thinking and you can't tell by looking." When some marchers asked a farmer for a drink of water, he begged them, "Please go away, we don't want no trouble!" A woman even refused to let King use her telephone. "If anyone sees you come into my house, my family will have trouble with the Klan once you have gone," she explained. "We just can't afford to take chances."[47]

In Coldwater, some white women at the public library insisted that their race relations were peaceful, pointing to the impending integration of the schools. But vandals had destroyed the town's two pay phones, one white businessman refused to let "any Yankee reporters" use his telephone, and some teenagers sat on a truck hood wielding homemade Confederate flags.[48]

Farther south, William Hardison, a fifty-eight-year-old man from Senatobia, stopped his white pickup truck in front of the marchers. Police waved him aside. The leaders, including King, approached within six feet of the truck. "I ain't going to move," sneered the burly, unshaven man. When police opened his door, they saw a semiautomatic .22-caliber rifle on the seat, and they charged Hardison with drunk driving and possession of a concealed weapon.[49]

Due to the late start and hot sun, the marchers covered just over six miles, ending north of Senatobia around five o'clock. While snacking on sandwiches and sodas, they listened to speeches by King, McKissick, Carmichael, and Fred Shuttlesworth before singing some freedom songs. They had not yet arranged for campgrounds with tents and latrines, so they rode back to Memphis. The first day of genuine mass marching was over.[50]

That night, James Meredith landed at LaGuardia Airport. As reporters again crowded around him, he looked exhausted. The hot television lights popped on, and a microphone grazed the raw wounds on his elbow, making him wince. Leaning on his walking stick and his wife, June, he thanked his supporters and reaffirmed his right to self-defense. His doctor had prescribed at least one week of rest. "I shall return," he vowed, citing his "divine responsibility."[51]

Meredith still believed that the march should be conducted by small groups of independent black men, not turned into a complicated, dangerous, large-scale operation full of logistical hurdles and political squabbles. "Two hundred and twenty-five miles is a long way," he warned. "The road to freedom is a long, long road."[52]

4

DAYLIGHT BREAKING
Senatobia to Como
JUNE 9, 1966

Armistead Phipps sat on a ridge shaded by a grove of trees, waiting to join the Meredith March. The fifty-eight-year-old man looked out over the Hill Country landscape. Green crops burst out of the thin, red, clay soil. The sound of insects hummed across the nearby fields. Warm breezes spread a sweet, dusty aroma. As he waited, the sun got higher and hotter. The temperature climbed toward ninety-five degrees. His companions checked on him. He was fine, he assured them, patting his bottle of pills.[1]

Phipps had grown up outside West Marks, Mississippi, working the same cotton fields as his sharecropper parents. He became a sharecropper himself. He and his wife, Beatrice, had six children, and they had scratched out a living, subsisting mostly on a common pot of pork and beans. Around 1957, near his fiftieth birthday, he began "taking spells." Doctors determined that he had heart disease and high blood pressure. Forced to stop farming, he moved to a three-room shack near the village of West Marks, where his family lived on $110 a month from Social Security and the Mississippi Welfare Department. His hair turned gray, his body frail.[2]

With time on his hands, Phipps got active in the movement. He attended church at Burr's Chapel in nearby Falcon, where pastor S. A. Allen preached about racial justice. Phipps started working for the Mississippi Freedom Democratic Party, and he and Beatrice also volunteered at a local youth center. He got excited for the Meredith March. Beatrice begged him to stay home, given his health problems. "I've got to go," he told her. "This is the greatest thing that has ever happened to our people in Mississippi. Now they won't be afraid to vote any more. I'll only march for a little. But I've got to be part of it."[3]

At 6:00 a.m. on June 9, Phipps walked to his neighbor's home and waited for Reverend Allen to pick them up. They piled into a car with other marchers, including Alex Shimkin, a reedy, bespectacled, white civil rights worker from Illinois, and drove forty miles to the north edge of Senatobia, where the march was scheduled to resume at 9:30. But Martin Luther King and his fellow leaders did not arrive until 11:45. They had spent the late night and early morning in another meeting at the Lorraine Motel. "We have decided to restructure the march to stress voter registration," King announced. His vision for the march was dovetailing with those of Stokely Carmichael, Floyd McKissick, and the Mississippi activists.[4]

Phipps listened to the speeches and joined the march into Senatobia, singing and waving to the people gathered at intersections. "Come and join us, even for half a block," urged McKissick. "Come and help us march for freedom." About one-third of the crowd joined in, swelling their number to about 250. Some whites waved Confederate flags and yelled "Go home, niggers," while one boy tooted "Dixie" on his clarinet. Just past the city limits, they heard gunshots. Four police officers burst out of their cars, rushed across a plowed field, and searched the nearby woods. It was a false alarm: some young boys had been shooting at turtles.[5]

Around this same time, Phipps stumbled out of the marching line, fumbling with his pill bottle. He fell onto the grass. His straw hat flipped off, and his head rested on the ground. He picked himself up to drink some water. Then he dropped again. When Dr. Alvin Poussaint arrived by his side, Phipps could barely breathe. His lungs were filling with fluid. "I'm all right," he said while getting lifted into a car. "I be all right."[6]

Those were his last words. Lying in the car, Phipps died.

Poussaint got word to Martin Luther King at the head of the line. At the first rest break, King called a press conference. Poussaint was flabbergasted. The doctor assumed that the media would blame civil rights leaders for letting an old, sick man walk in searing heat. But King placed Phipps in the pantheon of civil rights martyrs. He further laid blame upon larger social and political conditions: "His death means that he was probably underfed, improperly nourished, overworked and underpaid." Now Poussaint was impressed. Under an oak tree, dressed in a short-sleeved shirt and straw hat, King had turned a potential fiasco into an indictment of Mississippi's segregated, inadequate health care system.[7]

As the marchers sang spirituals, four men lifted Phipps into an ambulance. "He was a decent Christian man," said Shimkin. "I feel honestly that if he'd known he was about to die he would have done it this way." In his wallet they found a memento of his activism: a receipt for paying a poll tax. He had been a broken-down sharecropper without proper education, but Armistead Phipps had learned the meaning of freedom.[8]

The march's logistical hub was in Memphis. Nestled in the corner of southwestern Tennessee, the city offered critical amenities and resources, such as the Lorraine Motel. If the Peabody Hotel embodied the graces of the white southern elite, then the Lorraine Motel was its funky black cousin, with the clean, modular feel of a Holiday Inn. It hosted just about every black celebrity and political leader who swung through the city. Martin Luther King's favorite room was 306, which had a second-floor balcony overlooking Mulberry Street.[9]

Memphis also had a unique political texture. The city was both a racial oasis and an urban plantation—the way out of the Delta, and the way back in. It lacked the brutal repression of Mississippi: African Americans could register and vote, many public institutions were integrated, and it hosted no white demagogues in the vein of Bull Connor. Yet it had a paternalistic white power structure dating back to E. H. "Boss" Crump, whose political machine dominated the city in the first half of the twentieth century.[10]

Although most blacks were working-class or poor, the middle-class leaders of the NAACP ran black politics in Memphis. "The NAACP was *it*," recalled local photographer Mark Stansbury. "It was the voice of the black community." Ministers such as Benjamin Hooks, Billy Kyles, Harold Middlebrook, and James Lawson had affiliations with SCLC, but they worked locally through the NAACP. Executive Director Maxine Smith led a large, exceptionally active branch that registered voters, urged speedier school integration, fought job discrimination, and protested police brutality.[11]

The NAACP leadership often met with white businessmen, outlining their goals and plans. "You never saw it in the newspaper, and you wouldn't show it on television," said Kyles. "We weren't outlandish. We didn't ask for unreasonable things." Moderate leaders, both black and white, also served on the Memphis Committee on Community Relations (MCCR), which responded to black activism with measured concessions. Years before the Civil Rights Act of 1964, Memphis desegregated public facilities such as libraries, zoos, museums, parks, bus stations, and movie theaters.[12]

The Memphis NAACP was involved with the Meredith March from the beginning. After the shooting, A. W. Willis served as an especially critical liaison to Meredith. He had been the NAACP's attorney of record during Meredith's challenge to enter Ole Miss, and Meredith admired the intense, quiet, and practical man, who in 1964 became Tennessee's first black state assemblyman since the late nineteenth century. Willis marched, too. For the June 8 trek through Coldwater, he and his wife, Ann, brought their four children, aged eleven, seven, four, and two.[13]

That night, Willis spoke first during a mass meeting at Metropolitan Baptist Church. He described the eviction of Meredith at Bowld Hospital, stirring the congregation's outrage. Then Rev. Bill Smith announced a silent protest march to the hospital. As Floyd McKissick, Fred Shuttlesworth, and Martin Luther King stepped into the pulpit, Smith moved to the church's back offices, where an inspector communicated with police headquarters. They agreed that the protesters could march three abreast on the sidewalk. After the mass meeting, per their arrangement, an orderly group marched in silence to Bowld Hospital. It was a perfect example of racial politics in Memphis, accomplished through behind-the-scenes negotiations and mutual accommodation.[14]

Among the city's black leadership, the minister James Lawson offered the most potent critiques of these moderate, top-down tactics. His nonviolent workshops in Nashville had helped spawn the 1960 student sit-ins, and in 1962 he got assigned to Centenary Methodist Church in Memphis. Lawson wanted energetic direct action campaigns that appealed to the black masses, not "abortive" sit-in campaigns and legal challenges controlled by the NAACP. He urged Maxine and Vasco Smith to dissolve the MCCR, "a power structure committee" that funneled black grievances into token improvements. For Lawson, the church bore responsibility to foster racial justice and reconciliation. "This doesn't take place by people pretending the problems aren't there," he said. "It takes place in confrontation."[15]

At Centenary, Lawson preached about curing the city's persistent divides, about transcending token desegregation, about radical change through religious institutions. The Meredith March fulfilled his vision of an activist church. Though some members feared a white backlash, the board approved Centenary as the march's official headquarters, with only one dissenting vote. "I can't think of a better thing for the church to be doing," said one member. For two weeks, Centenary remained open day and night. Workers with armbands welcomed new volunteers. The lower level had a registration desk, food service area, press room, and office. A map on the wall charted the march's progress, while a bulletin board displayed messages for new marchers, who sometimes slept on the church's floor.[16]

Even if they never walked in Mississippi, black Memphians supported the march. They opened their homes to marchers, carried people and supplies in their cars, and volunteered their time at Centenary. Different churches hosted mass meetings. WDIA, the radio voice of black Memphis, kept people informed of the march's daily dramas. Culpepper's Barbecue and other black-owned restaurants donated food, as did Memphians who cooked in their home kitchens. "We just found people who would help us daily to fix food and do all the necessary things," recalled Harold Middlebrook. "This was their contribution to the movement."[17]

Hosea Williams of SCLC oversaw the headquarters at Centenary. Don Smith of CORE churned out press releases and solicited donations, while Bob Smith of SNCC ran the transportation center, an increasingly intricate endeavor as volunteers arrived from every state in the union—with the curious exception of Delaware.[18]

The precarious financial situation of all three organizations complicated the operation. Within a few days, the march was $4,700 in debt. Tents and portable toilets rented for $600 a day, and other expenses piled up. Mel Leventhal, an NYU law student representing the NAACP Legal Defense Fund, recalled Hosea Williams calling AT&T to install four WATS lines, which allowed unlimited long distance calls for a flat fee. Williams needed a $2,000 deposit. He had to bully, beg, and persuade his way into getting an advance.[19]

"This is not an outing for nuts, nor is it a pleasure cruise for some cats who like to get their kicks," Williams warned over fifty volunteers who had gathered at Centenary one morning. While supervising the practical details of a mass march, he reminded them to maintain nonviolent discipline. Before they left for Mississippi, a police car pulled up. Two officers approached a young man named Leon Howard. After a quiet talk, Howard dejectedly followed them back to the squad car. He slumped into the back seat. He was not getting arrested—he was only seventeen, and his mother had called the police. As the hangdog teenager explained, "My mama don't believe in civil rights."[20]

Back in West Marks, a housekeeper nicknamed "Sweetpea" said that Armistead Phipps had been brave. "Most of the older folks is afraid, not like him. They're scared of the white folks." She and her friends planned to join the march. "Lady I work for say she wants to get a big gasoline truck and pour gas on all the houses of the Negroes involved in the march. But I don't listen; I just turn up that old vacuum cleaner of hers and say, 'I can't hear you.'"[21]

On Highway 51, Tommy Brooks let the marchers rest on his lawn, use his outhouse, drink from his well, and conduct the impromptu memorial service for Phipps. He did not ask his white landlord for approval.[22]

Farther down the road, some white farmers placed the festering, fly-covered corpse of a massive dog along the path of the marchers. They stood upwind, giggling with expectation. But when a thin black man passed by, he stopped his truck, picked up the dog, dropped it in front of the speechless whites, wiped his hands on his overalls, and drove away.[23]

P. L. Elion watched the marchers while puffing on a cigar. He was eighty-seven years old, the son of a former slave. He had lived through dark times. "I think the daylight's breakin'," he said.[24]

The marchers covered nine miles on June 9. They stopped around four o'clock near a livestock auction barn, just south of Como. Martin Luther King and James Farmer delivered short speeches. King then hurried back to Memphis for an evening flight to Chicago. They still had no tents, so about seventy-five marchers rode south to Batesville and stayed with local families. From her front yard in Senatobia, Ida May Jackson watched other cars heading back to Memphis. "When they come by singin', why, we lit right in an' went singin' too," she recalled. "An' then some whites came by afterward, why, my husband, he told us to stand up tall so's we wouldn't look like we was afraid."

"Yes," she said, rubbing the worn edge of her shirt. "Lord knows we been tired of bein' low down. We want some freedom."[25]

Casting a dark shadow over such inspirational moments, believed Pete Hamill, were Stokely Carmichael and the young black radicals. The *New York Post* reporter filed his June 9 column from Senatobia, after the first set of speeches. The headline: "Black Power On the March."

"Once the kids who stormed the South were some of the most beautiful people in America," wrote Hamill. They suffered, they sacrificed. "They endured because they were better than we were. They had more courage and more innocence and the belief in the basic principles of this country that seemed for a while to be bringing it redemption."

But now, "something ugly and vicious has burrowed its way into the civil rights movement." Some black marchers refused to shake hands with whites, muttered rude responses to polite conversation, and growled at reporters. They glorified the slain Malcolm X, insisted on "black" over "Negro," and disdained black moderates, white liberals, and government institutions. In Senatobia, according to Hamill, Carmichael was "singing out the sweet blind lies of racism."[26]

What had Carmichael said? He had labeled Mississippi whites "a bunch of racists." He had implored that "this has got to be a march for the black people of Mississippi," since "our sweat and blood built Mississippi, and we got to take it over, because we deserve to have it." He wanted black people registering to vote and electing their own representatives. "We got to start building around black power," he said. "Because the only way you're going to stop getting black people being shot down is when we get black sheriffs."[27]

"Black power: That is the key to the brave new world," judged Hamill. "It combines dignity, pride, hatred of whites and Negro brotherhood." His column demonstrated how debates over black politics— and the meaning of the march—were starting to revolve around the new chairman of SNCC.[28]

Tall, dark-skinned, slim and strong, with intense eyes and an easy smile, Carmichael gave off an air, as Howard Zinn once wrote, that he

"would stride cool and smiling through Hell, philosophizing all the way."
His confidence bordered on cockiness. Born in Trinidad and raised in
the Bronx, his speech patterns and mannerisms shifted with the circumstances, allowing him to connect with sharecroppers, street toughs,
or idealistic activists. He loved to provoke and hated to compromise.
"He either mesmerized you or irritated you," recalled John Lewis. "There
was no middle ground."[29]

At Howard University, Carmichael joined the Nonviolent Action
Group (NAG), a Washington, D.C., affiliate of SNCC. If SNCC had been
born out of the idealism of the 1960 student sit-ins, Carmichael was
always sharpening its militant edge. He first went south for the 1961
Freedom Rides, spending his twentieth birthday in Mississippi's notorious Parchman Prison. During thirty-nine days of beatings and priva-
tions in Parchman, he kept questioning the long-term effectiveness of
turning the other cheek: it failed to convert racist whites, and it stifled a
full black humanity.[30]

Before the 1964 Freedom Summer, when volunteers descended upon
Mississippi to organize black voters, Carmichael spearheaded the opposition to inviting white college students, arguing that they would take
leadership roles and then abandon the state. That summer, stationed in
Greenwood, he energetically served as project director. He defied white
intimidation and inspired activists of all races. At Freedom Schools, he
urged children to take pride in themselves and their blackness. At mass
meetings, he celebrated the vote as a ticket to a better life.[31]

But Freedom Summer raised new questions about SNCC's identity.
SNCC had helped organize the new Mississippi Freedom Democratic
Party (MFDP), which demanded that its sixty-eight delegates, including
many SNCC workers, get seated at the Democratic National Convention
in Atlantic City. The MFDP maintained that it, not the "regular" all-
white delegation, represented the legitimate Democratic Party in Mississippi. The disillusioned delegates rejected a compromise proposal that
awarded them only two at-large seats. "They had struggled too long and
come too far to be chumped off like that," reflected Carmichael. "The
Democratic Party could, and would it seemed, try to treat them the way
the state of Mississippi always had."[32]

Carmichael left Mississippi after the disappointment of the 1964 convention. In 1965, in Lowndes County, Alabama, he helped build an
independent third party, challenging rather than integrating the state

Democrats. "We are trying to *build* Democracy," he wrote to a friend. "We have dedicated our lives to that task." The SNCC project formed Freedom Schools, advocated armed self-defense, won intervention from federal courts, and built the Lowndes County Freedom Organization (LCFO), an all-black third party with a black panther for its symbol. In early May 1966, the LCFO had its greatest triumph, achieving a high turnout for its nomination convention.[33]

The southern black man, wrote Carmichael, "has been shamed into distrusting his own capacity to grow and lead and articulate. He has been shamed from birth by his skin, his poverty, his ignorance and even his speech. Who does he see on television? Who gets projected in politics?" In Lowndes County, Carmichael was prescribing his cure for a hypocritical American democracy. SNCC, in his vision, could organize communities with black majorities, whether in the rural Black Belt or in crowded ghettoes.[34]

As Carmichael shifted from the Mississippi Delta to Lowndes County, SNCC workers engaged in existential grappling. "What is SNCC doing?" read the notes from one staff meeting. "Are we a revolutionary organization, or just another organization like the NAACP, SCLC, etc. etc.?" Given its radically democratic convictions, SNCC fostered a close-knit, consensus-driven culture. Yet as its "circle of trust" grew bigger, it got weaker. Many white, northern, middle-class volunteers from Freedom Summer joined as full-time staff, and SNCC had become financially dependent on white goodwill. At the same time, staff members confronted knotty challenges to social justice, illustrated by riots in Harlem and Watts, war in Vietnam, and freedom struggles in Africa. Were they political agitators or community organizers? Could they help local people without becoming traditional leaders? Could white people foster black freedom? If SNCC was against prejudice, why did it discriminate against its own women?[35]

By early 1966, SNCC was obviously alienated from establishment politics. On January 3, a SNCC activist and navy veteran named Sammy Younge got shot while integrating a gas station restroom in Tuskegee, Alabama. SNCC's statement blamed the federal government for the senseless deaths of both Younge and Vietnamese peasants. It further proposed civil rights work as an alternative to the military draft. With the antiwar movement still in its fledgling stage, this radical position inspired mainstream wrath. Julian Bond had left SNCC to win election as a state representative, but after his mild endorsement of the statement, the Georgia legislature refused to seat him.[36]

Meanwhile, SNCC's Atlanta Project advocated racial separatism. Many of its staff joined SNCC after working with other black nationalist organizations in northern cities. They organized in the Vine City ghetto by stressing the distinctiveness of black identity, and they refused to accept white volunteers. "Our everyday contact with whites is a reinforcement of the myth of white supremacy," stated their position paper. "Whites are the ones who must try to raise themselves to our humanistic level." If SNCC truly believed in black liberation, it should be "black-staffed, black-controlled and black-financed."[37]

At a May 1966 retreat in Kingston Springs, Tennessee, John Lewis originally won reelection as SNCC chairman. A man of unquestioned courage and moral fiber, Lewis had everyone's respect. Yet he seemed out of sync with SNCC's evolution. He had participated in the Selma March, attended the signing of the Voting Rights Act, and joined planning meetings for the White House Conference—all events disavowed by his organization. He also served on the governing board of SCLC. With his southern preacher's mien and faith in Gandhian nonviolence, Lewis seemed like a Martin Luther King, Jr., Jr.[38]

So someone challenged the election, and in typical SNCC style, a freewheeling late-night debate ensued. In the end, Carmichael won the chairmanship. If accomplished through dubious means, the election nevertheless gathered the forces building within SNCC. Notes from the Kingston Springs meeting captured Carmichael's larger point: "We assumed that we could organize around *ideals*, such as goodness, justice, etc. . . . We assumed that this country is really a democracy, which just isn't working."[39]

As the new chairman, Carmichael planned to stress grass-roots organizing, not launch a mass march through Mississippi. "I'm tired of marching, see?" Carmichael said in Senatobia. Marches meant appealing to the government, to the media, to liberals. Marches meant nonviolence, compromise. Marches blurred the focus on poor, working people. Yet Carmichael also embraced this unique opportunity to register voters and foster black unity. If they built enough political power, they could "really make this the last march."[40]

Earlier that morning, Carmichael and Cleveland Sellers had returned to Little Rock, where they wrestled with the consequences of SNCC's evolution. A small cadre of SNCC activists had fostered desegregation, voter registration, and education and job opportunities in Arkansas. Those same activists were now divided over their future and worn by fatigue. Ben Grinage, director of the Arkansas Project, resisted SNCC's new path. The African American minister told *The New York Times* that an all-black third party in a state that was only 22 percent black "could not ever bring the poor, both Negro and white, into positions of power that could bring about the relief of oppression."[41]

That public criticism irked SNCC's new leaders. Before Grinage arrived at the meeting, Carmichael asked seven staff members about the statement. Most disavowed it. Though about half the staff was white, they generally supported Carmichael's vision of blacks organizing blacks. Still, Mitchell Zimmerman quizzed Carmichael about how to apply the Lowndes County model. "Confronted with that question, he didn't really have an answer," recalled Zimmerman. The white organizer could see how an all-black party in Arkansas might create racial unity and cultural pride. But as a pure political strategy, it was toxic.[42]

When Grinage arrived, he resigned from SNCC. "It was clear then that SNCC as we had known it was coming apart," recalled Bill Hansen. The first SNCC organizer in Arkansas and its original project director, Hansen was once imbued with righteous faith in man's morality and America's goodness. He now saw national politics as inherently corrupt, entrenched inequality rooted in class, and domestic injustice connected to international colonialism. A white organizer committed to empowering local blacks, he nevertheless diagnosed a larger problem within SNCC: "We were a liberal reformist organization that was trying to become radical, and we didn't know how to do that."[43]

In Little Rock, Carmichael and Sellers tried to clarify some of the project's organizational issues and discussed the recruitment of more black staffers. Then they sped back to Mississippi in time for Carmichael to deliver his Senatobia speech. The following morning, they left for Atlanta. SNCC had just instituted a ten-person Central Committee to streamline the organization and establish its new direction. At the June 10 meeting at SNCC headquarters, the Meredith March dominated the Central Committee's discussions.[44]

Carmichael needed the committee's approval. He was leading a nonviolent mass march while representing an organization that now defined itself against nonviolent mass marches. In Atlanta, he argued that the march furthered SNCC's goals. It had the support of Mississippi blacks, pressured other civil rights organizations to indict President Johnson, elicited debates over nonviolence, and could inspire the creation of independent local organizations.[45]

Courtland Cox objected. Both he and Carmichael were born in Trinidad, grew up in New York, and joined the movement at Howard University. But Cox doubted that the march could stimulate genuine political organizing. "My opposition centered on it being an *event*," he recalled. "Once that event was over, we would have the same problems that we always had." In Lowndes County, they were building a strong black community from the bottom up. Cox argued that the Meredith March brought media attention, but once it was over, common black people would still lack control over their destinies.[46]

Carmichael and Sellers promised that they needed no resources from the Atlanta office, and after some debate and discussion, the committee agreed that the march could help spur independent black politics. Carmichael was optimistic. As notes from the meeting indicated, he believed that with SNCC's guidance, the march through Mississippi would get "people relating to the concept of Black Power."[47]

5

REGISTERING IS ALL RIGHT
Como to Pope
JUNE 10–11, 1966

It surprised no one in Sardis, Mississippi, when Henry Edmond joined the Meredith March. The thickly built, copper-hued man was vice chairman of the Panola County Voters' League, which encouraged blacks to register and vote. He lived in a tidy, five-room house with his schoolteacher wife, and he had worked as an auto mechanic for over twenty years at the local General Motors agency. His childhood education stopped after the eighth grade, but he had since taken seven training courses at the GM facility in Memphis. He was also president of the Negro Parent Teacher Association for North Panola County. On June 10, Edmond joined the march through the "colored" district of Sardis, winning many cheers.

As the parade turned into the main business district, it passed in front of the Chevrolet dealership, where Jim McCullough spotted his former employee. "The way these people carry on is disgraceful," said the middle-aged white man. That February, McCullough had learned that Edmond was running for the open seat on the North Panola School Board.

"Why do you want to run the white schools?" McCullough had asked. "Why do you want to mix with white people?" Edmond retorted that the school board oversaw all the students, black and white. Also, as his own light skin testified, it was white people who had mixed with blacks, not the other way around.

McCullough told him to withdraw the nomination. Edmond refused, saving his self-respect but losing his job. According to Edmond, McCullough fired him. According to McCullough, Edmond resigned.

"Although I would have fired him if he had not quit," added the white boss.

Along with a candidate in the South Panola School District, Edmond became the first African American to seek elected office in Panola County since Reconstruction. The local radio station kept mentioning his candidacy and disclosing his address. Crosses burned on his lawn. A white brick tied to tin cans, carved with the initials "KKK," crashed through his window.

On Election Day, North Panola's white junior high school held a special late-afternoon entertainment program, with free babysitting for white parents, to lure white voters. As election workers turned away some blacks with proper poll tax receipts, some whites voted even though the registration book did not list their names. A civil rights worker observed all the fraud. As the polls closed, a white man rushed up to the activist, pushed him over, kicked him, and punched him. Over thirty whites watched it happen.

After the election, Edmond could not find work, despite his skills. And yet, as Edmond walked among the Meredith Marchers through Sardis, it was McCullough who felt aggrieved. "Put yourself in my place," he said. "Would you let a nigger run for the school board?"[1]

Mississippi had the lowest rates of black voter registration in the South. By 1964, only 6.7 percent of the state's voting-age African Americans had registered, as compared to 38.3 percent of all southern blacks and 69.9 percent of Mississippi whites.[2]

In Panola County, fewer than one hundred blacks had registered by the summer of 1964. When SNCC began organizing there, it started to stimulate a black political consciousness. SNCC partnered with the voters' league, organized student protests for better school conditions, opened Freedom Schools, and ran candidates for a federal cotton allotment program. Panola County blacks learned how the Board of Supervisors distributed funds for schools, roads, hospitals, and public buildings. Clearly, political power shaped their quality of life.[3]

Thanks to the Voting Rights Act of 1965, the number of registered black voters in Mississippi jumped from 28,500 in 1964 to over 130,000 by April 1966. Yet progress differed from county to county, often depending on where the U.S. attorney general had appointed registrars. Civil rights leaders pleaded for more vigorous enforcement of federal law, especially for more mobile registrars and registration offices open on late nights and weekends. In Panola County, which had roughly equal numbers of blacks and whites, 2,060 blacks had registered by the spring of 1966, but so had 6,419 whites.[4]

In the midst of this political shift, Mississippi lawmakers found creative ways to weaken black votes. In the early days of the Meredith March, the State Senate held a closed-door session to approve a proposed constitutional amendment that gerrymandered a congressional district based in the black-majority Delta. The Senate divided it up within three separate districts, each with black minorities. In 1966, moreover, numerous Mississippi counties made changes that diluted black voting power, such as instituting at-large elections for county supervisors and school boards, or appointing rather than electing school superintendents.[5]

Whites also intimidated blacks out of political activity. Black teachers in Panola County, for instance, typically opted out of the Meredith March because they feared that whites would notice them, and then they would lose their state-funded jobs.[6]

Moreover, whites employed violence against politically active blacks such as Robert Miles of Panola County. After a car accident in late May, he and the other driver blamed each other. The police told him that "white women don't lie." They arrested him for refusing to say "Sir" and told him, "Nigger, this is the last ride you gonna take." After striking him from behind with either a gun or a blackjack, they beat him, stomped on him, and kicked him.[7]

The Meredith March arrived at the dawn of a new era: the Voting Rights Act had initiated the mass registration of blacks, but whites still possessed a stranglehold on power. James Meredith provided one more reminder about the risks and rewards of political action. One activist newspaper featured a cover drawing that replicated the now-famous photograph of Meredith writhing on Highway 51. The headline read: "Another reason for you to cast your vote."[8]

Some marchers were relieved that Martin Luther King was off in Chicago. When King walked, crowds flocked to him, and reporters implied that he was the leader, diluting the message of grass-roots empowerment. Now the focus turned more to local politics, and the demonstration included more young black men from SNCC. They talked about slowing down the march to register more voters. They also contemplated civil disobedience tactics such as lying across Highway 51.[9]

On the morning of June 10, the march left Como with 155 people. Five miles down Highway 51, it reached Sardis, a sleepy town of moss-hung oak trees, old homes, decrepit shacks, and small stores. On the grounds of St. Matthew Missionary Baptist Church, locals fed the marchers fried chicken, ham sandwiches, and apple pie. Then they moved on, picking up nearly a hundred more people in town, from young kids to old women. When Floyd McKissick teased, "I got my mojo on ya, you gotta come!" two young men jumped off a truck fender and joined the parade.[10]

All day, resentment rumbled back and forth between the patrolmen and the marchers. That morning, when Robert Green of SCLC pulled up in a "rest car" that provided supplies, Highway Patrol supervisor Charles Snodgrass ordered him to keep moving. "Stop the march!" yelled Green while bounding out of the car. Tempers boiled. Troopers complained that marchers called them "trigger-happy cops"; marchers raged that troopers called them "niggers." Fifteen activists linked arms across Highway 51 in protest. After Ralph Abernathy conferred with Snodgrass, they compromised that if policemen and demonstrators exhibited mutual courtesy, then two rest cars could roll alongside them.[11]

Yet as they walked in pairs along the left shoulder, cars kept whizzing past them, too close for comfort. They were approaching Batesville when McKissick again halted the line. He started complaining to troopers about the continuing problem. As if on cue, a big truck filled with sand rumbled into view. It was going about forty miles an hour, and it was barreling right at them. "Move! Move!" screamed Snodgrass. "Get out of the way! Watch it!" As everyone scrambled to the side, a brave policeman stepped onto the road, halting the truck about fifty feet past the head of the line. He arrested the driver. No one got hurt, although the truck's side-view mirror almost grazed a few people.[12]

The marchers turned off Highway 51 and crossed through Batesville's main square. Every store was closed. As they passed well-maintained homes shaded by magnolia, oak, and walnut trees (along with billboards calling Martin Luther King a Communist), about two thousand whites offered dull glares. Batesville policemen, outfitted in powder-blue helmets and night sticks, looked ready for a riot.[13]

For every hateful action, the marchers had a defiant reaction. White kids waved Confederate flags; "Ain't that cute?" they teased. A pistol-packing man threatened a young black photographer; "Freedom!" they chanted. "Whyn't you go back to the goddamn swamps?" jeered a woman in hair curlers; *Before I'll be a slave, I'll be buried in my grave,"* they sang. A gaunt-faced woman threw a rock; "Come join us," implored McKissick.[14]

The skinny rock-tossing white lady stood her ground, but hundreds of African Americans joined in—especially teenagers and children, who had less to lose and more to gain. They reveled in the freedom-singing heroes, television cameras, news reporters, and helicopters and light airplanes filming aerial shots. The march collected over five hundred people as it reached squat, brick Coleman Chapel AME Zion Church on the northwestern outskirts of town.[15]

Despite little advance warning, Batesville's black community prepared a feast of fried chicken, barbecue, sandwiches, beets, green beans, cornbread, cake, and fruit. Ralph Abernathy, the often-overshadowed lieutenant to King, showcased his own oratorical talents, mixing biblical allegories with constitutional rights, divine inspiration with low-brow jokes. A fifty-foot by fifty-foot tent had finally arrived, and some marchers bedded down there, a curtain modestly separating the men and women. It had been unseasonably cold and wet—Hurricane Alma had touched down on the Gulf Coast—so more people stayed in locals' homes. Many marchers, black and white, headed to a cafe and unwound into the wee hours, dancing the frug and the jerk.[16]

The next morning, they would hold their first voter registration rally.

On the Saturday evening before Meredith started his walk, officials of the Mississippi Freedom Democratic Party met in Jackson. Someone mentioned that MFDP supporters could register voters along Highway 51, but the organization was primarily concerned with Tuesday's Democratic primary elections. That same night, A. B. Britton, chairman of the Civil Rights Committee in Jackson, came to the house of Lawrence Guyot. Britton suggested that Guyot walk with Meredith. The stubborn, whip-smart chairman of MFDP refused: he considered Meredith's walk an ill-timed, unplanned distraction.[17]

The MFDP essentially grew out of SNCC's organizing in Mississippi. After the failed attempt to seat MFDP delegates instead of those from the state's white supremacist Democratic Party at the 1964 Democratic National Convention, the MFDP nonetheless supported the Lyndon Johnson/Hubert Humphrey ticket in that fall's presidential election. SNCC projects started falling apart, and some activists left the state. Disenchanted SNCC hardliners criticized the MFDP for working within the two-party system.[18]

At a November 1965 SNCC meeting, Guyot declared that the MFDP would chart its own course. He characterized the MFDP as both independent and the state's legitimate Democratic Party. During the march, Guyot remained on SNCC's staff, but his stance continued to anger leaders such as Stokely Carmichael, who favored total independence from the established parties.[19]

In June 1966, the MFDP ran candidates in all five congressional districts for the Democratic primary. It was Mississippi's first election since the Voting Rights Act. In the only statewide contest, the MFDP ran Clifton Whitley, a thirty-two-year-old minister, Korean War veteran, and former professor at Rust College. He challenged James Eastland, the sixth-longest-tenured United States senator, chairman of the powerful Senate Judiciary Committee, wealthy Delta plantation boss, and emblem of white supremacy. The state's newspapers rolled out endorsements for Eastland, who could best "cope with the Communist menace in which patriotic Mississippians are so vitally interested."[20]

Meredith got shot on Monday, June 6, the day before the elections. "We cussed him coming and going," recalled Ed King, a white MFDP official and chaplain of Tougaloo College. "We were trying to prove that people didn't have to be as afraid . . . The last thing we wanted was somebody getting themselves shot in the ass with rough shot like Meredith." MFDP attorneys filed a motion in federal court to delay the elections, to no avail.[21]

MFDP candidates lost all their elections. In the aftermath, civil rights workers noted how the Ku Klux Klan distributed intimidating leaflets in three counties, how the Justice Department assigned federal examiners in only fourteen counties, how armed sheriffs and deputies intimidated voters at polling places, and how election officials committed various types of racially motivated fraud.[22]

Yet in Eastland's own Sunflower County, a black woman named Ruby Davis reported that "some people have gone to join the march since James Meredith got shot, some people were afraid after the shooting, but most of us voted, some for the first time in our lives." In the southwestern counties of Jefferson and Claiborne, black candidates won more votes than their opponents, stoking white fears that as more African Americans voted, they would elect black officials.[23]

As Meredith's trek turned into a mass march, an opportunity arose to build on the MFDP's momentum. "We instantly associated it with registering people," said Guyot. On Election Day, party leaders such as Fannie Lou Hamer, R.L.T. Smith, and Clifton Whitley headed to Memphis to join other march leaders. The MFDP joined SCLC, CORE, and SNCC in signing the manifesto, as did two other Mississippi organizations, the Delta Ministry and the Madison County Movement. SNCC's philosophy of empowering local people had shaped these Mississippi activists, who helped push the march's agenda toward registering voters, organizing communities, and getting blacks into elected offices.[24]

On the night of June 9, Guyot brought a group north from Jackson, contributing to the character of the June 10 march to Batesville. On June 10 another carload of activists arrived from Lauderdale County, where they had been staging rallies, holding workshops, and gathering poll watchers to support Rev. Clint Collier, an MFDP candidate in the Fourth Congressional District.[25]

The MFDP was trying to make politics tangible for poor blacks. During the primary campaign, it had described how white congressmen voted against their interests: against education, against Medicare, against labor unions, against rent subsidies. Yet the primary election illustrated the continuing hurdles. "The psychological barriers to registration and voting are almost as prohibitive as the physical barriers," stated one MFDP report. The federal government could help, but it tended to move cautiously, appeasing state officials. "The events of the past few days—in particular, those of the march to Jackson—point up the dire necessity for wielded political power for Negro Mississippians," it concluded. "The MFDP sees as indispensable the need for political power in Mississippi to be in the hands of the people."[26]

On a typical Saturday morning in the summer, cars puttered past the tiny stores lining the aging main square of Batesville. A heavy heat sank upon the farmers arriving in town for their weekly shopping. The classical red-domed Panola County courthouse, built in 1877, loomed over them, its white paint fading and cracking.[27]

On the morning of June 11, however, Batesville hummed with anticipation. The Meredith March would parade through town, culminating with a voter registration rally at the courthouse. Several hundred blacks gathered by the Illinois Central depot. Old white ladies fanned themselves on front porches. Blond teenagers in madras shorts lounged on top of parked cars. Highway patrolmen glared down from the courthouse steps. Mimeographed broadsides from the Ku Klux Klan were scattered around town, calling the marchers "renegades," "outlaws," "parasites," and a "bunch of scum and alley rats."[28]

Charles Scott, a three-hundred-pound New Jersey longshoreman with a booming laugh, led the marchers down Panola Street. Into their ranks filed old women, joyous teenagers, and courageous adults. They swayed with a "Congo-like rhythm," according to one white observer. "Whites were singing those freedom songs to the Negro rhythm just as well as the Negroes themselves were singing, and a great number of the marchers were dancing or slapping their hands and appeared to be in a holiday spirit," he marveled. "It must be a great temptation to fall in line with them because the marchers appeared to be having such a jubilee time."[29]

African Americans lined up outside the courthouse. Eddie Ford, a young carpenter from nearby Courtland, had come to town for his errands, with no intention of registering—"But when I saw them marching, I decided I wanted my freedom." At a hand-clapping, freedom-singing rally, Rev. J. C. Killingsworth, the MFDP chairman in Clarke County, proclaimed that their individual claims to citizenship, taken all together, shattered the myth that black people were satisfied and complacent.[30]

With all the media and government attention, Batesville and Panola County police took pains to accommodate the demonstration. They just wanted the marchers to move on without incident. The first man in line at the courthouse was a retired sharecropper named Sam Flowers. The registrar treated him with courtesy. Flowers was illiterate and did not know his birth year, so he marked an X for his signature and guessed that he was sixty-eight.[31]

The most noteworthy registrant was El Fondren, a man so ancient that he probably had been born a slave. A friend said that he was at least 104 years old. He told reporters that he was 106 years and nine months old. His great-granddaughter later called the courthouse to say that he was 107. A farmer living outside Batesville with his children and grand-children, he was toothless, with a stubbly white beard that offset his dark skin. His mind remained sharp: upon request, he could quote virtually any Bible passage.[32]

Fondren's body trembled as he hobbled into the courthouse, leaning on a cane. "Have you come for your dinner?" asked the clerk, Hazel Weed. She gave him fifty cents, explaining, "We've known these old Negroes all our lives. They don't have much. It helps a little." People in the office often contributed to this fund, a form of paternalism that cushioned the harshness of racial privilege.[33]

Ten minutes after entering the courthouse, Fondren emerged a reg-istered voter. Marchers lifted him on their shoulders. "Hip hip hooray!" they cheered. It was a touching scene. Bob Fitch, a photographer for SCLC, had a near-mystical feeling. He snapped a picture just as Fondren raised his left arm, paralleling the courthouse pillars in the background. The image captured his sense of the moment's magnificence. Someone asked Fondren how it felt to register. "It's all right," he said, with gentle sur-prise. "Registering is all right."[34]

Over three hundred marchers left Batesville in midday, walking about seven miles before camping in an open, weed-strewn field near the tiny village of Pope. They left behind a dual legacy: Panola County whites dismissed this "circus," while blacks celebrated the boost to their free-dom movement.[35]

Compared to El Fondren, Willie Middleton was a spring chicken, but he was still eighty-five years old, so he had some historical perspec-tive. The wiry old insurance agent had watched the march pass through town. He described how the clerk had once blocked his own attempt to register, and how he gained his right to vote after winning a court case on appeal. Now the federal government banned practices such as poll taxes and literacy tests, giving blacks a fighting chance. "This march is waking not only Mississippi up, but waking the world up," he said. "If that man hadn't shot James Meredith, they'd have went on down to Jackson with anyone hardly noticing. But those shots were heard around the world."[36]

When Meredith got shot, Charles Evers rushed up from Port Gibson and spoke at the first mass meeting in Memphis. The NAACP field secretary admired Meredith's independence, courage, and adherence to armed self-defense. He vowed to deliver thousands of marchers.[37]

Three days later, Evers slammed the Meredith March. "I don't want this to turn into another Selma where everyone goes home with the cameramen and leaves us holding the bag," he said, characterizing himself as the champion of both local people and national allies. "Instead of spending all that money on airplane tickets and campouts, we should spend it on registration. That's what Meredith was shot for." He claimed that someone signed his name to the manifesto, which he rejected as "too critical of President Johnson."[38]

Evers's flip-flop reflected his paradoxical place within the Mississippi movement. He carried the legacy of his heroic brother Medgar, but he exploited that family tie. He represented the centrally directed NAACP, but he constantly defied the national office. He exhibited audacious courage and won loyal followers, but he acted out of self-interest. And while expressing the best ideals of racial fellowship, he shrewdly carved out a power base, balancing political pressures like some kind of Mississippi Machiavelli.

When Medgar Evers was organizing for the NAACP, Charles was in the Chicago underworld, running a numbers game while operating a liquor store and three bars. After Medgar was assassinated in 1963, Charles announced that he would replace his brother. Rather than publicly clash with the grieving brother of a martyr, Roy Wilkins allowed the unorthodox power grab. He regretted that decision. Evers followed his own instincts, not the directives of Wilkins. "They all sat up in New York trying to dictate," said Evers. "I never listened to them." As Evers endorsed political candidates, invited outside activists, promised jobs, and vowed armed retaliation to white violence, Wilkins chided him for "individual, unilateral, unauthorized moves by you as a member of the NAACP staff."[39]

Evers built his political foundation in the southwestern counties along the Mississippi River. In the fall of 1965, he declared a boycott of white businesses in Natchez while blasting MFDP and SNCC workers as "outside agitators." He gave stirring, fearless speeches and led boycotts, picket lines, and mass marches that kept pressure on federal and state authorities. By December 1965 the black community had won jobs in the public and private sectors, as well as the desegregation of city-run facilities, earning him a legion of loyalists.[40]

Evers had a gritty sensibility. He used threats to enforce boycotts, warning one crowd that "if we catch a Negro at any store, we will get his name, address, and phone number and take care of him later." Boycotts of potential competitors also fed his business ambitions. "You're in this to help people," he once told Lawrence Guyot. "I'm in this to make money."[41]

Evers nevertheless raised his national profile among white liberals. He praised Lyndon Johnson and the national Democratic Party, and the NAACP joined labor and liberal organizations at the July 1965 Mississippi Democratic Conference, an initial effort to find an integrated middle ground between white supremacist Democrats and the black, grass-roots MFDP. Those same moderates won control of the state's Young Democratic clubs. Unlike the MFDP, the NAACP tried to ally with white moderates to reform the existing Democratic Party.[42]

Throughout the spring of 1966, Evers led a boycott campaign in Fayette, the seat of rural, black-majority Jefferson County. On June 9, he announced a settlement: stores, city parks, and nine of Fayette's ten service station restrooms would be desegregated, the police force would have one black and one white officer with equal authority, roads in black districts would be improved, and city employees would address blacks by courtesy titles rather than "boy" or "auntie." Both he and the city mayor used the language of racial healing. More than ever, Evers appeared a charismatic leader of blacks and a responsible mediator with whites.[43]

Right up until the Meredith shooting, reports circulated that Wilkins was forcing out Evers. But the Fayette triumph reinforced that Evers was indispensable. After visiting a mass meeting in late May, NAACP attorney Jack Young reported back to New York that "Charles has the people in Fayette *completely under his control and domination.*"[44]

When Evers started criticizing the Meredith March, he not only distanced himself from SNCC, but also sprayed his MFDP rivals with the stink of black separatism. Political commentators now upheld him as one of the state's few hopes for a liberal, interracial Democratic Party—a potential alternative to "a white-black split dominated by the Eastlands on one side and the radical Mississippi Freedom Democratic Party on the other." Evers was positioning himself as the future of black politics in Mississippi.[45]

On June 7, Roy Wilkins sent telegrams to one hundred key branches and staff members across the country, urging them to hold mass meetings on Sunday, June 12. These demonstrations would protest the Meredith shooting, commemorate the third anniversary of Medgar Evers's assassination, and call for passage of the Civil Rights Bill.[46]

Even after Wilkins refused to sign the manifesto, Director of Branches Gloster Current urged that the NAACP exploit the Meredith March. Current suggested that they publicize the efforts of NAACP men such as New York's Eugene Reed, who delivered a hundred canteens to the marchers outside Batesville. Wilkins himself adopted a careful tone. "We reject the overt black racist notions freely and crudely expressed by some of the present shakers and movers," he stated. Yet he maintained that the march could highlight the importance of the Civil Rights Bill, and he welcomed individual NAACP members to participate.[47]

On June 12, as NAACP branches throughout the nation held rallies and marches, Wilkins joined Evers in Jackson, Mississippi. Thousands packed the Negro Masonic Temple, and then eight hundred people marched twenty blocks through downtown Jackson. The NAACP leaders defined themselves against racial separatism. "We and the white people must live together," said Wilkins. Evers admitted that he had considered leaving the NAACP, but as tears rolled down his cheeks and the audience cheered, he pledged, "I will never leave you as long as you need me."[48]

On this same morning, Aaron Henry went to the marchers' campsite in Pope. He was of the generation that poured the foundation for the Mississippi movement. Like Medgar Evers in Jackson and Amzie Moore in Cleveland, the Clarksdale pharmacist was a World War II veteran and worked through the NAACP. He had welcomed out-of-state activists in the early 1960s, and he had served as president of the Council of Federated Organizations (COFO), a short-lived coalition in Mississippi that included the NAACP, SNCC, SCLC, and CORE. Now, as the state president of the NAACP, he remained loyal to the Democratic Party and courted alliances with white moderates.[49]

Yet upon his arrival in Pope, Henry pledged his support to the Meredith March. His Coahoma County NAACP branch held its own march in memory of Medgar Evers, while also endorsing the larger march down Highway 51. He further promised that about a hundred of his NAACP people would attend the Jackson rally *and* join the Meredith March. Like others in the long fight against white supremacy, Aaron Henry could not afford philosophical debates or power struggles. He walked down any road that led to freedom.[50]

6

THE WORLD IS WATCHING
Pope to Enid
JUNE 12, 1966

Throughout the March Against Fear, its leaders gathered for late-night meetings. At the Lorraine Motel, and then later at the march's campsite or a nearby church, they planned their course, discussed logistical issues, and debated strategy. Almost daily, Mississippi state officials learned this inside dope. They had a spy. The Mississippi State Sovereignty Commission was receiving information from a confidential source called "Informant X."

Informant X had provided secret information about civil rights activities in Mississippi since 1964. Within a year, the spy was demanding $500 a month; Governor Paul Johnson authorized the salary. The Sovereignty Commission had other sources: some operated in the open, and others were clandestine infiltrators (including two Informant Ys and an Informant Z). But Informant X was especially valuable. According to a June 1965 report, "'X' has now been elected assistant to the director of the Direct Action Committee of SNCC, COFO, INC, and is second in command." It is unclear exactly what organization or office the report was referring to, but the person had influence in the Mississippi movement. Prior to the Meredith shooting, Informant X attended meetings in Jackson with the MFDP inner circle. During the march, this same person frequented the nightly sessions with leaders from SCLC, SNCC, CORE, and Mississippi organizations. Informant X then reported the news to a contact at the Sovereignty Commission.[1]

The Sovereignty Commission was a tax-funded government agency begun in 1956 with the express purpose of preserving racial segregation.

It had a large public relations arm: speakers and publicity materials denied white brutality, linked civil rights to Communism, and celebrated Mississippi as orderly and independent. It also had an investigative arm to keep tabs on civil rights activities and cultivate informants. By 1966, the commission lacked its earlier standing, but it remained a key state office for monitoring threats to white power.[2]

During the march, the Sovereignty Commission described who attended meetings, what they planned, and when leaders were coming and going. It shared the material with government officials and law enforcement. "We compiled information on all of the individuals and organizations who participated in the planning and carrying out of the James Meredith march of 1966," stated one report. "During the planning and carrying out of the march we were able to obtain advance information on plans of the leaders which assisted Governor Johnson in making decisions."[3]

The Sovereignty Commission also fulfilled its own stereotypes about the civil rights movement. Its memoranda were full of gossipy accounts of the march's financial debts and the marchers' sexual behavior. Painting the leaders as law-flouting publicity hounds, they paid particular attention to the weapon-wielding Deacons for Defense. They seemed to delight in arguments among the leaders. As one typical memo from June 9 illustrated, they linked the march to radical outsiders: "Bayard Rustin, the Negro who led the march on Washington D.C. and is a very strong Leftist, if not Communist, was communicated with this evening . . . Roy Wilkins has stated privately that his group should have nothing to do with this march because of its strong 'radical and leftist tendencies' . . . Stokely Carmichael is very much a revolutionary type."[4]

Such documents revealed the attitudes and anxieties of Mississippi's white officials. Yet its actual handling of the march demanded a projection of moderation and competence. Along with Informant X, the world was watching.

After James Meredith got shot, Mississippi governor Paul Johnson promised that "sufficient policemen and any other State forces will be used to see that these demonstrators get all the marching they want, provided they behave themselves, commit no acts of violence nor take a position of defiance." The governor would protect the marchers with the Mississippi

State Highway Patrol. Since taking office in 1964, he had arranged for investigators to receive FBI training, and he had transformed the Highway Patrol into a larger, more disciplined institution.[5]

On the March Against Fear, movement veterans noted how the state police exhibited restraint and used titles such as "Dr. King," a contrast to previous experiences with southern law enforcement. The policemen inspected passing cars and warned white rowdies against violence. Despite some early spats, they avoided using violence on activists.[6]

The highway patrolmen had not miraculously shed their racial prejudices. One officer, for instance, was Lloyd "Goon" Jones, an ornery hulk with a reputation for being "tough on niggers." Yet their professional conduct deflated the moral theater of nonviolent demonstration, dimming the media spotlight on the march.[7]

A disciplined Highway Patrol also forestalled the necessity of federal troops in Mississippi. The previous year, a federal court order had preceded the Selma-to-Montgomery march, so National Guardsmen and U.S. marshals oversaw that demonstration. On the Meredith March, the federal government offered no direct protection. State, county, and city policemen bore all the law enforcement responsibilities.

Attorney General Nicholas Katzenbach relished the Justice Department's role in racial progress, but he believed that if the nation asked the South to abide by the Constitution, then he needed to respect the line between federal and state authority. That cautious, legalistic approach vexed civil rights activists. He received criticism when Aubrey Norvell attacked James Meredith. "It was a tragic thing that he got shot, and we knew we would be blamed for it," reflected Katzenbach. "I suppose we could have put U.S. Marshals on the march with him, but if we did it for Meredith, we would have to do it for everybody."[8]

When the demonstration escalated into a mass march, Katzenbach still resisted a strong federal presence. He preferred that state and local authorities enforce the law. The National Guard or U.S. marshals were last resorts, a sword to be dangled over the South. As one federal official said, "Our big selling point is to tell the local people that either you protect these marchers yourself or we'll do it for you."[9]

John Doar spent the whole march puttering down the highway in a small red car, huddling with local police chiefs and county sheriffs, communicating with civil rights leaders. The young, level-headed assistant attorney general ran the Civil Rights Division of the Justice Department. He was cool and precise, respected by all. He felt satisfied as more blacks registered to vote and more whites adhered to the law. Doar nevertheless walked a tightrope between the marchers and the state authorities: civil rights workers wanted protection to exercise their constitutional rights, and southern officials griped about intrusion into state matters. Everyone constantly asked him about the federal presence along the march. "'Federal presence?'" he ruminated with quiet exasperation, talking more to himself than to reporters. "They'll put that expression—'federal presence'—on my tombstone."[10]

More than the Justice Department, civil rights advocates resented the FBI. Its director, J. Edgar Hoover, had considered black political activity subversive since the 1920s, when he targeted the nationalist leader Marcus Garvey. By contrast, Hoover classified white racist violence as a local problem, outside the FBI's jurisdiction. Only with the 1964 murders of three CORE activists in Mississippi did the bureau begin investigating and infiltrating the Ku Klux Klan. Still, when civil rights workers got harassed and beaten, agents did not protect them—they only conveyed violations of federal law.[11]

The FBI technically reported to Attorney General Katzenbach, who shared some of the activists' frustrations. For crimes such as bank robberies or Communist spying, FBI agents took the lead. Yet when it came to protecting civil rights demonstrations, he said, "they would only do exactly what you asked them to do." The agents acted without enthusiasm or initiative.[12]

The Meredith shooting again incensed the bureau's critics. "The FBI will shoot a man they find robbing a bank, but will only observe and take notes when they see a white man trying to kill James Meredith," cried the pacifist priest Richard McSorley. During the march, FBI agents filed detailed reports, but they would act only with clear provocation during a federal crime. For movement veterans who had endured years of stressful tension and unpunished violence, that restriction seemed racist and hypocritical. Instead of receiving protection, they were under surveillance.[13]

On June 10, an FBI memo relayed that James "Catfish" Cole, grand wizard of the North Carolina Knights of the Ku Klux Klan, planned to come to Mississippi to kill Martin Luther King. Cole actually told a reporter:

"I've seen too many people bungle the job of killing him. I'm not going to bungle it. I'll kill him myself if no one beats me to it. I've seen that Negro running up and down this country ruining our way of life for too long. I can and will put a stop to that Negro. Yes, I will die happy knowing that I have put a stop to that nigger." But the former carnival barker and circus-tent evangelist never acted on his ominous boast. Cole stayed in North Carolina, far from the Meredith March.[14]

While monitoring this threat against King, the FBI kept monitoring King as a threat. Since 1962, King had been on the FBI's "enemies list," subject to round-the-clock telephone surveillance. The scrutiny started because SCLC adviser Stanley Levison had past associations with the Communist Party, and it intensified as J. Edgar Hoover grew obsessed with King's marital infidelities. Out of some combination of racism, jealousy, priggishness, titillation, and a sense of political order, Hoover wanted to discredit King. By 1966 the FBI was curbing this fixation— during the march, in fact, the bureau cut its wiretaps at SCLC's Atlanta headquarters—but agents still maintained close tabs on King. They also kept a wiretap on Levison.[15]

The FBI surveillance of Levison showed SCLC's scramble upon Meredith's shooting. At first, people kept calling his Chicago home, wondering if they should go to Mississippi. Levison saw it as "a junior Selma, and nothing like Selma." Trying to fortify liberal support, he called contacts at religious and labor organizations while counseling patience, raising money, and urging attendance at the final rally in Jackson. He fretted, too, that friends of the movement were painting the march as radical, and he moaned about the Pete Hamill column that blasted Stokely Carmichael.[16]

Late at night on June 9, King returned to Chicago. SCLC's campaign sought to create an "Open City." King urged residents of the sprawling West Side to organize politically, winning the power to improve garbage-strewn streets, dilapidated tenements, and public transportation. He had just unveiled a series of sweeping demands at the city, state, and federal level: integrated and better-funded schools, rapid-transit facilities, open-occupancy laws, race-conscious hiring for upper-level jobs, improved police and sanitation services, and new public housing. As skeptics wondered about the cost, supporters cheered this ambitious, comprehensive vision of racial equality.[17]

The Open City plan revealed King as both practical and radical. He knew that no city official would approve such an extensive agenda, freeing him to initiate direct action protests. Yet even before the Montgomery Bus Boycott launched him into celebrity, King had conceived of injustice in terms of not only Jim Crow, but also colonialism, militarism, and materialism. With his gifts of intellectual synthesis and inspiring oratory, he framed the black freedom struggle in terms of the Constitution and the Bible. But this son of the Atlanta elite drew his inspiration from Gandhi, theologians such as Reinhold Niebuhr, and other socialist thinkers. King's foray into Chicago was not just about race, but about class—not just about civil rights, but about human rights.[18]

King intended to kick off the Chicago campaign on June 26, with a rally at Soldier Field and a march to City Hall. But after the "national emergency" of Meredith's shooting, King postponed the demonstration until July 10. "This in no way diminishes our effort to end the slums in Chicago," he insisted. "In Mississippi, Negro civil rights leaders are physically lynched or mistreated. In Chicago, Negroes are spiritually murdered and mistreated."[19]

Migrants from the Delta and Memphis had long brought their churches, blues music, and family bonds to Chicago. Now Chicago's black communities responded to the Meredith crisis. King spoke at a fundraising rally at Warren Avenue Congregational Church on June 10, and the next morning a busload of marchers headed to Mississippi. "You are the Moses for our people," one Chicagoan wrote to King. "I *will* be in the march to Jackson before it ends."[20]

In Chicago, King connected with both liberal institutions and poor blacks. On June 10 he conferred with members of street gangs at an SCLC workshop at the Sheraton Hotel, in a room reserved by the Unitarian-Universalist Church. King then headed to a luncheon at the LaSalle Hotel, where United Auto Workers president Walter Reuther drew parallels between the civil rights and labor movements, and where King praised the UAW for "embodying principles of civil rights."[21]

King was back at the Lorraine Motel by Saturday night. Early the next morning, he initiated a four-way conference call with Stanley Levison, Bayard Rustin, and SCLC's Washington, D.C., director Walter Fauntroy. King analyzed his high-wire act in Mississippi. He kept faith that the march would help pass the Civil Rights Bill and register voters, even as he mourned how the Vietnam War drained federal resources. While

Rustin and Fauntroy fretted about SNCC sabotaging any victory, King assured them that if masses of white liberals arrived for the final rally in Jackson, they could sustain political momentum. He recognized that Carmichael posed a problem, but they could work together.

"King says we're in it for good or ill," reported the FBI's surveillance notes, "and they have to make the best of the opportunity."[22]

SNCC workers sometimes referred to King as "*De Lawd*." The moniker poked fun at King's soul-stirring oratory, charismatic persona, and media-savvy leadership—traits that SNCC defined itself against, but also qualities that stirred its members' jealousies. Since the Freedom Rides, SNCC staffers complained that King refused to lay his body on the line, yet grabbed acclaim. When King won the Nobel Peace Prize in 1964, they grumbled with resentment.[23]

These festering emotions threatened to pop during the 1965 demonstrations in Alabama. SNCC had organized in Selma first, but SCLC turned the campaign into a dramatic march for national legislation. SNCC workers also criticized King's agreement to turn around during a second attempt to march across the Edmund Pettus Bridge. SCLC, for its part, agonized about SNCC's chaotic, police-baiting demonstrations in Montgomery, as well as the stubborn abrasiveness of organizers such as Carmichael.[24]

Yet at King's urging, SCLC donated money to SNCC that summer. In January 1966, King defended SNCC's antiwar stance at the Georgia State Capitol. Rebuffing recommendations from donors and journalists, King avoided criticizing SNCC. After SNCC boycotted the White House Conference, he did state that he rejected a black nationalist approach, but also cautioned that the boycott was "an indication of deep discontent, disappointment, and even despair among many black people."[25]

King wanted SNCC's participation in the Meredith March. SCLC had contributed to aspects of the Mississippi movement: it joined the original COFO coalition, sponsored citizenship schools that fostered political education, supported the MFDP's Congressional Challenge, imported King for morale-boosting visits, and maintained a small in-state staff. Yet SCLC lacked SNCC's network of MFDP organizers and knowledge of local politics.[26]

Striding through Mississippi, King reached out to the young activists who instinctively resented him. David Acey, a black student leader from Memphis, gravitated toward the fiery Carmichael, but he grew to appreciate King. "With Martin Luther King, you really had to walk with him to understand him," he said. Acey and others carried switchblades while marching. But King counseled that if they were doctors curing racism, they could not jump into bed with patients. "Better to enter heaven with a scarred-up body than a scarred-up soul," he told them. The young radicals might not have embraced nonviolence, but the more they walked with King, the more they understood his perspective. "King gave us a kind of spiritual, in-depth insight," said Acey. "He could see farther in this thing than we could."[27]

King gave the March Against Fear a moral authority. Mississippi blacks flocked toward the march, hoping to touch the hem of his garment. Old ladies handed him jugs of cold water, fed him apples, offered towels to wipe his brow—they had little, but they wanted to ease his burden. "I wanted to see him," said a housekeeper in Coldwater. "I've heard so much about him and I just wanted to see him."[28]

Stokely Carmichael witnessed this reverence firsthand: one time, a group of old women bowled him over while rushing toward King. Carmichael appreciated King's gifts. Rather than compete with the movement's most admired figure, he recognized that King drew people into marches, rallies, and voter registration. King also kept the media interested and respectful. Hosea Williams recalled overhearing SNCC workers complaining about King until Carmichael broke in: "The greatest mistake we could make is to drive Martin Luther King Jr. out. Because if you drive Martin out, we are going to lose the press and we will lose the platform to speak to the nation. Whatever we do, we must keep Martin in."[29]

The leaders also shared a personal affection. When Carmichael became SNCC chairman, King started inviting him to Sunday supper at his Atlanta home. On the march, King got exasperated with SNCC's rhetorical provocations, but he still liked Carmichael—a decade earlier, he had been Carmichael's age while leading the Montgomery Bus Boycott. In Mississippi, King chuckled when Carmichael teased, "You're in SNCC country now. You're going to bow to SNCC now." As for Carmichael, he loved the chance to walk alongside King, "trudging along, mile after mile, discussing every blessed thing under the sun."[30]

At one point, a television reporter walked between them at the head of the line. "Let me say first that this march is nonviolent," intoned King as the microphone pointed toward him. "It is a nonviolent expression of our determination to be free. This is a principle of the march and certainly we intend to keep this march nonviolent." The reporter then turned to Carmichael and asked if he shared King's commitment to nonviolence. No, he responded. "I just don't see it as a way of life. I never have. I also realize that no one in this country is asking the white community in the South to be nonviolent, and that in a sense is giving them a free license to shoot us at will."[31]

Guided by such brief scenes on the evening news, the public understood King as the spiritual force trying to repeat the triumphs of Birmingham and Selma, while Carmichael appeared the bitter challenger to liberal sensibilities. But the news footage obscured how King and Carmichael shared common principles. The March Against Fear kept evolving out of their creative tensions.

On Sunday morning, June 12, King arrived in Pope at ten o'clock, five minutes after the marchers had set off from the campsite. They were glad to be moving on. They had slept under two tents on the hard, rolling ground of a dust-choked cornfield. Flashlights, gas lanterns, and car headlights lent the only illumination. Almost everyone awoke at dawn, and they ate a spare breakfast of bologna and crackers.[32]

The big news concerned plans to change the march route. The previous night, while the campers bedded down, leaders gathered in a parked car and debated for two hours. Meredith's planned trek down Highway 51 passed small towns surrounded by farms, but the black populations were relatively small. Activists wanted to register more voters. A contingent from Bogalusa suggested that the march continue into southwestern Mississippi and Louisiana.[33]

SNCC and MFDP workers, especially, urged a more practical diversion into the Delta. "This was a march against fear," reasoned Charles McLaurin, an organizer in Sunflower County. "Our purpose in bringing it through the Delta was that there was as much fear—of white supremacy, of voter registration, of economic reprisals—in the Delta as anywhere." SNCC had established connections with blacks throughout the Delta. The proposed route would add some miles, but it would move across black majority districts. After passing through Greenwood and Yazoo City, it would loop back onto Highway 51 in Canton, just north of Jackson. "We still must talk over the new route with some people," cautioned King, "but I am certain we will take it."[34]

For now, the march continued down Highway 51. Bolstered by seventy-five new volunteers from Chicago, nearly three hundred marchers passed through rural Yalobusha County. At one crossroads, about thirty blacks waited under a chinaberry tree. Across the street, from the gravel driveway of a gas station, some whites said their "good niggers" had "more sense" than to join this silly march. But then the marchers paraded by, singing *"Oh Freedom, Oh Freedom, Oh Freedom over me."* The blacks weighed the costs of white dissatisfaction—lost jobs, denied credit, violence—against the benefits of a buoyed spirit. One middle-aged man pulled himself up, knocked the dirt off his pants, and started marching. Five others followed him, carefully avoiding eye contact with the glaring whites.[35]

By midday they reached Enid Dam. The federal property, operated by the Army Corps of Engineers, contained a huge concrete dam and an expansive reservoir. It provided a more comfortable resting spot than the Pope cornfield. They set up a tent two hundred yards from the water, ate lunch, and lounged on soft grass under shady trees.[36]

Fannie Lou Hamer led them in freedom songs, striking many marchers with her extraordinary presence. The youngest of twenty children in a poor sharecropping family, she possessed a deep Christian faith, seasoned by a harsh realism. In many ways, she epitomized the courageous women who were the movement's backbone. It was women who built political connections through churches and extended family networks. Men overshadowed them—on the March Against Fear, male leaders such as King and Carmichael stood before the television cameras and got quoted in the newspapers. But without women like Hamer, there was no Mississippi movement.[37]

Hamer's own epiphany had arrived in 1962, when SNCC workers came to Sunflower County, bent on empowering local leaders. This small, stout woman who walked with a limp proved an extraordinary organizer, using soaring songs, plain talk, and outright charisma to register her fellow Delta blacks. She burst into the American consciousness during the 1964 Democratic National Convention. During her nationally televised testimony, she urged the seating of MFDP delegates, recounting how she lost her job as a plantation timekeeper after registering. She recalled bullets fired into her home, and how in June 1963, on the way back from a political workshop, Mississippi police arrested her, June Johnson, and Annelle Ponder. In a Winona jail, these women suffered horrible beatings and sexual humiliation. "All of this on account of we want to register, to become first-class citizens," she said. "If the Mississippi Freedom Democratic Party is not seated now, I question America."[38]

Two years later, Hamer still had occasion to question America. Beads of sweat trailed down her face as she again recalled how in Winona, she "was beaten as hard as metal." It made her uneasy that the Highway Patrol was protecting them, "because it was a state highway patrolman that had me beat to my bottom as hard as nails." She also outlined an expansive notion of justice. "You don't march across Mississippi and leave people homeless, leave people hungry, leave people without food." They needed to register voters in the Delta. She wanted to march across the plantation of Senator James Eastland, who supported free elections in Vietnam yet denied them in Mississippi. "I'm concerned about democracy, but I'm sick of so much hypocrisy."[39]

Martin Luther King hit a theme of harmony. "No one organization in our movement can do the job in Mississippi alone," he said. "This isn't any time for ego battles over who's going to be the leader. We're *all* the leaders here in this struggle for Mississippi." He welcomed people of all races, regions, religions, economic classes, and educational levels: "This is a movement to free the soul of America, and we need *white* people to be in this march. We need each other. Our destinies are tied together. The white man is in dire need of the Negro to free him of his guilt, and the Negro is in dire need of the white man to free him of his fear."[40]

Then, under the protection of both the Highway Patrol and the Deacons for Defense, King drove thirty miles to Marks, Mississippi, to preach the funeral of Armistead Phipps, the man who had died while marching through Senatobia. In sticky, sweltering Valley Queen Baptist Church, King apologized: "I must confess that this is the first time I have stood in the pulpit without a tie or without the proper ministerial attire, but I believe you will forgive me today, because you know what we've been trying to do." He celebrated how Phipps carried his poll tax receipt, how he believed in the MFDP: "This was a man who loved freedom and was willing to suffer and sacrifice for freedom." King urged everyone to honor Phipps's legacy by registering to vote. Within hours, King had touched two audiences with distinct but intertwined messages, expressing man's best instincts and ideals.[41]

After the funeral, King left Mississippi to attend an SCLC meeting in Atlanta. That afternoon, many marchers stayed at Enid Dam, while fifty volunteers started walking again at 3:15. Cars returned them to the campsite after they covered five more miles. In the week since Meredith had left from the Peabody Hotel, the trek had gone over seventy miles. It had been called the Meredith March, the March Against Fear, the Mississippi March, and various combinations of those names. Because it united black organizations and compelled national attention, it was clearly a key moment in civil rights history, akin to the Freedom Rides, Birmingham Campaign, or Selma-to-Montgomery march. Yet its spirit of debate and improvisation clouded the meaning of what *The Washington Post* called "this strange parade—half army of liberation and half civil rights carnival show."[42]

The Sunday papers' week-in-review columns inevitably compared it to Selma. Yet months of demonstrations, considerable planning, and a federal court order had preceded the four-day march to Montgomery. This time, the illusion of organized unity cracked due to the departures of Roy Wilkins and Whitney Young, the quirkiness of James Meredith, the criticisms of Charles Evers, the long and meandering march route, the presence of the Deacons for Defense, and especially the militancy of Stokely Carmichael. This "radical leader," shuddered the *Los Angeles Times*, "has shouted about the need for 'black power' and displayed a truculence never shown in the Alabama demonstration." Liberals worried about such rebellious hostility, even if they applauded the march's greater mission.[43]

The resurgent right, by contrast, moaned about how liberals exploited the shooting of James Meredith. Resisting Lyndon Johnson's slate of Great Society programs, conservatives decried excessive limitations on the free market, state sovereignty, and individual freedom. They reserved particular disdain for the "open housing" provision of the Civil Rights Bill of 1966, which would ban discrimination in the sale, rental, use, or occupancy of private property—a legal measure that expanded federal authority over racist practices throughout the nation.[44]

Some columnists warned against using the Meredith attack to pass the Civil Rights Bill. David Lawrence likened Aubrey Norvell to another unbalanced loner, Lee Harvey Oswald. William White sighed with relief that Meredith survived, because otherwise, "extreme Negro leaders" and "a small, tireless minority of professional South baiters" would have further crushed the dissent against civil rights legislation. And William F. Buckley, Jr., the dean of modern conservatism, declared that "if the purpose of pending legislation is to extirpate all Norvells from south of the Mason-Dixon line, we shall have to have a civil rights bill every year for the next ten." Such legislation would bring about "the complete conversion of the South into a police state"—all because of some erratic would-be assassin. If the Civil Rights Bill did pass, wrote Buckley, it should be called "the Norvell law."[45]

Others assailed the march as hypocritical and dangerous. A Sacramento woman wrote to Martin Luther King that while Carmichael and Evers could scream seditious statements, "there has never been one word of acknowledgement that they [the Negroes] should act like American citizens." An Oakland judge huffed that he never allowed prejudice in his courtroom, yet the marchers promised violence. He wrote to Lyndon Johnson: "I urge you, with all the force at my command, to tell the Negro leaders of this country that they must stop this sort of thing." A Missouri editorialist linked the Mississippi marchers to the urban poor, assailing them all for promoting "hate, selfishness, greed, distrust, vengeance," employing "jungle law and anarchy," and betraying "faith and sacred heritage"—in contrast to the patriots protecting American freedom in Vietnam.[46]

Disgruntled editorials and letters to the editor recalled different instances of black-on-white violence, none of which resulted in a mass march. While criticizing the media for inflating an isolated attack into a "civil rights extravaganza," they cried that police guarded the Mississippi marchers, but no one protected a white person walking through a black ghetto. Others blamed Meredith and the marchers for provoking southern bigots. In their minds, the civil rights movement did not foster justice. It just aggravated the wounds of racial hatred.[47]

The Mississippi drama evoked the entire spectrum of political opinions, as illustrated by a pair of marches near the nation's capital. On Sunday, about thirty activists finished a four-day, sixty-six-mile hike around the Washington Beltway that protested Meredith's shooting and promoted open housing in the suburbs. It concluded with a 150-person rally in Lafayette Park. Many participants then attended a mass meeting at the John Wesley AME Zion Church. That meeting included some who had attended a memorial service for Medgar Evers in Arlington National Cemetery, and others who had paraded along Fourteenth Street to decry the Meredith shooting.[48]

On that same weekend, four Ku Klux Klansmen who opposed the Meredith March gathered in Gettysburg, Pennsylvania, to walk to Washington, D.C., and picket the White House—a protest of a protest. They delayed their start by spending hours looking for the Civil War battlefield's monument to Mississippi, which did not exist. On Saturday they covered only twelve miles. On Sunday they reached Baltimore, where they watched a CORE rally at War Memorial Plaza from across a police line. Then they returned to Pennsylvania. A Klan outfit from Prince George's County had preempted their White House picket. These Maryland Klansmen objected to the Pennsylvania klavern infringing on their turf—a protest of a protest of a protest.[49]

7

EVERYBODY SHOULD HAVE THEIR MARCH
Enid to Oakland
JUNE 13, 1966

Early on Monday morning, June 13, while roaming the grounds at Enid Dam, Theodore Seamans spotted a .45-caliber pistol on the seat of a car that belonged to Earnest "Chilly Willy" Thomas. The white minister from New Jersey confronted the black leader from the Deacons for Defense and Justice. "The movement is no place for guns," he scolded. Seamans also complained that newspapers were publicizing the presence of the Deacons on the march: "Many people who would have come down to join our march won't come now."

Thomas disputed that characterization of "our march." This march was for black people, he said. "We're the ones catching hell and are going to catch it even worse after the march is gone. You don't have any right to tell us how to defend ourselves if we're attacked." And if the public knew about the Deacons, that was good news: "Then maybe the Klan's heard about it too."[1]

Nonviolence asked its practitioners to occupy a higher moral plane. It demanded an extraordinary sacrifice, when most African Americans just wanted basic equality. As black people kept witnessing violence such as the Meredith shooting, their frustrations with nonviolence mounted. The Deacons, formed in 1964, started getting national attention by 1965. On the March Against Fear, for the first time, a national civil rights demonstration showcased and sanctioned blacks practicing armed self-defense.[2]

The Deacons rode along the march line, pistols on their front seats, communicating on two-way radios. They urged men to protect women by walking alongside them. When cars left for the airport, they provided an armed escort. At night they flashed headlights into the surrounding woods and guarded campsites with pistols, rifles, and shotguns. They did not reveal their numbers—they preferred the mystery, as it might deter attacks.[3]

This resistance had roots in the African American tradition. Frederick Douglass, Ida B. Wells, Marcus Garvey, and W.E.B. DuBois had all asserted a right to self-defense, as had the slain Malcolm X and exiled Robert F. Williams. Nonviolence won headlines and contributions, so it dominated the image of the civil rights movement. But grass-roots organizers saw a different picture. In Mississippi, for instance, SNCC worked with people like E. W. Steptoe, Hartman Turnbow, and Fannie Lou Hamer, who shot back when nightriders attacked their homes, or when cars tried running them off the road. After long debates in SNCC circles, many organizers bore arms out of practical necessity.[4]

Moreover, the Deacons were so tough and proud and unapologetic, they represented a kind of freedom. Jim Crow stripped black men of such masculine prerogatives as defending their family. Self-defense offered one way to reclaim manhood. "Any Negro or white has the right to defend themselves with arms," said Charles Ewbank Taylor, an AME bishop who blessed the marchers that day. "Any man who didn't ought to take off his pants and wear skirts."[5]

When Seamans confronted Thomas, the argument spread across the campsite. Bruce Baines of CORE pleaded, "If you want to discuss violence and nonviolence, don't talk around the press. This march is too important." Finally, the debate ended.[6]

It would be simplistic to divide the debaters into, on one hand, white liberals who embraced nonviolence out of spiritual purity or political calculation, and on the other hand, disgruntled blacks who asserted new prerogatives. But it was revealing that the white Seamans defined the march's goals as projecting a positive image and building interracial participation, while the black Thomas considered the march a vehicle for black empowerment. Those goals intersected, but they were not the same thing.

"Hey, boy! Come here!" a white policeman called to Alvin Poussaint. It was June 1965, and the black doctor had just come to Jackson, Mississippi.

Raised in New York, he had an M.D. from Cornell University and post-graduate training in psychopharmacology from UCLA. He retorted: "I'm no boy!"

"What d'ja say, boy?" The officer frisked him and demanded his name. When he responded "Dr. Poussaint," the officer frothed with rage, berating and bullying Poussaint until he gave his first name. "Alvin, the next time I call you, you come right away, you hear? You hear? You hear me, boy?" In front of his female secretary, in the heart of Jackson's black community, Poussaint had to say, "Yes, sir."[7]

Poussaint was the southern field director of the Medical Committee for Human Rights (MCHR), which brought physicians, nurses, dentists, psychologists, and social workers into the civil rights movement. Started in Mississippi during Freedom Summer, the MCHR expanded into other southern states by 1965. It provided medical care for activists, established clinics in black communities, and documented segregated hospitals for federal health officials. By June 1966, its Mississippi staff included Poussaint, four full-time nurses, and a rotating cast of volunteers.[8]

At first Poussaint considered his work distinct from political organizing. After the episode with the policeman, however, he better understood the psychological impact of Jim Crow. Robert Moses, SNCC's organizing guru in Mississippi, sometimes held meetings in Poussaint's living room. Over time, the doctor appreciated Moses's emphasis on developing black consciousness. "It was changing me," said Poussaint. "I began to see the nature of their conflicts, the debates that were going on." By 1966 new MCHR volunteers received specific instructions to listen to local people and avoid paternalist attitudes.[9]

The MCHR signed on as an official sponsor of the March Against Fear. While national headquarters solicited donations and volunteers from its seventeen northern chapters, Poussaint participated in the early planning meetings at the Lorraine Motel. Joyce Ladner, a black graduate of Tougaloo College, and Phyllis Cunningham, a white nurse from Minnesota, oversaw the Jackson office; they handled the comings and goings of marchers and volunteers, while also arranging daily deliveries of supplies such as gauze, hydrogen peroxide, sunscreen, and wrap bandages.[10]

Poussaint, the nurses, and visiting doctors tried screening out those with heart conditions and other ailments, especially after the death of

Armistead Phipps. They urged marchers to drink water, take breaks, and consume salt tablets to combat dehydration. While treating common ailments such as blisters, Poussaint also dealt with the marchers' mental strains. He had to sedate one man who was provoking policemen and alienating others with his rowdy, angry behavior.[11]

Civil rights workers endured extraordinary stress. Good organizers needed to be humble and practical. They could not be self-centered, naive, or cocky. Despite constant threats of violence, they had to show their faith and hide their fears. This tension led to what psychologist Robert Coles called "battle fatigue"—like soldiers, they experienced symptoms that included anxiety, insomnia, and wild anger. Unable to vent their rage upon southern authorities, they sometimes turned on each other.[12]

During counseling sessions, Poussaint kept hearing about black bitterness toward white civil rights workers. The MCHR staff found that blacks, conditioned by the racial climate in Mississippi, harbored deep-seated resentments and insecurities about whites, while white volunteers jumped into leadership positions and had "missionary attitudes." Neither blacks nor whites spoke comfortably about race. They were young, idealistic, and gathered together in pressure-packed circumstances. Sexual relationships, in particular, complicated their interracial alliances.[13]

One month before the march, Poussaint delivered a paper to the American Psychiatric Association called "The Stresses of the White Female Worker in the Civil Rights Movement in the South." It described how young white women faced hostility from not only southern whites, but also black activists. Black women complained that white women won admiration, acted superior, and stole the attention of black men. Black men wrestled with emotions: white women had been forbidden fruit, and now sexual attraction mixed with racial rage. "Whenever I'm around one of these white girls," confessed one man, "I don't know whether I feel like kissing her or punching her in the mouth!" Poussaint realized that white female workers faced an impossible situation, but thought that many acted like "White African Queens," seeing themselves as heroic do-gooders liberating the downtrodden natives.[14]

Poussaint's paper won national media attention. In movement circles, some accused him of airing dirty laundry. "It was like a betrayal," thought Phyllis Cunningham. The MCHR nurse recognized that the traumas of organizing, combined with the sexual activity typical of open-minded young adults, created racial tensions. But she believed that Poussaint laid blame at the feet of white women.[15]

Poussaint had not aimed to stir trouble. By illuminating the "unresolved psychological difficulties" among civil rights workers, he hoped to empower blacks. Through slavery and Jim Crow, African Americans had survived by acting submissively—at the cost, sometimes, of hating themselves. "The Negro has come to form his self-image and self-concept on the basis of what white racists have prescribed," he wrote. Even civil rights activists buried emotions underneath nonviolent discipline. In Mississippi, Poussaint saw their fury oozing to the surface. He knew that to cast off racism's shackles, blacks needed a positive sense of their history and capacity.[16]

During the Meredith March, black activists' frustrations fell under a national spotlight. They had long complained that whites assumed leadership positions, had paternalistic attitudes, and returned to cushy homes after their civil rights vacations. Now those grievances got a public airing. "We've received a lot of help from white liberals and we appreciate it," said Floyd McKissick. "But the situation is sort of like when you are sick and your neighbor comes in to help you. You need his assistance, but you don't want him to run your house or take your wife." Every marcher, black or white, brought his or her ideals, goals, and experiences to Mississippi. United by the goal of freedom, the marchers were still divided by race.[17]

Between towns on Highway 51, whites composed somewhere between 15 and 30 percent of the marchers. Most came for short spurts, such as Ray Goldstein, a nineteen-year-old engineering student in a summer co-op program in Chicago. He started driving with his roommate on late Friday night. They arrived on Saturday, marched on Sunday, and drove home on Monday.[18]

The white marchers fit no single profile. They included an Australian exchange student, a New York City waiter, and a seventy-two-year-old grandmother from Cleveland. John and Kathleen McKenna got married in Boston on a Saturday and were marching in Mississippi by that Wednesday. Another couple drove from San Francisco, got engaged along the way, had a wedding in Memphis, and spent their honeymoon on the march.[19]

A middle-aged factory owner had been watching the evening news in New York. After seeing coverage of the march, he went to Mississippi on an impulse. "I've never done anything like this in my life," he confessed to the elderly black maid walking beside him on Highway 51.[20]

David Dawley illustrated the idealism that many whites carried to Mississippi. A Peace Corps veteran and student activist at the University of Michigan, he faced his fears while marching through Mississippi. But he also experienced a moral clarity. While singing spirituals or filing into a church for a mass meeting, he felt "that we were walking together in history, hand-in-hand, black and white."[21]

Some whites served critical functions: Mel Leventhal had just finished his second year of law school at New York University when Marian Wright Edelman, head of the NAACP Legal Defense and Educational Fund, asked him to provide legal advice to march leaders. Others had less purpose: Eugene Nickerson, a Long Island Democrat running for governor of New York, flew south on June 10 to display his liberal credentials. By the time he reached Como, the marching was done. "Oh no," he said, before posing for pictures and driving back to Memphis for his flight home.[22]

For Jo Freeman, the Meredith March crystallized what she later identified as a feminist consciousness. After joining the Free Speech Movement at the University of California at Berkeley, she started to work as an organizer for SCLC, escaping the office work typically assigned to women through "willfulness and intentionally poor typing skills." In early June 1966, she was stuck at Atlanta headquarters, while SCLC's male staff joined the march. When a new volunteer showed up with a car, Freeman rallied her and two others for a trip to Mississippi. Hosea Williams saw her and shook his head: "When Atlanta told me a car full of women had left, I knew it was you."[23]

Freeman immediately sought a useful role. She called Centenary Methodist Church in Memphis from every available pay phone, updating Don Smith for his daily press releases. Sometimes she drove a car for the MCHR, and despite little experience with cameras, she took photographs for SCLC. She even produced the official march button. She conceived the design, negotiated with a New York company, and got five thousand buttons in ten different colors delivered to Jackson, where their sale raised funds for the march.[24]

The longer Freeman walked, the more she bristled at "male chauvinism," a term she first heard on the march. The emerging emphasis on manhood alienated her. Male photographers roamed outside the two-by-two column, but once, while she snapped pictures, a man literally dragged her back into the line. The official policy directed men to walk closer to the road, protecting the women from cars, but that rule meant that women walked on rougher ground, were more exposed to a road-side sniper, and were isolated from each other. Freeman said that the rhetoric of protection "made the men feel good," but "it didn't do a damn thing for the women."[25]

Moreover, no men protected women from insistent come-ons. Freeman recalled that young black men kept approaching white women, asking for sex without the usual preliminary flirtations. "It was an epidemic," she said. The movement had long fostered interracial sexual relationships—the ultimate taboo, smashed through idealistic affection—but these entreaties seemed unusually persistent and aggressive. At the campsites, women gathered together, complaining about constant pressure to "prove you believe in civil rights." They consulted march leaders, but no one wanted to confront such a thorny issue, especially if it leaked to the press. Freeman nevertheless called these sessions "the first women's group that I was a part of." Her personal efforts for racial justice had given her the experience, skills, and language to confront another form of inequality.[26]

Many other white marchers were clergymen. Rev. Elton Coleman, a thirty-nine-year-old Methodist minister in Moravia, Iowa, still had family in his native Mississippi. When he joined the demonstration, his mother "took it quietly." Still, Coleman had no regrets. "For a long time I've preached, 'Love your neighbor.' I've preached justice and Christianity," he said. "I felt it was time I started practicing it."[27]

The march posed new dilemmas for liberal religious organizations. The Selma March had included an open invitation for people of conscience, but in Mississippi, the stress on black leadership and grass-roots organizing diminished the potential role of white clergymen. Despite their support for the demonstration, neither the National Council of Churches (NCC) nor the National Catholic Conference for Interracial Justice (NCCIJ) issued a call for marchers.[28]

Religious liberals did contribute to the march. Jack Sisson, who covered seventeen states for the NCCIJ's Southern Field Service, volunteered for the publicity office in Memphis, relayed information through Mississippi, and organized support from Catholic parishes along the route.

Duncan Howlett, head of the Unitarian-Universalist Church, marched in Mississippi and arranged charter flights for politicians and clergymen. "I want to see if we shouldn't make an effort to duplicate Selma in order to push over the 1966 civil rights act," said Howlett's colleague Homer Jack. "If they get bogged down in voter registration, there won't be a national impact. Of course, we white folks have to be second class citizens when it comes to strategy."[29]

Jim Leatherer joined the demonstration at Enid Dam. The one-legged man shuffled down from the top of the dam, since the police had blocked his taxi from the campsite. "I was in Mexico, in a hammock enjoying life," he related, out of breath. His friend Dick Gregory had urged him to come to Mississippi. Despite losing his leg to a tumor, he had marched from Selma to Montgomery in 1965. In Mississippi he again hobbled down the highway on crutches, attracting attention from onlookers and authorities.[30]

A number of whites displayed countercultural fashions: beards, shaggy hair, guitars, berets, and peace symbols. Participation in the civil rights movement had radicalized many activists, and Lyndon Johnson's escalation of troop levels in Vietnam was arousing the passions of the emerging New Left. On June 11, in fact, the executive committee of the National Conference for New Politics, a radical-liberal alliance committed to ending the war and speeding racial justice, met in New York for the first time. It adopted a motion supporting the Meredith March.[31]

In 1966, though, antiwar sentiment had yet to filter into the mainstream, so the marchers tried to avoid a public association with this kind of political radicalism. When one man proclaimed, "There are more freedoms in China and Russia than there are here," his friend dragged him away from reporters. The press referred to another hippie as the "House Marxist."[32]

Journalist Renata Adler dubbed the white rank-and-file "The Drones." They arrived "with only the fuzziest comprehension of the issues but with a strong conviction that civil rights is a good thing to walk for." The last to learn about decisions and developments, they "trudge wearily along," reluctant to complain about the searing heat, logistical breakdowns, or nights in sleeping bags on hard ground in fetid tents. When a black woman lectured them not to throw away plastic spoons and forks, issuing heavy-handed hints that maybe whites should leave, they accepted her bossiness without complaint. They even laughed along when a black organizer sang:

> *All you Northern liberal white folks*
> *With all that excess fat*
> *A few days on the Mississippi highway*
> *Will sure take care of that.*[33]

Of course, whites exhibited courage and conviction by marching. Experienced activists, especially, appreciated the perspectives of their black colleagues. For instance, Dick Reavis had organized for SCLC in Demopolis, Alabama. It tested his idealism: Should he help a black farmer shoot back at Klansmen? Why did blacks from SNCC want whites out of the movement, even after white activists had bailed them out of jail? When Reavis came to Mississippi, he talked to black marchers along the route and in campsites, and he better understood that whites could help, but blacks needed to lead themselves. "It seemed like the logical conclusion to what the movement had been about," he reflected.[34]

At one point he walked alongside a ten-year-old black boy wearing oversized, hand-me-down boots. The child's feet burned with blisters, so Reavis put him on his shoulders for a few miles. He thought nothing of it until he saw the photograph in a newspaper. Then he regretted the symbolism—a white man's burden.[35]

"I'm not tired. I'm not tired," insisted Ada Orange as marchers guided her into the shade, just outside Senatobia. The petite, sixty-five-year-old African American grandmother wore wool stockings despite the mid-afternoon summer heat. As she drank from a water jug, her legs wobbled. But she resolved to keep marching. When asked why, she looked up from under her green straw bonnet. "For freedom," she said, nodding her head emphatically. "Yes, for my freedom."[36]

Local blacks swelled the march's ranks as it passed through towns along Highway 51. They marched to express anger, to conquer fears, to create a better future. Mary Jones promised to walk "to Kingdom Come," if necessary. Still seething at the attack upon Meredith, she proclaimed that "if I stop marching, I'm liable to do something else." She came across the Delta from Clarksdale, but only after voting for the first time in her life.[37]

Mississippi blacks did not have to walk down Highway 51 to embrace the march's spirit. After the Meredith shooting, twenty people in Hernando demonstrated outside the DeSoto County Courthouse, brandishing signs that demanded, WE WANT TO VOTE. Locals also housed and fed visiting marchers; one woman arrived at the Enid Dam campsite with a massive box of fried chicken and a pot of greens. Harmon and Earline Ellis hosted a rest break in their front yard in Oakland, even if it exposed them to retaliation. "Ah'm tired of standin' silent," said Harmon. "Ah don't care who knows. Earline feels the same way."[38]

The march lent Coby Smith a passage into manhood. He hailed from a politically active family in Memphis, and he, along with another young black man, had recently integrated Southwestern College, a Presbyterian liberal arts institution. He played football, acted in plays, joined an activist group called the Southern Student Organizing Committee, and stomached indignities such as a dean warning him to avoid white girls. In June 1966, he had just started his summer job as a draftsman for the Federal Aviation Agency. When Meredith got shot, he quit work and marched into Mississippi.[39]

At the first mass meeting at Centenary Methodist Church, the NAACP's Maxine Smith asked the audience for suggestions. After Martin Luther King pointed out his raised hand, Coby Smith urged leaders to recruit students from Memphis. As they marched, Smith grew only more appreciative of King. He discussed civil disobedience tactics and mass organizing with the famous civil rights leader, who seemed so down-to-earth.[40]

Smith's role model, however, was Stokely Carmichael. He first saw the charisma of the SNCC chairman during that mass meeting at Centenary. Instead of sermonizing, Carmichael spoke in a fierce, entertaining style that combined a rat-a-tat delivery with singsong tones. He also dressed like a particularly cool field hand—Smith admired his deck overalls, sandals, and dark shades. Exuding energy along the route, Carmichael connected with black youth. Smith now considered the federal government an enemy rather than a reluctant ally. Otherwise, as Carmichael asked, where was the protection from National Guardsmen or U.S. marshals?[41]

"This was not just a historical event," Smith reflected. "This was part of growing up for me." He swelled with pride when his father marched alongside him. Sitting around campfires, he heard folk songs that sounded nothing like Memphis soul. He met Floyd McKissick, Fannie Lou Hamer, and James Farmer. He also had his embarrassing and harrowing moments, such as when a salt tablet upset his stomach, and he had to drift to the rear—past marchers, reporters, troopers, and finally menacing white southerners—before turning a cotton field into his impromptu bathroom. More important was how the march's routines, friendships, stresses, and delights molded his future as a militant activist.[42]

Other African Americans came from beyond Memphis and Mississippi. Some were political celebrities, such as Harlem power broker Percy Sutton. Many worked for civil rights organizations, earning regular subsistence wages. Others arrived out of conscience, such as Thomas Edlin, an electrician who marched in two separate stints, taking vacation time and paying his bus fare to reach the South. "This is just something you have to do, because they need you down here. There is no other way to explain it," he said. "We're living a piece of history here that none of us will ever forget."[43]

Some marchers reveled in the spirit: "When I'm marching I like myself," explained Barbara Kay, a New Jersey woman walking alongside her fourteen-year-old daughter. Others showcased their bitterness: the Brooklyn bus driver Vincent Young carried a sign that proclaimed, NO VIET CONG EVER CALLED ME NIGGER. Still others learned important lessons: members of the Blackstone Rangers, a street gang marching under the auspices of SCLC, returned to Chicago with newfound respect for the guts of southern organizers.[44]

The march continued Barbara Jean Williams's involvement in the movement. Her father was SCLC's Hosea Williams, so she had participated in mass meetings, voter registration workshops, and marches. In Mississippi, her father moved up and down the line, "everywhere at the same time." Sometimes he popped beside her and commanded her to do some task. Usually she looked out for James Orange or "Big Lester" Hankerson, two massive SCLC men who lent a psychological reassurance of safety. More than fear, though, she dreaded the heat. Wearing a new dress with a bright-colored lining, she broke out in hives.[45]

Unlike Jo Freeman, Williams did not consider the march a catalyst for feminist consciousness. The civil rights struggle awakened women to gender inequalities, but as an African American, she identified first with the battle against racism. She had crusaded for freedom alongside black men. The emerging women's movement "was for white women who needed to be liberated, and I agreed that they needed to be liberated as women. But I did not see that as my primary oppression." Williams did not participate in women's discussions of sexism during the Meredith March. She would become a feminist, but later, and through different circumstances than the white female marchers.[46]

With its courageous efforts at grass-roots organizing since 1961, SNCC had forged strong ties to Mississippi's black population. When Meredith began his walk, Mississippi natives MacArthur Cotton, George Greene, and Hollis Watkins had similar reactions: the SNCC workers considered it the odd crusade of a solitary figure. But once he got shot, said Cotton, "we took it as a collective attack." They saw a way to advance their longtime mission of empowering the black community.[47]

Hollis Watkins walked the highways, booming out freedom songs. He also went into communities and talked about voter registration. For some, Meredith's shooting reinforced their fears. For others, it cast them off. Watkins leveled with people about the risks; he also explained the rewards. He emphasized that everyone could play a part: the organizers canvassing the streets, the celebrity orators such as King and Carmichael, the registrants entering the courthouse, and the people who cooked food, opened homes, and involved their children.[48]

Because SNCC had largely withdrawn from Mississippi by 1965, the march served as something of a reunion for staff members. They crashed in each other's rooms, traded war stories, and reconnected with local people. Courtland Cox had voiced the strongest objections to SNCC's participation, but he, too, came to Mississippi. He had once invested enormous energy in the March on Washington, and now, he saw that same passion among other activists. He left his doubts in Atlanta. "Everybody should have their march," he said.[49]

Stanley Wise, grim-faced and bitter, defied the Highway Patrol by walking on the pavement. He projected the militancy of the "new SNCC." He cared nothing about the pending Civil Rights Bill. "Why don't they use the legislation they already have on the books?" he asked. If the federal government was sincere, where were the mobile registrars in every county? Wise said that SNCC remained committed to nonviolence, though it was "re-defining" the term. They would not suffer violence without retaliation.[50]

SNCC reflected a more widespread attitude among young black people. In this atmosphere of black self-assertion, indications of white control inflamed racial sores. One white marcher, while helping with the tent at Enid Dam, exhorted, "Hey boys, come on, we generally get this thing down in ten minutes." A black man yelled back: "*Well*, you better get some of them *boys* you been working with."[51]

By refusing to pay lip service to white liberals, black activists not only expressed their disenchantment with the glacial crawl of legal reforms, but also defined freedom on their own terms. "We were seeking power," said Cox. "We were trying to bypass the whole issue of electoral politics and just participating in someone else's arena. We were trying to create our own arena." Most whites understood this development in negative terms, as a rejection of integration and nonviolence. More blacks considered it a positive growth, an affirmation of African American pride and self-determination.[52]

The movement needed white allies, white resources, and constitutional rights as citizens in a nation with a white majority and white leaders. Yet African Americans needed their own leaders and organizations— they needed to control their own destinies. Richard Haley of CORE realized the irony of asking whites for donations with no strings attached, but blacks had to slip the yoke of white paternalism. "We're going to swing wildly and hit somebody who doesn't deserve to be hit," he admitted. "It is inevitable. It is part of the process of finding our identity."[53]

Few negotiated the march's minefields with more skill than Floyd McKissick, the national director of CORE. Occupying the political ground between Martin Luther King and Stokely Carmichael, McKissick cast his arms wide, trying to pull everyone under the march's banner. On Sunday, June 12, while trumpeting the march's importance during television interviews and a CORE rally in the Bronx, he had emphasized that no single strategy could win black freedom. Back in Mississippi on Monday, he supported a route through the Delta that reached more African Americans, but insisted that no decisions were final: "It's a matter of reaching agreement and making a decision which everyone will accept."[54]

Unlike other national leaders, McKissick logged many miles through Mississippi. Ralph Abernathy, for instance, once stepped out of an air-conditioned car while wearing a white suit, walking just long enough for the news cameras to film him. McKissick, by contrast, served lunch, washed dishes, and set a quick pace through monotonous stretches of highway. While stressing black leadership and pride, he also affirmed CORE's older ethic of interracial fellowship. At Enid Dam, he locked into an earnest, hour-long discussion with a Mississippi woman about possible alliances with white liberals.[55]

McKissick put his family on the movement's front lines: his children had integrated North Carolina schools and participated in demonstrations, and they had just moved to Harlem to be near CORE's new headquarters. His wife, Evelyn, son, Floyd Jr., and daughters Andree, Jocelyn, and Charmaine joined the Meredith March from June 13 to June 15. They, too, had formative experiences in Mississippi. The Deacon who picked them up in Memphis in an old, disintegrating station wagon warned them to look out for snipers, since someone recently had shot at him. The younger children, Floyd Jr. and Charmaine, stayed with a black family in Grenada, appreciating their kind generosity. The precocious Charmaine, who had just finished the fifth grade, reveled in attention from Fannie Lou Hamer and mooned over Stokely Carmichael.[56]

Unfortunately, on June 13, their father presided over a day of grumbling discontent, organizational rivalry, and slowing momentum. The brouhaha over the Deacons preceded breakfast. The number of marchers peaked at about 200, down from Sunday's total of 290. People kept bickering about the route, and few locals cheered or joined them. A thunderstorm soaked them near the town of Oakland, and the Yalobusha County sheriff denied their request for shelter at a local black school. They waited on the shoulder, under pine trees. When the rain eased, most rode trucks back to the tents at Enid Dam, while eighty diehards marched on and covered over fourteen miles.[57]

During this moist Monday, resentments against Charles Evers and the NAACP floated to the surface. "I don't give a damn if the NAACP comes along. All they got is money," said one CORE official. He dismissed the NAACP as bourgeois snobs. "They're a paper organization in Mississippi. If they did come we'd have to have folding chairs and tea parties for them."[58]

Yet the day also featured Cecil Moore, who illustrated how the NAACP umbrella shaded various political viewpoints, depending on local circumstances and personalities. As NAACP branch president in Philadelphia, Pennsylvania, Moore employed the language and style of black nationalism. He lambasted moderates, the Democratic Party, and "Uncle Toms" while recruiting from the working class, launching aggressive all-black direct action campaigns, and fighting to improve city conditions. "I am the goddamn boss," he proclaimed.[59]

Moore's ad-libbing off the NAACP script, however, dismayed the national office. In 1965, Director of Branches Gloster Current announced that the Philadelphia branch would split into five local offices—a move that would curtail Moore's power. Moore delayed the breakup through the courts and his own guile. In June 1966, he demanded that Current postpone a midweek meeting in New York City to determine how best to divide the Philadelphia branch, claiming that his city's working people needed it moved to a weekend, so they could rally support to fight the change.[60]

Amid this controversy, Moore found time to march in Mississippi. He won attention while contrasting himself with the NAACP's old guard. At a Sunday rally in Memphis, he accused local NAACP leaders of refusing to let him speak, grumbling that "we have our 'safe' Negroes in Philadelphia, too." The next day on Highway 51, he boasted that the Philadelphia NAACP was "the only active branch they got." Marching at the head of the line, dressed in his old marine corps fatigues and brandishing a Grenadier cigar, he rejected Charles Evers's claim that the march was a publicity stunt. "This march is electrifying Negroes all over the country," he said.[61]

People walked through Mississippi to overcome fear, pass legislation, advance their own ambitions, achieve racial brotherhood, and/or realize black consciousness. After each day's trek, they massaged sore feet, bandaged up blisters, sang freedom songs, and talked about the movement. Of course, the campsites also hosted fleeting romances—sometimes discreet and sometimes obvious.[62]

That night, back at Enid Dam, Floyd McKissick hopped onto an oil drum. "There is a man's tent and a woman's tent," he lectured, sparking a few giggles. After Selma, an Alabama congressman had accused civil rights marchers of indulging in federally protected orgies. "Don't be surprised if your name is read into the Congressional Record for carrying on the process of integration," warned McKissick. Segregationists would exploit any suggestion of immorality. "You have a constitutional right to be human," he implored, "but this is a movement of the spirit."[63]

8

STANDING TALL
Oakland to Grenada
JUNE 14, 1966

Four days after the attack upon James Meredith, Claude Fuller called together the Cottonmouth Moccasin Gang. The "gang" had only two other members: Ernest Avants and James Jones. Based in Kingston, a small town in southwestern Mississippi, the group was an offshoot of the Ku Klux Klan—a government committee had recently identified Fuller and Avants as Klansmen. Jones, a hard-luck ex-convict, had just started working with them at International Paper Company in Natchez.

Jones drove his car to Fuller's house. While Fuller and Avants drank beer, Jones drank coffee. Unbeknownst to Jones, Fuller loaded the car with an automatic rifle and a shotgun. Jones then drove them to a grocery store, where Fuller and Avants drank another beer, while Jones had a Coke and a pickled sausage.

Fuller revealed his plan: they were going to murder a soft-spoken, God-fearing, sixty-seven-year-old black man named Ben Chester White. A handyman and cook for a white farmer, White had no connection to the civil rights movement. He depended on the good graces of white people. A few weeks earlier, Fuller had pulled up to White and started a conversation. He asked: Shouldn't black and white kids go to school together, share the same playgrounds, swim in the same pools? Accustomed to affirming white folks, White said yes. Fuller thus manufactured his own black agitator.

That evening, the three white men drove to White's home. Claiming that they were searching for a lost German shepherd, they asked for help.

White hopped into the backseat. They stopped again at the grocery. Fuller and Avants had another beer. White drank a red soda.

After driving for miles down a gravel road, looking for the imaginary dog, they crossed a bridge over shallow, clear Pretty Creek. Fuller told Jones to turn the car around. They stopped on the bridge. Fuller spun toward the backseat: "Pop, get out."

White saw the rifle. He started praying. "Oh Lord," he cried. "What have I done to deserve this?"

Fuller fired the rifle twice. Avants then blasted White with the shotgun. From the driver's seat, Jones felt a warm, wet sensation on his neck. It was a chunk of Ben Chester White's brain.[1]

Two days later, some children discovered White's corpse in Pretty Creek. His insides were ripped to tatters. Jones got arrested first. The day after the killing, he had left his night shift at International Paper, pretending to look for his car before reporting it stolen. In the gang's clumsy effort at a cover-up, they had burned the brain-splattered, bullet-strewn Chevrolet near the home of a county supervisor; Fuller then placed an anonymous call blaming White's death on the official. After the police traced the call to a service station telephone, the attendant confirmed that Fuller had made the call. By then, Jones had failed a lie detector test, and after stewing in his own fear and guilt, he confessed their crime. Wary of more bad publicity, Mississippi police arrested Fuller and Avants. The Cottonmouth Moccasin Gang never killed again.[2]

The murder of Ben Chester White displayed the nefarious depths of white supremacists, especially roiled by the Meredith March. After throwing White's body into Pretty Creek and burning the car, the three white men had stopped at another small store to eat barbecue. There, Fuller said that "he had orders from higher ups that the old darky had to go." According to the plan, White's killing would not only deflect attention from the march, but also draw Martin Luther King to southwestern Mississippi. Then, they could murder King, too.[3]

When whites spilled out of Oakland Baptist Church on June 13, they gawked at the marchers lounging in the shady yard of a tar-paper shack. Blacks and whites drank water from a common barrel on the front porch. A white girl sketched a black boy with charcoal. A white man passed his young son onto the shoulders of a black cotton picker. A priest wandered around with a hanging shirttail and dirty clerical collar. The local whites, dressed in their Sunday best, contrasted themselves with these un-washed, race-mixing radicals. It reaffirmed their sense of superiority.[4]

James Silver, a history professor who had befriended James Mere-dith at Ole Miss, characterized Mississippi as a "closed society," with rigid, state-enforced indoctrination of white supremacy at all levels, including political institutions, media outlets, family life, social inter-actions, schools, and churches. If most white people were not heckling the Meredith Marchers, they nevertheless lived in a segregated society, and they could not fully grasp the black freedom struggle.[5]

"As far as the Nigra having as much freedom as the white man, they do," insisted an Ole Miss student when asked about the march. "In fact, they have a lot more now than we have." Whites complained that federal legislation favored blacks for jobs, schools, and political offices. What about *white* rights? "The millions of dollars being spent to 'condone and support' these stupid, ignorant, Satanic so-called marches is nothing short of 'Satan's own work!!'" wrote a Neshoba woman to James East-land, after penning a similar rant to Paul Johnson. She catalogued the indignities, both real and fanciful: Her sick mother had to share a hos-pital room with a black person! Her car was broken-down, but blacks ate steak and drove fancy cars![6]

But by 1966, "massive resistance," such as defying federal authority or attacking black demonstrators, was losing legitimacy. Instead, many whites hoped to preserve the status quo with token concessions and stra-tegic adjustments. If the Baptist Church could no longer sanction Jim Crow, for instance, churches could focus on individual salvation. If federal law mandated school integration, whites could establish private schools or exploit "freedom of choice" statutes to keep most black chil-dren in all-black schools. If liberals condemned them as backwards rac-ists, they could define themselves as defenders of individual freedom, sharing concerns with conservatives nationwide.[7]

The Meredith March exposed a South in transition. On one hand, whites prided themselves on restraint. On the other, they howled about extraordinary provocations. Mayors, newspaper editors, and bystanders vowed to ignore this bloodthirsty "bunch of nuts." They blamed the media for inflating the march's importance. Why no similar outcry for black-on-white murder in the North? Why did their taxes support these "raggle-taggle elements" who bleated about discrimination instead of doing honest work? They kept insisting that conspiracies would overthrow their freedoms. One man complained to a Mississippi newspaper:

> The "war in Mississippi," and that is what it is, is being conducted by outsiders who are making our state their whipping boy to cover up their foul purposes. One organization of radicals send a few "marchers" to our state, and another sends a hatchet man to shoot up their leader, just as they used a man from Memphis, to shoot James Meredith with a few small bird shot which barely penetrated his skin, that the publicity boys with TV cameras might continue their slanders against white Mississippians and make them appear as unfeeling Negro haters, when the truth is that white and black people have lived side by side in our state for a hundred years in friendship, respect, and mutual helpfulness.

Such letters implied that despite these outrages, white southerners exhibited gracious, Christian behavior. They deserved respect, not blame.[8]

Their blacks, claimed many whites, were comfortable with segregation. "We have a good class of Negro here. We don't have any problems," said a Como man, echoing a common theme. They gloated when black Mississippians chose not to march, ignoring that local blacks were deterred by the fear of lost jobs or Klan attacks. They also portrayed the marchers as hailing from Chicago, New York, and other northern hotbeds of poverty and vice.[9]

Well-to-do whites assumed a lordly responsibility for poor blacks, even as they kept those same blacks poor and dependent. While in Pope, *Detroit Free Press* columnist Bill Porterfield profiled "Billy Jack," a plantation boss who paid his black workers one dollar an hour, offered free housing, footed bail money and doctor bills, and treated "my nigguhs" with gruff, parental warmth. Porterfield also described "Mule," a huge, illiterate black sidekick who avoided marching out of some combination of fear and love for Billy Jack.[10]

But the march frayed those paternalist bonds. "We don't know how to talk to our niggers and we don't know what they want anymore," lamented one farmer during the march through Como. Nearby, a bank president and wealthy landowner adjusted to the dawning black attitude: "Last year I was guardian angel to about twenty families living on my plantation, and they wouldn't go to the bathroom without checking with me. But I don't have them living there now. I just hire them by the day and I'm happy." Whether or not he actually preferred the new system, the old patterns had disintegrated.[11]

The spectacle of proud blacks parading through town, registering voters, and singing "We Shall Overcome" had a complicated effect on Mississippi whites. After the march left Batesville, whites sat in Brown's Café, mulling over the biggest event in recent history. "I don't ever recall seein' so many niggers at one time before," said a shell-shocked man. "It looked like a goddamn invasion." One man vowed to punch any more prideful black protesters, while another softly admitted that the march hastened an inevitable integration. The march was testing their principles, prejudices, and patience. Fred Ogg, the highway patrolman who earlier that week had shoved Martin Luther King, slumped onto a stool and ordered eggs, grits, and coffee. Someone asked how he felt.

"I'm just about overcome," he said.[12]

Virtually no Mississippi whites advocated racial integration, welcomed northern activists, or cheered civil rights laws. But not all whites were crude, foaming-at-the-mouth racists, either. Some refused to parrot the talking points of white supremacists. Every decent-sized community had some of these enlightened iconoclasts, who occupied a middle ground in Mississippi race relations. A few newspaper editors exemplified this unique political position.

Hazel Brannon Smith of *The Lexington Advertiser*, based in Holmes County, Mississippi, wrote editorials criticizing the Ku Klux Klan, the Citizens' Council, the Sovereignty Commission, political demagogues, and instances of gross racism such as the Ole Miss riot. This spirited woman endured advertiser boycotts and roughneck intimidation, but she kept promoting economic development and human decency. "If Mississippi could put aside its racial prejudices and concentrate on educating, training and developing the human resources of our state," she wrote, "a new and wonderful day would dawn for us all." She praised the interracial Young Democratic clubs and NAACP leaders such as Roy Wilkins, Charles Evers, and Aaron Henry.[13]

Smith valued civility, stability, moderation. When Meredith began marching, she considered it "provocative and dangerous." But she reserved disgust for his attacker, Aubrey Norvell, "who made it a little harder for whites and Negroes to live together in this, our common land, with mutual respect and trust for ourselves and each other and in common dignity." As the march continued, she lambasted whites for groaning about the incursion. "It is time for white Mississippians to wake up and throw off the blinders we have been wearing for so many years," she wrote. "Our house is on fire."[14]

Mississippi's dean of white moderates was Hodding Carter, Jr., editor of the *Delta Democrat Times*. He lambasted lynching in the 1930s, accepted the *Brown* decision in the 1950s, and guarded the peaceful reputation of his hometown Greenville. Carter, too, endured harassment from the Citizens' Council and Ku Klux Klan. Yet he objected to the label of integrationist. Immersed in the Delta's planter culture, he hosted out-of-town journalists at his comfortable estate, championing his state's gradual progress. Despite his plucky attacks on petty politicians and brutal bigots, the patrician editor disliked black protests and out-of-town organizers.[15]

Suffering from eye trouble, Carter endured bouts of depression and alcohol abuse. By June 1966, he had ceded editorial control to his son Hodding Carter III, a leader in the racially integrated Young Democrat movement. The *Delta Democrat Times* supported neither the marchers nor their enemies. An editorial worried how the "faction-ridden civil rights movement" would define its objectives, yet chided those who considered the demonstration some elaborate antiwhite conspiracy.[16]

On Friday, June 17, the NAACP launched a boycott of Greenville stores. Inspired by the Meredith March, the local branch called for businesses and city offices to hire more black workers. A *Democrat Times* editorial urged compromise: "Greenville's racial relationships have been the best in Mississippi. We have not been plagued or shamed by calculated acts of violence by either whites or Negroes." Behind the scenes, the elder Carter grumbled, viewing the protest with condescension. It delayed his vacation. "I am just about ready to join the Citizens Council, the Ku Klux Klan or the Knights of the Forest so as to get even with the people who are spoiling what we were looking forward to as the best part of our summer," he griped.[17]

If Hazel Brannon Smith and the Hodding Carters did not exactly embrace the Meredith March, they nonetheless distinguished themselves from other Mississippi editors. Most papers decried the marchers as lawless publicity hounds. Some urged calmness and reason, but others drew a line in the sand. "As long as we keep our segregationist attitudes intact, the enemy can never achieve his goal, which is the elimination of race consciousness," exhorted *The Meridian Star*. "No tyrannical federal government, no scummy marchers can control what we think and what we feel. If we remain segregationists at heart, we never need abandon our hope of restoring our Southern way of life."[18]

The two Jackson newspapers, *The Clarion-Ledger* and *Daily News*, were both owned by the influential Hederman family. Their columnists mocked the march with mean-spirited mischievousness. "You can hardly blame Martin Luther and the motley marchers for wanting to come into Mississippi for their parading," wrote Jimmy Ward. "Deep Harlem and South Side Chicago are pretty foul places all the time, but certainly no place to spend a 'long hot' summer. Here, there's plenty of fresh, clean air, open road and practically nobody interested in their overworked complaints."[19]

The Jackson papers pandered to whites' worst instincts. Their editorials blamed Communists, hoodlums, slobs, and "agitator leaders of the straggling publicity-seeking trek" for disrupting racial harmony. To refute popular portrayals of Mississippi, they printed letters from black people who claimed the march hurt race relations. The Hederman papers especially delighted in the racial unrest of northern cities, which reinforced black stereotypes without staining the South. One *Daily News* cartoon showed a scraggly black rioter, dressed in filthy clothes, swilling booze, and standing on a smashed-out car. He yelled: "Blood! Blood!"[20]

The Civil Rights Act of 1964 and the Voting Rights Act of 1965 promised to dismantle Jim Crow eventually. Yet as the Meredith March penetrated into the heart of Mississippi, its politicians staged energetic defenses of white privilege. They took different approaches. Some cried for old-fashioned massive resistance, fighting for every inch in the battle against racial integration. Others found violence distasteful, and they avoided any controversies that invited outside pressure.

Mississippi governor Paul Johnson embodied the new politics of racial accommodation. When Meredith started his walk, Johnson refrained from comment. He believed that Meredith would not win much attention, and he thought that his state had dispensed with crude racism. The shooting shocked him. "This is the kind of thing you pray won't happen," said the governor. "We were doing so well in Mississippi."[21]

Ironically, Johnson owed his position to Meredith. He was lieutenant governor during the Ole Miss crisis. When fog delayed Governor Ross Barnett's plane on September 26, 1962, it was Johnson who blocked Meredith, U.S. marshals, and Justice Department officials from entering the campus. This elaborate act of political theater, with a supporting cast of highway patrolmen and deputies, launched the star of the dour, balding, sharp-faced Johnson. He ran for governor in 1963 as a defender against federal tyranny. His slogan was "Stand Tall With Paul."[22]

Upon taking office, however, Johnson abandoned Barnett-style race-baiting. "We are Americans as well as Mississippians," he declared in his inaugural address. "Hate, or prejudice, or ignorance will not lead Mississippi while I sit in the Governor's chair." Touting "responsible Negro leadership," he distanced himself from the hard-right Citizens' Council. Under his orders, moreover, the Highway Patrol aided investigations against violent white supremacists. In no way did Johnson support racial equality. He did, however, understand business leaders' dissatisfaction with disruptive boycotts, seek out-of-state investment, and realize the inevitability of civil rights legislation. So he cast himself as a man of the New South, a champion of economic growth and social stability.[23]

By promising good protection from the Highway Patrol, Johnson hoped to move the Meredith Marchers down Highway 51 quickly, safely, and quietly. They might register some voters and stir some emotions, but they would leave Mississippi without attracting undue attention from the national media or federal government.

Yet Johnson still catered to his constituency: white people who preferred segregation, resented federal interference, and hated the march. When Meredith got shot, Johnson decried any attempt by "agitators and radical politicians" to manipulate "this isolated incident." The crime would be punished, but not through "a big production to foment strife and hate among peoples of the United States for the purpose of whipping up sentiments for civil rights laws." Johnson also spoke with Attorney General Nicholas Katzenbach, though White House officials kept that phone conversation out of the public record, lest white Southerners view the governor as a toady of federal power.[24]

Other Mississippi politicians, too, tried to defend the state against a civil rights onslaught. The Mississippi House of Representatives endorsed

Governor Johnson's statement, though one dissenter shouted that "if the nigger stayed in his place, he wouldn't be having this trouble." Attorney General Joe Patterson employed a more subtle misdirection, calling the Meredith shooting "just as irresponsible and senseless as the murder a few weeks ago of state highway patrolman Tommy Kendall by two Negroes." In a telegram to President Johnson, Senator John Stennis decried the "various militant civil rights agitators" descending upon his land. "I respectfully urge you as President of the United States to use your vast influence to call upon all extremists to stay out of Mississippi and thus enable duly constituted authorities to maintain law and order."[25]

Mississippi politicians also associated the March Against Fear with Communism—a familiar tool that tarred civil rights demonstrators as outside agitators rather than as local people with genuine grievances. Congressman Prentiss Walker, who was challenging James Eastland for his Senate seat, demanded that his rival investigate Communist influence on the demonstration. Rising to the red-baiting challenge, Eastland identified eleven Communists who participated in the march. He blamed them for fomenting a spirit of insurrection.[26]

On the Senate floor, Eastland called the march a "traveling circus" full of "beatniks, frauds, and persons wanted to answer for crimes in other states . . . whose personal backgrounds are so sordid and revolting that I must pass over them." He also lamented the plight of the Highway Patrol: "Out of concern that larger mobs would invade Mississippi, or use legitimate police action as fuel for their publicity machine, these officers have suffered in silence. My heart goes out to them." He mourned how the marchers, goaded by an unfair media, eroded standards of decency and order.[27]

Weeks after its conclusion, the march still riled up Congressman Thomas Abernathy, who bemoaned how "a light-minded citizen of Memphis" left "a few superficial wounds" in Meredith, and then "goateed riff-raff and just plain junks and punks from all over the nation swelled Mississippi's visiting horde," while the government and media had an "old fashioned field day kicking Mississippi." Of course, he added, "nothing was said about eliminating the bias and discrimination practiced against white Mississippians." The world cast them as villains. They saw themselves as victims.[28]

The Citizens' Council was the most "civilized" organ of massive resistance. Founded in the Delta town of Indianola after the 1954 *Brown* decision, it soon had 85,000 members in Mississippi, 60,000 members in Alabama, and influence throughout the South. The council printed material, aired television spots, and employed speakers that spread the doctrine of biblically sanctioned black inferiority. It resisted any threat to racial segregation, such as Meredith's admission to Ole Miss. It also choked black activism with economic reprisals, lobbied for laws that reinforced Jim Crow, and boosted hardline politicians. It remained a potent force: just before the march, Ross Barnett and James Eastland spoke at the council's luncheon in Jackson.[29]

The Citizens' Council argued that northern riots occurred because "we are dealing with a primitive people with primitive reactions." Segregation was the best avenue for blacks and whites alike, since it would not "force the Negro into unequal competition with white society." As for the Meredith March, it was the work of hate-spouting radicals who came south despite black discontent in northern cities. The Citizens' Council thus echoed Mississippi politicians and newspapers, only with a more frank endorsement of white supremacy.[30]

The Americans for the Preservation of the White Race (APWR) shared this ideology. "Racial integration is *genocide*, or *race murder*," stated one publication, "because when the blood of white people is mixed with the blood of colored people, *it can never be unmixed*, any more than you can unscramble eggs." It had chapters in Jackson and southwestern Mississippi, with a more working-class membership than the council. Operating on a local level, it intimidated black activists with economic reprisals. "Say we find a Negro agitating," explained the chairman of the Jackson chapter. "The first thing we do is tell his employer. Usually that takes care of it, and the Negro is fired. But if the situation isn't cleared up, we just pass the word. The 90 percent who feel as we do don't have to be told, they just stop trading at the place where the Negro works." The chapter prepared a news release asking Jackson merchants to close their businesses during the march, while APWR members took photographs and discussed the march's "Communist strategy."[31]

The Ku Klux Klan, of course, offered the most violent form of massive resistance. Ironically, the success of the Citizens' Council delayed the arrival of the modern Klan in Mississippi. The Louisiana-based Original Knights of the Ku Klux Klan started recruiting there after the Ole Miss crisis. By early 1964, the White Knights of the Ku Klux Klan dominated Mississippi's business of racial terrorism. Under its zealous Imperial Wizard Sam Bowers, the White Knights attracted thousands of members. Its klaverns operated in secrecy, employing rituals and code language. During Freedom Summer, they bombed churches, burned crosses, and harassed freedom workers.[32]

But by 1966, the Klan was in disarray. The FBI had established an investigatory White Hate Group, and its agents infiltrated klaverns. Many Klansmen defected from the White Knights to the rival United Klans of America. Other groups rose, as well, including the Universal Klans of America and Knights of the Green Forest. Infested with informants and rogues, the Ku Klux Klan in Mississippi was splintered and discredited— but still full of dangerous fanatics.[33]

In January 1966, Klansmen blasted shots into the home of Vernon Dahmer, the president of the NAACP in southern Mississippi's Forrest County. They then set the house on fire. Dahmer shot back, holding off the attackers until his family escaped, but died the next day from the effects of smoke inhalation. By June 23, the FBI had rounded up four-teen White Knights and one United Klansman connected to the fire-bombing, including Sam Bowers, and a federal grand jury had returned indictments against them.[34]

The Meredith Marchers witnessed the continuing dangers of the Klan. In Yalobusha County, they saw KKK painted in white on roads, bridges, buildings, trash cans, and picnic tables. On the highway near Oakland, they met a message painted in foot-high letters, as notable for its mis-spellings and illogic as its menace: RED [READ] NIGGER AND RUN. IF YOU CAN'T RED, RUN ANYWAY.[35]

Of course, most whites frowned upon no-count ruffians that tarred the South's name. But the Klan's harassment—and the killing of Ben Chester White—revealed the persistent influence of violent white su-premacy upon Mississippi. The institutions of the far right tilted the bal-ance of Deep South politics. By allowing other whites to contrast themselves against low-class hatemongers, it became acceptable to take otherwise extreme positions. If a white person believed that the civil rights movement was full of morally depraved Communists, that the federal government was an institution of repression, and that black people were satisfied with segregation, then they were simply wading in Mississippi's political mainstream.[36]

On Tuesday, June 14—Flag Day—the March Against Fear arrived in Grenada. No real local movement existed there. In 1965, an eleven-year-old mentally retarded deaf-mute black boy with his pants around his ankles strayed onto the property of a white man, who peppered the boy with bird shot. The all-white jury refused to indict the attacker. After that incident, SNCC tried organizing in Grenada, but it could not crack this nut. "If you come here tread softly among the Negroes," advised a friend of a SNCC organizer. "They seem to go directly to the City Manager every time anything happens. They tell on themselves!"[37]

Only 700 of the 4,300 eligible black voters in Grenada County had registered. Blacks had no access to the public library or swimming pool, no jobs at the post office, no students in the white schools. Despite the presence of various small factories, blacks had few jobs at low pay. Many whites lived on charming elm-lined avenues, most blacks in shack-strewn neighborhoods.[38]

The Meredith Marchers arrived over two hundred strong. They crossed the Yalobusha River Bridge, pulled left off Highway 51, and paraded down Pearl Street, through a black neighborhood. A news helicopter flew low, blowing six-foot sunflowers sideways. Some locals looked doubtful, others anxious. Some peered through their pulled-down shades or poked their heads out from behind trees.[39]

But hundreds spilled onto their front yards—the spirit was impossible to resist. They saw blacks and whites together, swaying in rhythm, singing "Come On Over Brother, Come On Over Brother." One young woman held her baby, her face betraying the battle between hope and fear; she pulled twice on her cigarette, flipped it away, grabbed her young child's hand, and joined the parade. "I was just looking," said another woman, "and all of a sudden I was marching."[40]

The column turned right onto Main Street, into the downtown business district, and the throng gathered in the center of town, by the ultimate symbol of white power: a monument to a Confederate soldier.

Unveiled in June 1910 and carved from Mississippi marble, the statue bore the inscription:

TO THE NOBLE MEN

WHO MARCHED NORTH

THE FLAG OF THE

STARS AND BARS

AND WERE FAITHFUL

TO THE END

GLORIOUS

IN LIFE,

IN DEATH SUBLIME

Similar monuments dotted town squares across the South, enshrining the legend of the "Lost Cause." White southerners canonized Jefferson Davis and Robert E. Lee as noble Christian heroes, cast Confederate soldiers as sacrificial and honorable warriors, and idealized the Old South as pure and peaceful. They recast the humiliation of the Civil War into a glorious, doomed, and holy crusade.[41]

If this myth concentrated on white virtue, it rested on a foundation of white supremacy. In this version of history, there was immoral chaos when blacks left slavery, and it took the Ku Klux Klan to restore virtue. The Lost Cause still seeped into the identity of southern whites. As countless Confederate battle flags along the march route attested, it shaped responses to the civil rights movement—even if its devotees could not articulate why. "I don't know if it accomplishes anything," admitted a Como teenager waving the Stars and Bars at the marchers, "but it makes me feel a hell of a lot better."[42]

For African Americans, the Civil War meant something else: a rebirth of American freedom, a possible avenue toward real democracy. The Confederate myth imprisoned them in the past.[43]

So in Grenada, the crowd roared with delight when Michigan State professor and SCLC official Robert Green climbed onto the statue's base. Above a bas-relief of Jefferson Davis, he placed an American flag. "We're tired of seeing rebel flags," he proclaimed. "Give me the flag of the United States, the flag of freedom." George Raymond of CORE then climbed up, pointed at the carving, and called Jefferson Davis "the joker up here."[44]

Whites looked on from the square's outskirts, absolutely stunned. "That's a white man's statue," someone cried weakly. Most seethed without a word. In the coming days, though, they would cry about the "desecration of our monument." From the Senate floor, James Eastland blustered, "I would not be surprised if Martin Luther King and these agitators next desecrate the graves of Confederate soldiers and drag their remains through the streets." Tom Ethridge of Jackson's *Clarion-Ledger* declared that "nothing said or done by uncouth riff raff can ever detract from the glory of Jefferson Davis."[45]

At the statue, Floyd McKissick spoke about, of all things, bathrooms. The county courthouse had restrooms labeled No. 1 (meant for whites) and No. 2 (meant for blacks). McKissick urged people to defy this backhanded segregation. "I wish we had a hundred more men like that McKissick," said a construction worker. An old lady nodded in agreement. "My father voted in slavery times, in Abraham Lincoln's time, but they killed him," she recalled. Now, fear seemed to fritter away. After the rally, a mass of people rushed across the square to the courthouse, lining up to register.[46]

Lewis Johnson took it all in. That morning, his mother had warned him to keep away from the march, but the young black teenager could not resist. When his mother left home, he sneaked away. Seeing these "Freedom Riders" walking alongside neighbors, friends, and relatives inspired him. He remembered "all of a sudden, out of nowhere, being injected with a sense of courage, defiance, outspokenness." He was old enough to recognize the past, and young enough to see the future. He had just seen Robert Green plant that American flag on the cherished symbol of the white South. There was Floyd McKissick calling for justice, and here were his elders heading toward the courthouse. As Johnson rushed back home, he knew that "being black in Grenada was never going to be the same again."[47]

9

POLITICS AND POVERTY
Grenada to Holcomb
JUNE 15, 1966

Grady Carroll watched the flood of black registrants, freedom marchers, note-jotting reporters, and television cameramen inundate the halls of the Grenada County Courthouse. Before the march came through, the policeman had assumed that blacks would disregard these outside agitators. Now so many people were registering that he had to find more forms. As Carroll guided the registrants, he insisted that this onslaught was unnecessary. "No reason they couldn't have come in before," he told a reporter. "They didn't have to have these demonstrations to register."

Carroll spied Albert Polk, an eighty-eight-year-old black man in overalls. "There's ol' Albert. Come on in, Albert," he said. "Now Albert, tell him. You could have registered before, couldn't you?"

"Yas suh," responded Polk.

"See?" said Carroll to the reporter.

When the officer turned away, the reporter asked Polk if that was true. "Naw suh," murmured Polk, cracking a nervous smile. "I know'd I couldn't."[1]

Grenada's white leaders were determined to follow a practical strategy: swallow pride, grant concessions, sidestep conflicts, and wave goodbye. They urged fellow whites to avoid clashes with the black invaders. "All we want is to get these people through town and out of here," said City Manager John McEachin. "Good niggers don't want anything to do with this march. And there are more good niggers than sorry niggers."[2]

County officials added four extra clerks and turned a courtroom into a waiting area. The registrars insisted that blacks were always welcome to register. Sheriff Suggs Ingram acted like a gracious host, insisting that the bathroom doors never had numbers, that anyone of any race could use any toilet. Police officers also warned some white ex-cons to keep their distance, and they kept a lookout for four men in a 1963 white Ford, who reportedly had a high-powered rifle and an appetite for trouble. Despite the audacious display at the Confederate memorial, the marchers encountered nothing worse than the grim-faced seething of Grenada whites.[3]

Over 150 African Americans registered on June 14, after the rally on the main square. Martin Luther King had returned to Mississippi that afternoon, and he and Floyd McKissick negotiated with City Attorney Bradford Dye at the courthouse. Among other concessions, Dye agreed to keep the registrars' office open until 9:00 p.m. A communication snafu with Hosea Williams, however, delayed the addition of more voters that night. Williams was preaching at a mass meeting at New Hope Baptist Church, and by the time he led over three hundred people to the courthouse, the clerks had gone home.[4]

The gaffe failed to dampen morale. *"If we can't registrate, we're going to demonstrate,"* the crowd chanted while shimmying and snake-dancing across the square. King addressed them near the Confederate memorial. With their demands won, he said, they should return to their homes or the tents. But too many hopes were stirring, too many spirits soaring. Hundreds walked through the streets of Grenada, proud and happy, their historic white intimidators nowhere in sight. King addressed them again at a late-night, encore mass meeting at New Hope Baptist Church.[5]

The next morning, a contingent of activists stayed behind in Grenada to help register voters. City officials set up registration offices in black neighborhoods and hired black schoolteachers as registrars. The courthouse opened at 8:00 a.m., and it again got overwhelmed with registrants. By nightfall, 814 blacks had registered. In the day and a half since the marchers had paraded down Pearl Street, the number of blacks on Grenada County rolls had more than doubled.[6]

The Meredith March inspired the beginnings of a genuine local movement. Civil rights leaders hailed Grenada as a model: "a dynamic and creative combination of mass demonstrations, mass meetings, and intensive grass-roots community organizing" that both registered voters and conquered fear. After Grenada, said King, "I'm convinced that Mississippi will never be the same again."[7]

"After they leave, everything will be the same again," countered a sheriff's deputy. When marchers and reporters left, the thin coat of courtesy melted. The numbers returned to the doors of the courthouse bathrooms. Police arrested SCLC staffers who tried to integrate the Grenada Theater, and white authorities harassed politically active blacks. Restaurants and stores remained segregated. Whatever concessions that whites made during the hubbub, they still possessed a stranglehold on power. The Meredith March, in their eyes, was a temporary insult. On the memorial in the town square, they had already replaced the American flag with a Confederate one.[8]

On the morning of June 15, the marchers headed west on Route 7, toward the Delta. Just as its path drifted from James Meredith's planned route down Highway 51, the march diverged from the vision of its creator. This same day, he forced himself back into the national conversation.

Meredith held a press conference at the Pleasantville, New York, estate of Juanita Poitier, the estranged wife of actor Sidney Poitier. Flanked by his wife, June, and the MFDP's Lawrence Guyot, he sat in a living room festooned with African sculptures, surrealist paintings, and an Academy Award. Meredith's statement supported the MFDP—a potential harbinger of an alliance between the quirky icon and the grass-roots party. Reporters ignored the possibility, instead focusing on his critique of the march. Civil rights organizations were marching in his name, but Meredith, as always, charted his own course.[9]

"Symbolically Highway 51 is too significant to give up entirely," said Meredith. His uneasiness about the route change reflected a larger frustration with the march. "It is not an arena for the national office of the NAACP to prove to the Johnson administration that they are truly his knights in armor," he said. "It is not a nonviolence demonstration," and "it is not an arena for experimentation in black nationalism." He resented the "free-for-all" structure and competing philosophies. "My military mind tells me there must be hierarchy and someone to head that hierarchy," he said. Did he mean himself? "Someone," he replied.[10]

Meredith had tried to stay relevant while recuperating in New York. One day after his flight home, he had dictated a press statement that Robert Weeks read from his building's front steps; it promised his quick return to Mississippi. Another of Meredith's original cadre, Claude Sterrett, spoke at a Harlem rally, urging volunteers to join Meredith's quest, though "they must be black and they must be men." Meredith also established the James Meredith Voter Registration Fund, administered by the Freedom National Bank, to channel contributions.[11]

Yet Meredith possessed no control over the news-generating demonstration bearing his name. In his mind, he had outlined a clear purpose: independent black men along Highway 51 would cast off fear, register to vote, and follow his leadership. Instead, the NAACP, SCLC, and SNCC had transformed the march into a tumultuous laboratory of black politics. He warned against "a publicity stunt or fund-raising contest among civil rights organizations." He believed that "the stress at all times should be on constructive results and less on slogans and emotions." He also complained that "now there are too many women taking part."[12]

Karl Fleming of *Newsweek* had first met Meredith in 1962, during the integration of Ole Miss. He had marveled at Meredith's steely pride in the face of murderous threats and social isolation. Only once did he see Meredith get emotional: after the reporter remarked that it was difficult for a white person to understand Meredith's experience, Meredith's eyes got moist. "You're right," he said. "But no Negro understands me either."[13]

Now Fleming called Meredith, and they spoke for an hour. Meredith recalled the shooting with bitter regret: "He shot me like I was a goddam rabbit . . . If I'd had a gun I could have got that guy." He also worried that a long, large, controversial march might expose Mississippi blacks to turmoil. He thus vowed to act as "mediator or peacemaker" upon his return. That ambition surprised Fleming. Meredith cherished his self-determination—he was fundamentally unsuited to bridging gulfs or forging consensus.[14]

Many were grappling with Meredith's motivations. "What kind of man decides to make this pilgrimage out of fear?" asked New York Congressman William Ryan before the House of Representatives. "He is a man we should all try to understand; a man from whom we all should learn." Liberal critics realized why he promised to carry a gun, but they feared its political consequences. FBI surveillance revealed that SCLC's Stanley Levison and Adele Kanter blamed Meredith for his headline-grabbing criticisms. They called him "a monster, a detriment to the movement."[15]

Media profiles described Meredith's characteristics of rigid certitude and bizarre unpredictability, but they also highlighted his affability, decency, and bravery. In an April 1966 review of *Three Years in Mississippi*, Martin Duberman had characterized Meredith as delusional and naive; now, he admired Meredith's iron will. Columnist Murray Kempton saw "a true figure of revolution," a black man from rural Mississippi who had transcended every limitation imposed upon him.[16]

No one totally understood James Meredith—not even his wife. June Meredith knew that a larger mission drove her husband. When they first met ten years earlier, they had discussed it, but she could not explain it then, and she could not articulate it now. He just acted according to his plan, whatever the dangers. "It's something I live with," she said.[17]

Meanwhile, the fog thickened around Meredith's attacker, Aubrey Norvell. On June 14, Norvell appeared before the Circuit Court judge in Ripley, Mississippi. His attorneys presented witnesses who cited his high blood pressure, weight loss, and nervous disposition after one week in jail. Norvell's wife also testified that they had only $500 in the bank. The judge nevertheless refused to reduce the $25,000 bond. Norvell said nothing. He just stared at the floor, fiddling with his wedding band. On the advice of his attorneys, he refused all interview requests, including those by the FBI.[18]

In the shooting's aftermath, segregationists flipped the burden onto Meredith, maintaining that he had provoked Norvell. Mississippi newspapers kept referring to his walk as "ill-advised." Whites complained that Meredith was "headline hungry," a "mentally defective masochist," and an unpatriotic rabble-rouser who deserved suspicion. "He must have known that his march into Mississippi was like a stroll through a lion's cage," contended a radio and television editorial in Charlotte, North Carolina. Jackson's *Clarion-Ledger* likened him to a Klansman marching through Harlem.[19]

Yet Aubrey Norvell's silence had an ironic effect: it let Mississippi whites distance themselves from the attack. If he never divulged a motive, they bore no collective responsibility. Newspaper editorials called the shooting "the act of a single, deranged man" and "the non-sensical attack of a sneak." One man pleaded that "there are nuts like this in every state." Another woman cried: "What a tragedy this Aubrey J. Norvell has brought on our state. Doesn't he have enough sense to know that he is doing Martin Luther King and Meredith a big favor? He's putting dollars in their pockets and bringing shame on our name. Hasn't Mississippi had enough smears? I think he should be punished to the 'nth' degree." In the eyes of Mississippi whites, they were Aubrey Norvell's real victims.[20]

Norvell was *not* from Mississippi, they emphasized. They lamented that Norvell committed the deed in Hernando. "I can't understand why a Memphian would come into Mississippi to do this thing," said state senator B. G. Perry. "It's unfortunate for Mississippi. We get enough bad publicity as it is!"[21]

They also cried conspiracy—*against* white southerners. Why had Norvell risked himself around so much law enforcement? Why the deliberate manner, the insistence that "I only want Meredith," the poor aim from an experienced marksman? Why just wound Meredith? White Mississippians kept suggesting that civil rights supporters paid this unemployed Memphis man to create a living hero out of Meredith, attract the national media, and crush the South under the weight of the federal government.

Their primary evidence of an antiwhite conspiracy was that Norvell fired bird shot. When discussing the shooting, they consistently mentioned the use of tiny pellets for ammunition. One columnist maintained that the pellets "were hardly big enough to kill a coon or snake at that distance." Alabama congressman Frank Boykin insisted that bird shot pellets "only sting a little." The first line of Governor Paul Johnson's official statement about the shooting noted that it was "with birdshot by an out-of-state resident."[22]

"James Meredith could have asked for nothing better," opined Prentiss Walker on the floor of the House of Representatives. "A few bird shot in his skin, a rest in a hospital, someone else to do his marching for him, and to be given credit for whatever success it may produce." Mississippi's political order thus staged its defense: undermining the politics of martyrdom, depicting the South as under siege, and floating its own conspiracy theories.[23]

The most extraordinary case of segregationist wishful thinking came from the Mississippi State Sovereignty Commission. While Norvell was appearing before the Circuit Court, the director, Erle Johnston, assigned Investigator Tom Scarbrough to a "very difficult and delicate assignment." Johnston admitted that the job "may be fruitful or fruitless, but worth the risk." He wanted Scarbrough to show that integrationists paid Norvell to shoot Meredith and spark a national incident. By proving this conspiracy, they could "right the wrong he had done by creating new tension in Mississippi."[24]

Johnston informed the office of Governor Paul Johnson that "I have authorized Mr. Scarbrough at the propitious moment to pledge a sum of money to Norvell's wife if the information can be obtained or publicized." In other words, Scarbrough could offer Mrs. Norvell a government-sanctioned bribe.[25]

After visiting the roadside south of Hernando, Scarbrough concluded that Norvell never planned to kill Meredith or to escape. He asked the DeSoto County sheriff to contact one of Norvell's lawyers. Scarbrough would not pay for information "if it was purely an act of stupidity on the part of Norvell." If someone had hired Norvell, however, the sheriff could offer $5,000. (Scarbrough lied "that the proposition I was making him did not include the state in any shape, form, or fashion.") Despite the long odds of finding any proof, it was worthwhile "if he could bring the truth out and expose this bunch of agitators as having hired someone to shoot Meredith."[26]

Scarbrough also met with the district attorney, two FBI agents, and an inspector on the Homicide Squad in Memphis—all of whom believed that integrationists had paid Norvell to create a crisis. According to the sheriff, attorney Boyce Lee Garner had said "that if he could prove the shooting to be a hired put-up job, he could get far more out of it in a monetary way than he could possibly get out of defending Norvell." So local, state, and even federal authorities based in the South all favored this far-fetched, antiwhite conspiracy theory.[27]

Scarbrough closed his investigation due to a lack of evidence. Norvell's attorneys had posted bond after establishing a "Norvell legal aid fund," directing contributions to a Memphis post office box. Norvell, his wife, his father, and his brother then left for an undisclosed location until his grand jury hearing in November. "We think the man's had enough publicity," said one of his lawyers. His home in suburban Memphis had its doors locked, its drapes down, and its lights dark.[28]

While reporting on the Meredith March, journalist Paul Good stopped off Route 12 near Belzoni. He found seventy-one-year-old Columbus

Thornton, who lived with fifteen family members in a desolate shanty. Only one daughter could read and write. A two-year-old boy lay on the filthy floor, eyes shut and body motionless, flies swarming his face. As Good drove away, he realized that "with eleven children in that shack, there had not been one toy. Not a ball, a rattle, a battered doll, or game. It seemed the darkest dimension of poverty."[29]

For generations, the backs of poor, black farm workers had carried Mississippi's prosperity, especially on the fertile cotton plantations of the Delta. Landowners trapped them in cycles of debt and forced them to stay on the land. By 1966, however, mechanical equipment planted and harvested 95 percent of the crops, chemical herbicides cleared weeds, and federal policies reduced cotton acreage. Human cotton pickers and choppers were becoming obsolete. Rural, unskilled black workers had two choices: wait for sporadic opportunities to make three dollars a day, or migrate away.[30]

As young adults went north, the remaining people endured extraordinary poverty. The median annual income of Delta blacks was $465. By 1966, an estimated 64 percent of the cotton labor force was unemployed. Some found scraps of work in the spring and fall, but borrowed to survive the winter. Wooden shacks had cracks covered with cardboard and tarpaper. Most homes had no tubs, showers, flush toilets, or running water. Children lacked basic nutrition and health care. Without surplus federal government commodities such as flour, butter, powdered milk, and split peas, many families would have starved.[31]

On January 31, 1966, during an unusually cold winter, about sixty poor farmers rushed into one of two hundred abandoned barracks at the deactivated Greenville Air Force Base. Others climbed over chain-link fences to join them. The demonstration embarrassed the federal government; the next day, 150 air police forcibly evicted the squatters. Attorney General Nicholas Katzenbach did, however, increase surplus food distribution and encourage more antipoverty programs. "If we do not do this," he warned Lyndon Johnson, "there is a real possibility that Mississippi will be the Selma, Alabama of 1966."[32]

That April, ninety black Mississippians went to Washington, D.C., to urge $1.3 million for home building, literacy classes, and job training. Frustrated with the tepid response from government officials, they camped out in Lafayette Square, across from the White House. They attracted some attention from tourists and reporters, but received no response from President Johnson. After four days, they packed up the tents and went home.[33]

Federal antipoverty programs were becoming the new civil rights battleground. Johnson's ambitious legislative vision included a "War on Poverty" administered through the Office of Economic Opportunity (OEO). Based on the principle of "maximum feasible participation," poor people helped plan and implement local programs. In 1965, under Operation Head Start, OEO granted almost $1.5 million to the Child Development Group of Mississippi (CDGM). Eighty-four centers in twenty-four counties provided preschools, health care, and food for six thousand poor children. Head Start distributed funds through CDGM administrators, almost all of whom were active in the Mississippi movement.[34]

Mississippi whites hated CDGM: it gave blacks positions of independence and influence, and its centers served as headquarters for civil rights activity. The *Jackson Daily News* compared Head Start to programs in Soviet Russia and Nazi Germany. School boards declined to rent out buildings for antipoverty offices, and stores refused to sell them food or supplies. A cross burned on the lawn of a preschool. Congressman John Bell Williams fulminated that antipoverty programs hired only administrators with "a background of agitation" and that "the oft-abused taxpayer will continue to contribute billions of dollars to the most colossal and collectively crooked raid on the treasury in this nation's history."[35]

By the time of the march, CDGM was both stronger and more vulnerable. Senator John Stennis, a powerful member of the Appropriations Committee, compelled the OEO to audit Head Start in Mississippi. The investigation revealed CDGM's sloppy record-keeping and use of public money for partisan politics. OEO urged CDGM to replace its director, move its headquarters, and employ more oversight of local centers. Yet OEO also awarded CDGM a new $5.6 million grant to run 125 centers for 9,125 children. Whatever its problems, this federally funded program educated thousands of children, employed adults in leadership positions, and put local institutions under black control.[36]

That success, however, portended CDGM's demise. OEO could defuse future controversies in Mississippi by funding programs controlled by moderates of both races. Even within CDGM, political tensions were fraying unity. Militants accused the CDGM board of co-opting the black freedom struggle. Distrusting federal money and resenting white administrators, they demanded more power in locals' hands. These young, disenchanted blacks did not have all the answers, but they were raising questions about black autonomy and white control that publicly surfaced on the Meredith March.[37]

In the men's tent at all-black Willie Wilson Elementary School in Grenada, some marchers shouted, cursed, and drank into the early morning of June 15. SNCC's Cordell Reagon tried to quiet them, leading to more back-and-forth jawing and a near-brawl. The chaotic spat stemmed from frustrations over the march's direction; in general, SCLC wanted to build momentum for a national demonstration in Jackson, CORE wanted to involve its organizing territories in central Mississippi, and SNCC wanted voter registration in the Delta. The press oversimplified the conflict as a debate over nonviolence. "We're going to carry on this march in the highest form of dignity," vowed King during the morning press conference, while Floyd McKissick promised a bus ticket out of Mississippi for anyone who broke nonviolent discipline.[38]

After breakfast at Bell Flower Missionary Baptist Church, Fannie Lou Hamer led the march west on Route 7, down a two-lane blacktop road in a sparsely populated, mosquito-infested region bordered by swamps and thick woods. The marchers feared a sniper attack. They started with only seventy-three people, although reinforcements arrived in the late afternoon. Some new arrivals rode along in trucks meant to carry water and supplies, annoying those who walked the walk.[39]

They reached Holcomb, a forlorn crossroads with three businesses and a population under 250. About fifty whites and fifty blacks stood on opposite sides of the road. Neither group reacted much as the tired marchers halfheartedly began freedom songs. After passing through town, they camped at a field near Rebecca Reed School, while thirty-four marchers knocked off another two miles, lending a head start for the next day.[40]

Other teams of activists fanned off in cars, urging rural blacks to register and march. They had started this mission four days earlier. Called the "Spectacular Task Force," they went door to door in Sunflower, Bolivar, Quitman, and Tallahatchie Counties, encouraging people to overcome white intimidation. "Up to now many of these towns were too hot to touch," said Fannie Lou Hamer. "But the people are moving with us now—and even those who don't register this week are at least beginning to think about it for the first time."[41]

But these mobile teams had little success. When a small crew arrived in the Delta town of Drew, for instance, the police tailed them, and local blacks kept their distance. One man in Drew had recently tried to register: his gas and electricity got cut off, and his children got trucked away from their plantation jobs. He could not find work. His family had to leave town.[42]

"What you're doing now, someone's going to get killed," scolded a black woman from her front porch. She refused to register until she had lasting protection. Mean-spirited whites controlled the jobs, courts, and police. "If you think he's wrong, you can't say it because he thinks he's always right," she boiled. "The only difference since slavery is we're not sold like cattle."[43]

SNCC's Willie Blue led an organizing team that went to his hometown of Charleston, the seat of Tallahatchie County, on June 13. He had since moved to Chicago, but his mother still worked on a nearby plantation. He parked his rusty 1952 Ford sedan in the black section of town, urged his team to knock on doors, and grimaced. "So far every time anyone has come to Charleston, they've been run out of town," he said. He looked at the reporters. "As soon as you-all leave, they'll probably start cracking heads."[44]

Blue found an old couple willing to register. The man was blind, so he held hands with both his wife and Blue as they walked along the main street, accompanied by not only freedom workers, but also some menacing whites in crawling pickup trucks with rifle racks. Photographer Charmion Reading gulped, thinking about his four daughters at home. When they reached the courthouse, the registrar refused to allow Reading in, so he waited outside, the camera his only weapon. After twenty minutes, the couple emerged as registered voters, and they reversed their frightening walk across downtown.[45]

The next day, a team stopped in Charleston to pass out leaflets. Ken Smith, known up north in Philadelphia as "Freedom Smitty," walked into Cook's Dairy Bar. "Get out of here, nigger, and get out fast," a white man demanded. Before Smith could react, he got punched in the face. As he fell, Smith grabbed the doorknob, which pried off. Out of rage and instinct, Smith cocked his arm, ready to throw the metal knob. He caught himself, and two friends rushed in to pull him away.[46]

On June 15, however, Charleston whites forsook violence. After briefly joining the marchers on the way out of Grenada, Martin Luther King came to Tallahatchie County. Now Charleston mirrored Grenada's strategy of temporary accommodation. After King and McKissick spoke at a rally, about 150 locals marched through town. The police created a security perimeter around the courthouse, isolating the demonstrators in the center of the tiny town. Whites leered from across the wide, circular street, leaning on storefront windows or sitting in their vehicles and talking on shortwave radios.[47]

King implored people to come forth and register. They seemed hesitant. King declared that they had the power to make whites "say yes when they want to say no." One or two came forward. Then three or four. In time, fifty people lined up. "This is wonderful; this is really beautiful," said King, leading two old women by the arm toward the courthouse.[48]

The number of black registrants in Tallahatchie County rose to about 1,100. Yet 6,500 voting-age blacks lived there, and 5,000 of 5,500 whites had already registered. One week later, when a reporter visited Charleston, he found whites still defiant and blacks still fearful. "When you have a custom of being afraid since you're a baby, it's hard to shake," said Thomas Tatum, a seventy-two-year-old man who attended the rally but declined to register. The invitation to King had created "a big hoop-de-do," reflected Willie Blue, but it also exposed those courageous new registrants to lost jobs and physical harassment.[49]

King had to go to Chicago, where a Puerto Rican district had erupted in violence: its community leaders reached out to SCLC, and King wanted to pull these working-class migrants into his summer campaign. Before flying out of Memphis, however, he crossed the Delta to Cleveland. Almost three hundred people stuffed into the tiny, clapboard-and-plaster Union Baptist Church. They crammed into pews, stood in aisles, and climbed onto shoulders to watch him through open windows. "If a man hasn't discovered something he will die for, he is not fit to live," intoned King. "Amen!" the congregants shouted back.[50]

The march was giving King this sweaty, spiritual connection to the people of Mississippi, one that was enriching his analysis of the nation's deep problems, compelling a reckoning with entrenched poverty. "We are not going to be intimidated and we are not going to be harassed and we are not going to be stopped," he declared. With the poetry of his words, the authority of the Constitution, and the spirit of Jesus, he inspired their dreams for justice. As the crowd spilled out of the sweltering church, a five-year-old girl sobbed. "I want to go with him," she cried. "*I want to go with him.*"[51]

10

DOWN TO THE CROSSROADS
Holcomb to Greenwood
JUNE 16, 1966

Stokely Carmichael bounded down a slope onto the grounds of Stone Street Elementary School, mocking nine police officers, two city commissioners, and the chief of police as "The Greenwood Welcoming Committee." He turned to someone from the march's advance team: "You got problems?" He learned that white officials had refused to allow the march tents on city property. "That ain't no problem," said Carmichael. "We'll put them up anyway." With their billy clubs drawn, the policemen circled the SNCC chairman.[1]

On the morning of June 16, the advance workers had tried to place the tents at the all-black school in Greenwood. The black principal of a local high school said that he lacked the authority to approve their request. He referred them to the Greenwood Board of Education, which refused to allow the campsite on school property. When the organizers returned up Route 7, march leaders told them to go back: they had camped at black schools in Grenada and Holcomb, and they deserved access to tax-supported institutions in the black community. "We are the people and it belongs to us," they explained.[2]

By 1:15, the crew was unloading the tents at Stone Street Elementary. The white officials arrived soon after, and police chief Curtis Lary read a letter from the Board of Education that denied use of the land. Police commissioner B. A. "Buff" Hammond had a message for the march leaders: "They are not going to put the tent on this school ground or any other school ground—not this place or any other city property inside Greenwood. Be sure and get that straight." He suggested some alternative sites, figuring that a black landowner could host them.[3]

Then Carmichael showed up, rejecting any compromise. "You are not putting those tents up here," said Hammond. "We are raising these tents up here," responded Carmichael. Hammond told the policemen to arrest Carmichael if he touched the tent. When Carmichael, Bob Smith of SNCC, and Bruce Baines of CORE grabbed the canvas, they got handcuffed. At 2:05, the three men were charged with trespassing and booked at the Greenwood police station.[4]

Afterward, Hammond sounded almost regretful. "There was no problem but for Stokely's mouth," he griped. He had wanted to avoid controversy, and the situation had been under control. "What's a man going to do? There are times when you have to hold your head up." Carmichael had provoked him, seemingly inviting the confrontation. As the police commissioner recalled, "Stokely said he was going to turn this town upside down."[5]

Carmichael had returned to Mississippi after a five-day stint at SNCC headquarters in Atlanta. After attending the weekend meeting of the Central Committee, he had devoted some attention to the Alabama project: planning to spread organizers beyond Lowndes County, helping secure a loan for someone, reassuring a concerned mother whose son got involved in the movement, and deflecting a young woman's lovelorn confession ("I am so busy I just don't have time to fall in love even with cute little girls like you"). Carmichael also urged activists around the country to participate in the March Against Fear. When SNCC organizers in West Point, Mississippi, complained about neglect from the national office, he replied that the march would invigorate projects throughout the state.[6]

Carmichael's correspondence reflected SNCC's strains and evolution. He touted SNCC's new orientation program to an organizer in southwestern Georgia who had suggested forming a committee to investigate new members—"particularly the white volunteers"—and stop infiltration from informants. Carmichael also replied to a black woman from New Jersey who complained that a beachside club called Sunshine Park had refused her admission. "One way to assure that this will not happen to anyone," he advised, "is for black people to get together and have their own Sunshine Park."[7]

Carmichael further reached out to whites who understood his perspective. "SNCC will never become a racist organization," he wrote to Lorna Smith, an older white woman who had volunteered during Freedom Summer. When blacks developed their own institutions, it would lead to "true racial integration"—instead of exceptional blacks entering white schools, for instance, whites and blacks should develop schools of equal quality, so each could integrate the other's schools.[8]

It troubled Carmichael that the media confused his stress on black autonomy with antiwhite hatred. "The press is trying to crucify me," he complained. He insisted that *Time* lied by printing that SNCC was purging white workers, and he objected that Pete Hamill of the *New York Post* mischaracterized him as racist.[9]

From SNCC's New York office, Elizabeth Sunderland agreed that the press warped Carmichael's words. But SNCC was enduring a backlash. "I just want to throw out the possibility that we might REDUCE this crap by adopting a special cool for the press," she wrote. She suggested that SNCC members avoid speaking with reporters or publications that demonstrated prejudice against them. "BEYOND THAT, it seems desirable—no?—to be very straight and cool and ASSUME we'll be misquoted, which means that you don't give them juicy quotes. Be a little more boring, if you want to put it that way." Sidestepping the suggestion, Carmichael replied that she should explain SNCC's position, not his quotes. He could not "be a little more boring." Like Malcolm X before him, he geared his words for black people. If he made whites uncomfortable, so be it.[10]

Carmichael returned to Mississippi on the evening of Wednesday, June 15. While the marchers rested in Holcomb, he went to Mt. Zion Missionary Baptist Church in Batesville, where he met with leaders from SNCC, CORE, MFDP, and the Deacons for Defense. Carmichael proclaimed that the Meredith March would exhibit "a new SNCC." According to the Sovereignty Commission, he stated that justice would arrive when "every black man in the South gets a gun and fights fire with fire." In alliance with the Deacons, SNCC would bring thousands of blacks to courthouses across Mississippi. If racist whites interfered, "my men will mow them down like dogs." Although these words were filtered through Informant X and the racial anxieties of Mississippi authorities, they revealed Carmichael's aggressive ambition.[11]

On the morning of June 16, prior to the confrontation in Greenwood, Carmichael led the marchers out of Holcomb. June Johnson rushed up to him, her eyes wet with tears: "Stokely, I gotta talk to you. Now. In private." Johnson was a tall, headstrong eighteen-year-old with deep experience in the local movement. Whenever in Greenwood, Carmichael stayed with the Johnson family. He charmed June's mother, Lulabelle, and he challenged June, rapping with his "little sister" about history, philosophy, politics, and culture.[12]

Now Johnson told Carmichael that she recognized one of the highway patrolmen. In June 1963, she had been among the women beaten in the Winona jail, along with Annelle Ponder and Fannie Lou Hamer. Four white troopers had punched Johnson in the face and stomach, stomped on her, and hit her with a leather-wrapped club. She spent three days in jail in a torn, bloody dress. At the time, the beatings of these women had outraged SNCC workers. Three years later, as word spread about the patrolman's presence on the march, some activists fumed. After listening to Johnson, Carmichael warned the supervising officer to remove the offending trooper.[13]

March leaders, however, remained furious with the Highway Patrol. About twenty cars had safeguarded the march along Highway 51. But after the triumph at Grenada and the turn toward the Delta, Paul Johnson complained that it had "turned into a voter registration campaign." The governor scaled back the protection. Now, only four cars patrolled alongside them. "We are not going to be in the position of wet-nursing a bunch of showmen," proclaimed Johnson.[14]

At 1:30, forty-five minutes after passing into the bayou country of Carroll County, SCLC's Robert Green halted the column. He told everyone to sit down. "We've had enough of that!" he yelled. Young white men had been driving back and forth in two cars, yelling such witticisms as "Look at that black boy walk!" Green refused to move until Highway Patrol supervisor Charles Snodgrass got there. A half hour later, Snodgrass told the Carroll County sheriff to remove the hecklers, but he rebuffed Green's demand for more officers.[15]

Later that afternoon, an advance team pulled off the road, looking for a rest stop. A white man named Eugene Neill burst out of his house, cursing and demanding that they leave his property. SCLC staffer R. B. Cottonreader could not stomach such hatred. He hopped off the truck and walked toward Neill. "We are both adults," he said. "You don't have to shout." Neill drew a revolver. Police interceded before the conflict escalated, but this incident, like the others, captured the mood heading into Greenwood: brewing frustration, fraying nerves, flaring tempers.[16]

The marchers crossed into Leflore County and entered the Delta. Remarkable for its vast stretches of flat and fertile land, the Delta possessed the largest black populations in Mississippi—and, with it, a long history of slavery and sharecropping, lynching and labor control, white wealth and black privation. It was no accident that the Delta had given birth to the blues, a musical expression of despair, alienation, transience, sexuality, and danger. In one pervasive legend, the bluesman Robert Johnson struck a late-night deal with the Devil at a rural crossroads—a forbidding and forsaken spot, but also a distinctive landmark amid the wide-open cotton fields. The crossroads presented choices with enduring consequences.[17]

Four years earlier, in June 1962, Robert Moses had dropped off Sam Block in Greenwood. "Now Sam," Moses warned, "do you know that the possibility is that you can be killed?" Tears welled in Block's eyes, but the young Mississippi native had resolve, if not money or food. He walked into grocery stores, pool halls, and Laundromats. He encountered plenty of fear, but he also found an older generation with long-standing grievances. He got them into an Elks Hall, taught them freedom songs, and talked about voting. So began SNCC's grass-roots organizing in Greenwood, a local movement with national ramifications.[18]

Greenwood was the epicenter of the Delta's cotton economy. A cadre of powerful planters dominated the seat of Leflore County. About two-thirds of the city's 50,000 residents were black, but only 250 could vote. When more organizers arrived to encourage voter registration, the County Board of Supervisors cut the distribution of surplus federal commodities. The SNCC office was ransacked and burned. Block got arrested seven times in eight months. Nightriders shot SNCC's Jimmy Travis in the shoulder and neck.[19]

Yet SNCC developed an organizational model in Greenwood. Its workers earned respect from the established black leaders of the Citizens' League. They started a national food drive to replace the commodities distribution, winning the loyalty of poor people. They nurtured new leaders, both young and old. Through rousing mass meetings and inspirational freedom songs, through patient conversations in cafes and on front porches, and through consistent and extraordinary bravery in the face of white terror, they demonstrated a commitment to the black community. Within a year of Block's arrival in Greenwood, SNCC had built a vibrant movement that was gaining national media coverage.[20]

During the 1964 Freedom Summer, SNCC moved its headquarters to Greenwood. The summer magnified SNCC's triumphs and tensions. Freedom Schools throughout Mississippi taught African American history, creative thinking, and self-pride to thousands of children, while demonstrations for voter registration and desegregation drew masses of black people. Yet as the jolt of well-educated, well-off white volunteers energized the movement, it also widened some interracial chasms. Whites arrived with sunny idealism and bustling know-how, while battle-hardened black activists complained about white paternalism. Although it was complicated by cultural gulfs and sexual tensions, inflamed by constant fear of racist violence, SNCC veterans and Freedom Summer volunteers together engaged in an audacious, impressive experiment in American democracy—even if, after the failed MFDP challenge at the Democratic National Convention, its immediate result was disillusion with the existing political system.[21]

"SNCC people had given all of the life they had but the last ounce of blood," recalled Ed King, a spiritual counselor to many volunteers. "They expected to die during Freedom Summer, and they were still alive!" Some drifted out of the movement, some developed drug problems, others lived the life of regular young Americans. Mississippi sapped their idealism.[22]

Only a few SNCC projects survived. Many organizers started working for the MFDP or CDGM. This "new, and rather unexciting, stage" of political campaigns and government programs illustrated SNCC's legacy of empowering locals. Yet without SNCC's sustained guidance, the Greenwood movement lost momentum. By 1966, a fire had destroyed SNCC's old headquarters, and vandals firebombed the car of James Moore, who had launched a selective buying campaign to demand desegregated facilities and black policemen. "The glamour is gone," wrote one MFDP worker. "The shadow of fear that was here in the pre-movement days has returned."[23]

When the Meredith March was redirected toward Greenwood, an opportunity arose to revive the old spirit in a new political climate. Jesse Harris, a SNCC veteran and CDGM administrator, was definitely guilty of accusations by Mississippi politicians that federal antipoverty projects harbored political activists. Greenwood had three Head Start centers. "I made it clear that all the people working in the Head Start centers should support the marchers," recalled Harris. CDGM workers and parents welcomed the demonstration. Many joined an organizing committee that arranged to feed marchers, pass out handbills, and recruit locals for freedom rallies.[24]

Another SNCC veteran, MacArthur Cotton, said that the advance preparation for the march "was just a matter of greasing the machine." SNCC already had laid the groundwork by establishing political contacts and local knowledge. Now working for the MFDP in Greenwood, Cotton was talking with his fellow organizers about the movement's next phase, about blacks controlling community institutions. Like others in SNCC circles, they called it Black Power.[25]

When Wiley and Jean Mallett joined the March Against Fear, the siblings had an eye-opening experience. Raised in James Meredith's hometown of Kosciusko, they were still in high school, but their older brother Luther was a political organizer, and their mother Lenora encouraged them to march. In the Delta, they saw families living in tiny shacks with outhouses, and they met marchers of all different backgrounds, including many nice white people. But what shocked Wiley, especially, was the venom of Greenwood whites. They knew racial prejudice in the Hill Country, but this, he thought, "was pure hate. It was the ugliest thing I ever saw."[26]

Greenwood sheltered some of the nastiest segregationists in the entire South. A plaque in the police commissioner's office honored the city's folk hero, a German shepherd named Tiger, for tearing into civil rights protesters in 1963. "We killed two-month-old Indian babies to take this country," said one man at the time, "and they want to give it away to the niggers."[27]

A local "civic group" demanded absolute resistance to integration. "The present so-called 'civil rights' movement is a brain child of the Communist Conspiracy," thundered a recent broadside. It lumped Governor Paul Johnson with President Lyndon Johnson as political elitists. It accused customers at the Holiday Inn—a national chain that accepted black customers—of "treason of the highest order." The propaganda targeted black activists, Head Start workers, and even white business owners who treated blacks with courtesy.[28]

Greenwood's white officials shared this distaste for racial equality. As the Meredith March approached, they feared it would overwhelm the city. On the morning of June 16, Mayor Charles Sampson had a heated telephone conversation with Governor Johnson about the scaled-back police protection. In a subsequent telegram, Sampson pleaded for more highway patrolmen: "Greenwood has for several years been a favorite target of racial agitators aided and encouraged by the Department of Justice, which is actively seeking and sponsoring this present unrest in our state." The city canceled leave for the local police, putting all thirty-three officers on twelve-hour shifts.[29]

A front-page editorial in *The Greenwood Commonwealth* oozed with racial paranoia. "King and Followers Should Be Ignored," urged the headline. The article likened Martin Luther King to Joseph Stalin and Mao Zedong. "This man has created more violence and left more hatred in his path than any other civil rights leader in the country's history," it stated, ignoring that whites perpetrated that brutality. The newspaper bade its readers to "let King walk his merry way down the highway."[30]

King was actually in Chicago, distant from this crisis. When he learned of the arrests at Stone Street Elementary, he considered it a possible turning point. He told Stanley Levison that until now, their interactions with the police had been so polite "that it just did not feel like Mississippi." Trying to exploit the arrest, he issued a statement calling for participants on the final leg into Jackson, as "this incident that happened today is indicative that Mississippi is still a state filled with terror, brutality, and hatred toward the Negro."[31]

An altercation between marchers and policemen seemed imminent. As evidenced by Carmichael's arrest at Stone Street Elementary, the City Council refused to allow the tents on a public facility. Nathaniel Machiesky, a liberal Catholic priest, offered the St. Francis of Assisi Mission, but march leaders insisted on a location in the black community, on grounds supported by tax dollars.[32]

Late that afternoon, the marchers stopped five miles northeast of Greenwood. They piled into cars and trucks, led by a U-Haul with tent poles jutting out the back. They drove into Greenwood and circled through the black district. The caravan arrived at Broad Street Park, which occupied an entire block. The burned-out remains of the old SNCC office stood at one corner.[33]

The U-Haul pulled onto the grass, scattering a baseball game. Out came the poles, stakes, and tent bags. "Are you glad to see us?" cried Robert Green. "Yes!" responded the gathering crowd. With help from an excited bunch of youngsters, the crew stretched out the canvas, pounded in the stakes, and assembled the tent.[34]

The police surrounded the park, billy clubs in hand. The marchers and community members stood their ground. "If any of us have to go to jail we want all of Greenwood to go. Are you with us?" Green asked the crowd. Again the people roared approval. George Raymond announced, "I don't care what the white people of Greenwood say, we're going to stay in this park tonight." It usually took one to two hours to erect the tent. This time, it took thirty minutes.[35]

Remarkably, the police let it happen. In fact, they satisfied Green's request to protect the park from hostile whites. Chief of Police Curtis Lary even told march leaders that the park lights typically turned on at 6:00 p.m. and off at midnight, but that the city could keep them on all night, if preferable. Also, the City Council rescinded the ban on Broad Street Park, and the bail for the three jailed activists was set at $100 each, well below the usual $500 or $1,000 bond for civil rights agitators. Greenwood's white authorities had shifted away from massive resistance, and the threat of violence cooled.[36]

While this drama played out, Stokely Carmichael was in jail, catching up on sleep. The earlier conflict at the elementary school had sharpened his frustrations: white authorities had dictated who used land in the black community, and local black leaders had no power. He got bailed out that evening, as hundreds and hundreds of people packed Broad Street Park. Carmichael walked out of jail and into history.[37]

Willie Ricks was a character, a provocateur. A self-described black nationalist, the SNCC field secretary had long questioned the utility of nonviolence and integration. If he lacked the intellectual clout of SNCC's college-educated leaders, "Reverend Ricks" knew how to rouse crowds. He told earthy jokes, showcased his fearless defiance, and drew people into action.[38]

Ricks danced on the line between courageous and crazy. According to legend, he once told a draft board that "if you can send me to Vietnam to defend Lady Bird Johnson, I can shoot some crackers here in the South to defend my Mama"—and the board dismissed him! Even within SNCC, Ricks was a troublemaker. On May 17, soon after the election of Stokely Carmichael, the Central Committee placed Ricks on its agenda. Apparently, he had disrupted staff meetings, and Ruby Doris Robinson suggested that he reexamine his attitude. The committee tabled the discussion, however, and the question of Willie Ricks was recorded as "undecided."[39]

Before Ricks joined the Meredith March, he stopped at Atlanta's SNCC headquarters, where he quizzed James Forman: "Suppose when I get over there to Mississippi and I'm speaking, I start hollering for 'Black Power'? What do you think of that?" The phrase was nothing new. Harlem politicians Jesse Gray and Adam Clayton Powell had employed the expression, and the Lowndes County Freedom Organization used the slogan "Black Power for Black People." SNCC had defined the phrase as an articulation of its new direction. Carmichael had said it during his speech in Senatobia, and while covering the march, the *New York Post* and the *Los Angeles Times* already considered the phrase a challenge to the established tactics of the civil rights movement.[40]

But Ricks recognized the visceral impact of "Black Power" as a rallying cry. In Mississippi, he led advance teams into neighborhoods and onto plantations, announcing that the march was coming. "I left the people hollering 'Black Power,' and they're still screaming," he reported to Stokely Carmichael and Cleveland Sellers. Ricks described farmers getting so excited that they dropped their tools on the ground. Carmichael was skeptical: "I said to Cleve, I said, you know, you sent the wrong man out because we need a clear analysis here and this man is given to exaggerations and talking all sorts of nonsense in hyperbolic terms." Ricks insisted that he spoke the truth.[41]

On the evening of June 16, as Carmichael left the Greenwood jail and headed to the Broad Street Park rally, Ricks sidled up to him, urging him to unleash the slogan. Ricks had been prepping people all day. It was the perfect venue. Greenwood illustrated both SNCC's achievements and the entrenched patterns of Jim Crow, and Carmichael was a local hero. The SNCC chairman hopped onto a truck bed that was serving as a makeshift stage. He looked upon a gathering of familiar faces and freedom fighters, one thousand strong. He sensed a mood of pride and defiance.

"Drop it now," urged Ricks. "The people are ready. Drop it now."[42]

"This is the twenty-seventh time I have been arrested," Carmichael announced. "I ain't going to jail no more. I ain't going to jail no more." He slashed at the hypocrisy of foreign wars for democracy: "They take black boys to fight in Vietnam. We shouldn't go fight in Vietnam. Our fight is here!" He chafed at calls for patient reform: "We begged the federal government. We begged and begged, we've done nothing but beg. We've got to stop begging and take power." He promoted black pride: "Ain't nothin' wrong with anything all black, 'cause I'm all black and I'm all good." And he demanded that black majorities exercise their political strength: "Everybody owns our neighborhood except us. We outnumber the whites in this county; we want black power. That's what we want—black power!"[43]

"The only way we gonna stop them white men from whuppin' us is to take over," thundered Carmichael. "We been saying freedom for six years and we ain't got nothin'. What we got to start saying now is Black Power!" He said it again and again: "We want Black Power. We want Black Power."

"*Black Power!*" roared back the crowd. Ricks had primed his people for this moment. He hopped onto the platform alongside Carmichael, encouraging the call-and-response.

"What do you want?" "BLACK POWER!" "What do you want?" "BLACK POWER!" "What do you want?" "BLACK POWER!" "What do you want?" "BLACK POWER!" "What do you want?" "BLACK POWER!"[44]

Black Power resonated with the audience because it captured, in two simple words, a generation of frustrations and aspirations: the slow pace of federal reform, the limits of nonviolence, the failings of white liberals, the need for political and economic control over black communities, the yearning for pride. The chant nonetheless suggested a new stage in the movement. While shooting photographs of Carmichael, Bob Fitch turned to a colleague and said, "We're watching history."[45]

Some older blacks in the crowd were rendered speechless—Carmichael was leading a loud, public chant that whites would interpret as a threat. "If Stokely lives through this march," whispered one man to his friend, "he'll live forever." They had uneasy looks on their faces, indicating how Black Power might erode the ideal of racial brotherhood.[46]

White marchers exhibited a gamut of emotions, from support to ambivalence to fear. David Doggett recalled that when the chant began, some whites looked at each other with surprise and a little confusion, though they ultimately chimed in. For David Dawley, the cry of Black Power was "chilling" and "frightening," tinged with "anger" and "hate," a message of "Go home, white boy, we don't need you."[47]

Lewis Zuchman agreed in principle with Black Power: blacks should lead their own movement, and whites should support them. He objected, however, to the atmosphere in which it was presented. The movement was changing, he thought; "it was losing its soul, in a way." A Freedom Rider who had admired Carmichael since their stint in Parchman Penitentiary, he arrived in Greenwood that day, driving down in a car organized through a New York CORE chapter. Now he heard stories of young African Americans stealing from white volunteers or acting sexually aggressive. That night, at a bar, an old movement friend suggested that Zuchman and his friend Art Spielman leave, because word was spreading that local blacks might attack white marchers.[48]

Zuchman and Spielman returned to the tent, where they heard a black militant insult the contributions of white liberals. More frightening, though, was the rumor of an impending attack by the Ku Klux Klan. Spielman woke up to see Zuchman trying to break two Coca-Cola bottles against a garbage can. In fact, the Klan stayed away. Thanks to the mayor's pleading, the Highway Patrol had dispatched fourteen officers to guard Broad Street Park until morning. Zuchman nevertheless felt caught between hostile whites and disgruntled blacks. "What the fuck are we doing here?" he asked himself. "This is insane!"[49]

Yet for black activists, Black Power had an invigorating energy. "It was kind of electric," said Quitman County project director John Summerall, recalling Carmichael's speech. Summerall understood the slogan as "people being able to decide their own destiny and doing what it takes to do that without being hindered, without being encumbered by those who might want to prevent it." It connoted a sense of self, a source of strength. That night in Broad Street Park, collection plates gathered contributions for the poor black people of the Delta. Someone flipped on a transistor radio, and even Cleveland Sellers danced the frug. Someone else gathered a group of children, joining their hands and forming a ring. On a land soaked in sweat and blood, they danced in circles, singing about "proud black power."[50]

11

THE CROW AND THE BLACKBIRD
Greenwood to Belzoni
JUNE 17–18, 1966

From the same platform where Stokely Carmichael called for Black Power, Charles Evers swore revenge upon his brother's killer. "If I ever lay my eyes on him, if I ever get my hands on him, he'll be through harassing Negroes," vowed Evers before the gathered throngs at Broad Street Park.[1]

Why was Evers there? One week earlier, he had made national news by denouncing the Meredith March as a wasteful show. But as the march won success, he changed his tune. The final rally in Jackson promised to attract national attention and lots of black voters. So he conferred with the Jackson police about the final demonstration, even as march leaders debated whether to accept the official participation of the Mississippi NAACP. He then joined the June 16 march from Holcomb to Greenwood, calling it "a good thing," and pledged to urge the participation of NAACP branches. His angry threat at the rally reinforced his connection to the martyred Medgar Evers, while also advancing his tough-guy reputation.[2]

Byron de la Beckwith took that threat as a challenge. The next day, Beckwith arrived at the marchers' campsite in Broad Street Park, looking for Evers. Beckwith was free despite substantial evidence linking him to Medgar's murder. Two juries had failed to convict him, thanks to $15,000 raised by Greenwood's White Citizens' Defense Fund, a legal team led by the local Democratic Party chairman, and a courtroom visit from former governor Ross Barnett. Welcome signs greeted Beckwith upon his return from jail. The unrepentant tobacco salesman, gun collector, and part-time police officer had recently won cheers at a local Klan rally.[3]

The police shooed away Beckwith, since Greenwood authorities wanted no trouble. Now, somewhat cheekily, Police Commissioner Buff Hammond insisted that the city had neither refused nor permitted the use of Broad Street Park. Once the marchers occupied the land, he said, "we were like the man who would rather take his wife to a convention with him than kiss her goodbye." But Greenwood leaders drew a harder line than those in Grenada; they rejected the marchers' requests for extended hours for voter registration and registrars in black neighborhoods. "These people are entitled to no more and no less than anyone else," said attorney Hardy Lott.[4]

That morning, the official march into Greenwood took place. While some volunteers stayed in town to canvass for voter registration, about a hundred people trucked up Route 7 to the previous day's stopping point, just south of the Leflore County line. Stokely Carmichael and Hosea Williams, along with the MFDP's James Moore, led them back. Near the city limits, local blacks doubled their numbers. By midday they had returned to the campsite.[5]

Martin Luther King came back to Mississippi that day, and in the afternoon, he led over six hundred people from Broad Street Park to the Leflore County Courthouse, intent on staging a voter registration rally. More Greenwood blacks swelled the streets as they approached the courthouse, a green-domed, gray-stone structure framed by pillars and shaded by magnolia trees. King, Carmichael, and Hosea Williams headed onto the courthouse lawn.[6]

A cordon of policemen halted them, ordering them off the grass and onto the sidewalk. The abrupt demand startled the leaders. After all, policemen had just escorted them through the heart of Greenwood. "We're going on that grass," said Williams in a deep-voiced rumble, while a deputy gripped his billy club. After King pulled Williams back, he pleaded that they were here to register voters. "Well, this ain't the door," responded an officer. "The door's back over there," he said, pointing his thumb at the main entrance.[7]

SNCC activists got testy with the deputies. "I've been in your jail more than you, and I don't even work there," snapped Carmichael.

"Why don't you move out of the way?" sneered Ricks.

"I got my jaw broken on those courthouse steps," grumbled another young militant.[8]

The police held their ground. Behind them stood Leflore County's Civil War monument, dedicated in 1918 by the United Daughters of the Confederacy. Topped and flanked by statues of Confederate war heroes, it also showed a nurturing white woman tending to a wounded soldier. After the incident in Grenada, no more altars of white southern identity would be desecrated. As an added deterrent, the state conscripted six black prisoners from Parchman State Penitentiary to guard the monument. The only people who walked on the lawn were three young white boys dressed in red sweaters.[9]

As one spark cooled, another hissed. King walked twenty yards along the sidewalk and turned up the courthouse steps. County sheriff George Smith waited with arms crossed. "You can't hold a meeting here," said Smith in a low tone. King insisted that they were staging a rally. "You can't hold a meeting here," Smith repeated. As sweat glistened on his forehead, King explained that he needed to invite people into the courthouse. "No meeting," said Smith. They stood just two feet from each other.[10]

The marchers massed right below King and Smith, at the foot of the short steps. A line of policemen faced the crowd. Few could hear the conversation, but everyone felt the tension. The marchers packed closer. Deputies grabbed their clubs. "Here we go," said an officer. "Somebody's going to get it." Sensing the impending disaster, SCLC's Andy Young walked around, urging calm in a soothing voice. King and Smith stood silently.

"All right, go ahead," the sheriff finally grunted, calculating that the cost of violence trumped the benefit of denying King.[11]

With the crisis defused, the marchers held a twenty-minute rally from the courthouse steps. It was their first public reckoning with the meaning of Black Power. SNCC activists clenched their fists and chanted the phrase, while some whites shuddered at its implications (Nicholas von Hoffman of *The Washington Post* called it a "totalitarian-sounding phrase"). Carmichael insisted that blacks would employ their voting strength just as Irish, Italian, and Jewish immigrants once did. "Black nationalism only means one thing in this country, that you're anti-white," he objected. "That's the trick bag the press is trying to get me into. But I'm not anti-white."[12]

King never uttered the words "Black Power," but he did try channeling the slogan into the democratic tradition: "You can always tell where the Negro community begins because that is where the pavement ends. We're going to change that when we get the ballot. That's what we mean when we say power." He embraced the positive messages of black pride and political strength, if not the implicit criticisms of nonviolence and interracialism. Straddling the widening gap between liberals and radicals, he promised that "when we get this power, we will try to achieve a society of brotherhood."[13]

In Greenwood, interracial brotherhood appeared a distant dream. After the rally, the marchers turned right onto Main Street and passed a service station. The attendant, Booker Riley, turned his garden hose on them. A teenager rushed at Riley, but a deputy pushed him away. "If you ever squirt water on a black woman again, I'll break your neck!" seethed another young man. Carmichael, who had been walking near the back of the column, bolted toward the conflict, only to be blocked by highway patrolmen.[14]

Hal York, a white waiter from New York City, grabbed the hose and turned it on Riley. The attendant retreated into the station, then emerged wielding a billy club, with a pistol jammed into his back pocket. Children fled down Main Street, screaming in fear, while six policemen rushed in before violence erupted.[15]

That afternoon King drove twenty-eight miles east to Winona to lead another rally. After parading to the Montgomery County Courthouse, he delivered an oration, and about a hundred blacks registered to vote. Meanwhile, about 150 marchers headed west. Children waved Confederate flags at them, a sound truck blared a song about the Ku Klux Klan, and Byron de la Beckwith drove up and down the line. At seven o'clock, ten miles outside Greenwood, the marchers rode back to Broad Street Park, where the tents still stood. That night they heard more speeches from King and Carmichael. The March Against Fear had lived up to its name. With courage and resolve, the itinerant protesters had braved the belly of the beast called Jim Crow.[16]

Yet the Leflore County clerk offered no special concessions, and blacks did not register at the courthouse. Only forty people signed onto the voting rolls at the federal registrars' office in the post office basement. The local political equation did not change: about seven thousand of Leflore County's eligible blacks were registered, as were eight thousand

On the second day of his walk from Memphis to Jackson, James Meredith was shot by a lone white man. The attack transformed his unique crusade into a civil rights extravaganza. (Jack Thornell, courtesy AP Photo)

During the march's first courthouse rally in Batesville, El Fondren registered to vote for the first time in his life. He said that he was 106 years old.
(Jim Peppler, courtesy Peppler and Alabama Department of Archives and History)

Blacks in Mississippi weighed many considerations when deciding whether to join the march as it passed through town. On the one hand, it could lead to costly reprisals. On the other hand, it bolstered their pride and buoyed their spirits.
(Jim Peppler, courtesy Peppler and Alabama Department of Archives and History)

Fannie Lou Hamer led marchers in freedom songs. A poor sharecropper who vaulted to national prominence, she epitomized the courageous women who lent the civil rights movement its backbone.
(Jim Peppler, courtesy Peppler and Alabama Department of Archives and History)

"When I'm marching I like myself," explained one participant.
(Jim Peppler, courtesy Peppler and Alabama Department of Archives and History)

"What we got to start saying now is 'Black Power!'" proclaimed Stokely Carmichael in Greenwood. The unveiling of the potent slogan signaled the beginning of a new direction in the black freedom struggle. (Bob Fitch, courtesy Bob Fitch Photo)

A flatbed truck filled with reporters, cameramen, and photographers led the procession down the highway. Civil rights veterans grumbled that the press exaggerated their internal conflicts and ignored Mississippi's poverty.
(Jim Peppler, courtesy Peppler and Alabama Department of Archives and History)

Robert Green and Martin Luther King, Jr., of the Southern Christian Leadership Conference consult with the Mississippi State Highway Patrol. The state troopers' protection forestalled the intervention of federal officials, but marchers constantly bickered with the highway patrolmen. (Jim Peppler, courtesy Peppler and Alabama Department of Archives and History)

White onlookers brandished the Confederate battle flag as a symbol of resistance against the Meredith Marchers. "I don't know if it accomplishes anything," admitted one spectator, "but it makes me feel a hell of a lot better." (Jim Peppler, courtesy Peppler and Alabama Department of Archives and History)

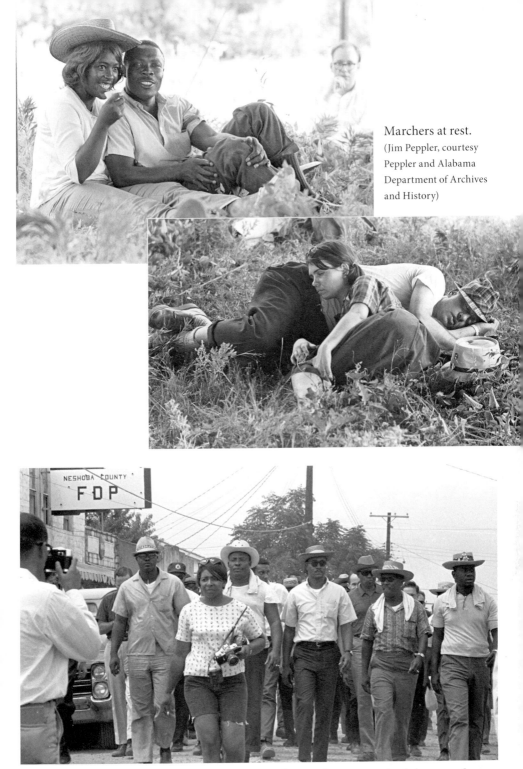

Marchers at rest.
(Jim Peppler, courtesy
Peppler and Alabama
Department of Archives
and History)

On a side trip to Philadelphia, Mississippi, the marchers recognized the second
anniversary of the deaths of civil rights martyrs James Chaney, Andrew Goodman,
and Mickey Schwerner. (Jim Peppler, courtesy Peppler and Alabama
Department of Archives and History)

In Philadelphia the marchers faced insults, projectiles, and outright violence. Three days later, they again marched through town, defying their intimidators. (Jim Peppler, courtesy Peppler and Alabama Department of Archives and History)

In Canton the Mississippi Highway Patrol launched a brutal tear gas attack upon the marchers. "It was like a scene of hell," described one reporter. (Courtesy Bettmann/Corbis)

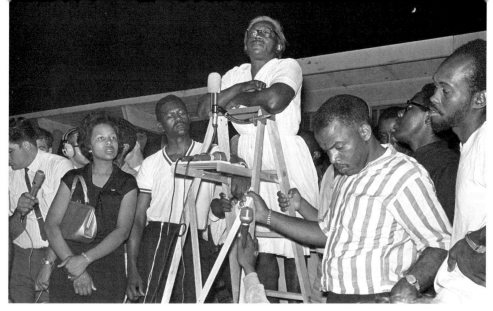

Annie Devine spoke from a makeshift stage near McNeal Elementary School in Canton, one day after the tear gas attack. The leaders' compromise with Canton authorities enraged the more militant marchers. (Jim Peppler, courtesy Peppler and Alabama Department of Archives and History)

Civil rights demonstrators from around the country converged on Tougaloo College for the march's final weekend. At a nighttime rally, James Brown, Sammy Davis, Jr., Dick Gregory, and Marlon Brando entertained the crowd. (Jim Peppler, courtesy Peppler and Alabama Department of Archives and History)

Whitney Young, Ralph Abernathy, Coretta Scott King, Martin Luther King, Jr., James Meredith, Stokely Carmichael, and Floyd McKissick led the march into Jackson. An estimated fifteen thousand participants made it the largest civil rights demonstration in Mississippi history. (Jim Peppler, courtesy Peppler and Alabama Department of Archives and History)

Stokely Carmichael at the podium at the back of the State Capitol. The march launched Carmichael into the realm of the radical celebrity. James Meredith would follow a more twisting and sometimes puzzling route. (Jim Peppler, courtesy Peppler and Alabama Department of Archives and History)

whites. A *Greenwood Commonwealth* editorial gloated that the police maintained order, whites ignored the circus, and black agitators accomplished nothing.[17]

The march's primary legacy in Greenwood, of course, was the unleashing of Black Power. It meant different things to different people, but the intricacies of its implications were sandwiched between two extremes, both found in Greenwood. The next broadside by the white "civic group" warned:

> The world first heard the revolutionary cry of BLACK POWER shouted from the mouth of a sunbaked Ubangi named STOKLEY CARMICAL [sic] right here in Greenwood during the "Mississippi March." If any of you should allow your selves to become intoxicated with this revolutionary brew, rest assured, you will be promptly sobered up with massive doses of BLACK POWDER, already in the hands of we white, Christians [sic] patriots. Do not be fools, black men. We will live here with you in the future as we have in the past or we will fertilize the soil of our beloved Southland with your remains.

Back in Broad Street Park, three young black girls rocked on a swing set, twisting new words into an old freedom song, reflecting more disillusion than hope, more bitterness than faith: *"I'm gonna bomb when the spirits say bomb . . . I'm gonna cut when the spirits say cut . . . I'm gonna shoot when the spirits say shoot . . ."*[18]

Sherwood Ross, the original press man for Meredith's walk, had stayed on the march as a reporter for radio station WOL. One day, while sitting on the press truck that puttered in front of the marchers, he interviewed the driver, Ted Alexander.

Alexander seemed like a character—when the sun got high and hot, he stripped off his shirt, revealing the words "Sweet" and "Sour" tattooed above his nipples. Now, with his tape recorder rolling, Ross learned that Alexander was a fanatical white supremacist. The Memphis man claimed that the Roman Empire fell after integrating with Africans, that Jesus Christ was not Jewish but Aryan, and that "nigger" was in the Bible: "It's spelled N-I-G-E-R." Into this twisted interpretation of history and theology, he interspersed biology: "Only mongrels integrate.

The birds don't integrate, and fish won't integrate. And God was certainly not colorblind. He put the yellow man in the East. He put the black man in Africa, and He put the white man here. He had no intentions of them mixing. If you put a crow in the pen with the blackbird, they will fight."[19]

Later, when reporters noted that his tattoo of a black panther symbolized the all-black party in Alabama, Alexander promised to add yellow ink spots and make it a leopard.[20]

Before the march ended, Alexander quit his job. "I was placed here by the Ku Klux Klan," he announced. He had relayed his observations, photographs, and recordings of the march to his fellow Klansmen, and he would donate his pay to "Klavern 777, Shelby County, Knights of the Ku Klux Klan."[21]

But Alexander was still driving the press truck as it rolled out of Greenwood. On that day, he and the reporters noticed a string-tied cardboard box sitting in the flatbed. Alexander decided to open it. Out popped a two-and-a-half-foot-long water moccasin. While others shot off in panic, a CBS News photographer smashed the poisonous snake with a wooden crate.[22]

The dangerous prank—even if it unwittingly targeted a Klansman— probably reflected white hostility toward the national press. A generation of reporters had cast black activists as heroes and white southerners as villains. How could they not? The papers delivered riveting images of mobs harassing schoolchildren in Little Rock and fire hoses blasting demonstrators in Birmingham. Bull Connor seemed a cartoon of racist hatred, Martin Luther King an archetype of Christian love. The press may have glossed over the nuances among both blacks and whites, but it conveyed the essential justice of the black freedom struggle.[23]

The Meredith shooting illustrated how the media's focus on dramatic conflict could still generate liberal goodwill: it cast blacks as noble victims of southern bigots. But when confronted by the rhetoric of black militants or the violence of ghetto blacks, the press offered the same surface coverage. Few journalists explored the roots of black rage or despair. By June 1966, black figures such as Whitney Young and Carl Rowan were writing syndicated columns that bemoaned how the media ignored the moderate black majority in favor of charismatic radicals such as Stokely Carmichael.[24]

The coverage of the Meredith March sometimes tilted toward sensationalism. If nonviolent demonstrations and voter registration seemed old hat, then reporters could seek juicy quotes from angry blacks, emphasize bickering among civil rights organizations, or portray the marchers as an exotic menagerie. Ed King of the MFDP had wanted the march to expose the depths of Mississippi's poverty, educating the American people and shaping White House policy. "The press never reported it, day after day after day," he lamented. "They were looking for something else."[25]

Most Americans got their newspaper updates from the wire services, which assigned reporters with little experience on the "Race Beat." Some of the newcomers lacked the requisite journalistic chops. The AP correspondents tended to misquote speeches, make uninformed speculations, and repeat egregious errors such as identifying Willie Ricks as an SCLC minister. A June 15 UPI report profiled a subset of radical white marchers, including a man proclaiming a "coming sexual revolution" centered upon homosexuality. According to the article, "most newsmen" agreed with the highway patrolman who called the march "a great assembly of kooks."[26]

One AP article featured Hank Coleman, a white graduate of Rice University. Before leaving the march to join the Peace Corps in Peru, Coleman slammed the white radicals in his midst. "If these white volunteers shaped up a little, shaved, their voter registration work would not arouse nearly so much animosity from white people in the community," he said. Yet Coleman contributed to the press's misunderstandings. Portraying the march as a logistical disaster, he claimed that at one campsite, they served canned dog food. The dinner was actually corned beef hash.[27]

Perceptive and experienced newsmen, such as Gene Roberts of *The New York Times* or Jack Nelson of the *Los Angeles Times*, also reported on the march. Renata Adler contributed a smart and salty piece for *The New Yorker*, painting the kaleidoscope of people that colored the demonstration. Paul Good wrote a long, thoughtful article for *New South*, but few people read the journal of the Southern Regional Council. Good had come to Mississippi as a freelancer, without funds or an assignment, and spent ten days there only because Arlie Schardt of *Time* shared his hotel room and his beer. Schardt, too, filed long and probing dispatches about the march and its meaning, but his editors chopped them into neat and simple summaries.[28]

A few photographers sought to portray human interactions among the marchers. Matt Herron of Black Star Photography, Jim Peppler of *The Southern Courier*, and Bob Fitch of SCLC all came to Mississippi as friends of the civil rights movement. Herron visited old SNCC friends and took one photograph of King and Carmichael in friendly conversation, transcending stereotypes about the march's divisions. Fitch and Peppler leapfrogged the column in their cars and then walked among the people, capturing personalities rather than scenes. Fitch once asked UPI's Joe Holloway why most photographers stayed on the press truck. "We have to be here," replied Holloway, "in case King gets killed."[29]

"The march reflected truths about America, north and south," wrote Paul Good. "If they shift in and out of focus it is because the country is shifting, trying to determine what it is and what it wants to be, while the question hangs whether there is enough time or inclination to truly reform what it was." Good captured the ambiguities of a traveling protest through a racist stronghold amid a changing national climate. He described soaring triumphs of the spirit, murky undercurrents of rage, shared goals of black freedom, and wide chasms of race, region, and ideology. Yet as the march wended through the Delta, few others conveyed that complexity.[30]

When they left Greenwood, the marchers wanted to stay on the campus of Mississippi Valley State University (MVSU), just outside Itta Bena. The location was perfect. The tax-supported facility for the black community had flat grassy fields and brick dormitories with kitchens and showers. An advance team came to the home of MVSU president James H. White. Flanked by eight highway patrolmen, White read a one-sentence letter denying use of the grounds.[31]

It may have seemed odd that an African American leader would resist a march for black freedom. Yet black conservatives did oppose the Meredith March. Syndicated columnist George Schuyler—the "Black Barry Goldwater"—accused Meredith of orchestrating national publicity, civil rights organizations of siphoning money, and radicals of eroding states' rights and individual freedom. Within Mississippi, Percy Greene, editor of the *Jackson Advocate*, condemned the march for causing racial conflict: "American historians may be forced to describe the Rev. Martin Luther King Jr. as the 20th century pied piper who led the people of his race over the precipice to be drowned and destroyed in a whirlpool of their own bitterness, hatred, frustration and disappointments."[32]

James H. White's own conservatism was rooted in his personal identification with the MVSU campus. When the institution opened in 1950 as Mississippi Vocational College, he presided over 450 boggy acres on a derelict cotton plantation with no buildings, roads, plumbing, or electricity. He erected academic programs and a physical infrastructure, and by 1966 the school's enrollment climbed over two thousand. Currying favor from white officials, he cultivated the school's growth. He could not afford any association with a freedom struggle, even if he got tarred as an Uncle Tom. White did not just discourage civil rights activity—he openly delivered information to the Mississippi State Sovereignty Commission. So when the Meredith Marchers wanted to use his campus, he sided with the powerful whites who funded his institution. One MVSU student tried to convince White to change his mind; he responded, "Hell no!"[33]

On Saturday, June 18, after an unusual breakfast of hot dogs, bologna sandwiches, and peanut butter, over one hundred marchers resumed the trek through the Delta. They began at the intersection of Routes 82 and 7, where a burning cross greeted them. As the marchers went south, George Raymond headed west toward MVSU. The CORE organizer found highway patrolmen guarding the main gate. The police had brought an old school bus, painted black, ready to serve as a huge patrol wagon. They also brought the same black prisoners from Parchman Penitentiary who had guarded Greenwood's Confederate memorial.[34]

Martin Luther King joined the march in the small town of Itta Bena. After a short rally, they pressed south toward the tiny plantation hamlets of Quito and Morgan City, fortified by an interracial busload from Chicago sponsored by the American Friends Service Committee. They received another reminder of Mississippi's threats: three cars driven by white men in white helmets, green shirts, and black ties. One car bore the sign KU KLUX KLAN—KNIGHTS OF THE GREEN FOREST. Its driver was Dale Walton, the imperial wizard.[35]

The marchers carried on without knowing that night's final destination. "I guess they'll have to sleep by the side of the road tonight with the mosquitoes," drawled a Leflore County deputy. He trailed the column in his Oldsmobile 98. "Those mosquitoes are big enough to pluck a hair out of your chest and put it back," he said before gulping his RC Cola.[36]

Andy Young shrugged off the uncertainty. The SCLC minister contrasted the Meredith March to Selma, when they had ten days to arrange a four-day march to Montgomery. "We just have no logistics and it works," said Young. The spontaneous spirit had hardened their resolve. During a break at the banks of the Muskegon River, King said that if they could not stay at MVSU, they could sleep in the Leflore County jail.[37]

Green Grove Baptist Church in Belzoni, fifteen miles down the road, offered its grounds for a campsite, but many activists wanted to force a confrontation at MVSU. Stokely Carmichael and Floyd McKissick had left for national commitments, and King left at three o'clock to catch a flight to Detroit, so the debate carried on absent the major leaders.[38]

At a meeting in Greenwood, SNCC's Bob Smith and CORE's George Raymond proposed to unload the tents at the campus gates—if they got arrested, the incident would spotlight Mississippi's racial injustice. Alvin Poussaint of the MCHR and Owen Brooks of the Delta Ministry questioned that idea's practicality, especially if it delayed their arrival in Jackson, which promised to be a national event. The debate got heated, but not as passionate as the one on Route 7. Glenn "Freedom X" Gurley, an excitable activist from Washington, D.C., had been arrested after the Meredith shooting for confronting guards outside the Justice Department. Now he favored a confrontation at MVSU, and he argued with "Big Lester" Hankerson of SCLC. The shouting devolved into a fistfight.[39]

The leaders ultimately settled on the Belzoni plan. That evening, after trucks deposited the marchers at Green Grove Baptist Church, they started a rally in a nearby vacant lot. Over three hundred people from Belzoni and the surrounding plantations joined them. They yelled, "Black Power! Black Power!" With no warning to the police, they began parading toward downtown. The impromptu evening demonstration headed toward the Humphreys County Courthouse.[40]

When the chanting, singing procession turned onto First Street, some young white men at a service station waved baseball bats and yelled such taunts as "Your mother's a nigger!" A muscular black man whipped back from the middle of the street. "Come on out here and say that!" he screamed, shaking his fist. An SCLC worker sprinted toward them, urging the marchers to keep moving, warning that the whites had chains and clubs. George Raymond put the marchers into a disciplined, two-by-two column. They headed for Belzoni's post office, where John Doar had arranged for federal registrars to open a late-night office.[41]

That night Raymond declared that the courthouse would change from "all-white to speckled," and activists circulated through the crowd, telling people to be brave. About seventy people registered to vote. Then they marched back to Green Grove Baptist Church, a trip that got scarier as it got darker. Yet peace prevailed. The historically repressive whites of the Mississippi Delta and the agitated Meredith Marchers had again neared a dramatic, traumatic confrontation. Again, they pulled back from the brink.[42]

After its first week, the March Against Fear had remained a national story, but it had drifted off the front page of most newspapers. Then Stokely Carmichael cried for Black Power, spurring new questions about American race relations. "Black Power meant a lot of things to blacks," cracked SNCC's Julius Lester, "but whites wanted to know only one thing: Does it mean y'all gon' kill white folks?"[43]

Liberal editorials feared that Black Power was "asking people to walk down a path toward an isolation that could be totally destructive." Critics, both black and white, equated the slogan with black supremacy. They portrayed it as a distorted mirror of the "mobs of white yahoos." While praising "intelligent moderates" such as Martin Luther King, they worried that Black Power would inflame northern ghettoes. "Racism," "ill manners," and "threatened violence" plagued the once-noble march, "trampling sympathy for civil rights into the Mississippi dust."[44]

Stokely Carmichael now served as a lightning rod for black pride, liberal anxiety, and conservative resentment. His reputation was a product of both his personal decisions and the media's interpretation.

At his finest, Carmichael electrified a folk epic. He exhorted crowds by saying a phrase softly at first and then repeating it with vigor—his dynamic eyes bulging, his knees bent, his long finger pointing down. "It is time to stop being ashamed of being black. It is time to stop trying to be white. When you see your daughter playing in the fields, with her nappy hair, and her wide nose, and her thick lips, tell her she is beautiful. *Tell your daughter she is beautiful.*" He had a genuine fondness for the people, putting young children on his shoulders or lugging water buckets for old women.[45]

When given time and space by sympathetic journalists, Carmichael framed Black Power in universal and democratic terms, as a logical outgrowth of the civil rights movement. He cited how black people could use local majorities to elect sheriffs and tax assessors. Black Power also meant taking pride in African American history and culture, understanding connections among oppressed and dark-skinned people throughout the world, and leading one's own freedom struggle. Only with this strength could blacks form real interracial coalitions. He said that he was not "anti-white," just "pro-Negro."[46]

Carmichael failed, however, to communicate his message through the mainstream press. Renata Adler captured his frustrating paradox: "When, as he saw it, he was continuously misrepresented by the press, he became obdurate and began to make himself eminently misrepresentable." As reporters focused on black violence and internal dissension rather than on white racists and voter registration, he demanded to be called "Mr. Carmichael" or "Sir," even by journalists whom he knew and liked. Whether speaking with a novice hack or a smart veteran, his press interactions dripped with contempt.[47]

Reporters thus accepted Carmichael's quotes at face value. "Every courthouse in Mississippi ought to be burned down to get rid of the dirt," he had proclaimed in Greenwood. "If they put one of us in jail, we're not going to pay a bond to get him out. We're going up there and get him out ourselves. Black Power!" Most blacks understood that he neither advocated revolutionary violence nor spewed racial hatred; many whites did not. One letter to an editor snickered that Carmichael's call for Black Power "reminds me of another catchy phrase of years gone by, 'Sieg Heil.'"[48]

On Sunday, June 19, Carmichael appeared on CBS's *Face the Nation.* Before a national television and radio audience, a panel of reporters fixated on the links between Black Power and black violence:

Q: This would seem to imply that you are advocating taking power by force and violence by the overthrow, in effect, of the government. Is that what you mean?

Q: Mr. Carmichael, do you reject the ultimate use of violence as a final last resort in bringing down the power structure?

Q: How can you not reject violence and be the head of the Student Non-violent Coordinating Committee?

Q: Are you a nonviolent person or are you talking in violent analogies because you want to see a violent Negro uprising?

Q: Would you agree, Mr. Carmichael, that the Watts riot and violence like that is irrelevant and doesn't make any sense?

Q: Can we pinpoint your feeling on violence?

Q: You are against the use of violence to achieve the objectives of the Negro movement?

Q: Are you telling us—are you saying the Negro can riot and take over—what do you mean by "black power"?

Carmichael neither endorsed nor denounced violence. He instead decried the poisonous effects of integrating white institutions rather than enriching black ones, and he again defined Black Power as independent, third-party politics in black-majority regions. Yet Carmichael also confused his own message when explaining his statement about burning down the courthouse. "I literally mean burn down," he said. In his next breath, he called the statement an "analogy."[49]

Back in Mississippi, during a rare quiet moment, Carmichael admitted that there was a chasm in perceptions about him. "When I talk about going to the courthouse, it's an allusion," he said. He knew, as well, that "whites get nervous when we don't keep talking about brotherly love. They need reassurance." But he refused to accept that task. His job was to empower blacks, not mollify whites.[50]

12

DELTA BLUES
Belzoni to Louise
JUNE 19–20, 1966

"The Mississippi Mau Mau are here to terrorize whites," announced a young black man into the microphone of Sherwood Ross. The same radio reporter who had interviewed the undercover Klansman driving the press truck was now surrounded by young black men who had formed a new group promising violence against white supremacists. "We decided that Negroes need to retaliate, and now's the time," said the man. Ross asked if they would use guns and bombs. "If necessary, yes."

The Mississippi Mau Mau refused to give their names—"We don't even want the black people to know who we are," said one. They were not from Mississippi, but they planned to stay for at least five years. They distinguished themselves from the Deacons for Defense, who protected black people. Instead, they planned to "come in to take over and do the things that need to be done"—including the aggressive targeting of Klansmen.[1]

One thousand miles away, Jean Chaney joined a protest march from Harlem to the Upper East Side. Originally from Neshoba County, Mississippi, she had moved her family to New York City after the Ku Klux Klan murdered her brother, James Chaney, in 1964.

The marchers alongside Chaney carried signs such as NONVIOLENCE IS A TACTIC, NOT A DOGMA and DON'T MAKE US VIOLENT. Organized by the Harlem branch of CORE, the march headed toward a neighborhood where whites had thrown eggs and vegetables at black protesters. The marchers bubbled with anger, almost spoiling for a fight. A group modeled on the Deacons for Defense guarded them. A reporter asked Chaney if she saw big differences between New York and Mississippi. "No," she responded. "Everybody I know is getting violent."[2]

June 1966 looked like the start of a "long, hot summer." As the Meredith March entered its third week, a white grocery store owner slapped a black boy in Pompano Beach, Florida, leading blacks to storm the streets, crash rocks through plate-glass storefronts, light a car on fire, and spar with white teenagers. That same week, the Cleveland district of Hough endured four days of rioting; black youths tossed glass jars stuffed with gasoline-soaked rags while battling police and hostile whites, and one white man driving a convertible shot a nine-year-old black boy in the stomach.[3]

Like the riots during the previous two years in Harlem, Philadelphia, Rochester, and Watts, these violent outbursts exposed black people's festering grievances about police brutality, job discrimination, poor schools, and dilapidated neighborhoods. Rioters targeted symbols of oppression, such as policemen and white-owned businesses. They also reflected how the civil rights movement had shifted the perceptions of all black people. Northern blacks, too, wanted access to the American dream.[4]

The March Against Fear funneled the hopes and furies of blacks throughout the nation. During the march's second weekend, civil rights organizations from across the country protested not only Meredith's shooting, but also their own local problems. For instance, the Oklahoma City NAACP organized a hundred-mile march to Lawton, both to support the Meredith March and to protest a segregated swimming pool at an amusement park.[5]

In Boston, the all-white School Committee was delaying racial integration, despite recent legislation outlawing de facto school segregation. When School Committee Chair Louise Day Hicks appeared at a middle school graduation in Roxbury, SCLC's Virgil Wood branded her "the Hitler of Boston." At a subsequent street rally, civil rights groups from the NAACP to SNCC backed Wood. While raising funds for black Bostonians to march in Mississippi, they arranged an alternative "Freedom Graduation" for the students. "What we are dealing with is a form of 'black power,'" said one minister. "It is something which can't be given; it must be seized." Almost every speaker used the slogan of Black Power.[6]

Bill Strickland, the new president of the Northern Student Movement (NSM), visited Mississippi during the march. Begun as a fundraising arm for SNCC, the NSM started tutorial programs in Harlem and North Philadelphia. Then its activists turned to grass-roots organizing in the urban North, and it developed an all-black orientation. Strickland saw models for northern politics in the Black Belt. Upon his return to New York, he wrote to Mississippi activists. He proposed such ideas as creating a federation of independent black parties, planning active resistance to the Vietnam War, deploying black students as organizers in the Delta, and turning the Deacons for Defense into a national organization.[7]

The roots of African American militancy stretched deep and wide. "There is always a strand in black history from Nat Turner on up that seeks confrontation or mutiny or rebellion," reflected Strickland. "What radicalized us was the same thing that radicalized Marcus Garvey." Malcolm X, in particular, had inspired Strickland's generation. The recently published *Autobiography of Malcolm X* chronicled his early life as a "hustler," prison stint, religious conversion, rise to prominence, rift with the Nation of Islam, voyages to Mecca and Africa, and evolving ideology. With eloquence and charisma, Malcolm X lambasted white liberals, internationalized the racial struggle, and exuded a proud black manhood. After his 1965 assassination, he stood as a founding father of Black Power.[8]

Well before Stokely Carmichael spoke those words in Greenwood, activists used the language and strategies of Black Power. Yet the concerns of the South reflected upon the North. When the cry of Black Power burst out of Mississippi, it echoed in the ears of black militants. It gave them a name, a recognition, a sense of a movement.[9]

"We are tired of white folks killing black folks. We're going to get some black power," proclaimed Willie Ricks. He was standing atop a car, leading a rally that blocked off Route 7 north of Belzoni. As cries of "Black Power!" echoed back, Ricks promised that "from now on, it's not gonna be all black blood. We're gonna get some of that white blood!"[10]

The improvised protest on Sunday, June 19, mixed two streams of marchers, one heading south and the other north. That morning, the official contingent had trucked back to the previous day's stopping point. On the walk back down, Route 7 offered reminders of the Delta's poverty and paternalism. When the marchers stopped near three sharecropper cabins to rest and drink water, plantation owner J. W. Gamlon left his dinner table, rushed to the scene, and ordered them off his property. *"Come on off the bigot's land!"* they sang while walking away. *"Oh yeah! Come on off the bigot's land!"*[11]

Later that day they passed through Pugh City, where a few hundred blacks lived in shanties near a tiny row of sagging stores, all owned by plantation boss Joe Pugh. Some old, semiblind, dirt-poor farm workers with crooked teeth asked for a ride into town. They, too, wanted to experience a civil rights jubilee.[12]

Back in Belzoni, Green Grove Baptist Church hosted a daylong rally. The black majority in this Delta town of 4,200 people grew excited. Crowds dressed in church clothes waited for the march's return to town, until some could wait no longer. Around four o'clock, hundreds of African Americans—from respectable ladies twirling parasols to excitable young children to stiff-jointed sharecroppers—started walking north. Twenty minutes later, they were listening to Ricks preach about Black Power.[13]

They walked en masse into Belzoni. It was the march's largest demonstration yet. Black people skipped off sidewalks, hopped off porches, and spilled out of stores. They strode toward Green Grove Baptist Church for another rally, where Ricks bragged about occupying Route 7, called for blacks to control Mississippi politics, celebrated the Deacons for Defense, and said that "the U.S. flag represents a bunch of lies."[14]

"That's the way to win, ain't it?" an old black woman beamed to her friend as they watched the parade through town. Her friend nodded back. The display promised new political opportunities, new self-images. It warned of something else, too. As the grand procession moved through the main streets, some people chanted, *"Whites must go!"*[15]

The cry might have targeted powerful whites in Mississippi, but it also sharpened attention on the place of white marchers. Especially after Greenwood, young militants openly advocated a black nationalist approach. It alienated those who considered the civil rights movement an interracial undertaking. Some whites felt punished for their generosity. "SNCC has cut me out," groused a white teenager from Chicago while moping around the Belzoni campsite.[16]

Veteran white organizers showed more composure. Joe Morse had arrived in Lauderdale County during Freedom Summer, after his junior year at a Minnesota seminary, and stayed for two years. While campaigning for the MFDP, he tried taking his cues from local leaders, not the other way around. As he marched through the Delta, he realized that Black Power was expressing new ideas, but he never felt out of place. The march urged blacks to improve their lives by unifying around protests and ballot boxes. Like the black organizers, Morse had been working toward those same goals.[17]

If white marchers felt insulted by chants such as "*Hey hey, what do you know, honky got to go*," many also accepted Black Power in terms of political unity, economic strength, and cultural pride. When the media characterized Black Power as violent, white liberals helped point out that Mississippi whites were the violent ones. Homer Jack of the Unitarian Universalist Association insisted that whites still felt welcome. They needed to understand the frustration of black activists. "Black power is not black racism, not black nationalism, and not black extremism," he said. "At least not yet."[18]

For now, black militants could grumble about white liberals, and white marchers could feel unappreciated. Those same blacks might admit the necessity of white participation, and those same whites might yell for Black Power. "We do need black power," said Leon Hall of SCLC, "but we don't need black power to take over and do to the white folks like they done to us." The middle path forged by Hall and other liberals still seemed possible, even if a walk through Mississippi could not resolve all of the movement's problems.[19]

The constant chant of "What do we want?" now received competing answers: the old "Freedom Now" and the new "Black Power." Proponents on both sides tried enlisting "Kicker," the blond-haired, barely supervised, three-year-old son of two hippie marchers. On this debate, Kicker stayed true to his principles. "What do we want?" they prompted.

"A kitty cat!" he answered.[20]

If the Delta was a sea of hardships, then black people found refuge on its islands: the front porches of clapboard shacks in dirt-road shanty-towns; the hand-clapping jubilations, soaring spirituals, and sweaty ser-mons in tiny wooden churches; the low-down blues, whiskey slugs, and hip-hugging dances in juke joints. The cotton fields contained the basis of their livelihoods and the seeds of their oppression. Crop dusters dumped clouds of insecticide. Billboards called Martin Luther King a Communist. Poor black families walked down flat, lonesome roads toward nowhere. When the Meredith March came through, it conjured all the old fears, but it also conveyed the possibility of a better life. Of course they chanted for Black Power: they were poor, they were black, and they had no power.[21]

But what did Black Power mean? How did black people in Missis-sippi understand it? Joyce Ladner, a Mississippi native and SNCC veteran, tried to answer those questions. She saw blacks' swelling dissat-isfaction with the pace of change, and she heard the grumblings about whites in the movement. Her own optimism had deflated after the 1964 Democratic National Convention. "It made sense to shift from inte-gration as the sole goal," she said. "What began to make sense to me was to leverage the potential power that lay within black people." In connec-tion with her Ph.D. work in sociology at Washington University, she started interviewing black activists in Mississippi.[22]

Ladner divided Black Power advocates into two groups: "cosmopoli-tans" and "locals." The cosmopolitans tended to be college-educated young men working through SNCC and CORE, often from the North, influenced by revolutionaries such as Malcolm X, Frantz Fanon, and Kwame Nkrumah. They considered Black Power in ideological terms of race consciousness and anticolonialism. They bemoaned the move-ment's incremental gains and questioned their own past tactics. Only through psychological liberation, they believed, could blacks have an equal stake in society.[23]

The Mississippi Mau Mau—who disappeared from the historical re-cord after their interview with Sherwood Ross—offered an extreme example of this outlook. It also could be found in the zealous oratory of Stokely Carmichael or Willie Ricks, in the scowls and outbursts of black marchers, or in march signs with the slogan MOVE ON OVER—OR WE'LL MOVE ON OVER YOU. A posture of dramatic, public defiance was part of its very philosophy.

Ladner's "locals," by contrast, tended to be Mississippi-bred supporters of the MFDP without many educational or financial resources. They had always lived in a world divided by race. Black Power provided a language for achieving "bread and butter" goals such as jobs, voter registration, and political offices. They cheered the speeches by Carmichael and Ricks, but they cared more about community programs than philosophical arguments.[24]

Like the MFDP, the Delta Ministry adopted this practical application of Black Power. Established in 1964 by the National Council of Churches (NCC), the Delta Ministry established seven projects with an interracial, interfaith staff. Partnering with local blacks, it helped register voters, train political candidates, deliver federal antipoverty funds, and picket employers and school boards. By 1966, it had the largest staff of any civil rights organization in Mississippi.[25]

In a May 1966 report, the NCC praised how the Delta Ministry tended to the repressed poor and compelled the church to consider its larger purpose. The NCC criticized the Delta Ministry, however, for closing lines of communication with white moderates. The report further suggested that projects such as black-controlled antipoverty centers perpetuated racial segregation.[26]

But activists on the ground believed that blacks *had* to control their own institutions, and they *had* to demand revolutionary change. Anything less meant piecemeal gains and the psychological stigma of powerlessness. "People like myself were not intimidated by the use of the term Black Power," reflected Owen Brooks, the associate director of the Delta Ministry. "It was an important aspiration of the dispossessed to acquire political and economic power." As the organization's key representative on the March Against Fear, Brooks allied with other Mississippi activists in focusing the march on voter registration and community organization. Yet he rued that Black Power appeared under a national media spotlight, so multiple camps defined and distorted it. The march inflated the slogan's significance but confused its meaning.[27]

Throughout Mississippi, people adapted Black Power to their experiences and aspirations. In the Delta town of Tribbett, a black student from Rhodesia spoke at a civil rights rally. While urging participation in the Meredith March, he compared white supremacy in Africa and America, pulling together local and international ideas about Black Power.[28]

By joining the March Against Fear, sixteen-year-old Jean Mallett got to eat breakfast with Martin Luther King, sleep in a cemetery, and endure grueling stretches of highway with a sense of accomplishment. She walked alongside whites, which taught her that they could be good people. But she also loved hearing Carmichael's speech in Greenwood. She remembered counting change for an illiterate clerk when she was a little girl in Kosciusko; the store owner had employed this unqualified white woman, yet refused to hire blacks. She thought that if black people had some power, then whites would have to treat them better. Here was Black Power in pure and personal terms. "It meant a lot to me," she said. "It helped me reaffirm who *I* was."[29]

On the morning of June 20, Robert Green of SCLC gathered another crowd outside Green Grove Baptist Church in Belzoni. While he urged everyone to stay in line and cooperate with white officers, Willie Ricks interrupted him with calls of "Black Power!"[30]

Green wanted to rally around the Confederate memorial at the Humphreys County Courthouse, but Parchman prisoners again guarded the statue. Sixty highway patrolmen—the largest police force yet—were also on hand. They offered to send registrants through the back door of the post office, but Green refused the arrangement. He staged a rally in front of the courthouse. Then he led a small group into the building, threatening a sit-in unless the sheriff unlocked all the white bathrooms. "This toilet is symbolic of all the things the Negro has been locked out of in Mississippi," proclaimed the activist professor.[31]

The restroom integration provided the sole, rather dim highlight of a difficult Monday. Federal registrars did sign about forty more blacks onto the rolls while Green and Ricks led the marchers south down Highway 49. They carried new, colorful signs for the MISSISSIPPI MARCH 1966 but encountered only a few unenthusiastic people in the cotton fields. The only two towns on the route, Silver City and Midnight, were plantation villages with populations under five hundred.[32]

Yet the March Against Fear exposed these poor, rural people to the civil rights movement. In Midnight, whites locked up the town's two stores, two soda machines, and one outdoor water spigot. The amassed deputies and farmers stiffened as advance cars rolled into town, and they gasped when two white women emerged from the same car as black men. They seethed, too, at the local blacks who waved and danced during the processional; "Them's the ones can starve to death from now on as far as I'm concerned," grimaced one man. They watched the marchers' backsides with relief—unaware that the march had inspired a group of Midnight blacks to register.[33]

By this time, Ricks had left for a rally in Lexington, the seat of Holmes County. Unlike the stretch of plantations along Highway 49, Holmes County had landowning black farmers who led a local movement, allied with SNCC workers, and shot back at white intimidators. Ricks was tilling fertile soil. Move closer, he urged the crowd. "You're black and the sun can't hurt you," he declared to their delight. His speech lambasted exploitative whites, Uncle Toms, the Ku Klux Klan, and "Nigger preachers." "We have black power and we intend to use it," he said. "We are going to make them pay for every black person they've beaten, murdered, killed."[34]

A few hours later, the marchers finished their hot slog. They had covered seventeen and a half miles, their longest hike yet. When they heard "What do you want?," more than a few shouted back, "A little rest!" Although 247 people had left Belzoni, only 90 reached the final destination. The stalwarts included about fifty whites. It was ironic: as the march got associated with Black Power, it had, for one moment, a slight white majority.[35]

Their host that evening was H. L. Montgomery, a remarkable exception to the region's rule of black poverty. In the nearby town of Louise, white plantation owners ran all the stores and offices. Most blacks were poor tenant farmers with no idea if the planter-dominated town council was elected or appointed—they actually referred to it as "the White Citizens' Council." Yet Montgomery had inherited 250 acres from his father, a former slave who bought land after the Civil War. Montgomery had fifteen employees and leased five hundred more acres. He raised cows, hogs, chickens, and turkeys, planted cotton, beans, and corn, and traded mink, beaver, raccoon, and opossum hides.[36]

Montgomery was not particularly enthusiastic about the possible complications of hosting a civil rights cavalcade, but he "had an intuition" that the march would stop there, even before it was rerouted through the Delta. He chased his pigs into an unused pen, opening high and dry land for the tents.[37]

At a late-night meeting on Montgomery's land, Ricks chafed at the moderation of Martin Luther King, while Green relayed King's displeasure that some whites felt unwelcome. For now, however, they tried to shield any dissension or controversy. That night, a patrolling Deacon found a black man and white woman naked together in a car. Safeguarding the march's image, he ordered them back to their separate tents.[38]

The Sovereignty Commission relayed gossip from Informant X: "The consensus is that if not for all the nationwide publicity and financial support, a large percentage of these groups participating in this 'March' would like to call a halt to it. However, they are committed and cannot do anything about it."[39]

The spiritual integrationists of SCLC were frustrated. Instead of appreciating the march's impact in Mississippi's black communities, the media was gravitating to the exciting threat of Stokely Carmichael and hyping the violent fantasies of Willie Ricks. Textured by their southern upbringings and religious training, the SCLC men understood the depths of human sin, but they cherished the bonds that united humanity, and they held faith in nonviolence. They disagreed less with Carmichael's definition of Black Power than with his prickly, vengeful presentation of it.[40]

"I just don't know what to do," confessed Andy Young in private. "We got so many irresponsible and erratic characters around." The march was in debt, and SNCC's radical image made joint fund-raising impossible.[41]

On Saturday night, Martin Luther King headlined a rally at Cobo Hall in Detroit sponsored by thirty civil rights, labor, and religious organizations. It included speeches by United Auto Workers president Walter Reuther, Detroit mayor Jerome Cavanagh, and Aaron Henry and Charles Evers of the Mississippi NAACP. The twelve thousand entrants paid a one-dollar fee, and pledges raised additional funds for voter registration campaigns in the South.[42]

King urged people to come to Mississippi for the final march into Jackson. While describing the persistent horrors of the Deep South, he discussed the structural barriers to equality in northern cities, such as jobs and housing. He called for blacks to not only express racial pride, but also ally with poor whites. Alluding to the new battle cry, he stated that the "powerlessness of the Mississippi Negro must be transformed into economic and political power." But he also reaffirmed his principles. "I don't care if every Negro in the United States comes down and urges using violence," he said. "I will still be the last one to cry against it."[43]

Two days later, from SCLC headquarters in Atlanta, King confronted Black Power. He had been harboring misgivings that the slogan was alienating and divisive. Now, in a statement for widespread public consumption, he said that "it is absolutely necessary to gain power, but the term 'black power' is unfortunate because it tends to give the impression of black nationalism." Interracial cooperation and nonviolent protest paved the road to freedom. He downplayed the radical ideas of a small minority. "Black supremacy would be equally as evil as white supremacy," he said. The floor underneath black politics was shifting, but before returning to Mississippi for the march's final stretch, King had staked his ground.[44]

13

BROTHERLY LOVE
Louise to Yazoo City; Philadelphia
JUNE 21, 1966

On the morning of June 21, Martin Luther King and his SCLC associates took a chartered, twin-engine plane from Atlanta to Meridian, Mississippi. Policemen flanked him as he walked into the tiny airport's coffee shop and bathroom. On the heels of his anti–Black Power statement, he downplayed any rifts among march leaders, instead emphasizing their common goals of voter registration, federal protection, and a national commitment to alleviating poverty. "Violence creates many more problems than it solves," he added. "Nonviolence is still the most potent weapon in the Negro's struggle for freedom."

Upon learning that Philadelphia had a long enough airstrip, the SCLC contingent got back on the plane and flew to the town in nearby west-central Mississippi. King was leading a protest march in recognition of the second anniversary of the murders of three civil rights workers.[1]

King's presence in Philadelphia was a double-edged sword. He had an unrivaled drawing power, luring in demonstrators for marches and rallies. Yet he also attracted violent racists, creating dangers for everyone involved. Some Mississippi organizers thought that King was inviting an assassination attempt.[2]

A little before noon, the marchers gathered in Philadelphia's black district, Independence Quarters. A small group had driven over from the Meredith March's campsite in Louise, while a larger crowd of local blacks and MFDP activists joined them outside Mt. Nebo Baptist Church. Matt Rinaldi, a white civil rights worker in Attala County, walked into the church just as the march leaders wrapped up a meeting. He was surprised to see the expression on King's face. The great leader looked scared.[3]

The actual Meredith March was happening eighty miles to the west, on the stretch of Route 16 between Louise and Yazoo City. Sixty-one people had set out early that morning, walking briskly but with a methodical, almost resigned air. Yazoo City was eighteen and a half miles away. By eleven o'clock they had already gone twelve miles. Few plantation workers greeted them, but they were too tired to care. They ate lunch in near silence. Some slept in the thin strip of shade provided by parked trucks.[4]

The most newsworthy moment was another calculated cameo by Charles Evers. The previous evening, he had urged the audience at a mass meeting in Port Gibson to join the final rally in Jackson. While armed guards patrolled outside the church, Evers had proclaimed that blacks would fight back against intimidation; his force in Claiborne County was even calling itself the Deacons for Defense, despite no affiliation with the Louisiana organization. Around the press on the Meredith March, though, he appealed to liberal integrationists: "If we are marching these roads for black supremacy, we're doomed. I never will be anti-white. I would be just as guilty of the racism and bigotry we've been fighting all these years."[5]

The marchers crossed the Yazoo River Bridge at 1:25 and soon entered Yazoo City, where about eighty black teenagers joined them. They feared a violent response. Straddling the Delta and the Hill Country, Yazoo City had a long history of racial terror. Civil rights workers often got run out of town. Only about 1,000 of Yazoo County's 8,700 eligible black voters had registered. The county sheriff won election in 1964 based on his reputation for "cracking niggers in the head."[6]

Yet Yazoo City maintained white supremacy under a shady tent of civility. The Citizens' Council met every Friday at a local restaurant. The leading whites abhorred disruptions to their community of broad boulevards, stately old homes, charming storefronts, and verdant trees. As rumors spread that the march's "outside agitators" would provoke a conflict, the council had the city's Board of Aldermen and the county's Board of Supervisors issue a joint public announcement. Published in the local newspaper, it urged whites "to demonstrate the wisdom, maturity, solidarity and calmness of mind that have been of such great benefit in the maintenance of peaceful racial relations in the past." No heckling or violence, it pleaded. "Any citizen who violates this advice is a worse enemy of the county and does it more harm than the marchers themselves."[7]

There were no incidents. The marchers were too exhausted, the local whites too cautious. FBI agents and Justice Department officials watched as the police escorted the procession down Main Street and Broadway. They reached a recreational area on West Seventh Street, where an advance team had won approval to camp. Although the city had drained the swimming pool, the marchers rested and took much-needed advantage of the shower facilities.[8]

Like their counterparts in Grenada and Greenwood, the white leaders of Yazoo City had opted for the conciliatory approach, and they worked with state and federal authorities to ensure security. Their strategy ensured a day of relative peace—a far cry from the drama then occurring in Philadelphia.

Exactly two years earlier, on June 21, 1964, Neshoba County deputy sheriff Cecil Price had arrested James Chaney, Andy Goodman, and Mickey Schwerner in Philadelphia. Like his boss, Sheriff Lawrence Rainey, Price was a member of the Ku Klux Klan. After releasing his prisoners late that night, he joined local Klansmen in chasing down the activists. Price led a caravan to an isolated clearing surrounded by thick piney woods, where Klansmen shot the men dead. They buried the bodies in an earthen dam.[9]

The victims were CORE workers from nearby Meridian. Their disappearance set the nation's gaze upon Philadelphia. Goodman and Schwerner were out-of-state whites, and the murders occurred just before the arrival of Freedom Summer volunteers. The FBI began a massive investigation. Before they found the three bodies that August, authorities discovered a host of discarded black corpses, unknown casualties of southern justice. The FBI further learned that Rainey and Price engaged in such unsavory activities as bootlegging, financial scams, and the torture of prisoners. The federal case against the killers stalled until 1966, but on June 17, while the Meredith March was leaving Greenwood, a trial date of September 26 was set for eighteen men, including Rainey and Price.[10]

To the region's unreconstructed bigots, the sheriff and his deputy were popular heroes. An advertisement in *The Meridian Star* showed a chiropractor shaking hands with Rainey; the caption read, "World Famous Neshoba County Sheriff Says, 'Civil Rights Got Him Down in the Back.'"[11]

Moderate whites—the kind who frowned upon Klan violence, rejected simpleminded racists, or respected the law—were tarred as "nigger lovers." "It seems a bunch of roughnecks and Ku Kluxers took over the community, and intimidated all those fine, decent people we used to know," mourned Turner Catledge, a Philadelphia native who was editor of *The New York Times*. After a white woman named Florence Mars testified about the case, Rainey arrested her on a trumped-up drunk driving charge, and community pressure forced her to resign from leading a Bible class and youth group.[12]

In this climate, COFO and MFDP built a political movement. They established a new Freedom House in Philadelphia. Cecil Price often cruised past it, brandishing a shotgun, yet Neshoba County blacks started registering voters, staging demonstrations, and filing desegregation suits. In early 1966, the black community launched an economic boycott and demanded the firing of Tripp Windham, a brutal black officer who patrolled Independence Quarters.[13]

Clint Collier led the Neshoba County crusade. Most recently, he ran for Congress on the MFDP ticket. The steadfast, nonviolent minister had been fired from his public school teaching job, endured constant surveillance from Rainey and Price, and suffered a beating after buying a cup of coffee at a segregated cafe. Once he got thrown in jail while working with Nina Boal, a white volunteer from Chicago. Rainey and Price brought in their Klan buddies, who got so enraged by the sight of a black man with a white woman that Boal thought that they would become Philadelphia's "civil rights martyrs #4 and #5."[14]

The murders of Chaney, Goodman, and Schwerner lent an important touchstone for local organizing. On June 21, 1965, fifty Neshoba County blacks marched twelve miles from Philadelphia to the charred remains of Mt. Zion Baptist Church, where the three civil rights workers had gone one year earlier to investigate an arson. In 1966, as the March Against Fear coursed through the Delta, activists worked with march leaders and did extensive advance organizing. On June 19, the MFDP organized a motorcade from Meridian to James Chaney's gravesite, where a crowd gathered to hear speeches. The next night, Mt. Nebo Baptist Church hosted a mass meeting. "They died for you," implored Leah Jones, a peppery, sad-eyed old woman with deep roots in the movement. "Every one of us oughta be in the march tomorrow."[15]

Despite the plans for a big demonstration under a national spotlight, only about ten ill-prepared city police and a few Neshoba County officers handled its security. The Deacons for Defense were guarding the main body of marchers on Route 16. Although some FBI agents and Justice Department officials were observing the Philadelphia march, only one car from the Mississippi Highway Patrol got assigned there. "Philadelphia local officials are handling march," a Highway Patrol memorandum reported that morning. "They have *not* requested assistance."[16]

Moreover, the county sheriff, Lawrence Rainey, had skipped town for El Paso, Texas. Authority lay with Cecil Price, the weak-chinned, pot-bellied deputy sheriff at the center of a civil rights murder conspiracy set for trial in federal court.[17]

"Ain't gonna let nobody turn me 'round," sang the marchers as they left Mt. Nebo Baptist Church. Red dust puffed up from the unpaved streets of Independence Quarters.

The trouble started at the bottom of Depot Hill. A black sedan barreled toward the marchers and braked, skidding and scattering them. A red convertible buzzed down the column, nearly grazing a few people. A passenger in a pickup truck swung a wooden club at them. When an ice-blue Mustang drove up, its two young female passengers—*Time* described one as a "button-cute blonde"—yelled: "I wouldn't dirty my Goddamned car with you black bastards!"[18]

As the march approached Philadelphia's main square, a gauntlet of angry whites screamed insults from sidewalks, second-story windows, trees, and rooftops. Andy Young advised Alvin Poussaint to keep close, in case King got attacked and needed emergency medical attention.[19]

At the county jail, Ralph Abernathy led a brief memorial service. Few could hear the prayers as the surrounding crowd jeered, motorcycle engines revved, and car horns honked. A sandy-haired white man in his early twenties sprayed the marchers with a garden hose. Running on a cocktail of hate and adrenaline, he then pointed at ABC cameraman

George Romilly and announced, "I'm gonna get him." He rushed toward Romilly and jerked the camera, forcing Romilly to topple over. Despite the marchers' outraged pleas, the policemen just grinned as the attacker ran away.[20]

The marchers displayed a fierce spirit, further enraging the mob. "Freedom! Freedom!" they shouted at their hecklers. An old woman proclaimed: "You done killed our boys! But we on the march ain't turnin' round. Ain't *nobody* gonna turn us 'round. You *cain't* turn us 'round!" A housekeeper saw her longtime employer, an outraged white woman jabbing a finger at her. "Yes! It's me and I've kept your children," yelled the black woman. "I could've spit in their milk for all you know!"[21]

They reached the Neshoba County Courthouse, where King and Abernathy came face to face with Cecil Price. The two squat ministers in dark suits, white shirts, and sunglasses stared up at the tobacco-chewing, blackjack-wielding lawman. "Oh yes, you're the one who had Schwerner and the other fellows in jail," said King. "Yes, sir," responded Price, his voice flecked with pride. Price blocked the courthouse steps. The registrar's office was closed until one o'clock, he said. King stated their intention to hold a prayer meeting. Price crossed his arms and glowered.[22]

Over two hundred demonstrators massed in front of the courthouse. At least three hundred whites, resentful of King and emboldened by the lack of law enforcement, surrounded them. Roy Reed of *The New York Times* was standing just behind King. "*This is the day he will die,*" thought Reed.[23]

"Today we face the violence of misguided men," spoke King. "In this county Andrew Goodman, James Chaney, and Mickey Schwerner were brutally murdered. I believe in my heart that the murderers are somewhere around me at this moment."[24]

"They're right behind you!" shouted a white boy. The surrounding spectators cheered, chuckled, and hooted agreement. Price, standing behind King, smirked.[25]

King later admitted that he had never been more scared. He had endured death threats, southern jails, police dogs, and assassination attempts, but the hatred in Philadelphia seemed so palpable. MFDP workers Matt Rinaldi and Luther Mallett were scanning the trees and rooftops, looking for snipers. Mallett recalled how the hairs stuck straight out on Rinaldi's neck. Rinaldi was inspired, however, by King's calm, powerful, self-assured demeanor. He had seen King's fear in the church, but not here, in front of his people.[26]

"I am not afraid of any man," King continued. "Whether he is in Mississippi or Michigan, whether he is in Birmingham or Boston. I am not afraid." Price whispered to a deputy, who passed along the message, and soon the news spread to other whites. BOOM! BOOM! BOOM! It sounded like a shotgun—at least one marcher clutched his chest, looking for blood. In fact, the mob had tossed cherry bombs, apparently at Price's order. While firecrackers exploded at his feet, King pressed on: "We are going to work together for freedom. We are here to save America. We are here to save you. Why don't you whites understand this?" Through the cacophony of jeers and firecrackers, he prayed: "The Lord is my shepherd, the Lord is my shepherd . . ."[27]

As King uttered a final prayer—"Father, forgive them, for they know not what they do"—Price grabbed Clinton Collier. Policemen wrestled the local leader to the sidewalk and arrested him on four outstanding traffic violations. Collier writhed and screamed. "Don't let them put me in there," he pleaded. "They'll kill me." While police dragged him away, city police chief Bruce Latimer warned the marchers: "Now you better GIT!"[28]

The final, slender threads of order snapped. The spectators tossed eggs, rocks, and soda bottles at the marchers returning down Main Street. A rock struck one man in the chest. Amid the fusillade of insults and projectiles, a middle-aged black marcher staggered off, spun around, and collapsed. He was having an epileptic seizure. A nurse named Dorothy Williams tended to him while surrounded by men with clubs and switchblades. They cracked cruel jokes: "There's a Mississippi slave for you—can't stand a little Mississippi sun." When a truck pulled up, they shouted, "Come on, roll over, kill him!" After loading in the patient, Williams got dragged back into the crowd. A volunteer in the truck pulled her over the tailgate, away from the mob.[29]

One hundred yards behind King, a big fight broke out. A marauding white man had wrenched the shoulder of a television cameraman, and a black teenager named Eddie Lee Turner intervened. Another white man ran across the street, bounded off a car hood, and landed feet first on Turner. A half-dozen blacks then traded roundhouses with a group of whites in a rowdy, tumbling scuffle. Meanwhile, a larger mass of whites waded onto the street carrying knives, pliers, ax handles, chains, and wrenches. One man had a five-foot club; another brought a hoe. Philadelphia approached the brink of an all-out riot.

At last, the police intervened, and the fistfights stopped before the weapon-wielding crew got too close. Somehow, the marchers reached the safety of a black neighborhood.[30]

By the bottom of Depot Hill, Martin Luther King's brave facade had crumbled. He looked shaken. "This is a terrible town, the worst I've seen," he said. "There is a complete reign of terror here." He worried, too, that Clinton Collier would meet the same fate as Chaney, Goodman, and Schwerner. He turned to Andy Young. "We've got to find a way to protect these people," he said.[31]

After gathering themselves in Independence Quarters, King and Abernathy returned to the Neshoba County Courthouse with $400 to bail out Collier. The MFDP leader left jail unscathed. "We'd like to work you over, and we would have worked you over if that crowd hadn't been out there," Cecil Price had told him. "And we will work you over yet."[32]

The next morning, Highway Patrol investigators met with city leaders. "The situation could have been handled in a more satisfactory manner if the local officials had made arrangements to control the local troublemakers," concluded A. L. Hopkins of the Sovereignty Commission, who fretted that such attacks would escalate the pressure on Mississippi. After requesting an FBI investigation, John Doar of the Justice Department pressured the Highway Patrol to force cooperation with Philadelphia and Neshoba County officials.[33]

From the march's new headquarters in Jackson, Don Smith sent out press releases detailing the white-on-black violence. National newspapers offered blow-by-blow accounts. For the first time since the Meredith shooting, the media clamored for federal intervention on the march. "Yesterday was a tragic anniversary compounded by a new national shame," lamented the *New York Post*. *The New York Times* noted the irony of the literal translation of "Philadelphia"—instead of "brotherly love," the Mississippi town flaunted racist hatred.[34]

Yet if the mob attack revived the politics of black victimhood, it also steeled a black commitment to self-defense. After the brawl on Main Street, one large black man walked off with his shirt torn, and a writer described how his fellow blacks "watched him with hot eyes and proud smiles, feeling the fight, rejoicing in their young man's open anger." Describing the Philadelphia march in his official project report, Joe Morse of the MFDP wrote that "it would take someone *extremely dedicated* to the *philosophy* of nonviolence to remain nonviolent under the circumstances."[35]

On the night of June 21, after most of the Meredith Marchers had left Philadelphia, local activists protected themselves from more attacks. About twenty-five people had gathered within the Freedom House in Independence Quarters. Many were armed. Others were stationed on the flat roof of a wooden store that overlooked the Freedom House. At one point, the unpopular black officer Tripp Windham told the guards to climb down, but they jeered him away. Later, a truck drove down the dirt streets dragging something large and black—perhaps an effigy, though it might have been a dog. At 8:10, a group of whites drove up to a street corner and exchanged insults with a group of blacks. One of the whites fired a gun, and the car sped off.[36]

At 8:25, another car roared by the Freedom House. Four shots rang out. This time, the activists fired back from both the street and roof-tops. About twenty minutes later, the first car returned, and whites blasted eight to ten shots into the Freedom House. Again, the activists shot back. Their return fire struck the car and superficially wounded the driver, Stanley Stewart, a middle-aged factory worker with a history of alcohol abuse. Stewart drove himself home, and his wife took him to the hospital.[37]

SNCC field secretary Ralph Featherstone narrated the conflict in real time over the telephone to a reporter, who then relayed the news to five other reporters crowded into a Yazoo City motel room. At one point, Featherstone asked him to hold, went to the window, and shot back at a car full of roving white thugs. Featherstone also called the FBI office in Jackson. "We are armed and returning fire," he said. "You can do anything you want about it."[38]

By 10:40, two FBI agents had arrived to investigate. One was inside the Freedom House talking to Featherstone, and the other was on the porch quizzing Jim Leatherer, the one-legged activist who had been hob-bling through Mississippi. Johnnie Mae Walker, an MFDP leader, thought that the FBI men were skeptical of their stories. Then a black pickup truck pulled up. Four more shots blasted through the air.[39]

According to Leatherer and another witness, one agent dove behind a parked car, unable to pull his gun from his holster. "I pay my taxes! Protect me! Protect me!" shouted Leatherer. The incident deepened their distrust of the government: the FBI agents had not appreciated the danger until getting shot at themselves, and they displayed a fumbling inaction (though they dismissed the story as "propaganda" and "a pile of crap"). The Justice Department report, moreover, questioned whether whites fired more than a single shot the entire night, contradicting the specific testimony of multiple eyewitnesses.[40]

The media described the horrors of the day's march, but also sensationalized the evening's conflict. "White Man Shot as Battle Flares in Mississippi March," proclaimed *The Atlanta Constitution*, equating self-defense by freedom workers with brutality by white hooligans.[41]

Philadelphia mayor Clayton Lewis denied knowledge of any attack. He blustered that he might learn something about it on the evening news with Walter Cronkite. The police questioned two men but arrested no one. They also took Stanley Stewart's pistol—which had a spent cartridge—but declined to even question the wounded man.[42]

"I know the men who drove the car," admitted city police chief Bruce Latimer. Confessing on the record that he had no intention of enforcing the law, Latimer said: "I know their mammas and their papas and I know THEIR mammas and papas. I think they started drinking and wandered over where they had no business and somebody took a pop at them. I don't think they were mad at no nigger and I don't think no nigger was mad at them."

Anyway, he claimed, only the county police could arrest them, and Cecil Price showed no inclination to do so. Latimer could fine them, but he would not. He just wanted the attacks to stop. Of course, he blamed outside agitators: "We got good nigger people here. They will fight back, but we don't push our niggers."

"I know you are going to say that three civil rights workers were killed here," he acknowledged, "but don't let's bring that up."[43]

Fresh from the horrors of Philadelphia, Martin Luther King flew to Sunflower County, in the heart of the Delta. It was the birthplace of the Citizens' Council, the site of Parchman Penitentiary, and the home of James Eastland. The powerful head of the Senate Judiciary Committee also owned a massive cotton plantation. "Congress is determined to force an integrated society upon the south simply to placate the northern liberals and demagogues," Eastland told a Lions Club in May 1966. "Everybody's hollering for free government money, but they don't stop to realize that those dollars have a rope attached that'll hang us." Meanwhile, under an agricultural allotment program, the senator personally received hundreds of thousands of dollars in federal subsidies.[44]

Yet Sunflower County reflected the movement's possibilities. SNCC organizers had empowered local leaders such as Fannie Lou Hamer, and although only 13 percent of voting-age African Americans had registered, a federal court had recently voided a racially discriminatory municipal election. A "National Committee for Free Elections in Sunflower County" demanded the presence of federal registrars.[45]

That day, Charles McLaurin of SNCC and Joe Harris of the Delta Ministry organized a minimarch in Sunflower County. Hamer led 130 people along the ten-mile route from the tiny town of Sunflower to the county courthouse in Indianola. Unlike the rowdy mess in Philadelphia, this demonstration lacked violent drama. The police chief even lent McLaurin his bullhorn. The local newspaper later lauded the police for maintaining order while "out-of-state agitating rabble" staged a "dubious show," allowing a quick return to "the old way of friendly relations."[46]

The June 21 protest nevertheless invigorated the local movement—thanks, especially, to King. "It was like the messiah walking through the community," recalled McLaurin. King attracted three hundred people to the voter registration rally. He pointed to the freedom-wielding powers of the ballot, noting how black votes could end James Eastland's reign of terror.[47]

McLaurin led the crowd in enthusiastic calls for Black Power. Upon hearing those hollers, Ralph Abernathy of SCLC grimaced. During his own speech, he urged: "Say Freedom!" Just as enthusiastically, the crowd bellowed "Freedom!" The people cared more about practical concerns, anyway. Their signs proclaimed WE WANT A NEW C.A.P. BOARD IN SUNFLOWER and WE WANT INTEGRATED SCHOOLS. Another sign folded the movement's new cry into the old one: FREEDOM IS BLACK POWER.[48]

That night, a huge crowd arrived at St. Benedict the Moor Catholic Church in Indianola, ready to hear King. By then, however, he had left for Yazoo City, where a nighttime rally was turning into a public debate over Black Power.[49]

Almost a thousand people had pressed into the park on West Seventh Street in Yazoo City. They roared for the militant thunder rumbling out of Willie Ricks and Ernest Thomas. "Negroes in Mississippi will never have anything until they show black power," declared Ricks. "When a white man attacks us, attack him back!" Most blacks could not embrace nonviolence, said Thomas. "We do not intend for any redneck to abuse any black people anymore," warned the leader from the Deacons for Defense. "If they do, there'll be a blood-red Mississippi. *Just don't mess with this march.*"[50]

Other speakers tried to soften these vengeful impulses. Ralph Abernathy and Andrew Young cautioned against rhetoric that offered emotional satisfaction instead of concrete results. Floyd McKissick endorsed the basic principles of Black Power, but upon following Thomas to the stage, he offered a moderate message. The crowd roared loudest for Thomas.[51]

Then Martin Luther King walked toward the stage. In the darkness, in the thick summer heat, after the trials of Philadelphia and the appearance in Indianola, King waded through the masses. Old women jostled each other to touch him. Weathered farmers in overalls pressed their hands into his.[52]

Once again, it fell to King to explain not just the right choice, but the righteous choice. He described the poverty and violence of Mississippi, and he asked how they could respond. Apathy would not work. Neither would anger. "Somebody said tonight that we are in a majority," he said. "Don't fool yourself. We are not in a majority in a single state in the United States." Even in Mississippi, blacks were 43 percent of the population. "I can't fool you tonight. I can't fool the Negro in America. We are 10 percent of the population of this nation, and it would be foolish for me to stand up and tell you we are going to get freedom by ourselves." Segregation destroyed them all, black and white. The only remedy was "a coalition of conscience."[53]

SNCC workers rolled their eyes and traded cracks about "De Lawd." They were tired of these love-thy-brother speeches. "Blessed Jesus!" yelled one man, mockingly pointing at King. But no one laughed. Actually, some nodded in approval. "Listen, listen," murmured the elders. "Can't he talk, Lord, can't he talk!" Indeed, King had extra silver on his tongue this night. "Speak on!" they cried.[54]

They could never achieve freedom through violence, preached King.

Armed struggle would cause tragic and pointless deaths. "Now," he added, "I'm ready to die myself."

> When I die I'm going to die for something, and at that moment, I guess, it will be necessary, but I'm trying to say something to you, my friends, that I hope we will all gain tonight, and that is that we have a power. We can't win violently. We have neither the instruments nor the techniques at our disposal, and it would be totally absurd for us to believe we could do it. The weakness of violence from our side, the weakness of a riot from our side is that a riot can always be halted by superior force. But we have another method, and I've seen it, and they can't stop it.

To a crescendo of whoops and amens, he recalled the campaign in Birmingham, when Bull Connor used police dogs and fire hoses, and they responded with dignity and freedom songs. That spirit was coming to Mississippi. "Don't worry about getting your guns tonight. Don't worry about your Molotov cocktails tonight," he exclaimed. "You have something more powerful and if you work with it, morning will come." In the language and rhythms of the pulpit, King had linked the black experience to the highest ideals, touching people in their souls—and maintaining his slippery, one-handed grasp on the march's message.[55]

14

THE PRIZE BULL
Yazoo City to Benton
JUNE 22, 1966

The afternoon after his impassioned speech at the West Seventh Street campground, Martin Luther King sat in an overstuffed chair, with his fellow march leaders forming a half circle around him on chairs, couches, and the floor. He was at the parish house at St. Francis of Assisi Church in Yazoo City. Days earlier, Father John Kist had offered his grounds as a campsite, only to rescind the offer out of concern about a white backlash. Then, out of conscience, he opened the parish house's living room for this meeting, which King had called because of a "widening split in our ranks."[1]

Black Power had become a powerful rallying cry. Using "black" rather than "Negro" reversed the common negative associations with blackness, suggesting a pride in African American culture and history. Moreover, as Owen Brooks of the Delta Ministry said, "the acquisition of political power was part of all of our missions." The press might have inflated its menace to whites, but Mississippi leaders such as Brooks wanted to help the poor and dispossessed, and Black Power provided a simple lingo to lift themselves up, as a people.[2]

Still, King implored them to stop using the slogan. Adopting a professorial style, he discussed the difference between *denotative* and *connotative* meanings. He accepted Black Power's denotative meaning—its literal definition. "There is nothing essentially wrong with power," he reflected. It was good for black people to pool their votes and economic resources. But King rejected Black Power's connotative meaning—the suggested ideas behind the words. The media's obsession with violence meant that Black Power implied black separatism and bloody revolution, whether they liked it or not.

King suggested "black consciousness" or "black equality," which evoked their positive aspirations without the negative consequences. Neither Stokely Carmichael nor Floyd McKissick accepted the change. Black Power was in the air, on people's lips, a spiritual and emotional force. Plus, SNCC had defined the slogan as its new direction. King did manage to wring one compromise out of the meeting: for the rest of the march, the leaders would chant neither "Black Power" nor "Freedom Now." Still, marchers and local people would say whatever they pleased.

King was juggling the discontent of militants, the alienation of liberals, the scorn of conservatives, the headline-hungry press, dangerous white supremacists, and a detached federal government. His presumed allies in SNCC and CORE laid more burdens upon him. "Martin," admitted Carmichael, "I deliberately decided to raise this issue on the march in order to give it a national forum, and to force you to take a stand for Black Power."

"I have been used before," chuckled King. "One more time won't hurt."[3]

That morning, the marchers had paraded from the campsite to the Yazoo County Courthouse, where nearly five hundred people heard speeches, and over one hundred African Americans registered to vote without incident. The large crowd of local whites abstained from taunts or assaults, even as cries of "Freedom!" and "Black Power!" rang through their eardrums. By noon hundreds of marchers were trudging up the big hill on Broadway, heading east on Route 16.[4]

White authorities sighed with relief. The Citizens' Council strategy had spared Yazoo City the mayhem of Philadelphia. The Board of Aldermen and Board of Supervisors issued another resolution, this time congratulating whites for "the good judgment, the respect for law and order and the excellent cooperation all of you displayed during our recent visit from civil rights demonstrators."[5]

As the leaders debated at the Yazoo City parish house, about 150 marchers covered the thirteen miles toward Benton. After the debacle in Philadelphia, the mood was tense and bitter. They camped that night at Oak Grove Baptist Church, on the outskirts of town, where church members and nearby landowners fed them.[6]

Though the press never reported it, a contingent of organized labor representatives had arrived that day to provide additional protection. Jesse Clear and his father-in-law Slim Rossignol, both members of the National Maritime Union, drove through the night from New Orleans. They formed part of a tough, interracial, armed band of union workers that blended into the march. According to Clear, they repelled a late-night attack at the Benton campsite, fighting off "peckerwoods" with chains and nunchucks and firing warning shots from pistols and shotguns. The union men left the next morning after detecting resentment from black militants, who presumably favored protection from the Deacons for Defense.[7]

In Benton, many leaders convened at the church, talking and arguing until four in the morning. King, however, stayed in Jackson. Worn by the strains among the leadership, troubled by the many faces of white resistance, he sank into despair. In a conference call with three SCLC advisers, he called the Meredith March "a terrible mistake."[8]

"The rag-tag march moves on toward Jackson," seethed an editorial in Memphis's Commercial Appeal. "Let those who might be inclined to follow the leadership of the bitter, arrogant and vindictive individuals be warned that they will have only themselves to blame for the consequences that will flow from any shedding of blood precipitated under these circumstances." The Philadelphia mob attack had underlined the depths of white resistance. More than ever, the march leaders wanted federal protection—a visible demonstration of their rights as American citizens. They turned to the White House.[9]

One year earlier, in the summer of 1965, some officials had asked Lyndon Johnson about his vision for the White House Conference on Civil Rights. Johnson took a dramatic pause. Then he started reminiscing about his ranch in the Texas Hill Country. On spring mornings, he said, the sun rose early. The grass steamed. The trees dripped sap. And in a pen, "you see my prize bull."

> He's the biggest, best-hung bull in the hill country. In the spring he gets a hankering for those cows, and he starts pawing the ground and getting restless. So I open the pen and he goes down the hill, looking for a cow, with his pecker hanging hard and swinging. Those cows get so Goddamn excited, they get more and more moist to receive him,

and their asses start quivering all over, every one of them is quivering,
as that bull struts into their pasture.

The officials stared at him with dropped jaws. "Well, I want a *quivering*
conference!" boomed Johnson, punctuated by a loud clap of his hands.
"That's the kind of conference I want. I want every damn delegate quivering with excitement and anticipation about the future of civil rights
and their future opportunities in this country."[10]

The moment captured the stew of ambition, crudity, ego, righteousness,
and persuasiveness simmering within the president of the United States.
He had risen from poor circumstances in central Texas by embracing
the dirty business of political campaigns, engaging in legislative horse
trading, and cultivating sponsors and allies. The masterful Senate majority leader had become an unlikely vice president, but after assuming
the Oval Office upon the assassination of John F. Kennedy, Johnson
spearheaded an impressive record of Great Society legislation, including
the twin pillars of racial reform, the Civil Rights Act of 1964 and the
Voting Rights Act of 1965. During the Selma demonstrations, the big
Texan had even appropriated the movement's language, ending a nationally televised speech by saying, "We Shall Overcome." Black leaders had
been skeptical when Johnson took office, but at that moment, confessed
Roy Wilkins, "I loved LBJ."[11]

As indicated by the tale of the lascivious bull, Johnson kept seeking
civil rights triumphs. He announced the White House Conference during a remarkable commencement address at Howard University in June
1965. He did not just celebrate how black demonstrators and the federal
government became "allies of progress"; he also recognized the tragic
legacies of slavery and problems of poverty. "It is not enough just to open
the gates of opportunity," he said. "All our citizens must have the ability
to walk through those gates. This is the next and the more profound
stage of the battle for civil rights." The Howard audience cheered this
expansive blueprint for racial equality.[12]

The president appreciated moderate black officials who understood
the give-and-take of national politics. When considering the appoint-
ment of Robert Weaver as secretary of housing and urban development,
Johnson described him as "decent, respected, and not arrogant." Before
making Weaver the first black cabinet member, he told Roy Wilkins
that "I liked Weaver, just like I like you." Forging personal bonds

strengthened his grip on power. "Don't you have the feeling that this man would be loyal to me if I named him?" he asked. "Wouldn't he be to his dying day grateful that I made him a Cabinet officer?"[13]

The president had a more complicated relationship with Martin Luther King. Any perceived partnership between Johnson and King enraged white conservatives and annoyed black radicals, yet the passage of civil rights legislation depended on both King's moral stature and Johnson's clout. Each sought common ground with the other. In August 1965, for instance, Johnson solicited advice about inner city unrest, while King lauded the Howard University speech "as the best one you have ever made and the best analysis of the problem I have ever seen anywhere— and certainly no President has ever said it like that before."[14]

In that same conversation, however, Johnson lamented the perception that "you are against me in Vietnam. You better not leave that impression. I want peace as much as you do and more so, because I am the fellow that wakes up in the morning with a report that fifty of our boys died last night." In 1965 and early 1966, Johnson sent hundreds of thousands of American troops to Vietnam. Despite the military stalemate and the corrupt regime in Saigon, Johnson steered a futile middle course: refusing to pay the political cost of withdrawing American forces, yet avoiding the declaration of all-out war. Instead, he gestured toward peace while intensifying the conflict.[15]

Johnson expected his allies in the Great Society to support him on Vietnam, but King opposed the war. "I'm tired of the press and others trying to brainwash people and let us feel that there are no issues to be discussed in this war," said King from the pulpit at Ebenezer Baptist Church in January 1966. He abhorred militarism, and Vietnam siphoned resources away from the War on Poverty. The draft, moreover, placed disproportionate numbers of blacks in combat positions. One week before the Meredith March, King said on *Face the Nation* that the United States should cease bombing North Vietnam and pursue peace negotiations.[16]

Yet King still sought good relations with Johnson. During one SCLC strategy session, he resolved to praise the U.S. senators who opposed a bombing campaign, but cautioned that "I don't think it is necessary for me to personally attack the President." In January 1966, after SNCC issued its statement condemning the war, Roy Wilkins and Whitney Young worked with the White House to soften its impact. King could not do that, but after the State of the Union address, he lauded Johnson for seeking the continuation of Great Society programs and peace in Vietnam.[17]

Every week in June 1966, thousands of antiwar letters arrived at the White House, dwarfing the correspondence that protested the shooting of James Meredith. That same month, Johnson's approval rating dipped to an all-time low of 46 percent. Most Americans did not identify with the antiwar movement, but they disliked the lack of military progress, the factional disputes in Saigon, and the draft at home. Political critics noted Johnson's "credibility gap" with the American public. The slowing economy and rising inflation exacerbated his political problems. Headlines told the story: "LBJ's Sagging Image" . . . "Confidence in LBJ Dwindles" . . . "Popularity of President Takes Nosedive."[18]

Johnson was also disengaging from the fight for racial equality. Ghetto uprisings, especially, stoked his predilection for self-pity. During the Watts riot of August 1965, African Americans in south-central Los Angeles burned buildings, looted stores, and fought police, leading to thirty-four deaths and almost one thousand injured. Johnson felt *personally* betrayed. "How is it possible," he cried, "after all we've accomplished?" Though he understood the genuine frustrations that ignited these violent explosions, he never crafted effective, large-scale responses to the problem of urban poverty.[19]

Federal momentum on civil rights further slowed with the controversy over Daniel Patrick Moynihan's "The Negro Family: A Case for National Action." The so-called Moynihan Report was a political debacle. The assistant secretary of labor ascribed the "cycle of poverty" and "tangle of pathology" in black ghettoes to breakdowns of the nuclear family, a crisis with roots in the era of slavery. After Watts, the media oversimplified his thesis as a shorthand explanation for race riots. Civil rights leaders resented the implication that black people bore the chief responsibility for their degradation. "We are sick unto death of being analyzed, mesmerized, bought, sold, and slobbered over while the same evils that are the ingredients of our oppression go unattended," wrote James Farmer.[20]

The snarled mess of race and class demanded a complex response, one with a heavy price tag. Yet the American electorate was shifting to the right. On June 8, for instance, Ronald Reagan won the Republican primary for governor of California. Reagan had opposed the Civil Rights Act and Voting Rights Act without using the racist language of southern demagogues. He instead tied big-government activism to liberal egg-heads, dirty antiwar hippies, lazy welfare recipients, and the wild denizens of Watts. Blaming riots on the "philosophy that in any situation the public should turn to government for the answer," he appealed for low taxes, individual enterprise, and law and order, exploiting a weariness with the perceived excesses of the Great Society.[21]

The conservative tide pulled the debate over Johnson's Civil Rights Bill of 1966. As the march moved through Mississippi, a House sub-committee ignored the bill's controversial "fair housing" provision, which would ban racial discrimination in the sale, lease, or rental of housing. The legislation reached beyond the South, and even northern liberals hoped to kill the provision. "It is one thing to cheer the Meredith march-ers in Mississippi from a comfortable metropolitan apartment or a lawn in suburbia," wrote James Wechsler, but fair housing legislation asked northerners to tie their actions to their principles. *The Sun* in Baltimore quipped that the provision might have survived if James Meredith had gotten shot while buying a house in the suburbs.[22]

By June 1966, then, the civil rights movement operated in a different context than one year earlier, when Lyndon Johnson had demanded a "quivering" White House conference. By the time "To Fulfill These Rights" convened in Washington, D.C., on June 1 and 2, Johnson's ardor had cooled. At a November 1965 planning session, Floyd McKissick had bickered with Attorney General Nicholas Katzenbach over the govern-ment's responsibility to register black voters. Then SNCC announced its boycott, and militants planned an all-black protest against "more con-ferences with the two-faced white power structure." Johnson wanted gratitude for leading bold charges against racism and poverty. Instead, he endured this discord.[23]

"To Fulfill These Rights" thus managed, as much as expressed, black aspirations for freedom and equality. The planning council distributed a 104-page report as the basis for discussion in twelve different working groups. White House officials scrupulously vetted the delegates, ensur-ing that no radicals disrupted the proceedings. And although McKissick urged his antiwar resolution, moderates preserved the image of unity. At one point, conference chairman Ben Heineman saw McKissick approach a podium, but before the CORE leader could air any dissent, Heineman ordered the microphone shut off.[24]

The conference panels resulted in a list of recommendations for employment, education, housing, and justice, most of which were never adopted. It was a well-scripted, well-intentioned affair, more like a political convention than a civil rights protest, politely avoiding the yawning gap between government officials and grass-roots activists.

Johnson made no commitment to attend the conference, but once it started without radical theatrics, advisers urged him to make a surprise appearance. He agreed to introduce Thurgood Marshall, the main speaker at an evening banquet. The audience stood, clapped, and chanted *"LBJ! LBJ!"* He shook hands and exchanged warm greetings with Ben Heineman, A. Philip Randolph, Roy Wilkins, and, in a key gesture, Martin Luther King. Applause kept interrupting his address, which celebrated a common commitment to justice. "Those who have built castles of prejudice have seen them crumble," he said. "Those who have whispered the counsel of despair—the counsel of separatism—have been ignored." After his speech, he shook more hands and basked in more applause, confirming his faith in liberal government programs and the integration of American life.[25]

By then, however, one particularly quirky delegate had announced his upcoming walk from Memphis, Tennessee, to Jackson, Mississippi.

The contrast between the White House conference and the Meredith March was stark. The White House provided a tight script for the political establishment; the trek through Mississippi was freewheeling, open to anyone with the conviction to march, full of freedom songs and sweat-soaked rallies and late-night arguments. What the march lacked in order, it compensated for in energy. "The conference, in itself, was meaningless if it didn't move into the field of action," stated King while walking down Highway 51. His gifts surfaced in Mississippi. The black political experience was rooted in protest, in a commitment of body and soul.[26]

Johnson, for his part, considered the march some sort of metaphysical retribution for his ambition. "To Fulfill These Rights" had projected the illusion that he possessed control over the civil rights movement, but the militant cries in Mississippi left him, in one analyst's phrase, "treading on eggs." He could not associate with Paul Johnson, even if he appreciated the governor's practical approach. Nor could he endorse a traveling demonstration full of firebrands who denounced his leadership. Just as Vietnam trapped him between escalation and withdrawal, the

march imprisoned him between white segregationists and black sepa-
ratists. He could no longer sustain his brand of consensus politics.[27]

Through most of June, Johnson avoided any connection to the march.
Once its manifesto criticized the federal government, he could not tie
the Civil Rights Bill to the events in Mississippi. Moreover, unlike the
march from Selma to Montgomery, no federal court order had precipitated the Meredith March. When Paul Johnson temporarily scaled back
the Highway Patrol presence in the Delta, Floyd McKissick wrote to the
White House urging "adequate federal protection to the marchers in
lawless Mississippi." The president ignored him.[28]

After the mob attack in Philadelphia, however, civil rights leaders
pressed the federal government for action. On June 22, with the backing of Carmichael and McKissick, King sent Johnson a telegram that
described the "clear and absolute breakdown of law and order in Philadelphia." They had scheduled another march in Neshoba County for
June 24. "We therefore implore you to send the necessary federal protection to Philadelphia, Miss. to protect the lives and safety of the citizens
seeking to exercise our constitutional rights." The White House Situation
Room received the telegram early on June 23, the same day that King
and his associates filed a suit in federal district court seeking an injunction to protect the second march through Philadelphia.[29]

Attorney General Nicholas Katzenbach wrote a response for the pres-
ident's approval. "Nick suggests that this wire should be sent by you to
Martin Luther King," prefaced Harry McPherson in a note to Johnson.
"He believes King is useful to us and needs the prestige of a reply by
you." Despite his stance on Vietnam, King offered a counterweight to
Black Power.[30]

Yet Johnson rejected the request for federal protection. His reply
telegram was polite and indirect, but it was a rejection all the same. "I
understand and sympathize with your concern over the incidents which
occurred at Philadelphia, Miss. last Tuesday," it began. It affirmed that
"personnel of the Department of Justice will be present" and that John
Doar would remain the administration's point man. But the message
implied that no more federal personnel were coming to Mississippi:
"The Attorney General informs me that Governor Paul Johnson has assured him that law and order will be maintained Friday in Philadelphia
and throughout the march, and that all necessary protection can and
will be provided."[31]

That day, Deputy Press Secretary Robert Fleming deflected questions about the Meredith March. He gave no specifics about the Justice Department's presence in Mississippi. Six different times, Fleming said, "I do not know." When asked why the White House had not distributed either King's telegram or Johnson's response, he said, "We do not choose to put it out. It is not being released." A reporter later called to see if Fleming had learned anything about federal protection in Mississippi. "The White House does not answer," he replied.[32]

In the march's final days, Johnson turned away a delegation of prominent clergymen who were concerned with the lack of federal protection; they instead met with Katzenbach, who brushed them aside after eighteen minutes. Johnson then ignored a thousand-person rally at Lafayette Park in support of the Meredith March, where, before representatives from all the major civil rights organizations, Lena Horne sang a sassy version of "This Little Light of Mine" and Josh White belted out his classic "Freedom Road."[33]

The administration's stance equated white racists with black militants. Aides prepared talking points for the president in response to potential questions about Mississippi. If asked about the march's effects, he could state, "It is too early to tell. If it awakens people in Mississippi to the right and responsibility to register and vote, that is good." He might also reinforce that "real progress cannot be achieved in an atmosphere of intolerance and hatred—either of the white for the Negro, or the Negro for the white."[34]

Johnson did make one final, secret effort to manage the crisis. King received another telegram from the White House, inviting him to Washington, D.C., for "an informal (off the record) visit with the President" on Thursday, June 23, at 5:30 p.m. A. Philip Randolph, among other leaders, received a similar message. The White House later confirmed that it had invited major participants from "To Fulfill These Rights," as well as Stokely Carmichael.[35]

But Johnson could no longer gather the civil rights leadership in his wide embrace. On the evening of June 23, instead of meeting in the White House, King was arm in arm with Carmichael and McKissick outside the Madison County Courthouse, in the heart of Canton, Mississippi, looking over a sea of black faces. He chose protest over politics.[36]

15

THE SHADOW OF DEATH
Benton to Canton
JUNE 23, 1966

C. O. Chinn talked tough and shot straight. Most blacks respected him. Many whites feared him. "He was the type of person," wrote Anne Moody, "that didn't take shit from anyone." The forty-six-year-old military veteran had run a cafe and underground bootlegging operation. Then, after CORE workers came to Canton in 1963, Chinn threw his support behind the movement. He pulled in others by virtue of his rugged, charismatic personality. He had run afoul of the law throughout the 1950s, but by the 1960s his rap sheet reflected the hazards of black political leadership in Canton.[1]

Chinn spent the afternoon of June 22 on the march. That evening, while driving back from Benton, he stopped at the Freedom House on the northwestern edge of town. The phone kept ringing with hostile telephone calls. Three times, Chinn traded insults of "peckerwood" and "black son of a bitch" with a crank caller. Around nine o'clock, the man warned Chinn that he was coming there.[2]

About twenty minutes later, civil rights workers and local blacks were standing outside the Freedom House when a dark-colored Ford Ranchero cruised by. A passenger tossed a homemade bomb from the far window, over the car roof. It rattled under a parked vehicle. It sounded like *shhhhhhhhhhh*, then *poof!* Smoke billowed out. There was no explosion, but everyone scattered.[3]

Every time movement workers reported this kind of harassment, the police insisted that they needed the car's plate number. This time, Chinn pursued the "peckerwoods." His posse searched Canton in three cars. At the Southland Café, a white establishment on Highway 51, they spotted the Ranchero in the parking lot. About seventy young whites were loitering there. Chinn's Oldsmobile rolled in, with the other two cars close behind. "There's them black sons of bitches!" they heard. Cans and bottles rained down on their cars. Then: BOOM! BOOM! They drove off, unsure what they had heard. Firecrackers? Gunshots?[4]

They had heard gunshots. One bullet grazed the arm of a twenty-six-year-old white man, William Longgrear. The other bullet ripped his shirt but missed his body.

According to Longgrear, Chinn twice fired a revolver while driving through the parking lot. White eyewitnesses corroborated the story, though with various contradictory details. Assistant police chief C. R. Jolly later testified that Chinn's second shot passed through Longgrear's shirt and deflated a car tire, even though no shot from Chinn's car could explain the impact and angle of the tire's bullet hole.[5]

In truth, the black activists were the victims. Chinn had kept the car windows up, and he had stopped carrying a handgun since a trumped-up concealed weapons charge in 1963. After hearing the shots, he drove back to the Freedom House. When Jolly inspected Chinn's Oldsmobile, he found no weapons. He nevertheless charged Chinn with assault with intent to kill. With the Meredith March arriving the next day, Canton authorities were not appeasing civil rights workers. They arrested Chinn, not the white rogues who tossed the smoke bomb or fired the shots. "Whether there is any connection between the two incidents, we have not been able to determine," said city attorney Robert Goza.[6]

The hostility of whites, the resistance of blacks, and the disingenuous response of city authorities—the past was prologue for the coming racial tempest.

In Canton, the march reconnected with James Meredith's original route. Highway 51 ran through its main square. The town of 9,700 people, just twenty-five miles north of Jackson, was the seat of Madison County. The county was nearly three-fourths black, with many landowning farmers. Yet most blacks lived in poverty. Whites controlled the allotment system that governed cotton production, and the Citizens' Council dominated local politics.[7]

In the early 1960s, while SNCC organized in the Delta and elsewhere,

CORE took the Fourth Congressional District, which included Madison County. The stocky and intense George Raymond started canvassing black neighborhoods. Soon came more organizers such as Matt Suarez and Anne Moody. By 1964 the Canton project had staged three "Freedom Days" for voter registration, a one-day school boycott, and a selective buying campaign at downtown businesses. Canton became a civil rights hotbed.[8]

The involvement of local black leaders was critical. If C. O. Chinn lent one model, Annie Devine provided a counterpoint. The former schoolteacher and insurance saleswoman drew people into politics with soft-spoken, sweet-tempered strength. In 1964, she had run for Congress as an MFDP candidate. The next year, she went to Washington, D.C., with Fannie Lou Hamer and Victoria Gray during MFDP's Congressional Challenge, which demanded legal recognition of their election in the House of Representatives. Although the challenge failed, 149 United States congressmen supported the seating of three black women from Mississippi. To her fellow Madison County blacks, Devine gave the movement an aura of respectability.[9]

Canton's civil rights workers had various personality conflicts, resulting in what one field report called "a very serious staff polarization." Local blacks complained that leaders ignored their concerns. Disillusioned CORE workers, like their SNCC counterparts, started leaving the state. Yet their efforts at community organization paid dividends. Through 1965 and early 1966, local people joined campaigns for school desegregation and welfare rights, established a Head Start center, and supported a three-week economic boycott of downtown businesses, called a "blackout."[10]

Led by a tall, defiant preacher named James McRee, the Madison County Movement now served as Canton's primary organ of civil rights activity. Also, the long-defunct Canton branch of the NAACP had reopened. By June 1966, Madison County had a slim African American voting majority: about six thousand blacks and about five thousand whites were registered.[11]

A few whites, guided by faith and conscience, supported racial justice. Father Luke Mikschl oversaw the Holy Child Jesus Mission; as elsewhere throughout Mississippi, the Catholic Church served black communities, though it typically avoided controversial activists or direct action protests. At Valley View, a village just north of Canton, the Mennonite Central Committee established a community center and work camp. Its volunteers staffed tutoring projects, voter registration workshops, and a library.[12]

As the march approached, the Freedom House became a beehive of activity. The Madison County Movement coordinated with area churches. Local people prepared meals, opened their homes, and donated quilts, blankets, and sleeping bags. Father Mikschl volunteered the grounds of the Catholic mission for a mass meeting or campsite. George Washington, a black grocery store owner, also offered his rural land.[13]

The Meredith Marchers preferred to demonstrate their citizenship by camping on a public, taxpayer-funded black institution. In Grenada and Yazoo City, they had stayed on public property, since city leaders wanted to avoid conflict. In Greenwood, Stokely Carmichael was arrested for pitching the tents at Stone Street Elementary School, but the police relented when the marchers took over Broad Street Park. As they approached Canton, the march leaders asked Mayor Stanley Matthews for the use of a public park. He refused. That land was already a civil rights battleground; after some recent attempts to integrate the city parks, a court order had closed them all.

So the focus turned to McNeal Elementary School for Negroes, four blocks west of the county courthouse. On the morning of June 23, C. O. Chinn, who had been released on bail the previous night, was at the Freedom House with the march's advance team. He called Charles Snodgrass of the Highway Patrol, who was fine with the proposed campsite. Snodgrass suggested, however, that they get permission from local authorities. Annie Devine contacted School Board official E. D. Morgan, who lodged no objection to marchers camping at McNeal. In a subsequent conversation, however, Morgan hedged on his earlier approval, telling Devine that he would research the situation.[14]

Around 10:30 that morning, the tent crew arrived at McNeal. The city police chief was waiting there. He told the representative of the tent rental company to keep his materials on the truck. When Superintendent of Schools Lamar Fortenbury arrived, he insisted that the field was only for "school-sponsored events." The tents had to go.[15]

An hour later, the crew returned to the school with reinforcements from the Freedom House, led by Hosea Williams and C. O. Chinn. They started rolling out the tents. Policemen pulled up and ordered them to halt. An officer gave Williams an official letter from Fortenbury denying use of the school grounds. Williams handed it back to the officer, who read the entire letter out loud. Williams maintained that they needed only the permission of local blacks, since their taxes funded Jim Crow institutions. The police threatened to arrest them.[16]

A crowd gathered. Children drifted over from their games, and reporters sniffed out a good story. Some onlookers yelled "Freedom!" and "Black Power!" About twenty policemen arrived, as well. "This is our ground," said Chinn. "We're going to put up the tents or else. We're tired of being pushed around by the white folks."[17]

The police moved in. Three officers pulled a raging, twisting Chinn toward a squad car, arresting him for the second time in twelve hours. Williams, an SCLC man trained in nonviolence, submitted with more serenity. The police arrested ten men for trespassing, including Chinn, Williams, SNCC's George Greene, a black marcher from New Jersey, three white volunteers, and three other Mississippi blacks.[18]

Glenn "Freedom X" Gurley—the Washington, D.C., man arrested at the Department of Justice after the Meredith shooting, and the same man who fought "Big Lester" Hankerson while marching through the Delta—got arrested for not only trespassing, but also assault and battery. Gurley had rushed over from the tents and collided with a policeman. In response, an officer struck Gurley on the head. Another elbowed him in the stomach. Policemen punched him, dragged him into a squad car, and kicked him in the rear, while Madison County sheriff Jack Cauthen waved his revolver and called him "nigger boy." The eleven men went to county jail, where bail was set at $100 for everyone except Gurley, who needed $350.[19]

At first, Charles Evers refused to help post bond. The NAACP field secretary had again injected himself into the march, as the big rally in Jackson promised local and national exposure. Yet Evers also undercut the march leaders. "He would run to the Highway Patrol with information, you see, that was prejudicial to King, or what Carmichael said about somebody in the patrol, or how they were acting," recalled Governor Paul Johnson. "He kept things in turmoil as much as he could."[20]

While in Canton, Evers had offered to secure permits to use public grounds. He cautioned against an altercation with police. He also sparred with Stokely Carmichael, who said that Evers controlled only thirteen to fifteen counties in Mississippi, and that SNCC and MFDP would "take them too." So when the marchers called for help, Evers reminded them about ignoring his advice. He let them stew in jail for a while.[21]

Evers eventually contributed $300 to the bailout fund. With the exception of Gurley, the arrested men left jail by 2:00. Both the activists and the authorities had established their resolve. With McNeal Elementary School for Negroes serving as the stage, the drama's first act came to a close. The violent climax was next.[22]

The heat hung in the air, wet and thick. The blaring sun was punctuated by low, gray, rolling clouds that dropped fat dollops of rain. Around five o'clock, the marchers were resting on Route 16, still a few miles north of Canton. From there, a caravan of trucks relayed two hundred people into town, while fifty stalwarts pressed south on foot.[23]

Stokely Carmichael sauntered through the streets of Canton, a pied piper for the upcoming rally at the Madison County Courthouse. He cajoled the hesitant with a clap to the back, attracted old women and young ladies with flirtatious eyes, and sizzled with anticipation for the coming clash. By 6:15, the last of the marchers reached the Freedom House. They paraded through town, three abreast.[24]

The marchers entered the town square singing "Go Tell It on the Mountain." They met a crowd of black locals that had been waiting across the street from the courthouse, mustering up the courage to walk onto the lawn. Everyone assembled on the south side of the courthouse, 1,500 strong.[25]

Paul Good had reported on Canton's first Freedom Day in 1964, and he remembered the intimidated looks on the faces of black people that day. Policemen had waved around rifles, bullied people, and kept registrants in line for hours. "Now," mused Good, "blackness spread over the courthouse lawn wherever it wanted to go." There was a mood of triumph, as if the black majority might finally exercise its power. Tonight, together, they would challenge the direct orders of the white establishment. Carmichael took the microphone last. "They said we couldn't pitch our tents on *our* black school," he exclaimed. "Well, we're going to do it *now!*"[26]

Again they snaked through Canton's black district, stirring even more excitement. The grand procession lured new marchers off their front porches. By the time they reached McNeal Elementary School for Negroes, they had collected around 3,500 people. A few highway patrolmen flanked the column, but no one blocked the school grounds.[27]

An eighteen-wheel U-Haul truck rolled onto the field and dropped off the tents. The march's marshals, identified by red armbands, guided the crowd into a large circle. The lack of police resistance seemed like a victory, along the lines of their occupation of Broad Street Park in Greenwood. People crowded close, wanting to help, staking their claim to freedom. "The Lord said the tents will go up," cried an old man.[28]

Amid this jubilation, though, some newsmen suspected a looming disaster. The occupation of the park seemed too easy. Were the police spoiling for a fight? Deputies were carrying rifles, shotguns, and semi-automatic weapons.[29]

Around 7:20, dozens of Mississippi Highway Patrol cars rolled into view. These were state policemen, under the authority of Governor Paul Johnson. They stopped at a field just south of the school, and about seventy-five officers assembled into a two-column formation, fifty yards upwind from the tents. First, the police had allowed the demonstration onto the school grounds. Now, the Highway Patrol, with support from Canton, Madison County, and Mississippi Game and Fish officers, prepared to attack. "Have you ever seen a more profound fix?" grumbled one reporter.[30]

The patrolmen performed final checks on their firearms, producing ominous warnings of snaps and clicks. They edged closer, in formation. They wore riot helmets, and each of their belts had a ring of small canisters. The officers released the bolts of their carbines, unleashing a cascade of metallic clunks. They advanced to within ten yards of the marchers and donned gas masks. They looked mechanical, something less than human.[31]

Many people slipped away, but at least two thousand remained on the field. Some backed up, casting wary glances toward the police. Others lay on the ground or joined hands in a line between the patrolmen and the tents. A team of marchers kept stretching out the canvases and arranging the tent poles.[32]

The leaders had climbed atop the truck to address the crowd. Floyd McKissick gave a crash course in nonviolent discipline: "When we say lock arms, lock arms. When we say sit down, sit down." Carmichael roused their pride: "The time for anybody running has come to an end! You tell them white folk in Mississippi that all the scared niggers are dead! You tell 'em they shot all the rabbits—they gonna deal with the men!"

Then King took the bullhorn: "I want to get this over because this is important. We're gonna stick together. If necessary, we are willing to fill up all the jails in Mississippi. And I don't believe they have enough jails to hold all the people!"[33]

"You will not be allowed to erect that tent on this lot," warned city attorney Robert Goza from a county sheriff's car. "If you continue doing so you will be placed under arrest."[34]

By now Carmichael had hopped off the truck and was circulating through the crowd, leading the chant: "*Pitch the tents! Pitch the tents! Pitch the tents!*"[35]

John Doar watched from the outskirts, brimming with frustration. If the police attacked, the state would reinforce its racist reputation, and the federal government would have another crisis on its hands. But the assistant attorney general could not negotiate a middle ground. "What can I do?" he said. "Neither side will give an inch." The tents were going up, and the troopers were advancing.[36]

King pleaded for calm. He reminded the audience that fighting the police would make a bad situation worse. More people edged away. King started to sing "We Shall Overcome," his gaze distant and uneasy. He stopped. A canister had landed by the truck, emitting a thick, nasty smoke. "It's tear gas!" he cried.[37]

The time was 7:42 p.m. The rain had left the ballfield a rich, dark green, while the late-setting sun had colored the hanging storm clouds salmon-pink and hazy purple. Now the red-white-and-blue canisters sailed into the twilight. *Psssssssst . . . Pop!* The projectiles flashed with an orange spark, and then a gray smog hissed onto the surreal canvas.[38]

The troopers had fired both conventional tear gas and canisters labeled "riot grenade irritating agents." When it was used for crowd control, officers shot tear gas high up and along a line—that way, the smoke created obvious exit paths. The Highway Patrol, however, shot its canisters all over the field. "Get some more on the inside over there, get some over there, get in there," ordered an officer. A massive cloud covered the field. Troopers shot tear gas right into the crowd, turning the canisters themselves into dangerous projectiles. They even gassed victims who were staggering away. They were *punishing* the Meredith Marchers.[39]

Half-blinded marchers ran in every direction. Some disoriented victims ran toward the column of policemen, right into a swinging rifle butt. A mass of people rushed toward a chain link fence, and as they scaled it, it collapsed under their weight. People were screaming, crying, vomiting. Some squirmed on the ground, quivering and wailing. The gas had an acrid stench. It burned their eyes and skin, and it choked their lungs. They panicked, gasping for what seemed like a last breath.[40]

At least twelve people passed out from the fumes. Others suffered cuts, bruises, and broken bones. A young boy coughed blood. When Charles Meyer, a medical volunteer for the MCHR, treated a four-year-old child and then ran back to help more victims, five troopers struck him with rifle butts, kicked him, and dragged him into a ditch.[41]

Veteran activists knew to drop to the ground, to let the gas rise away. But on this night, they suffered the worst. The police attacked those in the no-man's-land in front of the tents. They grabbed one tall woman by her long blond hair, and as she caterwauled in anguish, they threw her into a ditch. They beat the stuffing out of one-legged Jim Leatherer. They kept kicking a young man who vomited uncontrollably. When a trooper hit a priest with his shotgun, another marcher cried, "He's a man of God!" The trooper sneered, "I'll put him with his God," and hit the priest again.[42]

That afternoon, *New York Post* columnist Murray Kempton had considered the white officers gracious, even gentle. Now he witnessed an astonishing brutality. Some terrified blacks lined up against the school's brick wall, out of the smoke; policemen threw three canisters right at them. Other troopers knocked down the tent poles and deployed tear gas under the collapsed canvas, trapping those who had taken shelter there.[43]

"You niggers want your freedom—well, here's your freedom," an officer told Odessa Warwick, a mother of eleven. He kicked her, fracturing her tail bone.[44]

"It was like a scene of hell," recalled Arlie Schardt of *Time*. Amid the smog and panic and tears and darkening sky, the marchers caught brief glimpses of the terror around them: the jab of a rifle, the bloodied face of a friend. And as the smoke rose and the crowd dispersed, there was a chilling quiet, broken by one sound, like a gloved hand hitting a heavy punching bag: *Thud! Thud! Thud!* The police were kicking and rifle-butting the remaining, helpless people on the field.[45]

By eight o'clock the Mississippi Highway Patrol had cleared the grounds around McNeal Elementary. They gathered the tents and impounded the U-Haul. A dazed young woman walked toward a line of officers. "Can't you see I'm a human being, just like you?" she cried. "Can't you see it? Can't you see it?"

"I couldn't see it, friend," drawled a policeman as she staggered away. "I couldn't see it."[46]

At first, Jo Freeman tried to take photographs, but it was too dark and smoky. Her eyes, she later wrote, "felt like they were being massaged by two hot pokers." She started crawling away. "My whole body felt blistered; my scalp felt like every hair was being pulled out one by one, and my lungs as though I was inhaling molten steel." She pressed her face to the soggy ground, waiting for the gas to clear. When highway patrolmen poked at her legs, she forced herself off the field.[47]

Freeman ran to a nearby street, where people sobbed and moaned. Their faces looked blank, their souls in shock. Nearby residents offered their garden hoses. She washed her face and arms with cool water, but for hours afterward, "my body still felt like it was being bathed in liquid fire."[48]

Clarice Coney had watched the rally from the north edge of the field, holding her baby girl. She, her husband Eddie, and their six children lived across the street from the school. Once the teargassing started, she went back across the street, and at least a hundred retreating demonstrators packed into her tiny home. Unfortunately, the wind blew the tear gas toward them. It seeped through the walls and windows. People were choking. Children cried, men cursed. Eddie walked onto the porch with his gun—his friends had to drag him back inside. Clarice soaked towels, sheets, and pillowcases and draped them over people's faces. So much water ran out of the faucets that the floor got soaked.

"Oh my God, something's wrong with your little boy!" someone yelled to Coney. The child was convulsing. Coney grabbed him and ran out the back door, stepping over people who were crawling in her backyard to avoid the drifting gas. A man grabbed her leg and pulled her down. "Lady, give him to me!" he said. "I just got back from Vietnam, and I know what to do for him." He scooped up mud and rubbed it in the boy's face, scrubbing out his eyes until he felt better.[49]

Alvin Poussaint realized that the MCHR lacked the resources to handle this crisis. The medical student Charles Meyer had broken ribs and a punctured lung, and their ambulance driver had been knocked unconscious. Poussaint established a triage clinic in the convent at Holy Child Jesus Mission, with the nuns serving as extra nurses. He also called

Jackson funeral director Clarie Collins Harvey, who sent a fleet of hearses to Canton. These "ambulances" ferried the severely wounded to a hospital in Jackson. In Canton, MCHR doctors and nurses spent the entire night treating victims. "We were all enraged," recalled Poussaint. "There was just so much rage."[50]

Andy Young had been on the U-Haul, shouting instructions to stay low and calm. Through trials such as Birmingham and Selma, the SCLC minister had kept his head and heart. He always anticipated the next logistical step, always looked out for Martin Luther King, always taught that love bound humanity together.[51]

Then he caught a whiff of tear gas. He jumped off the truck. Instead of moving against the wind, he ran into more smoke. His eyes burned, his throat stung, and his mind went to pieces. Finally he bounded over a chain link fence. With gas still burning his lungs, he realized that the Highway Patrol had assaulted two thousand men, women, and children for occupying the ballfield of an elementary school. That moment was his brush with pure, visceral hatred. "If I had a machine gun," he thought, "I'd *show* those motherfuckers!"[52]

Young took deep breaths, cleared his head, and reassumed his traditional role. Willie Ricks was standing atop a car, shouting about torching the Highway Patrol cruisers. Young reminded him that matches, bottles, and bricks were no contest against semiautomatic guns. More violence would endanger women and children. "If you want to fight someone, fight me," said Young. He might not have convinced Ricks, but he got him off the car.[53]

Something shifted inside Floyd McKissick, both literally and figuratively. He fell off the U-Haul truck after a tear gas canister hit him in the knee. He heard a crack—a disc in his spine had moved. Throughout the march, the CORE leader had occupied the space between SNCC and SCLC with earnest patience. But now he shed tears of fury. "I'm tired of having to *negotiate* for our constitutional *rights*," he said. "You didn't *want* that school, but they made it yours. They don't call it *white* power. They just call it *power*. I'm committed to nonviolence, but I say what we need is to get us some *black* power."[54]

A canister struck Stokely Carmichael in the chest, and then he inhaled gas. His cool, militant persona disintegrated. While staggering off the field, he saw a policeman hitting a black woman. He started rushing back into the fray. King grabbed him, counseling that he could not fight violence with violence. Carmichael's emotions switched from rage to pathos—he stumbled in circles, blubbering with tears. "Don't make your stand here," he cried. "I just can't stand to see any more people get shot." Carmichael had spent six years on the movement's firing line, and the March Against Fear had thrust him before the masses, burdening him with huge responsibilities. The Canton chaos exposed his vulnerabilities. For a moment, it broke him.[55]

Charles Evers took smug satisfaction in Carmichael's panic. "Stokely ran like a scolded dog," he later grinned. Evers had warned against risking a battle with the Highway Patrol, and he considered Carmichael an empty pair of overalls, more inclined to outrageous statements than hard negotiation. Yet the attack reaffirmed Carmichael's radicalism. Black Power's proponents had been arguing that white society was inherently racist, inherently brutal. The assault bolstered their contention. Alvin Poussaint believed that until Canton, Carmichael "was still ambivalent" about SNCC's new direction. "The teargassing made him more militant," maintained Poussaint.[56]

Late that night, Charles McLaurin walked back to his parked car on the outskirts of Canton. He worried about an ambush from angry whites, but he also felt good, "like a new awakening." Black Power was here to stay. He and a fellow organizer would call this night "the Valley of the Shadow of Death." The state of Mississippi had arrested them, beat them, and gassed them, but as the Twenty-third Psalm assured, they had strength. They feared no evil.[57]

Martin Luther King stood on a street near McNeal Elementary, his cheeks streaked with tears. "We've *got* to be nonviolent," he told a television reporter. "How could we be violent in the midst of a police force like that?" He stated that the attack "represents the kind of brutality, the kind of violent hatred still residing in the state of Mississippi, and it is quite ironic and interesting that we were tear-gassed today by the very same state patrol that President Johnson said today would protect us."[58]

King huddled with march leaders at the home of George Raymond, just one block from the school. They needed to act fast, since so many victims were dazed or frantic. Soon organizers moved onto the streets, shouting, "March to the Asbury Methodist Church!" They shepherded the displaced demonstrators toward the church, singing mournful spirituals along the way. *"Nobody knows the trouble I've seen . . ."* At Asbury, the marchers calmed down and ate dinner. Then they moved next door to the Holy Child Jesus Mission.[59]

At Asbury's parsonage, the leaders debated the next step. The attack had stirred the black community, and that energy could be harnessed for political activism. They established three plans for the next day: a one-day work stoppage, a new blackout of downtown businesses, and a return to McNeal Elementary to pitch the tents.[60]

An audience of seven hundred gathered at the Holy Child auditorium. McRee and Raymond announced the boycott and blackout. McKissick no longer cared about an audience with the president: "I said the hell with it. We're sick and tired of begging. That man thinks you don't bleed, you don't cry, you don't suffer." Carmichael found his bearings; the crowd roared, stomped, and shouted "Black Power!" as the Howard University philosophy major exclaimed, "Johnson, you ain't never was our friend!"[61]

"We've got to do something tonight," intoned King. "We cannot wait until the morning. Tonight we are going to march around this city!" A night march, though dangerous, funneled their swirling, popping emotions into nonviolent action. So in the hour before midnight, about six hundred people marched four abreast through Canton. Considering the earlier trauma, they showed remarkable resilience, singing old union anthems such as "Which Side Are You On?" and patient spirituals such as "We Shall Overcome." The Black Power types went along, but they shot militant sparks, trying to ignite a confrontation. "Downtown!" they clamored. *"Whitey got to go! Whitey got to go!"*[62]

The curtain drew on the day's final act. Late that night, NBC staged a press conference at Holy Child. Television reporters interviewed the nuns who helped the MCHR doctors and nurses. Over four hundred marchers slept on the concrete floor of the auditorium, cushioned only by a blanket or bedroll. Others slept on the church's wet lawn.[63]

Local people found spots for other marchers on beds, couches, and floors. Connemara Wadsworth, a white student from Friends World College, shared a bed with a marcher who had suffered a beating that night. With the smell of tear gas still wafting inside her nose, she fell asleep to her bedmate's anguished moans.[64]

"The state had nothing to do with this," said city attorney Robert Goza. Local officials accepted responsibility for the teargassing, but their claim deserved heavy skepticism: city and county leaders had no authority over the Highway Patrol. Justice Department representatives stated that Paul Johnson must have ordered the attack. The next day, in fact, Charles Snodgrass of the Highway Patrol admitted that the governor was adopting a new "get tough" policy on the Meredith March. By declining to intervene after the Philadelphia fracas, the White House had essentially written Governor Johnson a blank check for violence against the marchers.[65]

Mississippi whites developed their own perverse narrative about the attack. The Sovereignty Commission report blamed it entirely on the provocations of Carmichael and King. Madison County sheriff Jack Cauthen lauded the state troopers for handling civil rights marchers "who intentionally, flagrantly and, in my opinion, unlawfully attempted to usurp local authority and totally disregard the peace and dignity of our community." In a lie as bald as his head, Governor Johnson said that no one got hurt. He even made the astonishing claim that the teargassing "was the humane thing to do."[66]

Few Canton whites had any firsthand knowledge of the injustice. The *Madison County Herald* ignored the march until it passed, and then it just ran an editorial praising the police for preserving order. Years later, prominent white citizens in Canton still ignored the factual record. "They liked to have had a riot that night," recalled reporter O. D. Crawford. "Some whites went by and shot firecrackers and they thought it was guns, you know, and scared them pretty well. There actually never was any blood shed or anything like that here during that time."[67]

The attack did elicit another round of liberal outrage. Letters to Martin Luther King conveyed shame for racism. Telegrams to Governor Johnson demanded an end to his "reign of animalistic terrorism." Most of all, Lyndon Johnson received more pleas for federal protection of the marchers. They came from Roy Wilkins, NAACP branch presidents, United States congressmen, newspaper editors, humanitarian organizations, and liberal clergymen. "What happened at Canton is an affront to human sensibility," proclaimed *The Washington Post*. "If Federal marshals can provide the protection, let them be sent to Mississippi. If the National Guard is needed, let it be called up immediately. If nothing less than the United States Army can do the job, let it be sent there right away."[68]

Yet if the brutality in Canton mirrored that at Selma, it failed to arouse the national conscience. Bloody Sunday had taken place in the morning, and the Edmund Pettus Bridge had provided a perfect backdrop for the graphic footage that interrupted television broadcasts—it looked like troopers beat a long, somber procession toward some faraway church. The Canton attack, by contrast, occurred in a darkening chaos. Photographers and cameramen were running away from the tear gas, too, making it difficult to capture iconic images of the night's horrors.[69]

More important was the negligence of the White House. President Johnson met with Attorney General Katzenbach late on June 23 and then again the next morning, but he never commented on Canton. According to Deputy Press Secretary Robert Fleming, Johnson had "no specific reaction" to the attack.[70]

Katzenbach's own statement had all the zest of lukewarm milk. "I'm sorry it happened," he said. "It always makes the situation more difficult." He did not condemn the Highway Patrol, and he did not commit more federal officials to Mississippi. He expressed confidence that state authorities would protect the demonstration. He explained to the president, moreover, that the marchers had refused alternative campsites before seizing the prohibited school grounds. The attorney general blamed no one, but he emphasized that civil rights leaders defied the law. Instead of exploiting liberal indignation, the White House nudged the tear gas victims off the moral high ground.[71]

On the night of the attack, Martin Luther King stayed up well past midnight, meeting again at Rev. McRee's parsonage. He learned that the Deacons for Defense were trying to acquire gas masks; in the event of another attack, they might fire guns over the heads of the Highway Patrol, perhaps instigating a shootout. The tear gas had driven too many people too far. The next day, King seemed unsteady, even despairing. "I don't know what I'm gonna do," he said. "The government has got to give me some victories if I'm going to keep people nonviolent." If he could not translate moral clout into federal action, the floodgates would open for Black Power.[72]

16

UNINVITED GUESTS
Canton to Tougaloo
JUNE 24, 1966

Late on Friday morning, Albert Turner of SCLC led forty-five marchers out of Canton. When they reached their planned stop eight miles down Highway 51, they decided to keep going. By five o'clock they had covered the eighteen and a half miles to Tougaloo College, the designated stop for Saturday. A caravan then ferried them back to Canton.[1]

It was the nineteenth leg of the hike from Memphis to Jackson. It was also the least interesting, least important aspect of the Meredith March Against Fear on June 24. On this same date, the marchers endured scary tests, met surprise guests, and debated controversial compromises. The real action was elsewhere, at the touchstone battlegrounds of the past few days: the streets of Philadelphia and the schoolyard in Canton.

Since Tuesday's mob violence, Martin Luther King had vowed to return to Philadelphia. His SCLC lieutenants showed particular caution to keep the protest nonviolent. When Ralph Abernathy led an advance team on Thursday, he recruited only volunteers committed to nonviolence. That night, during a mass meeting at Mount Nebo Baptist Church, he preached that "if you can't come without a knife or gun in your pocket, don't come at all." Hosea Williams and Robert Green both took pains to note that Stokely Carmichael would be walking down Highway 51, not going to Philadelphia.[2]

In fact, Carmichael led the second excursion to Philadelphia alongside

King and Floyd McKissick. Although he accepted its nonviolent strategy, he argued for the presence of the Deacons for Defense. At the Benton campsite, after Williams had debated with militants over the return march, Carmichael organized a vote that approved the Deacons' participation. They would avoid detection by drifting into Philadelphia in scattered cars with Mississippi plates, and they would bring along women to smuggle guns in dresses and pocketbooks.[3]

The march leaders had sought a court injunction that provided federal protection, but to their chagrin, the court did not act by Friday. Assistant Attorney General John Doar instead urged the state, county, and city to coordinate a response that ensured law and order, so they could halt the cries for federal intervention. Highway patrolmen thus established police lines around Philadelphia's black district of Independence Quarters, while Mayor Clayton Lewis permitted a rally on the steps of the Neshoba County Courthouse.[4]

Congressman Prentiss Walker warned Philadelphia whites that Martin Luther King "cannot succeed unless he can create some sort of violence." Every half hour, a radio station aired statements from the mayor and sheriff that encouraged peaceful conduct. A front-page editorial in Philadelphia's *Neshoba Democrat* entitled "Let's Hold Our Tempers" urged readers to ignore the marchers, even though "we know it is hard to take a lot of the lies, insults, and actions of beatnicks who are worked up to fever pitch by their leaders with sessions of 'prayer.'"[5]

Yet Philadelphia remained a racial tinderbox. FBI agents learned that Norman Stevens, Exalted Cyclops of the United Klans of America in Philadelphia, planned to have unrobed, armed Klansmen retaliate if marchers disobeyed laws or uttered "wise remarks." White mobs lingered outside of Independence Quarters, and rumors spread that two hundred blacks were armed. At the same mass meeting where Ralph Abernathy pleaded for nonviolence, local leader Johnnie Mae Walker reminded the congregation that after the march, they still had to deal with Lawrence Rainey and Cecil Price: "We have to be ready to protect ourselves." Ralph Featherstone, SNCC's organizer in Philadelphia, predicted that this time, many locals would carry guns.[6]

At 11:45 on Friday morning, about seventy-five Neshoba County blacks greeted King and Abernathy at Mount Nebo Baptist Church. Soon, fifteen cars arrived from Canton. They left the low-lying, white-shingled church and marched through Independence Quarters, gathering more people along the way. Clouds of red clay dust billowed up, settling on their heads and shoulders. Their freedom songs slowed down a beat—they were almost mournful, more steadying than uplifting, as if acknowledging the dangers ahead. As they pressed onto the paved streets of downtown Philadelphia, whites again lined the sidewalks.[7]

It was the most people in town since the last Neshoba County fair. The crowd included farmers from the surrounding area, rambunctious teenagers, and a biker gang. Some leaned out of windows, screaming insults. Others spit on marchers who passed near the rope barricades. When a well-dressed black man held out his hand to help an old white woman over a curb, her husband yelled, "That black bastard touched my wife!" and repeatedly punched the black man.[8]

This time, however, the Highway Patrol was out in force, separating the marchers from the mob. It was surreal. Seventeen hours earlier, in Canton, while wearing the same riot helmets and carrying the same weapons, the same men had tossed tear gas canisters and pummeled helpless victims. Now they provided extensive protection.[9]

Just as striking, Neshoba County officials accommodated the protest. As the marchers approached the courthouse, a deputy officer expressed confusion about whether to allow them on the steps. MFDP leader Clinton Collier casually flipped his hand while walking past him. "It's all right," said Collier. County sheriff Lawrence Rainey, back in town from his Texas trip, watched from the courthouse steps, spitting tobacco and brandishing a cowboy hat, while a group of whites gathered outside the Ben Franklin store with crossed arms, stony glares, and barely suppressed rage. Mayor Lewis took the bullhorn and warned the surrounding whites to behave themselves.[10]

The mayor's instructions proved hard to follow. When Collier delivered an opening prayer, whites hooted in derision. Glass Coke bottles sailed into the crowd. "We have been dictated to long enough," preached Collier. "You can tell about these people who are yelling at us because, if they had decent things to do, they'd be home attending their own business." That defiance stoked the onlookers' outrage. A policeman patted his friend on the shoulder, commiserating that all white people felt the same way about this invasion.[11]

In this atmosphere of hate and heat, the leaders kept their speeches short. Carmichael and King continued their ideological jockeying. "The people gathered around us represent America in its truest form," said

Carmichael, seeing the nation's essential racism in these bigoted red-necks. "We will start representing ourselves in our way, and we will do it in our way." If King diagnosed a similar illness, he kept faith in a cure. He repeated a favorite quote from the nineteenth-century abolitionist Theodore Parker: "The arc of the moral universe is long, but it bends toward justice."[12]

But King, too, displayed bitterness. Climbing toward his speech's pinnacle, he lifted spirits with a soaring, preacherly cadence—and then broke it suddenly. "We're gonna win," he proclaimed, "because the Bible is right when it says, 'Ye shall reap what ye sow.'" Then he stopped. For a half second, everything was quiet. And in the moment, perhaps, the taunting onlookers realized the ultimate implications of that scriptural passage.[13]

But these were the same people just yelling, "Go to hell!" and screaming, "Nigger—you're a nigger!" and chanting, "*We're gonna kill King! We're gonna kill King!*" The silence broke, and the jeers returned. As the parade moved back through town, a teenager yelled that he wanted to fight King. Others made hog calls: "*Soooee! Soooee!*" When a bearded, mop-topped white man and a black woman tweaked the racists by holding hands, they heard threats of "Wait till tonight, you black bastards, we'll find you then!"[14]

As the procession entered Independence Quarters, the four-abreast column loosened, with marchers drifting a little farther apart. Just then, a Ford sedan barreled toward the column. It was going about thirty miles an hour. Marchers dove to both sides of the street, like waves parting. Somehow, the car just missed them. At the end of the block, a Highway Patrol officer stood in front of the vehicle, with a shotgun aimed at the windshield. The car stopped. The police charged the driver and passenger, R. E. Wolf and Felix Crossland, with reckless driving and interfering with an officer. Had the marchers still been in tight formation, Wolf and Crossland might have caused one of the great tragedies in the history of the civil rights movement.[15]

Despite the officer's courageous action, the marchers' distrust of the Highway Patrol deepened. In the midst of the action, the police had pulled out their guns and pointed them—at the marchers! They had instinctively identified the scattering, diving, screaming protesters as a greater hazard than a car on a kamikaze mission.[16]

The incident lent an appropriate conclusion to a politically ambiguous excursion. King called the demonstration a victory: "We planned to march to the courthouse and have a rally and we did it." Yet King also faulted the federal government for its inattention, and the hecklers provided another glimpse at bigotry's ugliest face. "It revealed Philadelphia to me," said Nancy Burnside, a woman from nearby Stallo. Pulled by the presence of King, she had joined her first civil rights demonstration. "I just couldn't believe it. We all lives here, was raised here, my foreparents stayed here all my days. It don't make me feel good walking up the streets now."[17]

Before the convoy returned to Canton, one car had already left Philadelphia. Father Richard McSorley, a professor of social justice at Georgetown University, drove back with two Boston priests and Jesse Turner, a black NAACP official from Memphis. Leaving early and alone was a mistake. The interracial carload, made even more conspicuous by their clerical collars, passed through rural Leake County. In anticipation of the Meredith March, local Klansman Roscoe Robinson had offered support to the Canton and Philadelphia klaverns. The Klan had also been threatening teachers and igniting dynamite at St. Joachim Catholic School for Negroes, which used federal antipoverty funds. That very morning, arsonists had burned the school down.[18]

A pickup truck tried to run McSorley's car off Route 16. McSorley jammed on the brakes and the truck pulled ahead, blocking the highway by swerving back and forth. Another car rushed in from behind, threatening to ram them. So McSorley slammed the gas, and for the next ten miles they raced at high speeds. Finally, the thugs peeled off. Back in Canton, McSorley saw his fellow priest Luke Mikschl. "Father, I was ready to die," he said. "A better way I can't think of—a priest witnessing for justice."[19]

The adjacent churches of Asbury Methodist and Holy Child served as the march's staging ground. Asbury's James McRee, a state official for CDGM, used some of that federal funding to feed marchers with chicken, mashed potatoes, and string beans, while the nuns at Holy Child served soup, sandwiches, milk, and Kool Aid. Father Mikschl loved the giving spirit and praised the mission's Sisters, whose "Christian kindness seemed to melt away even the coldness of the new extreme radical left."[20]

Canton nevertheless pulsed with Black Power. The Madison County Movement ran off flyers urging a "Black Out for Black Power." Activists picketed downtown businesses and urged a one-day work stoppage. They also engaged in small acts of civil disobedience, such as blocking traffic with their bodies. Some carried signs reading WE ARE READY FOR BLACK POWER and BLACK POWER BY ANY MEANS NECESSARY, while others wrote BLACK POWER on their T-shirts. A Pennsylvania pacifist huffed that militants should go home rather than damage the civil rights movement. "We're *already* home, baby," someone responded, "and we *are* the civil rights movement."[21]

The Highway Patrol and local police blocked a morning pilgrimage to the courthouse; "We've had enough of this," announced one official. On a second attempt, the city attorney Robert Goza stopped them a few blocks from the courthouse, stating that downtown traffic made it impossible to clear the streets. Goza did agree to let Madison County residents walk single file on the sidewalk up to the courthouse. Although the circuit clerk was "out to lunch," forty-six citizens registered at the nearby office of a federal voting examiner.[22]

Throughout the day, no protesters set foot on the grounds of McNeal Elementary. March leaders wanted to return and pitch the tents, but highway patrolmen guarded the field. By early evening, spotlights illuminated the field, and troopers stood on the school's roof, armed with guns and tear gas. The police had the tents. The school board upheld its policy.[23]

Some activists tried to raise money to buy more tents. Volunteers even sewed together ten bedsheets, creating a symbolic tent to pitch in protest. They talked about raising a tent and then taking it down, just to defy their oppressors. One way or another, they promised, "there will be a tent set up tonight."[24]

Another confrontation on the school grounds seemed inevitable— even if it damned the white authorities, even if it cost the marchers' blood. A peaceful resolution depended on compromise around a conference table, before everyone took to the streets. Since the beginnings of the Canton movement, however, African Americans had lacked open lines of communication to city officials. Finally, with another disaster looming, negotiations began.[25]

Highway Patrol chief Charles Snodgrass called some local black leaders to police headquarters. Snodgrass, who lived in Canton, assured them that the authorities were reasonable. Moreover, white merchants groused that the teargassing had precipitated another "blackout." So Snodgrass again offered alternative sites for a campground. In response, George Raymond softly reiterated the black community's need to see the tents at the school. The marchers were definitely returning to McNeal Elementary. But no one knew what would come next.

"What are you going to do tonight?" asked Snodgrass.

"Are you going to use tear gas again tonight?" responded Raymond.[26]

That evening, the march leaders packed into the sweltering, tightly packed, and heavily guarded living room of grocery owner George Washington. The meeting included national organization heads such as Martin Luther King, Stokely Carmichael, and Floyd McKissick; state leaders such as Lawrence Guyot and Aaron Henry; and local people such as Annie Devine, James McRee, and Flonzie Goodloe. Raymond relayed the gist of the conference with Snodgrass: there was a possibility of concessions from Canton's white leaders.[27]

Carmichael still favored pitching the tents, arguing that even if it provoked another brutal response, the Deacons for Defense would protect them. King was more willing to compromise. More important, the local leaders resisted another confrontation. Although a faction led by C. O. Chinn sided with SNCC, leaders such as Devine and Goodloe felt responsible for the safety of Madison County blacks. They also would have to deal with white officials after the march moved on. SNCC had long believed in listening to local people, while criticizing SCLC for a heavy-handed, top-down approach. On this occasion, though, King strengthened his hand by allying with Canton's leaders. Carmichael seethed as they voted to send a delegation to meet with Mayor Stanley Matthews and city attorney Robert Goza.[28]

By then, somehow, the picture had become even more muddled. The march's unpredictable namesake was back.

James Meredith had stayed out of Mississippi while the march detoured through the Delta. *His* march went down Highway 51. Until the marchers looped into Canton and merged back onto his planned route, he let his wounds heal.

In the interim, he had remained active in New York politics. His new, Harlem-based James Meredith Voter Registration Fund asked for volunteers and business support to enroll 175,000 unregistered voters. Meredith also condemned the Harlem Democrats for Action for withdrawing his nomination as a delegate for the state's constitutional convention, and he endorsed Justice Samuel Silverman as a reform candidate for Manhattan's Surrogate Court. In both cases, he presented himself as a free-thinking challenger to elitist party politics.[29]

During the march's final week, Meredith went to Washington, D.C., to appear on *Meet the Press*. Two weeks earlier, he had left Memphis with minimal fanfare, as a once-iconic figure whose personal eccentricity had eroded his importance. Now he fielded questions on one of television's signature programs, a Sunday morning forum for national public affairs.[30]

The reporters quizzed Meredith about the march's many controversies: the swelling of black nationalism, the perceived inadequacies of state and federal authorities, the competing agendas of civil rights groups. Despite his individualism, he stated his respect for the contributions of different organizations. The panel especially probed him about his promise to carry a gun in Mississippi. He responded that federal, state, and local authorities bore the duty to protect citizens. "When these people fail, then the ones who are affected have responsibility, and I will never relinquish that responsibility."[31]

Because Stokely Carmichael appeared on *Face the Nation* that same day, press accounts of the Sunday programs smashed together their ideologies, even though they shared little more than a commitment to armed self-defense. Both men, according to *The New York Times*, "refused to reject violence by Negroes to obtain their goals." Their justifications got conflated, sensationalized, and contrasted to Martin Luther King's nonviolence.[32]

Three days later, Meredith spoke before the National Press Club. He again outlined his principles of personal responsibility and military order. He saw no connection between Vietnam and the civil rights movement, and he dismissed Black Power as just another call for black freedom. Then a newsman asked, "Will you be packing a gun, and what caliber is it?" Once the laughter died down, Meredith spoke in sober tones: "If the government refuses to protect Negroes, there is no choice left to the Negro but to provide protection for himself. A man should never be helpless." He won a standing ovation.[33]

The next morning, after visiting the graves of John F. Kennedy and Medgar Evers at Arlington National Cemetery, Meredith drove back to New York and said goodbye to his wife and child. Along with his original marching companion Claude Sterrett, he flew to St. Louis, where he met with backers of his voter registration fund. Meredith then caught a plane to Memphis. At every stop, reporters asked him about guns, and he kept reiterating that people had to protect themselves if governments did not.[34]

Dick Gregory and his wife, Lillian, joined Meredith and Sterrett on the flight to Memphis. Since his one-day "reverse walk" from Hernando to Memphis, the activist comedian had gone to prison on charges of obstructing traffic and disorderly conduct during a June 1965 demonstration in Chicago. During a previous jail stint, Gregory had conducted a hunger strike and sparked inmate protests at a crowded House of Corrections. This time, he got assigned to a farm facility in suburban Cook County, where he tended crops and slopped hogs. He was released in time to finish the march with Meredith.[35]

On June 24, Meredith's group drove into Mississippi, stopping in Kosciusko to surprise his mother. The next day was his thirty-third birthday, so Roxie Meredith sent someone to buy a cake. Meredith also gathered opinions about the march. He surmised that most Mississippi blacks considered it a good thing, though it reflected the concerns of national organizations more than of local people.[36]

Meredith arrived in Canton during the meeting at George Washington's home. Ralph Abernathy greeted him with a clap on the shoulder. "You've got to come," said the SCLC minister, telling Meredith that he was the guest speaker for that night's rally. They went inside. Some time later, Meredith walked out alone. "I don't know what is happening over there," he said. "I think something is wrong. The whole damn thing smells to me." He picked up his mother and drove to Tougaloo College, where they stayed as guests of the dean.[37]

Meredith had various grievances. Given his emphasis on discipline and order, he abhorred the violence in Philadelphia and Canton, which had endangered helpless people. He also resented that marchers had proceeded to Tougaloo, because he expected to lead the procession down Highway 51. Perhaps, as Cleveland Sellers reflected, "Meredith had been outgrown by his own march." But this tired, emotional man refused to let civil rights organizations exploit his status as the protest's original hero, especially in this atmosphere of chaotic debate. If the Meredith March was his in name only, he refused responsibility for it.[38]

Paul Murray arrived in Canton on Friday morning, while the marchers slept off the effects of the tear gas attack. A recent graduate from the University of Detroit, he and his fellow white volunteer Jim Atherton had driven through the night to reach the work camp at Valley View, just north of Canton, where they would participate in antipoverty and voter registration summer projects. Murray tried to avoid the stereotype of a white student radical. He buzzed his hair close and dressed in a button-down sport shirt, khakis, and sneakers. His plan collapsed at a bus stop in Columbus, Ohio, where he met Atherton, a bearded, shaggy-haired beatnik in paint-stained pants and sandals.

Driving south, they heard radio reports about the Canton mayhem and read an early edition of *The Commercial Appeal*. Before checking in at the camp, they explored Canton. After breakfast at the Derby Café, a seedy spot filled with white truckers, Murray saw a message scratched above the bathroom's urinal: "*Take a stand, join the Klan.*" He had no previous experience in the southern civil rights movement. The March Against Fear was his baptism by fire.[39]

Murray returned to Canton late that afternoon, as marchers lounged on the grounds of Holy Child. That day, they had either walked to Tougaloo, gone to Philadelphia, or canvassed Canton on another humid, ninety-degree day. Though tired, they had a nervous energy. Everyone was talking about the tear gas attack, and they expected to pitch the tents again at McNeal. Some people saw Martin Luther King leave Canton in a big black sedan, though they had no idea where he was going or what it meant. By early evening, about a thousand local blacks joined a few hundred marchers in Holy Child's auditorium. The crowd hummed, full of resolve and spirit.[40]

"We're going to the schoolyard," announced Annie Devine. Before anyone could explain the details, the audience roared, leaped up, and clapped. The gymnasium shook with their exuberance. They soaked their handkerchiefs in case of more tear gas, and they filed outside to start the mile-long parade toward McNeal. They sang, held hands, and called for bystanders to join them. Feeling conspicuous, Murray walked among blacks rather than whites. He had no idea what would happen. There were rumors of highway patrolmen with machine guns and tear gas, and more rumors of Deacons prepared to ambush state troopers.[41]

Then they reached the school. The Highway Patrol had pulled back. The spotlights were gone. There were no tents.

The leaders had negotiated a deal: the marchers could hold a rally on the school grounds, but they could not raise the tents. Both sides had reasons to accept the agreement. Canton's white officials had proposed the deal under pressure from local merchants, the state government, and Justice Department officials; the city could not afford another black eye. Annie Devine emphasized that it was an important breakthrough— the black community needed to establish lines of communication with powerful whites. A refusal to compromise, moreover, meant more violence. "Civility prevailed. Reason, I suppose, prevailed," said Flonzie Goodloe. "They would have killed us."[42]

But no one warned the marchers about any compromise. "I guess you're wondering what happened to the tents," said Devine. One man yelled back: "We been sold out, that's what." Ralph Abernathy tried to portray the rally as "a proud moment for us," and marchers hooted back, "Get the tents!" They complained that leaders ignored the rank-and-file. It was a dismal scene. The sky was darkening. The speakers had to use a ladder as a podium. Neither King nor Meredith was there. As a final insult, policemen had opened a fire hydrant, rendering the field a muddy mess.[43]

In a lame attempt to mollify the crowd, Abernathy announced a "surprise": a speech by John Lewis. The somber, squat man had arrived in Mississippi that day with misgivings. Losing the chairmanship of SNCC had bruised his pride. In his mind, Black Power was an empty slogan. He hated, too, how SNCC's new leaders exploited King and alienated liberals. He had already offered his resignation from SNCC, and he officially left the organization after the march.[44]

"The whole man must say no nonviolently, his entire Christian spirit must say no to this evil and vicious system," said Lewis. The audience trudged away through the mud. The rhetoric of militant love, of redemptive suffering, of sit-ins and Freedom Rides—in that time, in that place, in that circumstance, the words seemed lost in a simpler past. "I felt like the uninvited guest," reflected Lewis. "By the time of Canton nobody knew what would be enough to make America right, and the atmosphere was very complicated, very negative."[45]

Stokely Carmichael glowered from the fringes, his arms crossed and his head shaking side to side. He led the disillusioned masses back to Holy Child, limping slightly from the bruise caused by a tear gas canister. He leaned into the young woman by his side, sizzling with charisma despite his grim expression, warning her to hold her tongue around reporters. "Tell us about the sellout!" cried his fellow militants.[46]

The marchers gathered in Holy Child's auditorium, where, free from reporters, Carmichael blasted the compromise. After listening to this continued outrage, James Lawson interrupted. The Memphis minister had attended the meeting at George Washington's home. Lawson, too, wanted to pitch the tents. But no one presented an alternative to another teargassing. "You are as much to blame as anyone else," Lawson told Carmichael. "If other leaders were not prepared to do it because they were scared, you should have been prepared then to suggest how it could be done." The local leaders made their decision based on politics, and national leaders had to respect that choice.[47]

Around 2:00 a.m., marchers bedded down for another night on the cold, concrete floor at Holy Child. Like many Canton blacks, they felt cheated and empty. As Paul Murray rode back to Valley View, however, he felt relieved. The new volunteer had wanted nothing to do with tear gas. Yet he wondered about his place. On the march back to Holy Child, he had been surrounded by a loud call-and-response: "What do you want? *Black Power!* What do you want? *Black Power!* What do you want? *Black Power!*" In the months to come, the young white idealist would immerse himself in Madison County's racial politics, and he would understand the slogan's goals. But at that moment, he was worried. "What am I doing here?" he asked himself. "Is this my show?"[48]

17

WE'RE THE GREATEST
Canton to Tougaloo
JUNE 25, 1966

Wendell Paris wanted to come to Mississippi for the march's final weekend, but he had no car and no money. The SNCC organizer was stuck at his home base in Macon County, Alabama. Then, at around nine o'clock on Friday night, his friend Thomas "Tippy" Jackson rolled into town in his souped-up Chevrolet Impala. By ten they were driving west on Highway 80 toward Jackson. A white woman named Susan Solf, who had worked with SNCC in New York, lent them money for the trip, provided that she could come. They took along Norman "Duke" Barnett and an associate that Paris identified as "Cool Phil from Miami."[1]

Paris had grown up with a friend named Sammy Younge, whom he loved like a brother. Both had exhibited a restless energy, engaging in hijinks such as joyriding in stolen cars. After Younge served in the navy, they both entered the Macon County movement. They picketed businesses, confronted white churches, and joined SNCC to register rural voters. Once a hostile cafe owner tried to whack Younge with his pistol, and Paris jumped in, getting hurt himself. On January 3, 1966, Younge tried to use the whites-only restroom at a Tuskegee service station. After a prolonged argument, the attendant shot Younge in the head.[2]

The murder of a military veteran and civil rights worker helped spawn SNCC's anti–Vietnam War statement. By then, too many black activists, like Paris, had lost faith in the redemption of southern whites, the goodness of the federal government, and the philosophy of nonviolence. On the night of Younge's death, Paris's mother gave him a pistol. "If you go down," she said, *"you go down fighting."*[3]

On the drive to Mississippi, Paris had an upset stomach. Well past midnight, before crossing the state border, he pulled into a service station. At the small lunch counter, Paris bought an Alka-Seltzer. The white clerk handed him a packet, poured a Styrofoam cup of water, and told him to drink it outside. Paris refused to accept the indignity. He tore open the packet and dropped in the tablet. The cup stayed on the counter.

When the clerk reached for a pistol, Paris whipped out his own gun. Cool Phil flipped out a switchblade. Duke Barnett grabbed two Coke bottles, ready to swing them like clubs. Weapons drawn, everyone waited for the tablet to dissolve. "Here's the longest-fizzing Alka-Seltzer in the history of this country," thought Paris.

Finally, the tablet melted. Paris laid down his gun, seated himself, and drank.

"It's a new day now!" he announced while walking out. "Black Power is here, and we're not taking any more of white folks' bullshit!" He felt good. He remembered his mother's warning after Younge's murder. He had been ready. White folks respected violence, and that clerk *had* to respect him. Paris got back in the Impala, floored the gas pedal, and sped through the dark night into Mississippi.[4]

The last leg of the march into Jackson was collecting people from across the civil rights spectrum, from Black Power militants to idealistic white liberals. Somewhat surprisingly, it prompted the return of one of the march's original cynics: the executive director of the National Urban League, Whitney Young.

Since that first late-night meeting at the Lorraine Motel, Young had withheld the Urban League's participation in the March Against Fear. But he kept looking for a way back in. His instinct was to use this opportunity. Roy Wilkins had left Memphis in an imperious fury, but Young told Martin Luther King to contact him if necessary. His organization depended on alliances with the government, corporations, foundations, churches, and people at the grass roots. The man knew how to build consensus.[5]

In a newspaper column and a radio address, Young sidestepped the Urban League's withdrawal from the march, instead focusing on the Meredith shooting and the Civil Rights Bill. At a press conference, however, he indicated that the Urban League would join the march on two conditions: if James Meredith approved, and if civil rights organizations displayed unity. Even after SNCC unleashed Black Power, Young sought a working harmony. He supported power "based on the ability to compete economically, socially, and educationally," yet deplored any inference of separatism. "Our goal is to be in the mainstream of American life."[6]

Young cared about "the meat and potatoes issues for every Negro citizen—voting, jobs, housing, education." For all the hysteria over Black Power, the Meredith March advanced concrete goals. It dramatized the evils of racism and the courage of ordinary people. It registered voters. It revealed an interracial commitment to American ideals. Also, it needed money. SNCC and CORE were already broke, and the march would finish $20,000 in debt. Young planned to announce a new branch in Jackson, so after winning cautious consent from his executive board, he promised to help cover costs for tents, lavatories, food, and transportation. He bought his place on the dais in Jackson.[7]

Young arrived with a desire for "a frank and meaningful dialogue" with white moderates, appealing to these "men of good will" who wished to scrub the historical stain of racism. In his mind, the Urban League would not just improve lives for black people, but also help well-meaning whites uplift the South.[8]

James Meredith had his own faith in white people. In the face of Jack Cauthen, he saw a changing Mississippi. Months earlier, when Meredith wrote to ten officials about his walk down Highway 51, only Cauthen had responded. The Madison County sheriff assured Meredith that he would provide appropriate protection, "so long as you and your associates conduct yourselves in such a manner as not to disturb the peace and dignity of this community."[9]

On Saturday morning, June 25, Meredith returned to Canton. He wanted to lead his own march down Highway 51. Cauthen invited him into his office and leveled with him, man to man. His deputies had barely slept over the past three days, and he had received no advance warning for this new demonstration. Cauthen nevertheless pledged to protect a two-mile march to the city limits. "He might not have liked me, he might even have hated me; but he treated me as a citizen," reflected Meredith. African Americans were gaining political power, and the sheriff's stance acknowledged this new reality.[10]

Cauthen corroborated Meredith's account of a cordial, reasonable meeting. But years later, when describing the announcement of their agreement outside the Madison County Courthouse, he added a twist. "I just rub James on the back, you know," said Cauthen, "and his back was just smooth as silk." When they met, Meredith still had a shaved patch of hair, visible pellet wounds, and a limp. Yet long after the turbulence of the civil rights era, the sheriff floated an extreme version of a conspiracy theory. He absolved whites of guilt while blaming outside agitators for elaborate, nefarious schemes. "There hadn't been no pellets or shots in James's back," he insisted. "I don't think he was shot, no sir."[11]

Meredith had left Tougaloo by car that morning. "I am alone," he said, though he welcomed others to join him. Dick Gregory, Claude Sterrett, and Philadelphia minister William Bentley accompanied him from the outset. In Canton, where many marchers had spent another night at Holy Child, 126 people set out with Meredith from the courthouse.[12]

The man at the helm was as enigmatic as ever. Meredith wore the same faded-yellow pith helmet and carried the same ebony walking stick. He walked with solemn, testy determination. He cut off questions from reporters, and when marchers started singing, he barked, "Tell them to shut up back there." At one point, Andrew Young conveyed regrets from Martin Luther King, who was stuck in meetings in Jackson; Meredith whispered in Young's ear and then pushed him away. A confused, horrified Young drifted away. Later, Robert Green tried to relay the same message; Meredith shoved him as well.[13]

Why was he marching? "I had announced that I would rejoin the march in Canton," Meredith explained in a deliberate monotone. "Nobody consulted me about any changes in the plans." While fulfilling his pledge to the people of Mississippi, he also reclaimed his original vision: he would walk down Highway 51 as an independent citizen, and people would flock under his leadership. As the column grew to about three hundred marchers, he considered his endeavor a success, a contrast to the "shenanigans" of the bickering, ad-libbing leaders acting in his name.[14]

Meredith planned to stop at the city limits, but Charles Snodgrass offered Highway Patrol protection for a continued march down Highway 51. Feeling proud and strong, Meredith accepted. But after the hype surrounding Meredith's earlier statements, Snodgrass needed one clarification. "Are you armed?" he asked. Meredith said no. He lifted his arms high, extended his cane skyward, and exposed himself for a pat-down. Dick Gregory chuckled, since the Deacons for Defense were shadowing Meredith and patrolling nearby with carbines resting on their cars' backseats.[15]

As Meredith led the way out of Canton, cars from Tougaloo dropped off more marchers. When the pace quickened, the pellet wounds in Meredith's leg got inflamed. His limp grew more pronounced, and for one stretch, he rode in a car. But as the procession moved south, his resentments mixed with his pride. "This is my march," he said. "They can join me if they like."[16]

Late that afternoon, Martin Luther King took six hundred marchers north out of Tougaloo College, and he met Meredith one mile north of the campus. Together, they led everyone back to Tougaloo. King regretted the recent communication snafus, and Meredith put his arm over King's shoulder. "I hope this is in light of what you wanted," said King. As they passed under the iron gates at the campus entrance, Meredith looked back at nearly a thousand people filing along Highway 51. With King by his side, he felt validated. "This," he said, "is the most beautiful thing I have seen in a long time."[17]

Tougaloo College sat on the northern edge of Hinds County, distant enough from downtown Jackson to be an oasis from hostile segregationists. A private school founded through the American Missionary Association, it provided a liberal arts education for generations of Mississippi blacks, and in the 1960s it attracted a handful of idealistic whites. Its autonomy enraged white politicians; Lieutenant Governor Carroll Gartin called it a hotbed of "queers, quirks, political agitators and possibly some communists."[18]

In the early 1960s, a small cadre from Tougaloo energized Jackson's freedom struggle. The "Tougaloo Nine" staged the city's first sit-in, and the "Tougaloo Four" were its first Freedom Riders. SNCC and CORE workers recruited, studied, and recuperated on campus. The Tougaloo

Movement launched demonstrations against segregated public facilities. A white professor, John Salter, organized direct action protests; its white chaplain, Ed King, campaigned on the MFDP ticket; its white president, A. D. Beittel, supported the movement. "It represented safety," said Joyce Ladner. "It was a secure place, a welcoming place."[19]

George Owens replaced Beittel in 1965. The college's first black president approved the Meredith March's stop at Tougaloo. Although nervous about the marchers, officials, and enemies descending upon his campus, he kept his commitment. "An institution like Tougaloo is a cultural apparatus for black people and through black people for this country," he said. "There's no other role that it can have. It's got to be that. If anything it's got to be that."[20]

On Saturday, marchers arrived from all over the country. Black Mississippians came in packed cars or rickety church buses. People rested under shady oak trees. The MCHR set up a medical facility in the basement of Woodworth Chapel, and marchers used the restrooms and showers in Brownlee Gymnasium. Volunteers sold pennants and buttons commemorating the "Meredith Mississippi March for Freedom," while SNCC workers affixed bumper stickers with a black panther logo that proclaimed, WE'RE THE GREATEST.[21]

After Canton and Philadelphia, the march's militant faction felt more embittered than ever. SNCC's Cordell Reagon tried to preserve unity and discipline. Gathering a crowd under the blazing sun, he insisted that Black Power meant political representation, not black racism or violence. A man in a straw hat and a WE'RE THE GREATEST T-shirt jumped off the ground. "I came to Mississippi to die if necessary," he proclaimed. "But when the white power structure makes decisions for us, we might as well give up the God-damn ballgame."[22]

That evening, everyone migrated to the football field, where they sat on trampled grass and dirt, staking out positions for a celebrity-studded rally. An estimated ten thousand spectators filled the field and surrounding embankments. Thousands more tried to come, but the police blocked a long line of cars from entering the college. A Hinds County officer claimed that they were preventing congestion, but they provided no alternate way into campus—for them, this fuss was big enough already.[23]

"It is a gas to be here," said Sammy Davis, Jr. The star of Broadway's *Golden Boy* had chartered a plane from Los Angeles, bringing along champion decathlete Rafer Johnson and movie stars Marlon Brando, Burt Lancaster, and Tony Franciosa. At Tougaloo, the public address system was broken, and the spotlights filtered through a thick haze of bugs. But Davis was a professional. The crowd hushed as he performed pop standards and show tunes, and it clapped in rhythm during his trademark scatting. "*What kind of man is this?*" he crooned, gliding across the stage in a denim jacket, khaki pants, and low-cut black boots.[24]

Davis battled his demons all the way to Tougaloo. Given his stardom and white wife, he feared that stepping into the South was a death sentence. He later claimed that Robert F. Kennedy warned him about a potential assassination. Davis thus vowed to leave before the march to Jackson. Martin Luther King, Stokely Carmichael, and Dick Gregory all tried cajoling him into marching on Sunday, but he demurred. "I have a commitment," said Davis. "I've got to make bread, man."[25]

Brando exuded a more romantic appreciation of his time in Mississippi. The impulsive actor loved the authenticity of the civil rights movement, its distinction from the plastic world of Hollywood. In Jackson, he chatted with marchers, offered to carry a photographer's equipment, and slapped a SNCC sticker on his forehead. He even proclaimed, "Black Power!" from the stage. "I haven't really participated in this movement, not in the way that my conscience gnaws at me that I should," he confessed to the audience. He promised to march to Jackson. "You are the heroes of America," he said. "You know what suffering is. You really know it."[26]

The pop culture stars created a common ground, a sense of interracial possibility. March organizers had tried getting Nina Simone and Eartha Kitt, and King had wanted Frank Sinatra. Even without those celebrities, the rally attracted popular attention—even from the movement's enemies. For years, Mississippi radio stations had refused to air a whisper about civil rights. Now, WOKJ broadcast not only live performances by the entertainers, but also uncensored speeches, from Martin Luther King's rolling orations to Stokely Carmichael's dynamic exhortations.[27]

James Meredith limped onstage to a huge cheer. He had turned thirty-three on Friday and Carmichael would turn twenty-five that Wednesday, so the crowd sang "Happy Birthday." Meredith beamed that it was "the happiest birthday I've ever had." Carmichael, against type, appreciated the serenade with a goofy shyness.[28]

Dick Gregory further diffused the lingering tensions. The evening's emcee joked about Black Power: "When y'all get to saying it down here, it sounds like you're saying Black Powder! You don't want Mr. Ku Klux Klan to think you're calling him." He wished that President Johnson was the pope, "so that way folks would only have to kiss his ring." Throughout the night, he displayed his signature mix of brashness and hilarity. Committed to nonviolence, approving of Black Power, and loyal to Meredith, Gregory pulled together the march's fraying strands.[29]

But no one galvanized the crowd more than Soul Brother Number One, Mr. Dynamite, The Godfather of Soul: James Brown! A decade ago, "Please Please Please" had vaulted Brown into stardom. *Live at the Apollo 1962* made him a cultural phenomenon. He led the most frenetic, soulful, ornate show in the business, and his music jerked away from Motown's crossover pop—young audiences embraced its sweatier, funkier style.[30]

At his career peak, Brown came to Tougaloo. He was friends with SNCC's Cleveland Sellers. Brown bought dinners and gave backstage passes to SNCC workers, while Sellers arranged meetings between Brown and Martin Luther King. When Sellers called to ask about performing at Tougaloo, Brown promised, "I'll be there." Sellers asked what arrangements he required. "I'll be there," he repeated.[31]

Brown arrived in Jackson in a Lear Jet, along with his entire band. The Meredith March was his first public engagement with the civil rights movement. Dressed in a form-fitting suit and an open, ruffled shirt, he belted out "Try Me" and "I Got You (I Feel Good)." The audience leaped to its feet as Brown shimmied and shook. "This is Black Power, baby!" exclaimed Dick Gregory.[32]

In the coming years, Brown's thinking would encompass both patriotic liberalism and separatist disenchantment. Right now, he projected one way that the Meredith March was shaping and reflecting African American culture. Being black was nothing to worry about. Black was good, black was beautiful. Brown translated Black Power into popular, universal terms. "*Say it loud,*" he would soon sing, "*I'm black and I'm proud.*"[33]

For weeks, Martin Luther King had pinned high hopes on the parade into Jackson. "It will rival the Alabama pilgrimage from Selma to Montgomery," he promised, predicting a gathering of 25,000 people. Privately, he hoped that number would reach 45,000, or even 75,000. At one point he even suggested delaying their arrival in Jackson until July 4.[34]

Unlike the Selma March, the Meredith March had not issued a general invitation to people of conscience. During the final week, however, Carmichael and McKissick joined King in "a call for the clergy and citizens in all walks of life to join in the final stretch of the walk to Jackson, Mississippi." This culminating event could reaffirm King's original mission of a mass demonstration that aroused the nation's conscience. "Everyone is invited," stated the official press release, implying that whites were welcome. A willing marcher just had to reach Jackson and "agree to conform to the basic philosophy of nonviolence."[35]

King had asked Bayard Rustin to coordinate the final spectacle, but the organizational mastermind remained wary of radical theatrics. Indeed, SNCC workers had discussed using tactics of mass civil disobedience, such as blocking buses and trains with their bodies. While walking south, they kept winking to reporters: "Watch SNCC when we get to Jackson."[36]

Walter Fauntroy, SCLC director in Washington, D.C., assumed Rustin's role. At the Jackson headquarters at Pratt Memorial Methodist Church, he worked with pastor Allen Johnson. Fauntroy also oversaw a seven-member coordinating committee representing a spectrum of civil rights organizations.[37]

During a locally televised press conference, Fauntroy and Johnson appealed to the black community to open homes, drive marchers, donate money, and prepare meals. As local merchants donated goods, Pratt Memorial hosted a mass meeting on Wednesday night, and Masonic Temple did the same on Thursday and Friday nights. Black churches would hold Sunday services, serve a midday meal, and then get parishioners to the Capitol. Also, the MFDP planned its statewide convention for Sunday morning; after nominating candidates for that November's general election, delegates would march downtown.[38]

Black Jacksonians bubbled with excitement. Many felt a personal connection to James Meredith, who had attended Jackson State before integrating Ole Miss. Local people drew inspiration, as well, from out-of-state activists. The political energy had waned since Freedom Summer, so now they wondered: How many people were coming? Would it revive the local movement?[39]

The National Pilgrimage Coordinating Headquarters, based in Washington, D.C., sent out train schedules, established fourteen regional coordinators, and encouraged press releases, mass meetings, and fund-raising efforts to get people to Jackson. Caravans left from thirty different cities. Bayard Rustin arranged a chartered flight from New York City, and fleets of buses rode south from Chicago.[40]

On Friday night, two hundred people attended a prayer vigil at King's Atlanta pastorate, Ebenezer Baptist Church, and then left for Mississippi. Thirty-eight passengers boarded a chartered Trailways bus, but soon balked when the air conditioner broke down. They returned to the bus station, where repairmen tried fixing it. After going one block, they turned around again. The air conditioner still did not work. The Trailways manager offered either a refund or a hot bus. The Atlantans instead launched a nonviolent demonstration, blocking the counter. "*Leave the driving to us*," they sang, "*We just want an air-conditioned bus*." After two hours, Trailways caved to their demands and found a new bus. They rode to Jackson in cool comfort.[41]

"It takes about ten drinks for me to say what I think," confessed a white woman from Jackson. "Why, we've never done anything that's right for the Negro. All we did was starve him, and work him, and shoot him in the back. I don't see how they could run their counties any worse than the whites have been running them."[42]

If some whites saw the future, others were stuck in the past. The Americans for the Preservation of the White Race encouraged "all Southern Christian people to fly their Confederate flags" to express defiance against this "planned publicity plot." The Jackson chapter president proclaimed that "we do not intend to stand idly by and be trampled on or see our city and state taken over." A white woman told a British reporter about the ills of the march and the movement: it was run by Communists, put millions in Martin Luther King's pocket, lied about black people (who had equal rights, but were too lazy to hold steady jobs), and orchestrated the shooting of James Meredith.[43]

Yet if barbarians were at the gates, white politicians would accommodate the invasion. "These people thrive on publicity," said Jackson mayor Allen Thompson on Thursday. "They cannot bear to be ignored." On Friday and then again on Saturday, Paul Johnson issued similar statements. Soon, promised the governor, this "sad little show" would leave Mississippi. "They will inflict their hate and hostility on other Americans as they sow strife and discord across this Nation, which needs to be united behind the brave men who are following our flag in Viet Nam." A front-page editorial in Jackson's *Clarion-Ledger* echoed the officials, as did a statement by the Citizens' Council.[44]

That weekend, 275 of Mississippi's 300 highway patrolmen got assigned to the Meredith March, along with 450 local officers. The FBI had learned that leaders from the White Knights of the Ku Klux Klan and United Klans of America met in Laurel, Mississippi, to consider an attack upon Martin Luther King. A South Carolina klavern also planned a mischief-raising trip to Jackson.[45]

But state authorities seemed more concerned with civil rights activists than hate groups. The Highway Patrol monitored the arrival of outsiders, from New England ministers to Lowndes County "Black Panthers." Sovereignty Commission investigator A. L. Hopkins spent Saturday checking hundreds of cars in Canton, Tougaloo, and Jackson for tags registered to CDGM, hoping to prove that marchers were abusing federal antipoverty funds. He failed to find any CDGM cars.[46]

The Capitol building inspired a particular paranoia. March leaders wanted to speak from its front steps. One year earlier, after the MFDP staged a protest march to the Capitol, Jackson police stuffed 482 demonstrators into paddy wagons, hauled them to the state fairgrounds, and caged them in primitive cattle barns. More marches and more arrests ensued. Over a thousand prisoners spent weeks on a concrete floor in a livestock hangar; one investigation compared the site to a concentration camp.[47]

The state legislature had since banned political demonstrations at the Capitol. Most leaders of the Meredith March urged a defiance of the law, assuming that Paul Johnson could not stomach the bad press of mass arrests in Jackson. King, however, sought to avoid any messy surprises. During the meeting at the parish house in Yazoo City, he had slipped into the bedroom to call the governor, who assured him that he would not enforce the statute. Yet the Sovereignty Commission was relaying Stokely Carmichael's threats about occupying the Capitol, and Johnson faced pressure to rebuff black militants.[48]

On Friday, June 24, the governor's office ordered the construction of a wire fence around the entire Capitol. As quickly as the fence went up, it came down. Charles Evers had brokered a deal: the state allowed a rally on the back side of the building, which had a big parking lot. Bulldozers cleared the lot of rocks and other debris, and the governor's staff established specific zones for the stage, press, and audience.[49]

The marchers were still barred from the front of the Capitol. The front steps were the site of governors' inaugurations, not civil rights rallies. The front lawn, moreover, had a grand statue of the women of the Confederacy. It lauded the contributions to the Lost Cause by "Our Mothers," "Our Wives," "Our Sisters," and "Our Daughters." Johnson avoided the political repercussions of black men defiling this monument to white womanhood. By restricting the rally to the rear grounds, Mississippi whites saved face. Politicians snickered that "we're gonna make the niggers use the back door."[50]

Some sympathetic white friends told Ed King about this bragging, but the white MFDP official kept it to himself. He wondered if he had made the right decision. But if he relayed this racist smugness to march leaders, then militants might demand a confrontation on the Capitol steps. And then, he feared, the march's last possibilities for positive change "would disappear in a pool of blood."[51]

Along its winding course through Mississippi, the march had mixed the issues of a national demonstration with the politics of local communities. In some places, it inspired blacks never before touched by the civil rights movement; in others, it built upon legacies of grass-roots organizing. Now it entered a new arena. Jackson was the only major city in Mississippi. Though it operated within the confines of Jim Crow, the black community had more middle-class professionals, educational and cultural opportunities, and political weight. By June 1966, African Americans constituted about 20 percent of Hinds County's eighty thousand registered voters.[52]

Like Memphis, Jackson was an NAACP town. Field Secretary Medgar Evers had worked with college students in the sit-in movement, and an NAACP youth council boycott of downtown merchants launched the Jackson Movement. By 1963, direct action protests were inspiring a genuine mass movement. As Martin Luther King won national publicity in Birmingham, Roy Wilkins saw a similar opportunity in Jackson. But Wilkins never liked confrontational protests, and he negotiated a conservative agreement with city officials. Then Medgar Evers got murdered, and the Jackson Movement lost momentum.[53]

When Charles Evers replaced his brother, he ignored the more established NAACP officials in Jackson. The branch's Executive Committee complained that Evers pitted the youth council against adult leaders, branded community pillars as Uncle Toms, handled finances with abandon, and acted rude or outrageous. "He is just plain sick," concluded one official.[54]

The Meredith March had the potential to revitalize the Jackson branch. A local man, John Frazier, ran a three-week recruitment campaign. Frazier produced a newsletter, enlarged the Executive Committee, and reorganized the finances. "Let us remember the scars of Mr. Meredith," stated the newsletter. "The march is good for Mississippi and well timed." NAACP members joined the mass meetings at Pratt Memorial and Masonic Temple. The Jackson branch office stayed open from 7:00 a.m. on Saturday until 4:00 a.m. on Sunday to find housing for visitors, and its members worked with local churches to feed thousands of marchers.[55]

For all his objections, Roy Wilkins knew that the march advanced the NAACP's agenda. Testifying before the Senate Judiciary Committee, he described African Americans' anger after the Meredith shooting. He also endorsed branch demonstrations in conjunction with the Jackson march. But in his nationally syndicated column, he criticized SCLC, SNCC, and CORE for ignoring the Civil Rights Bill. He described the "tough talk" of the "new militants" as "separate and suspicious," driving the races apart.[56]

Cecil Moore, the Philadelphia branch president who had marched in Mississippi, urged that Wilkins cancel the NAACP's upcoming national convention. He pleaded that "we immediately cast aside organizational jealousies in order to make the Meredith March a success," rather than "dissipate funds in frivolity" at a convention. Moore failed to mention that the convention agenda included an item about dividing his branch into five smaller units, which would erode the power of Philadelphia's militant black "boss."[57]

Wilkins did not cancel the convention. Nor did he go to Mississippi. He reflected that the march "was a tragedy for the civil rights

movement." Black Power "couldn't have been more destructive if Senator Eastland contrived it." He rejected the slogan's implication of violent
revolution, its undefined connection to third world anticolonialism, and
its invitation of a white backlash. The Meredith ambush was a gift from
heaven, he thought, and militants had wasted it.[58]

Late on Saturday night, after all the excitement of Sammy Davis, Jr., and
James Brown, the march leaders reviewed the final arrangements for the
parade into Jackson. Besides King, Carmichael, Floyd McKissick, and
Mississippi activists, the meeting included James Meredith, Dick Gregory, and Whitney Young. They planned to have forty marshals keep the
formation in line, and the Deacons for Defense would put one hundred
men among the marchers.[59]

The big debate concerned the place of Charles Evers, who wanted a
speaking slot at the Capitol. He had joined the seven-person coordinating committee in Jackson alongside representatives from SCLC, SNCC,
CORE, MFDP, MCHR, and the Delta Ministry. He applied for permits
to use public space, leased the truck that served as a speakers' platform,
and arranged transportation and housing for dignitaries such as Congressman Charles Diggs and United Auto Workers president Walter
Reuther. He also negotiated with city officials about the march route,
including the placement of the final rally behind the Capitol.[60]

But Carmichael and McKissick argued that the NAACP had disavowed the manifesto, and Evers had acted only out of political calculation. Representatives from the MFDP and Delta Ministry echoed SNCC
and CORE, given their rivalry with the Evers-led political machine.
Martin Luther King pleaded the other side, urging harmony. Alvin Poussaint, who backed King, recalled Carmichael's reaction: "He started
yelling at King, cursing at King." According to Poussaint, Hosea
Williams had to restrain the SNCC leader. In the end, they voted to ban
Evers from the dais.[61]

Roy Wilkins huffed about the lack of recognition for the NAACP's
work, and he condemned the march's dissension and "fanfare." Evers,
however, took the high road. He wished for black unity, called for interracial cooperation, and positioned himself as a responsible power broker. Ironically, the Meredith March benefited no politician more than
Evers. His tough talk earned him black support, his interracial pleas

won him liberal backing, and the march fed him with enthusiastic audiences and registered voters. This final slight reinforced his stature. When he learned of his banishment, he had been down at the Capitol, overseeing some final arrangements. "It's all right," he responded. "I'll be here when they're all gone."[62]

18

DREAMS AND NIGHTMARES
Tougaloo to Jackson
JUNE 26, 1966

After sitting through Sunday school, Frank Figgers skipped church. The black teenager from Jackson kept seeing a contradiction: religion taught that they were all God's children, but in reality, black people got treated as something less than human. Even basic jobs seemed off limits. "The gas*man*, the fire*man*, the police*man*," he recalled. "Anything that had 'man' attached to it was for white people."

Figgers and his friends headed for the Meredith March. Growing up, his heroes were the young activists of the Jackson Movement. Now he was sixteen years old, and he had just finished eleventh grade at Lanier High School. He knew all about the shooting of James Meredith, the terror in Philadelphia and Canton, and the impending arrival of thousands of freedom marchers. On Saturday night, he and his brother-in-law hitched a ride to Tougaloo, and while watching the music and speeches, he got so excited. Here was his chance to really participate in the black freedom struggle.

By early afternoon on Sunday, Figgers was walking among the great leaders of the civil rights movement, as well as labor leaders and judges, black organizers and white hippies, ministers and priests and rabbis and nuns, housekeepers and sharecroppers, old people and college students and young kids. By the thousands, they filled the streets of Jackson. They were part of the largest civil rights demonstration in Mississippi history.

"Black Power!" he shouted. As they headed toward the Capitol, Figgers reveled in hollering the slogan. *Black* . . . it was more real, more authentic, more his identity than "colored" or "Negro." "And then, to put *Power* with that? You knew you had been power*less*. Now you have some *Power*?" It felt like the old movement spirit, but also like the dawning of a new day.[1]

Every marcher had a journey and a story. Elizabeth French arrived at Union Station in Washington, D.C., on Friday night. She identified her fellow travelers from their walking shoes and light luggage. The white housewife from Virginia had long sympathized with the civil rights movement, but never before participated. She stated that she joined the March Against Fear "to save my own soul."[2]

Her group had twelve people: nine whites and three blacks, eight northerners and four southerners, eight men and four women. Some were old, some young. Eight had participated in the march from Selma to Montgomery. They included the memoirist Sarah Patton Boyle, the minister of a Unitarian church, a nurse at a Catholic settlement house, a schoolteacher who would get fired if her community found out about her participation, and a retired army officer whose last march was twenty-four years earlier, in the Philippines—the Bataan Death March.[3]

They rode a train for seventeen hours, finally stopping in Birmingham, where SCLC's Joseph Lowery took them to St. Paul United Methodist Church and fed them at the Gaston Motel. French saw constant reminders of the movement's dangers: three years earlier, that same motel had been firebombed, and near St. Paul, a dynamite explosion at Sixteenth Street Baptist Church had killed four little girls. After the meal, they packed into two rented cars and drove for five and a half hours to Tougaloo. As they reached campus, hundreds of cars headed in the opposite direction, since the Saturday night rally had just finished. French's group joined more than a thousand campers at the college. Some slept on the floor of Brownlee Gymnasium, others in tents or under the stars.[4]

Sunday, June 26, dawned under a hot, heavy haze. Marchers began stirring at daybreak, and a muffled buzz of energy droned across campus. After breakfast, they started gathering at the Tougaloo gates. By late morning it was steamy. Nurses handed out salt tablets and suntan lotion. Marlon Brando and Burt Lancaster circulated through the crowd, encouraging the marchers. Robert Moses, the guru of Mississippi organizing, lurked on the fringes, somber and quiet.[5]

French sat on a curb next to an old African-American woman from

Holmes County, whose worn-out shoes testified to nine straight days of marching. The longer they talked, the more French learned about black life in Mississippi: cotton workers displaced by mechanization, a Social Security system administered by racist local officials, brutal reprisals against voting registrants, sexual exploitation of black women by white men, and naked violence such as the Meredith shooting, the Philadelphia mob attack, and the Canton teargassing. The White House's hardhearted response was just as discouraging. As French later reflected, "there was, among Negroes, a bitter cynicism about the Administration's concern for human life—Negro human life."[6]

By eleven o'clock, the last leg of the Meredith March Against Fear was under way. Nearly two thousand people left from Tougaloo, singing, *"We've got the light of freedom."* James Meredith, Floyd McKissick, Hosea Williams, and other titans led the way, all dressed in hats and short-sleeved white shirts. Stokely Carmichael marched in denim overalls. Martin Luther King walked alongside his wife, Coretta, who noticed the march's toll on her husband. The Kings walked with three of their four children, ages five to ten. From here, Coretta would take them to Chicago, where they would publicize SCLC's open housing campaign by living in a slum apartment.[7]

From the outset, the Highway Patrol and the Hinds County police patrolled the trek. At the city limits, the Jackson Police Department added its manpower, including eleven black officers. The route mostly passed through black neighborhoods in North Jackson, but it also skirted a middle-class white district. A white doctor who had treated some Canton tear gas victims stood with his family, displaying a hand-drawn sign: GOOD LUCK. Marchers hailed them and beckoned them to walk, but they looked away, shy and hesitant.[8]

The temperature climbed into the midnineties. Marchers wore straw hats, wrapped bandannas around their heads, and ingested salt tablets and prunes to combat dehydration. Soda machines along the route got emptied. Trying to stave off overheated engines, the accompanying cars popped their hoods. From their lawns and porches, black spectators passed out water, lemonade, and encouragement. "It was so fucking hot," recalled SCLC staffer Bruce Hartford. When he saw an automatic ice machine, he popped in a quarter, and after smashing a five-pound block on the ground, he and other marchers wrapped the shattered ice in bandannas and towels against their necks.[9]

Tom Ethridge of Jackson's *Clarion-Ledger* snickered at the "mixed couples and much nasal whining and twanging in non-Southern brogues." He wrote that whites might understand why blacks marched, or even respect their determination. But he could not fathom the motivations of white marchers, "whose ranks included quite a few beatnik, weirdo-looking types such as you might see at the police lineup of any big city, or on the campus at Berkeley, California."[10]

The *Jackson Daily News* ran two "man on the march" columns. The reporter Charles Overby smiled at his reflection in a plate-glass mirror: with his handkerchief-wrapped head and open shirt, he looked like a hippie! When hecklers called him "white trash," though, a shiver of fear coursed through him. If he could not grasp the purpose of all this marching, Overby also described the protesters' idealism. His fellow correspondent, Lincoln Warren, walked among some black youths. At first they viewed him with suspicion. But as the march progressed, a young boy sidled up and started a conversation. He asked if Warren had many friends. "Before or after this march?" cracked the reporter.[11]

Walter Reuther and his wife, May, logged five miles. The president of the United Auto Workers defied the advice of his bodyguards, who warned him to slip away after a short stretch. In the Deep South, newspapers painted Reuther as a crazed Bolshevik. In fact, he was the ultimate establishment liberal, a big-time NAACP contributor who urged the MFDP compromise at the 1964 Democratic National Convention. He was marching to support SCLC. "The alternative to Dr. King's leadership in this kind of non-violent struggle is frightening to contemplate," he warned.[12]

Another white dignitary, Pennsylvania Supreme Court justice Michael Musmanno, got pushed to the ground by a furious white spectator after the judge walked on his lawn. Young black men came to Musmanno's aid, surging off the street and yelling, "Get that whitey! Kill that whitey!" Although Musmanno was unhurt, controversy kept following the flamboyant jurist. A longtime NAACP member and former prosecutor at the Nuremberg Trials, he marched in Mississippi to promote the Civil Rights Bill. His presence sparked a vigorous debate in the Pittsburgh media; his detractors claimed that he flouted the canons of judicial ethics, while his supporters defended his liberal conscience.[13]

CORE produced posters that proclaimed FREEDOM NOW. SNCC workers slapped WE'RE THE GREATEST stickers on those posters, as well as on telephone poles, street signs, clothes, railroad trains, and police cars. The competing chants of "Black Power!" and "Freedom, Freedom" got louder and more frequent.[14]

When SCLC's James Orange bellowed "Freedom!," James Meredith glowered and pointed his walking stick. "Shut up," he instructed. Orange looked befuddled: "We can say Black Power, but we can't say Freedom?" Some reporters figured that Meredith supported Black Power, but in fact he hated any expression that undermined his principles of discipline and order. His wounds made him especially cranky. He looked tired and weak, and he soon climbed into a yellow-and-black Chevrolet along with Dick Gregory, Lillian Gregory, and A. W. Willis.[15]

At the tracks of the Illinois Central Railroad, a white engineer started rolling his diesel locomotive toward the crossing. SCLC's Robert Green rushed in, stood on the tracks, and demanded that he stop. Then Willie Ricks and some teenagers hopped onto the cowcatcher and banged on the windows. "Black Power! Black Power! Black Power!" screamed Ricks from the side of the train, his fist raised in triumph. Green cussed out Ricks, while Stokely Carmichael drifted back to calm the teenagers. "Black Power stops the train!" howled one amped-up young man.[16]

SCLC workers stationed themselves off the two-lane streets heading toward the Capitol, holding armfuls of small plastic American flags. Many marchers grabbed one, including William Hohri, who had spent the World War II years at Manzanar, a Japanese American internment camp. That ordeal motivated his continued involvement in political causes. In June 1966, he was attending a Methodist conference that voted to send delegates to Jackson. Hohri recalled his pride as an Asian American marching for freedom alongside whites and blacks. He loved carrying that flag. "It was the first time in my life," he said, "that I felt proud to be an American."[17]

When Willie Ricks saw black people wielding flags, he surged into the march column. "Give me those flags," he declared. "Those flags don't represent you." An Episcopalian leader named John Morris pleaded with Ricks. Then an SCLC man intervened. "Those are our flags," he said, passing them back to marchers.[18]

Farther south, the march passed into a white working-class neighborhood, where spectators waved Confederate flags, creating another battle in this war over identity and citizenship. Defiant blacks chewed out their hecklers and even snatched the Stars and Bars right out of the hands of astonished whites. Marchers ripped up flags and sang a modi-fied, mocking version of "Dixie." Later that afternoon, after the rally at the Capitol, Ricks and his cohorts pulled out a big Confederate flag and set it ablaze.[19]

Some whites spewed crudities, others oozed a grumpy disgust, and a few opined that the march was a flop, or a Communist plot, or a money-making scheme for that rascal Martin Luther King. One man stood by a NO TRESPASSING sign, wielding a brick. The police arrested another white spectator for punching a black man. When an elderly white woman in a red wig screamed epithets at marchers, a white man tried to cover her mouth, but she had infuriated some black teenagers. "March! March!" barked the marshals, keeping the riled-up young men in formation.[20]

Yet this final march was not defined by white racists. It was not de-fined by white liberal visitors, and it was not defined by organizational squabbles. It was defined by a spirit of black pride. Coby Smith loved it. The college student from Memphis had walked almost the entire route, and he remembered despairing stretches with dwindling numbers and eroding morale. Now people cheered him, handed him cups of water, and sneaked him cans of beer. He had begun this odyssey as a callow kid who emptied his bowels in a roadside cotton patch, and he finished it feeling like a hero.[21]

Even during the heyday of the Jackson Movement, no one could have imagined thousands upon thousands of African Americans marching through the city. Now black people sauntered off their front porches and onto the streets, jubilant and uplifted. At one point, a brass band moved in, and as the sun glinted off the gyrating trombones and tubas, they played a jaunty, exultant rendition of "When the Saints Go Marching In." Organizers had created eight gathering spots around the city, so different tributaries fed into the march's main stream. Marchers poured into the massive procession, singing and laughing, sometimes even spilling ahead of the column, turning narrow streets into churning rivers of humanity.[22]

"The ragged band that had begun as one mystical prophet in Mem-phis, that became 100 in Hernando, that became 1,000 after the baptism of spit in Philadelphia and tear gas in Canton, had become 15,000 Sun-day afternoon," rhapsodized Jack Newfield. He saw clergymen and "New Left types" and "a handful of dreamy Dylanesque kids," but the black domestics, fieldworkers, manual laborers, and students composed the huge majority. They were "giving a great movement the rare gift of a second chance to redeem its country's greatest sinner."[23]

The uplifting spirit buoyed many marchers. "If my daddy had done this it would have been a lot better for me," said seventy-eight-year-old Monroe Williams, who shambled down the street while leaning on his cane. "Now all of this ain't going to help me none—it's too late for that—but I'm doing it for the children." James Coleman, a dean at Tougaloo College, had a pearl-handled .22 pistol tucked into the back pocket of his shorts. He started walking with a wary eye on the police, but over time, the spectacle overwhelmed him. "That march," he recalled, "looked like forever."[24]

And those magic words: *Black Power!* "It gave me a new vision," said Frankye Adams, a Tougaloo College student. Stokely Carmichael and Willie Ricks were telling young blacks to resist brutality, to control their own destiny. Black Power scared some of the older generation, but anyone could grab on to the idea. It could inspire and exhilarate. As an old domestic named Mollie Gray waited for the marchers under a mimosa tree, SNCC workers drove by and exhorted, "Say Black Power!" She yelled back, "Black Power!" and giggled to herself, shaking her glass of ice cubes, just a little astonished by the thought of it all.[25]

After two hours on Highway 51, Elizabeth French was on the verge of heatstroke. She packed into a passing car that took back roads into downtown Jackson, where French rested on a black family's front porch, drinking water and talking to a local woman. Then they walked to the Capitol, waiting for the masses to arrive. "Any one of us who isn't scared to death is crazy," muttered French's companion. "Anything can happen this afternoon and probably will." The black woman said that when Lyndon Johnson refused the march leaders' request for federal protection, he gave the state of Mississippi "a license to kill."[26]

A phalanx of blue helmets and white faces guarded the Capitol. The state assigned hundreds of Mississippi highway patrolmen, Hinds County and Jackson policemen, and Mississippi Game and Fish officers to ring the edifice. They carried not only clubs and firearms, but also gas masks. Governor Paul Johnson called out two hundred state guardsmen to protect the front of the Capitol, where the verdant grounds and Confederate memorial were off-limits.[27]

Crowds of sullen-faced whites gathered, including fifty men in green shirts, white ties, green pants, and white belts. They were the Knights of the Green Forest, a disaffected splinter of the United Klans of America. "We would never object to our local niggers coming out here," said Imperial Wizard Dale Walton. "But these outside agitators . . . it's disgusting."[28]

Teenagers cruised around on motorcycles. Some spat at the feet of civil rights sympathizers. A CBS reporter interviewed two young white men. "They're acting like a bunch of monkeys out there," said one. "I don't like the niggers," added his friend. "They stink." As cars drove by waving Confederate flags, even policemen gave the rebel yell. When Elizabeth French passed by, an officer made a crude joke about "white women and black power."[29]

A little before four o'clock, the heralds arrived. Cheeky teenagers ran up and down, yelling "Black Power! Black Power!" Then came wave upon wave of people, pouring toward the Capitol. Freedom songs rang through downtown Jackson. The Highway Patrol estimated 10,000 to 12,000 participants, the Justice Department figured 15,000, and the Jackson police guessed 16,000. It was a massive and theatrical rejection of Mississippi's racial past, and it seemed to stun the assembled whites.[30]

The marchers amassed at the back of the Capitol. Some people scaled trees for a better view, and others packed close to the stage. The police guarded an imaginary line two hundred feet from the building. Some SNCC workers bickered with the Highway Patrol, but the troopers refused to budge. "The governor draws the line, and we've got to keep it," said one. After a woman provoked a confrontation by running up the hill toward the Capitol, SNCC's C. J. Jones saw a trooper load a shell into his shotgun. His protective instinct kicked in. He chased after her. The next thing he knew, he was on the ground. An officer had smacked him across the chin with a gun butt.[31]

The final speeches proved anticlimactic. The back of the Capitol offered neither a majestic backdrop nor symbolic significance. Exhausted marchers baked in the late-afternoon sun, and over time, those on the fringes peeled away. A flatbed truck served as the platform, and the sound system was feeble. Andy Young, the emcee, had to ask television helicopters to hover farther away. ABC broadcast only clips in its weekend news coverage, and NBC ran only two five-minute segments. CBS did a live one-hour special, but it cut away before the final speeches.[32]

Still, there were moments of inspiration and signs of progress. May-belle Smith sang the Negro national anthem, "Lift Every Voice and Sing." Clifton Whitley of the MFDP announced his third-party candidacy for the Senate in November's general election. Whitney Young revealed that the Urban League was establishing a branch in Jackson. Harold DeWolf, Martin Luther King's theology professor at Boston University, had dropped from heatstroke that afternoon, and on the way to the hospital he heard taunts of "We don't need whitey." But he recovered in time to intone before the masses, "O God, father of all mankind, we see spread out before Thee the red and black soil of Mississippi, an altar on which a great burnt offering has been laid."[33]

James Meredith won the loudest cheers. He looked awkward, some-times losing his words and once referring to SNCC's chairman as "Michael Carmichael." But he struck a generous tone, recalling his father's words about white people in Mississippi: "These people can be decent." He had started his walk from Memphis to conquer black fears, and this mass demonstration affirmed his goal. That triumph was the legacy of his march, not media-hyped controversies over black political divisions. "From what you've seen on television and what you have read in the newspapers," he said, "you might assume that I had been shot by a Negro."[34]

Lawrence Guyot of the MFDP thundered that blacks should learn three terms at birth: "One is white supremacy, one is neo-colonialism, and one is Black Power." Alvin Poussaint of the MCHR proclaimed that "the civil rights movement is doing more for the mental health of the Negroes and of all Americans than any other force in this nation." The even-tempered doctor got a little carried away when he called for replac-ing "We Shall Overcome" with "We Shall Overthrow," which earned him a raised-eyebrow smirk from Andy Young.[35]

After Owen Brooks represented the Delta Ministry, Stokely Car-michael stepped to the podium. He refrained from cries of Black Power, but he outlined its principles. "We have to stop being ashamed of being black!" he said. "We have to move to a position where we can feel strength and unity amongst each other from Watts to Harlem, where we won't ever be afraid!" he exclaimed. "And the last thing we have to do is build a power base so strong in this country that it will bring them to their knees every time they mess with us!"[36]

"There's nothing wrong with black power," added Floyd McKissick.

"It's just an adjective inserted before a noun . . . you can call it orange power, green power, or whatever you want. But we want power." He remembered the desperation after Meredith's shooting: How would they organize a massive human rights demonstration that spanned hundreds of miles, surrounded by the threat of racist violence, and with no advance planning? "And so we sent word down the road that these black folk are coming down the line." Local people fed them, housed them, walked with them. The march's significance, he told everyone, "was what you did, what you did."[37]

Finally, Martin Luther King riffed on his iconic "I Have a Dream" speech. At the March on Washington, he had eloquently married American democracy with Christian morality. Three years later, his oration had a darker edge. "I have watched my dreams turn into a nightmare," he mourned. On the march through Mississippi, he met people who barely survived on sporadic wages of two or three dollars a day, and he despaired at such poverty in such a rich nation. Recalling the biblical parable of Dives and Lazarus, he said that it was sinful to ignore a poor man's suffering.[38]

"I still have a dream this afternoon," continued King. This dream outlined his evolving vision: schools will be integrated, "rat-infested slums will be plunged into the junk heaps of history," blacks and whites will live side by side in decent housing, and "the empty stomachs of Mississippi will be filled." Poverty will become a national priority, and Americans will recognize each other as God's children. "This will be a new day. This will be the day of all men living together as brothers. It will not be the day of the white man. It will not be the day of the black man. It will be the day of man, *as* man!"[39]

By six o'clock the rally was over, and so was a civil rights epic. Elizabeth French went home to Virginia, grappling with the march's meaning. "Liberal whites are being faced with a major test of their commitment, of their ability to understand in depth what is happening and why it is happening," she reflected. Mississippi blacks were "proclaiming a declaration of independence from white paternalism," an imperative guided by cultural pride, the necessity of self-defense, the slowness of antipoverty programs, and the hypocrisy of Vietnam. She acknowledged that well-meaning whites might feel shut out. "There is, above all, the wish that we could emphasize a common humanity and forget all about color. But those who deplore the Black Power movement can never argue or ignore it out of existence. It is now a force in our society."[40]

Melvyn Leventhal of the NAACP Legal Defense Fund was more cynical. Upon Stokely Carmichael's speech in Greenwood, he immediately considered Black Power counterproductive. "We lost the upper hand," he said. "The demonstration was no longer about concrete issues of discrimination." In his eyes, the march lacked the cohesiveness of previous mass campaigns, failed to focus on national legislative remedies, and invited a conservative backlash. He left Mississippi feeling detached and listless. "This march was so different than the Selma-to-Montgomery March that it had to signal something: the beginning of the end."[41]

Media postmortems mixed French's generosity with Leventhal's pessimism. Some applauded how the march registered voters and involved local people, and others analyzed the sources of black militancy. Most betrayed ambivalence and anxiety. In one typical assessment, *The Washington Post* portrayed the march as necessary and impressive, especially if Black Power was applied "as the organized political activity of an outraged minority seeking its rights under the law." The same essay warned that black leaders should "recognize that the great social reform so nearly within grasp by lawful action can yet be thwarted and destroyed by lawlessness."[42]

Predictably, James Eastland called it a "flop," an opinion echoed by his fellow Mississippi politicians. Paul Johnson demanded television time on CBS, ABC, and NBC to rebut the Capitol speeches, even though he had refused interview requests from all three networks and a slot on *Face the Nation*. The governor was descending into old-fashioned demagoguery. That summer he called the Meredith March a "wandering minstrel show" and said that Black Power "harbors the seeds of a hurricane of hate and hostility that could sweep sanity aside and introduce an era of anarchy that would represent a real and present danger to the very fabric of society in the United States."[43]

Southern newspapers delighted in conflicts between King and the militants, blamed protesters for provoking whites, and linked the march to Communism. "The sovereign State of Mississippi has survived the ordeal without being intimidated by those who chanted their demands for 'black power' and the destruction of courthouses and the violent overthrow of county governments," editorialized *The Commercial Appeal*.

"The march accomplished nothing of consequence for the self-appointed leaders of the civil rights movement that could not have been accomplished without the hullabaloo." Even moderate white editorialists, such as Hodding Carter III and Hazel Brannon Smith, painted Black Power as dangerous.[44]

Martin Luther King left Jackson on Monday morning, exhausted and disillusioned. He appreciated the surge in voters and spirit, but he mourned the inability to concentrate attention on poverty. He also considered Black Power needlessly divisive. "We've learned a lesson from this march," said SCLC's Bernard Lee. "We can't work with SNCC, or for that matter CORE either." SCLC lieutenants raged at how militants exploited the news cameras following their leader, attacked nonviolence, decried the Canton compromise, and ignored their financial debts.[45]

SNCC faced its own challenges. Charlie Cobb called the march "a stressful time for SNCC, organizationally." Long defined by grass-roots politics, SNCC had to adjust after Stokely Carmichael's compelling articulation of Black Power. "Stokely was SNCC's first charismatic leader, and that radically changed the nature of the organization," said Cobb. To his admirers, Carmichael embodied a new black spirit. To his detractors, he personified rebellion. As a whole, he represented SNCC's uncertain future and Black Power's unsettled meaning.[46]

Late on Sunday night, SNCC held a staff meeting at Tougaloo College. Well past midnight, Carmichael strutted onto the terrace of the Student Union. "I'm going to give you some black power-r-r-r," he laughed, squirting a reporter in the eye with a water pistol. SCLC's Hosea Williams walked toward him. "Black Power!" hooted Carmichael, shooting water at Williams. "My God!" bellowed Williams as he wiped his face dry, "and he's a national civil rights leader!"[47]

Fatigue, jealousy, confusion, and ugliness plagued the civil rights organizations. SCLC, SNCC, and CORE considered future projects in Mississippi, but none established an efficient plan in the march's aftermath. They also bickered over finances. The $1,500 collected in big liquor boxes at the Capitol barely dented the deficit. SCLC paid $14,000 in expenses, and several staffers needed reimbursements for personal credit card payments. Near the Holiday Inn pool on Monday evening, a dispute over march debts among CORE and SNCC workers led to a fistfight, drawing a big crowd and police cruisers.[48]

That same night at Pratt Memorial Methodist Church, SNCC's Bob

Smith argued with Hosea Williams. Four boxes full of contributions, each containing at least $200, had been stolen. Williams vowed that SCLC bore no responsibility. According to the Sovereignty Commission's Informant X, Smith hit Williams, and then four others helped beat up the SCLC leader. An arriving SCLC man shot a gun into the air three times, warning the SNCC workers to stay away from Williams.[49]

The major organizations never again worked together on a mass demonstration. In popular memory the Meredith March won resonance for the rise of Stokely Carmichael, the evolution of Martin Luther King, the bizarre crusade of James Meredith, the alienation of Lyndon Johnson, and the rage of black militants. It was an end and a beginning: the last great march of the civil rights movement, and the birth of Black Power.[50]

But it was also a march of the people, a unique mass phenomenon. The black press championed the marchers' courage, the continuing battle against white supremacy, and the brimming spirit of black Mississippians. Op-ed pieces frowned upon white journalists who hyped Black Power as violent and threatening. "Despite the reaction of much of the press to the March on Mississippi," judged *The Baltimore Afro-American*, "objective historians may well record it as one of the pivotal points of the civil rights movement in this country."[51]

Black people defied Jim Crow's culture of intimidation by marching. Moreover, 4,077 African Americans registered to vote in the counties along the route. Federal examiners registered 1,422, and county clerks performed the rest. Approximately 1,200 registered in Grenada County, where a large crowd had already attended the first meeting of the Grenada County Movement.[52]

For Mississippi activists, the march was another step on a long road. Their freedom struggle started before Medgar Evers, and it continued after Martin Luther King. It had less to do with nonviolence and white consciences than with oppressed people controlling their destiny. Looking back, black veterans of the Mississippi movement praised how the march mobilized voters, with political and cultural effects beyond 1966. Civil rights organizations might have showcased different philosophies, but they shared a larger purpose. Whatever its controversies, the march expressed both the depth of black grievances and the height of black possibilities.[53]

On the march's final day, L. C. Dorsey had found someone to watch her young children—"in case it was a bloodbath." Growing up on a Delta plantation, she had learned lessons about using the back door at white people's homes, calling whites sir and ma'am, and hiding the women when white men came around. She also had strong parents who toiled for her future. Her father walked ten miles to a barbershop for smuggled copies of *The Chicago Defender* and *The Pittsburgh Courier*. He carried a gun in the bottom of his cotton sack, in case some white boss demanded that his children leave school to work the fields.

Dorsey got married at age seventeen and had six children in succession. But she was smart, and she had the movement. In 1964, she registered to vote with a white woman from SNCC by her side. She then attended citizenship workshops and organized voters for the Delta Ministry. She also worked as the manager on a three-hundred-acre plantation, avoiding economic dependence on any man, including her husband. But when the plantation mechanized, she lost her job and moved to Jackson.[54]

During that walk to the Capitol, Dorsey kept thinking about her parents, and she regretted not bringing her children. "It was like a spiritual awakening," she recalled. "There was an energy that I have not felt before or since." She felt so close to her fellow marchers. Her whole body pulsed with awareness: at any moment, hostile whites might attack, and bullets might fly. But there was also a purity, a joy. The feeling reminded her of a mass meeting in a country church or a Mason hall. She might have shared the streets of Jackson with fifteen thousand people, but when those freedom songs rang out, she swore that she heard the individual voices of June Johnson and Hollis Watkins and other heroes of the Mississippi movement.

As they approached the Capitol, the singing faded out. The only sound was the *crunch, crunch, crunch* of all their footsteps. Then the marching stopped. For a moment, it got quiet, as if everyone had hushed all at once—as if even the birds had stopped flying—and there was something so good about that heartbeat of perfect silence.[55]

EPILOGUE: HIGHWAY 51 REVISITED
Hernando to Canton
JUNE 24–JULY 4, 1967

One year after the grand march, James Meredith was back in Mississippi, standing at the spot where Aubrey Norvell shot him. On the morning of June 24, 1967, he was a few miles south of Hernando, on the red clay shoulder of the two-lane highway, under the shade of a big oak tree, decked in sunglasses and a rain hat, passing out mimeographed sheets to reporters. Then he started another walk through Mississippi, following his original path down Highway 51. He invited only men who took responsibility for themselves. "Every man is his own man on this walk," he said.[1]

As Meredith headed south, it evoked scenes from his 1966 trek. He left with four college students, two black and two white, and a number of reporters. Black people greeted him, handed him cups of water, fed him sandwiches, and pressed dollar bills into his hand. Lawrence Guyot drove up and down the route, drumming up support for the MFDP. Some white onlookers jeered, but police discouraged such nastiness around television cameras. A few out-of-state visitors joined in, including two black engineers from the Manned Spacecraft Center in Houston.[2]

According to one white Mississippian, Meredith was "still more hated here than Martin Luther King and Stokely Carmichael all wrapped up together." The Sovereignty Commission relayed that Meredith had bought a bulletproof vest, that the Deacons for Defense had offered protection, and that George Lincoln Rockwell of the American Nazi Party was in Mississippi. It was way too hot for bulletproof vests and the Deacons stayed away, but the police did arrest six Nazi sympathizers, forestalling any trouble.[3]

By this time, Meredith's old attacker was in prison. Aubrey Norvell had emerged from seclusion for a November 1966 court date. Unlike previous trials involving Mississippi's racial crimes, it attracted minimal attention. Norvell sat quietly, wearing a brown suit, smoking, folding and unfolding his hands. After three unsuccessful motions by his attorneys, they surprised everyone by pleading guilty. *Newsweek* reported that local white leaders had urged him to avoid a trial, because the jury might have ruled Norvell innocent, which would have fueled more national outrage. After the trial, one of Norvell's lawyers hinted at a handshake deal with Governor Paul Johnson that reduced his jail time.[4]

Norvell received a five-year sentence for assault and battery with intent to kill, with three years suspended and parole eligibility after eighteen months. Because he pled guilty, prosecutors never learned his motives. "He has given me a reason, but that is in confidence," said attorney Edward Whitten. "He did have a personal reason for what he did. A reason that probably no one has thought of." Norvell left the Mississippi State Penitentiary at Parchman in June 1968. He has never explained why he shot Meredith.[5]

Meredith was pleased that Norvell went to prison, but he cared more about fulfilling his original mission. Three days after resuming his march, Meredith arrived in Grenada, leading a column of men singing freedom songs. One thousand people turned out, the walk's biggest crowd by far. But after Grenada, Meredith's hike never escalated into a big spectacle. There was no horrible shooting, no great outcry. The worst that he suffered were painful blisters; he limped much of the way, often dousing his feet in baby powder or rubbing alcohol.[6]

On July 4, Meredith arrived at his final destination of Canton. He had about fifteen followers, and a few more joined the walk into town. The courthouse square was practically empty, a naked contrast to the events of 1966. He shook a few hands, then sat on steps at the edge of the courthouse lawn. "We made it," he said.[7]

Meredith had failed to inspire the masses along Highway 51, which disappointed him. Yet he had compelled good protection from local law enforcement, which recognized his citizenship. He also proved something to himself. "This spot marks the completion of the 220 miles

I started over a year ago," he said. Indeed, in three trips over thirteen months, he fulfilled his promise to walk Highway 51 from Memphis to Jackson. "I had to continue," he said, "to be sure that I was not afraid."[8]

The immediate legacy of the Meredith March was a raging controversy over Black Power. "No matter how they try to explain it, the term 'black power' means anti-white power," proclaimed Roy Wilkins in July 1966. "It is a reverse Mississippi, a reverse Hitler, a reverse Ku Klux Klan." At the NAACP's annual convention in Los Angeles, he attacked the March Against Fear. Instead of exploiting Meredith's shooting for the Civil Rights Bill, said Wilkins, SNCC and CORE advocated black separatism and invited white violence: "'Black power' in the quick, uncritical, and highly emotional adoption it has received from some segments of a beleaguered people can mean in the end only black death."[9]

Whitney Young expressed similar frustrations: "The National Urban League does not intend to invent slogans, however appealing they may be to the press." The hubbub over Black Power diverted attention from the problems of jobs, housing, and education. He wanted "full equality in a pluralistic society," not "the shadow power of self-segregated black reservations."[10]

Loyalists of the black establishment—newspaper editorialists, college professors, prominent ministers—echoed Wilkins and Young. Thurgood Marshall called Black Power "Jim Crow thinking." Carl Rowan's article in *Ebony* had the subtitle, "Isolation is a trap; 'black power' is a phony cry, a plain old-fashioned hoax." That October, Wilkins, Young, A. Philip Randolph, Bayard Rustin, and three others bought a full-page *New York Times* advertisement that reaffirmed ideals of integration, nonviolence, and the democratic process. It never mentioned Black Power, but it obviously repudiated the slogan.[11]

The facade of black political unity was melting. After the Meredith March, Randolph and Rustin considered calling an all-black, closed-door conference, but they failed to bring the leaders together. Elijah Muhammad of the Nation of Islam tried arranging a similar meeting, also without success.[12]

Hyped by the mainstream media, Black Power seemed inherently threatening. "Freedom Road has taken a disconcerting turn," fretted *News-*

week. Newspaper editorials ripped SNCC and CORE. *The New York Times* published the entire, earlier position paper of SNCC's separatist Vine City Project, labeling it a blueprint for Black Power.[13]

The press also highlighted declining contributions to CORE, SNCC, and even SCLC; waning interest in civil rights on college campuses; racial unease among northern whites; and denunciations of Black Power from prominent liberals such as Hubert Humphrey and Robert F. Kennedy. Was the civil rights movement dead? As historian C. Vann Woodward mused, "Who can quite imagine now another March on Washington, another Selma, another joint session of Congress rising to give a standing ovation to a President who intoned, 'We shall overcome,' or the same President or another one intoning it again?"[14]

Alongside "Black Power," the new buzzword was "backlash." Polls revealed a surging white resentment of street demonstrations, civil rights laws, and black radicals. Urban violence widened the racial chasm: that summer, police clashed with black protesters in Los Angeles, Atlanta, and Providence, while blacks rioted in Baltimore, Philadelphia, and Minneapolis. William F. Buckley, Jr., demanded a moratorium on demonstrations and legislation. George Wallace contemplated a presidential run. Richard Nixon helped position himself for one of the great comebacks in American political history by avoiding race and calling for law, order, and respect—contrasting himself with liberals who coddled wild-eyed militants, lazy welfare recipients, and bloodthirsty rioters.[15]

The Civil Rights Bill of 1966—considered a fait accompli upon the shooting of James Meredith—never passed. After a watered-down version emerged from the House, the bill died in the Senate. During the November midterm elections, Republicans won key Senate seats. Ronald Reagan became the new governor of California.[16]

Lyndon Johnson eschewed his typical congressional bull-wrangling during the debate over the Civil Rights Bill. Black Power and ghetto violence eroded the liberal consensus, while Vietnam and the white backlash threatened his legacy. Out of some combination of personal sensitivity and political calculation, the president grew only more alienated from the civil rights movement.[17]

While Roy Wilkins savaged Black Power at the NAACP meeting, Floyd McKissick championed it at the CORE convention. In Baltimore, the delegates adopted resolutions opposing the Vietnam War, and they advocated bloc voting in majority-black communities. Martin Luther King had planned to speak, but he withdrew after SCLC advisers objected that radicals would exploit his popularity, just as on the Meredith March. Stokely Carmichael took his place.[18]

"This is the Congress for Racial Superiority," shuddered a white nun as the convention hall echoed with chants of Black Power. Author Lillian Smith resigned after nine years on the advisory committee. Critics attacked CORE for scaring off white allies, while *Time* and *Newsweek* painted the proceedings as chaotic and extremist.[19]

McKissick responded with frustrated fury. Blacks got press coverage only for disagreeing with other blacks or for uttering provocative statements. The debate over Black Power, he charged, had been "twisted by knaves to make a trap for fools." During a sweaty press conference in the basement of a Harlem YMCA, he combined radicalism with pragmatism. "Black Power is no mere slogan," he stated. "It is a movement dedicated to the exercise of American democracy in its highest tradition; it is a drive to mobilize the Black communities of this country in a monumental effort to remove the basic causes of alienation, frustration, despair, low self-esteem and hopelessness." He soon outlined a Black Power program rooted in consumer boycotts, third-party politics, proud black identities, vigorous enforcement of federal laws, an end to police brutality, and energetic black leadership.[20]

As McKissick illustrated, fire-breathing provocateurs had no monopoly on Black Power. Black newspapers, letters to *The New York Times*, and civil rights workers all panned the mainstream media for exaggerating Black Power as violent and hateful. The philosophy had positive, reaffirming qualities—even if white America could not comprehend them. And while many NAACP members cheered Wilkins's speech, others wrote him angry letters, including a ninety-six-year-old minister who exclaimed that "'Black Power' means self-determination, self-respect, and self-protection for black people—nothing else!" For its proponents, the slogan captured the soul of black people, paving a concrete path toward real democracy and total humanity.[21]

In time, Black Power adopted many guises. It found cultural expressions in soul music, street style, works of art, and religious thought. Black Studies programs arose on college campuses, and the "Revolt of the Black Athlete" rocked the sports world. Cultural nationalists such as

Ron Karenga emphasized African traditions and heritage, while revolutionary nationalists such as the Black Panthers employed Marxist-
Leninist ideology. If Black Power meant the political mobilization of
black communities, then it helped shape electoral politics, as well, as
evidenced by the 1967 victories of black candidates for mayor in Gary
and Cleveland.[22]

Whitney Young urged interracial coalitions, though he recognized
the changing landscape. The Urban League announced a "New Thrust"
to build economic and political power in black ghettoes. As Young admitted in 1969, Black Power was the language of his people. Instead of
condemning it, he would "reinterpret it, redefine it, sanitize it a bit if
you will, and give it a positive connotation."[23]

McKissick followed another of Black Power's winding trails. In 1968
he left an unraveling CORE and founded McKissick Enterprises, which
promoted black economic development. Upon the election of Richard
Nixon, McKissick allied with the Republican Party. He had long held a
vision for Soul City, a new all-black town in eastern North Carolina.
With federal backing, his project broke ground in November 1973. The
feat required compromises, though, such as courting white residents.
Moreover, Soul City failed to recruit enough industrial development. As
the state Republican Party drove off its moderates, politicians on the
right blasted it as a boondoggle. Soul City lost federal funding in 1979. It
had stood at the intersection of Black Power and liberalism, and it crumbled amid a rising conservatism.[24]

The Meredith March catapulted Stokely Carmichael into celebrity. He
was a lightning rod for both admiration and fear, a human symbol of
Black Power. After the march, he embarked upon a national speaking
tour. He urged blacks to control their own destiny, because appeals to
white consciences sapped blacks of confidence and control: "Every
white man in this country can announce that he is 'our friend.' Well,
from now on we are going to pick our own friends. We're going to decide whether a white man can be our friend or not. We don't want to
hear any more words; we want to see what they are going to do. The
price of being the black man's friend has gone up."[25]

Carmichael exuded coolness. In northern cities he favored crisp suits and dark glasses, looking the part of the modern philosopher-activist. At political rallies and college forums, he sprinkled drops of humor onto spiky indictments of Vietnam and the ghetto. He danced on a rhetorical tightrope: venting black frustrations and aspirations, neither celebrating violence nor blaming rioters, always delivering an emotional release. While stimulating the thinking of receptive whites, he tailored his ideas to black people.[26]

In speeches, interviews, press releases, essays, and a coauthored book with political scientist Charles Hamilton, Carmichael demanded that blacks abandon coalition politics in favor of all-black organizations, quit begging whites for good treatment, and focus more on structural inequities than on racial integration. If the United States was fundamentally racist, only black people could address black concerns. He chafed when Black Power was interpreted in terms of antiwhite violence, but his own words enabled that interpretation: "When you talk of 'black power,' you talk of bringing this country to its knees. When you talk of 'black power,' you talk of building a movement that will smash everything Western civilization has created."[27]

Carmichael thus served as a bull's-eye for the backlash. After a riot in Atlanta in September 1966, critics blamed his incendiary leadership. Southern politicians trumpeted his emerging association with third world Communism, highlighted by journeys to Havana and Hanoi. Liberals painted him as a destructive revolutionary. The FBI amassed bulging security files on SNCC and its leader.[28]

Carmichael's stardom pulled attention away from SNCC's grass-roots organizing. "There is no SNCC," lamented one staffer, "there is only a Stokely Carmichael with a group of followers behind him." Central Committee members complained about the new direction, and Lowndes County activists asked for more help, but SNCC frayed apart. An aborted stunt to picket the wedding of President Johnson's daughter Luci diminished its stature. Contributions dried up, replaced by letters from liberals who judged Black Power as naive, inconsiderate, or disgusting. In December 1966, SNCC expelled its few remaining whites.[29]

"Yeah, SNCC worked for Black Power, and Black Power killed SNCC," ruminated Carmichael. The organization collapsed in a storm of disputes, rivalries, and negativism. "As the chairman of SNCC, I tried to educate the masses, to add fuel for the urban rebellion, to encourage a new way of thinking. But there was no organization capable of meeting the challenge." In the year after the march through Mississippi, "it became clear that SNCC had run its course."[30]

After an ill-fated alliance with the Black Panther Party and a short-lived stint in Washington, D.C., Carmichael moved to Africa. He soaked up lessons from Guinean president Sékou Touré and deposed Ghanaian leader Kwame Nkrumah, shaping his own ideology of pan-African socialism. (In 1981, he honored his two mentors by changing his name to Kwame Ture.) The government surveillance and media manipulations sometimes wore him down, and he occasionally revealed his tendencies for rhetorical bombast and repetitive dogma. Before he died of cancer in 1998, he got gray and tired, but he still emitted that baritone laugh, and his eyes still danced with electric energy. His intelligence, creativity, and charisma had inspired a generation of activists.[31]

Martin Luther King sought a middle ground. He worried that Black Power alienated the mainstream, and he considered it somewhat nihilistic. He never used the slogan. Yet he insisted that "the allure of 'Black power' in its extremist or moderate sense stems from real, not imaginary causes. It is a mood of millions of Negroes, tormented and frustrated with broken promises." King endorsed a Marshall Plan for the ghetto, a massive government investment to combat slums and poverty. Nonviolent demonstrations, he believed, could still dramatize radical agendas while capturing liberal consciences.[32]

But the middle ground was crumbling. Political forces buffeted King from all sides. Radicals blasted his moderation, while skeptical advisers urged him to attack Carmichael. Yet he refused to demonize the Black Power apostles, even if he endorsed the integrationist principles of leaders like Roy Wilkins. His greater concern was the election of reactionary governors, the frustrated rage within the inner city, the hunger of poor children.[33]

SCLC's summer campaign in Chicago highlighted the barricades before the Promised Land. Thirty thousand people sweated through a July 10 gathering at Soldier Field, culminating with a march to City Hall, where King posted thirty-two demands to create an "Open City." Yet Chicago's freedom movement suffered from the manipulations of a well-oiled political machine run by Mayor Richard J. Daley, who, in private conversations with Lyndon Johnson, maligned King as a disloyal troublemaker.[34]

Throughout the summer, King received letters from white Chicagoans who claimed to support racial equality, but who labeled blacks as shiftless, dirty, and immoral. "Tell them to educate themselves, not to gamble too much, not to act like animals, not to be so loud," wrote one person. "Tell them to act more civilized. Get ambitious. Save money. And not be lazy." They further blamed King for rabble-rousing among the ignorant masses.[35]

King expected naked bigotry in Mississippi, but not Chicago. During SCLC demonstrations, onlookers yelled "Nigger!" and "Hate!" and "White Power!" On a march through Marquette Park, a mob waved Confederate flags, brandished swastikas, and screamed "Nigger go home!" King got hit by a rock. He had experienced real fear in Philadelphia during the Meredith March, but in Marquette Park, he recalled, "I faced the inevitability of death for the first time." He had planned a march into the notorious all-white suburb of Cicero, but feared that racists would massacre his flock. He negotiated a weak compromise that ended direct action protests. SNCC and CORE workers branded him a sellout.[36]

That November, at an SCLC retreat in Frogmore, South Carolina, King used the metaphor of a "freedom flight," celebrating the "marvelous tail winds" that had propelled racial justice: the ethical purity, interracial spirit, and governmental backing compelled by nonviolent direct action. Then, "we ran into unexpected turbulence." Black Power might have been shortsighted and suspect, but it also expressed a genuine pain. "We have a long, hard struggle," he warned, "and we must honestly let the people know how difficult it is."[37]

King reckoned with the nation's fundamental flaws. He grew more explicit and public in his denunciations of the Vietnam War. He kept addressing the poverty of the urban North, annoying the big-city mayors who once hailed him as a hero. He sought transformative solutions for poverty: not only a government-sponsored full-employment plan, but also a "revolution of values" to reset the nation's moral compass. Guided by conscience, he tacked into the political winds, sailing forward as a true American prophet.[38]

His journey returned him to the scenes of the March Against Fear. In March 1968, SCLC was recruiting volunteers for the Poor People's

Campaign, a mass caravan to Washington, D.C., that would demand government solutions to poverty. In the Mississippi Delta town of Marks, where he had once preached the funeral of Armistead Phipps, King now cried at the sight of starving schoolchildren. He resolved that a train of mule carts would leave from Marks for the nation's capital. During this same period, King had been supporting a sanitation workers' strike in Memphis. Ignoring his advisers' practical warnings, he embraced the poor workers' struggle for dignity. On April 4, 1968, he stood on the balcony of the Lorraine Motel, where he had presided over the feisty planning meetings for the Meredith March. Then a gunshot rang out, and he never marched again.[39]

A mule train left from Marks in the aftermath of King's assassination. As it passed through Mississippi, it confronted an evolving political landscape. For all the local impact of the March Against Fear, it claimed few pure triumphs. In Grenada, for instance, SCLC workers and local blacks initiated boycotts, sit-ins, and night marches to win the concessions promised during the march. Once the cameras and reporters moved on, however, white authorities resisted their demands. Police teargassed and billy-clubbed demonstrators, and hostile whites tossed bricks and fire-crackers at nonviolent blacks.[40]

That September, a mob wielding ax handles and clubs attacked black children after their first day in an integrated classroom. Some white men shoved a girl to the ground, threatened to shoot her, and hit her legs with a metal pipe. She was eleven. And she had polio. Like the Canton tear gas attack, the Grenada violence should have inspired a national uproar. Like Canton, it compelled only token liberal outrage. The White House virtually ignored it.[41]

In Canton, the blackout, or economic boycott of white-owned businesses, continued through the summer of 1966, accompanied by Saturday protest marches. But relations between police and activists kept deteriorating, while conflicts festered between Black Power acolytes and middle-class types. In both Grenada and Canton, the local movements suffered from brutal repression and internal exhaustion.[42]

After the March Against Fear, organizers returned to their local projects, discussing the meaning of Black Power. The MFDP referenced the catchphrase while promoting its brand of popular democracy. "For the first time in 90 years, Black people are seeking power in Mississippi," proclaimed a 1967 pamphlet for black candidates. Mississippi blacks might have eschewed Stokely Carmichael's militant style, but their world was divided into black and white. By early 1967 the MFDP had virtually no whites. Black Power, said MacArthur Cotton, "was the only agenda we could have at the time."[43]

White organizers generally accepted these developments. They had long aspired to develop black leaders, tilt the local political balance, and foster black pride. Black Power carried that agenda forward—but without them. After the Meredith March, many white activists left Mississippi. They saw their projects decline, which stirred regret, but acknowledged that local people had to control their own destinies. Many adapted their civil rights experiences to other movements such as protesting the Vietnam War, organizing for unions, or fighting for women's rights.[44]

Running as third-party independents in the 1967 elections, the MFDP achieved a milestone when Robert Clark of Holmes County became the first African American congressman from Mississippi since Reconstruction. But most of the twenty-two black victors in the 1967 elections hailed from the southwestern counties, where Charles Evers presided over his political machine. By 1968, the MFDP had opted for a practical, if unlikely, partnership with the NAACP; Lawrence Guyot even managed Evers's campaign for governor. The alliance nurtured some gains, but the old movement spirit faded away.[45]

Other developments, too, signaled both headway and retreat. By late 1966, federal antipoverty funding went through Mississippi Action for Progress (MAP), which had an integrated leadership of NAACP officials and white moderates. The OEO stopped funding the grass-roots CDGM, which was tied to MFDP, SNCC, and Black Power. Among CDGM's abuses, charged Senator John Stennis, was using federal resources to feed and transport the Meredith Marchers.[46]

Over time, the walls of Jim Crow eroded, but the fortress of white privilege stood its ground. More whites sent their children to all-white private schools or public schools with token integration. The increasingly conservative, increasingly dominant Republican Party made little effort to court black votes. Mississippi still has the nation's highest rates of poverty and infant mortality, with a disproportionate impact on its black population. Both locally and nationally, the civil rights movement empowered African Americans with constitutional rights and new self-definitions. But there is a longer road to freedom, and it still must be walked.[47]

James Meredith walked his own path. Before the march, his notoriety had diminished. After the march, he was on the cover of *The Saturday Evening Post*, which published his first-person account of the trek through Mississippi. A company agreed to market the "James Meredith Freedom Cane" and the "James Meredith Freedom Hat." MFDP officials contemplated running him for governor. He spoke at huge freedom rallies in Chicago, Philadelphia, and Los Angeles. "Starting with the Mississippi March, the Negro Movement is on the move and nothing is going to stop it," he proclaimed. "I plan to be a part of that movement." He envisioned starting a corporation, calling an "All Minority Conference," and leading a liberation army to combat white supremacy in Rhodesia and South-West Africa.[48]

There was no one else like Meredith. He made outlandishly ambitious statements, but he embodied self-reliance. He supported the Vietnam War, but he had no relationship with the White House. He criticized integration and nonviolence, but he was no Black Power radical. His independence touched a chord in Black America.

In August 1966, a special ninety-minute *Meet the Press* assessed the civil rights movement. NBC invited Wilkins, Young, King, McKissick, and Carmichael, who represented the "Big Five" organizations. The network also invited Meredith, who represented only himself. "Mr. Meredith, you have been described as a loner, as a man with no organization and no clearcut philosophy," said Carl Rowan. With whom did he align himself? "The group with which I most closely associate myself," responded Meredith, "is the Negro."[49]

"He is a loner. He has charm. His appeal is almost innocently demagogic," marveled one writer. "He talks self-help, political pressure, alienation, accommodation, all at once." He exhibited deep faith in his own powers, his own mission, his own importance. "In a way, Meredith is the Bobby Kennedy of the civil rights movement."[50]

But Meredith frittered away his political capital. In March 1967, he announced his candidacy as a Republican against Adam Clayton Powell, the legendary twelve-term Democratic congressman from Harlem. He

believed that Powell's monopoly on the seat turned black voters into political tokens. Yet blacks mostly resented that the House of Representatives refused to seat Powell while investigating his financial improprieties.
Meredith looked like not only a guaranteed loser, but also a race traitor.
Constance Baker Motley begged him to reconsider. Claude Brown called
him "an ass, an absolute ass." In Harlem, rumors circulated of Meredith's impending assassination.[51]

On March 12, Floyd McKissick and Charles Evers advised Meredith
to quit the campaign. "Adam Powell is a bastard, but he's our bastard,"
said Evers. "Don't sacrifice all that you have suffered and fought for. The
Negroes in Harlem hate you." Meredith cried with anguish. Late that
night, he issued a terse statement of withdrawal. Harlem's rumor mills
now churned that he dropped out for a bribe, or because he feared for
his life.[52]

Meredith's intertwining penchants for self-determination, self-
importance, and self-promotion cast him down a bizarre path. He endorsed the 1967 gubernatorial campaign of Ross Barnett, his foil during
the Battle of Ole Miss, and supported Richard Nixon in 1968. He endured terrible publicity for business failures, a bankruptcy declaration,
and the harassment of tenants in a Bronx apartment building that he
owned. After moving back to Mississippi in 1971, he opened a small
nightclub and dealt Amway products. He ran as a Republican for the Senate in 1972, won as a Democrat in a 1974 House primary, and then withdrew to campaign as an independent in the general election (the State
Supreme Court prohibited the maneuver).[53]

Meredith always claimed to be "the elitist of elites," a type of messiah. In a 1973 *Ebony* article, he compared himself to Jesus Christ. As
his status waned, he aligned himself with far-right conservatism. In the
late 1980s, he joined the staff of North Carolina senator Jesse Helms. In
the early 1990s, he stumped for Louisiana state representative David
Duke, a former leader of the Ku Klux Klan.[54]

Still, he walks. Since the March Against Fear, Meredith has kept staging long and lonely treks, for causes both specific and esoteric. He once
walked through New York City "to expose the city to itself, all the contradictions, hypocrisies, and contrasts." In 1969 he completed an amaz-
ing thousand-mile journey from Evanston, Illinois, to New York City to
inspire black community organization. In 1974, he hiked from Jackson
to Vicksburg, maintaining that if he could walk that far, then other

blacks could register at the courthouse. By the 1990s, he was walking to promote public libraries, emphasize education, and encourage blacks to speak standard English. On June 4, 1996, he again left Memphis on Highway 51. He called it a March Against Illiteracy. Despite recent surgery for prostate cancer, he reached Jackson by July 4, covering the familiar ground of thirty years earlier.[55]

James Meredith may fit no classic definition of a civil rights icon. His mind may be askew. Certainly, his extraordinary trials scarred him—on his scalp and neck, he still has hard, tiny lumps of embedded bird shot. Yet it took Meredith's singular audacity to integrate Ole Miss and to start the March Against Fear. He remains his own man, following his own course, walking down a Mississippi road.[56]

NOTES

Abbreviations in the Notes

AMP	Amzie Moore Papers; Wisconsin Historical Society, Madison
APRP	Papers of A. Philip Randolph; microfilm collection, accessed at University of Memphis
APWR	Americans for the Preservation of the White Race, Jackson, MS Chapter, Collection; Department of Archives and Special Collections, University of Mississippi, Oxford
ARC	Anne Romaine Collection; King Library and Archive, Atlanta
BGRC	Betty Garman Robinson Collection; Schomburg Center for Research in Black Culture, New York City
BRP	Bayard Rustin Papers; microfilm collection, accessed via interlibrary loan
CCC	Citizens' Council Collection; Department of Archives and Special Collections, University of Mississippi, Oxford
CDGM	Child Development Group of Mississippi Collection; Schomburg Center for Research in Black Culture, New York City
CORE	Papers of the Congress of Racial Equality; microfilm collection, accessed at University of Memphis
CORE-A	Papers of the Congress of Racial Equality—Addendum; microfilm collection, accessed at University of Memphis
CRJA	Civil Rights during the Johnson Administration; microform collection, accessed at University of Memphis
CRM-VET	Documents and Interviews, Civil Rights Movement Veterans Website; www.crmvet.org
DDPJ	Daily Diary of President Johnson, 1963–1969; microfilm collection, accessed at University of Memphis

DLC	Debbie Louis Collection on Civil Rights, 1949–1971; Special Collections, Charles E. Young Research Library, University of California, Los Angeles
DMR	Records of the Delta Ministry; King Library and Archive, Atlanta
DVHC	Densho Visual History Collection; Densho Digital Archive, www .densho.org/archive
EHP	Eugene Hunn Papers; Wisconsin Historical Society, Madison
EPI	Eyes on the Prize Interviews; Washington University Digital Gateway, www.digital.wustl.edu/e/eyes
FBI-RR	Federal Bureau of Investigation Electronic Reading Room; www.fbi .gov/foia/fbi-headquarters-reading-room
FBI-SNCC	FBI File on the Student Nonviolent Coordinating Committee; microfilm collection, accessed via interlibrary loan
FBMP	Floyd B. McKissick Papers; Southern Historical Collection, University of North Carolina, Chapel Hill
FLHP	Fannie Lou Hamer Papers; microfilm collection, accessed via interlibrary loan
HBWCP	Hodding II and Betty Werlein Carter Papers; Special Collections, Mississippi State University, Starkville
HJP	Homer A. Jack Papers; Swarthmore College Peace Collection, Swarthmore, Pennsylvania
HTD	Harriet Tanzman Documents; Wisconsin Historical Society, Madison
HWC	Hosea Williams Collection; Auburn Avenue Research Library, Atlanta
JBP	Jacqueline Bernard Papers; Wisconsin Historical Society, Madison
JFP	Jake Friesen Papers; Wisconsin Historical Society, Madison
JFPP	Jo Freeman Personal Papers; selected documents in author's possession
JHMC	James Howard Meredith Collection; Department of Archives and Special Collections, University of Mississippi, Oxford
JOEC	James O. Eastland Collection; Department of Archives and Special Collections, University of Mississippi, Oxford
JWCRC	Jill Wakeman Civil Rights Collection, 1964–1968; McCain Library and Archives, University of Southern Mississippi, Hattiesburg
KKK	Ku Klux Klan Collection; Department of Archives and Special Collections, University of Mississippi, Oxford
LBJ	Lyndon Baines Johnson Library; University of Texas, Austin
LBJ-MS	Office Files of Mildred Stegall; Lyndon Baines Johnson Library, University of Texas, Austin
LBJ-RT	Recordings and Transcripts of Telephone Conversations and Meetings; Lyndon Baines Johnson Library, University of Texas, Austin
LFCRC	Leesha Faulkner Civil Rights Collection; McCain Library and Archives, University of Southern Mississippi, Hattiesburg
MCHR	Medical Committee for Human Rights Records; Schomburg Center for Research in Black Culture, New York City
MDAH	Archival Reading Room, Mississippi Department of Archives and History, Jackson

MFDP	Mississippi Freedom Democratic Papers; Wisconsin Historical Society, Madison
MFDP-LC	Mississippi Freedom Democratic Papers–Lauderdale County; microfilm collection, accessed at Wisconsin Historical Society, Madison
MLK-FBI	The Martin Luther King, Jr., FBI File; microfilm collection, accessed at University of Memphis
MLKP	Papers of Martin Luther King; King Library and Archive, Atlanta
MMP	Honorable Michael A. Musmanno Papers; Duquesne University Special Collections, Pittsburgh
MS-NAACP	Maxine A. Smith NAACP Collection; Memphis/Shelby County Public Library, Memphis
MSSC	Mississippi State Sovereignty Commission Collection; mdah.state .ms.us/arrec/digital_archives/sovcom
MSU	Special Collections, Mississippi State University, Hattiesburg
NAACP	National Association for the Advancement of Colored People Collection; Library of Congress, Washington, D.C.
NAACP-B	Branch Papers of the NAACP; microfilm collection, accessed via interlibrary loan
NCCIJ	National Catholic Conference for Interracial Justice Records; Marquette University, Milwaukee
NSM	Northern Student Movement Records; Schomburg Center for Research in Black Culture, New York City
NULP	National Urban League Papers; Library of Congress, Washington, D.C.
OHC-MC	Oral History Collection, Madison County-Canton Public Library, Canton, Mississippi
OHJA	Oral Histories of the Johnson Administration; microform collection, accessed at University of Memphis
PBJFP	Paul B. Johnson Family Papers; McCain Library and Archives, University of Southern Mississippi, Hattiesburg
PCM	Paley Center for Media, New York City
RBP	Robert Beech Papers; Wisconsin Historical Society, Madison
RRC	Race Relations Collection; Department of Archives and Special Collections, University of Mississippi, Oxford
RWP	Roy Wilkins Papers; Library of Congress, Washington, D.C.
SCLC	Records of the Southern Christian Leadership Conference; microfilm collection, accessed at University of Memphis
SC-LDS	Stokely Carmichael–Lorna D. Smith Collection; Special Collections and University Archives, Stanford University, Palo Alto
SCRBC	Schomburg Center for Research in Black Culture, New York City
SCRLR	Southern Civil Rights Litigation Records, 1960s; microfilm collection, accessed via interlibrary loan
SNCC	Papers of the Student Nonviolent Coordinating Committee; microfilm collection, accessed via interlibrary loan

SNCC-AR   SNCC Arkansas Project Records; Wisconsin Historical Society, Madison
SRC   Southern Regional Council Papers; microfilm collection, accessed via interlibrary loan
SRTR   Sherwood Ross Tape Recordings; selected recordings in author's possession
SSC   Sanitation Strike Collection; Special Collections, University of Memphis
TBP   Taylor Branch Papers; Southern Historical Collection, University of North Carolina, Chapel Hill
TCSC   Tougaloo College Special Collections, Tougaloo, Mississippi
UMASC   University of Mississippi Archives and Special Collections, Oxford
USM   University of Southern Mississippi, Special Collections, Hattiesburg
USM-COH   University of Southern Mississippi, Center for Oral History and Cultural Heritage, www.usm.edu/oralhistory/collections.php
USM-CRM   University of Southern Mississippi, Civil Rights in Mississippi, www.lib.usm.edu/~spcol/crda
VGA   Victoria Gray Adams Papers; McCain Library and Archives, University of Southern Mississippi, Hattiesburg
WCBUT   "Will the Circle Be Unbroken?" Transcripts; Manuscript, Archives, and Rare Book Library, Emory University, Atlanta
WFMP   Wilson F. Minor Papers; Special Collections, Mississippi State University, Starkville
WHCF-HU   White House Central Files, Human Rights; Lyndon Baines Johnson Library, University of Texas, Austin
WHCOF   White House Confidential Files; Lyndon Baines Johnson Library, University of Texas, Austin
WHS   Wisconsin Historical Society, Madison
WLBT   WLBT Newsfilm Collection; Mississippi Department of Archives and History, Jackson
WWP   William Winfield Papers; Wisconsin Historical Society, Madison
WYP   Whitney Young Papers; Rare Book and Manuscript Library, Columbia University, New York

Prologue: A New Day

1. Harry McPherson to Lyndon Johnson, 12 May 1966, Part 1, Reel 12, CRJA.
2. Roy Wilkins, "The Civil Rights Bill of 1966," *Crisis*, June–July 1966, 302–306, 330; Kevin L. Yuill, "The 1966 White House Conference on Civil Rights," *The Historical Journal* 41, no. 1 (1998): 259–82; *The Courier-Journal* (Louisville), 3 June 1966; *Los Angeles Times*, 9 June 1966; Memorandum for the President, 24 August 1966, Part 1, Reel 6, CRJA.
3. On the nation's black political spectrum and racial mood see John K. Jessup, "An Urgent New Reach to Be Equal," *Life*, 3 June 1966, 88–101; Russell Sackett, "Plotting a War on 'Whitey,'" *Life*, 10 June 1966, 100–12.

4. Richard H. Rovere, "Letter from Washington," *The New Yorker*, 18 June 1966, 143.

5. *The New York Times*, 1 June 1966.

6. *The New York Times*, 2 June 1966, 3 June 1966; Ben Heineman interview, Part 3, Reel 2, CRJA.

7. *The New York Times*, 3 June 1966.

8. *The New York Times*, 3 June 1966, 5 June 1966; *The Commercial Appeal* (Memphis), 7 June 1966; *The Philadelphia Inquirer*, 2 June 1966; *Los Angeles Times*, 7 June 1966; *The Washington Post*, 3 June 1966, 6 June 1966; Yuill, "The 1966 White House Conference on Civil Rights," 278–79; David C. Carter, *The Music Has Gone Out of the Movement: Civil Rights and the Johnson Administration, 1965–1968* (Chapel Hill: University of North Carolina Press, 2009), 93–97; FBI memorandum, 3 June 1966, Box 71B, Folder 3, LBJ-MS.

9. Press Statement, 24 May 1966, Reel 3, SNCC.

10. *The Washington Star*, 1 June 1966; *The Clarion-Ledger* (Jackson), 27 May 1966; *The Citizen-News* (Hollywood, Calif.), 6 June 1966; *The Atlanta Constitution*, 2 June 1966.

11. "Thinking Big," *Time*, 27 May 1966, 22; Stokely Carmichael with Ekwueme Michael Thelwell, *Ready for Revolution: The Life and Struggles of Stokely Carmichael (Kwame Ture)* (New York: Scribner, 2003), 486–88; "Is Integration Irrelevant?," *The New Republic*, 4 June 1966, 7.

12. *The Washington Post*, 3 June 1966, 7 June 1966; *The New York Times*, 3 June 1966; Ben Heineman interview, Part 3, Reel 2, CRJA.

13. *The New York Times*, 2 June 1966.

14. *The Washington Post*, 7 June 1966; FBI memorandum, 3 June 1966, Part 1, Reel 10, MLK-FBI.

15. See Carter, *The Music Has Gone Out of the Movement*, 91–92; David J. Garrow, *Bearing the Cross: Martin Luther King, Jr., and the Southern Christian Leadership Conference* (New York: Morrow, 1986), 473; Taylor Branch, *At Canaan's Edge: America in the King Years 1965–68* (New York: Simon and Schuster, 2006), 472–73. On King see also Taylor Branch, *Parting the Waters: America in the King Years 1954–63* (New York: Simon and Schuster, 1988); Taylor Branch, *Pillar of Fire: America in the King Years 1963–65* (New York: Simon and Schuster, 1998); Adam Fairclough, *To Redeem the Soul of America: The Southern Christian Leadership Conference and Martin Luther King, Jr.* (Athens: University of Georgia Press, 2001); David Levering Lewis, *King: A Biography*, 2nd ed. (Urbana: University of Illinois Press, 1978; original 1970); Stephen B. Oates, *Let the Trumpet Sound: A Life of Martin Luther King, Jr.* (New York: HarperPerennial, 1994; original 1982); Stewart Burns, *To the Mountaintop: Martin Luther King's Mission to Save America, 1955–1968* (San Francisco: HarperSanFrancisco, 2004); Harvard Sitkoff, *King: Pilgrimage to the Mountaintop* (New York: Hill and Wang, 2008); Thomas F. Jackson, *From Civil Rights to Human Rights: Martin Luther King, Jr., and the Struggle for Economic Justice* (Philadelphia: University of Pennsylvania Press, 2007).

16. Martin Luther King, Jr., "Behind the Selma March," *Saturday Review*, 3 April 1965, 16–17, 57; Martin Luther King, "Nonviolence: The Only Road to Freedom,"

Ebony, October 1966, 27–34. See also Eric J. Sundquist, *King's Dream* (New Haven: Yale University Press, 2009), 43–44.

17. "Leaders Laughed at Meredith When He Bared Miss. March Plans," *Jet*, 23 June 1966, 26–27.

18. *The New York Times*, 1 June 1966; "Statement—My Walk from Memphis to Jackson," 31 May 1966, Box 14, Folder 2, JHMC.

19. Tape Recording by Sherwood Ross, copy in author's possession; "Statement—My Walk from Memphis to Jackson," 31 May 1966, Box 14, Folder 2, JHMC.

20. "Leaders Laughed at Meredith When He Bared Miss. March Plans," 26.

21. Sherwood Ross, interview by author, telephone, 27 January 2010.

1. The Bible and the Gun

1. David Cohn, *Where I Was Born and Raised* (Cambridge, Mass.: Riverside, 1948), 12–14.

2. James Meredith to James Silver, 15 January 1966, Box 10, Folder 2, James W. Silver Collection, UMASC; *The Washington Star*, 7 June 1966.

3. Sherwood Ross, interview by author; *The New York Times*, 6 June 1966.

4. Robert Palmer, *Deep Blues* (New York: Penguin, 1982), 122–23, 225–31; Sherwood Ross, interview by author; Maxine Smith, interview by author, Memphis, 22 August 2011; *The Washington Star*, 7 June 1966; NAACP Press Release, 11 June 1966, Group IV, Box A56, Folder "Meredith, James 1966," NAACP; *The Sun* (Baltimore), 6 June 1966.

5. Robert Weeks, interview by author, telephone, 28 April 2010; *The New York Times*, 6 June 1966; *The Washington Star*, 7 June 1966.

6. Rob Bowman, *Soulsville, U.S.A.: The Story of Stax Records* (New York: Schirmer, 1997), 88–107; Charles L. Ponce de Leon, *Fortunate Son: The Life of Elvis Presley* (New York: Hill and Wang, 2006), 101–105.

7. Sherwood Ross, interview by author; Robert Weeks, interview by author; *The Washington Star*, 7 June 1966; *Newsday*, 6 June 1966.

8. Charles Snodgrass to T. B. Birdsong and A. D. Morgan, 6 June 1966, Box 147, Folder 4, PBJFP; *Newsday*, 6 June 1966; Maxine Smith interview, 13 June 1968, Container 24, Folder 216, SSC; *The Washington Star*, 7 June 1966.

9. Sherwood Ross, interview by author.

10. Frank Lambert, *The Battle of Ole Miss: Civil Rights v. States' Rights* (New York: Oxford University Press, 2010), 13–14; James Meredith with William Doyle, *A Mission from God: A Memoir and Challenge for America* (New York: Atria, 2012), 32.

11. James H. Meredith, *Three Years in Mississippi* (Jackson, Miss.: Meredith Publishing, 1996; original 1966), 18–20; Charles W. Eagles, *The Price of Defiance: James Meredith and the Integration of Ole Miss* (Chapel Hill: University of North Carolina Press, 2009), 207–208.

12. Eagles, *The Price of Defiance*, 202–207; Meredith, *A Mission from God*, 25–27; Meredith, *Three Years in Mississippi*, 17–18, 61.

13. Eagles, *The Price of Defiance*, 208–13; "Statement from Army Air Force Record," SCR ID# 1-67-3-79-1-1-1, MSSC.

14. For the most complete explanation of the Ole Miss crisis, see Eagles, *The Price of Defiance*. For a blow-by-blow description of the riot, see William Doyle, *An American Insurrection: James Meredith and the Battle of Oxford, Mississippi, 1962* (New York: Anchor, 2003). For a concise take, see Lambert, *The Battle of Ole Miss*. For chronicles from the 1960s, see Walter Lord, *The Past That Would Not Die* (New York: Harper & Row, 1965); Russell H. Barrett, *Integration at Ole Miss* (Chicago: Quadrangle Books, 1965); and Meredith's own *Three Years in Mississippi*. For modern journalistic accounts that use the riot as a departure point, see Nadine Cohodas, *The Band Played Dixie: Race and the Liberal Conscience at Ole Miss* (New York: Free Press, 1997); Paul Hendrickson, *Sons of Mississippi: A Story of Race and Its Legacy* (New York: Vintage, 2003).

15. James H. Meredith, "I'll Know Victory or Defeat," *The Saturday Evening Post*, 10 November 1962, 14–17; James H. Meredith, "I Can't Fight Alone," *Look*, 9 April 1963, 70–78; "Though the Heavens Fall," *Time*, 12 October 1962, 19–20; "Life on the Campus," *Time*, 9 November 1962, 19; Larry Still, "Man Behind the Headlines," *Ebony*, December 1962, 25–35; *The New York Times*, 21 September 1962, 28 September 1962, 10 October 1962, 4 December 1962, 8 January 1963, 31 January 1963; *The Baltimore Afro-American*, 6 October 1962, 27 October 1962; *Atlanta Daily World*, 20 August 1963; *The Chicago Defender*, 22 August 1963.

16. "Negro Dissenters—Two Students Speak Out Against Leaders," *U.S. News and World Report*, 22 July 1963, 14; "Meredith's Advice to Negroes," *U.S. News and World Report*, 22 July 1963, 89; *The Chicago Defender*, 6 July 1963, 8 July 1963; *Los Angeles Sentinel*, 11 July 1963; *Call and Post* (Cleveland), 13 July 1963; *The Philadelphia Tribune*, 13 July 1963.

17. James Meredith, interview by author, Jackson, Miss., 24 August 2009; James H. Meredith, *"Me and My Kind": An Oral History with James Howard Meredith* (Jackson, Miss.: Meredith Publishing, 1995), 15, 54–63; *The Philadelphia Tribune*, 29 October 1963; "A Look at Nonviolence—Is This the Way to Solve the Negro Problem?," Box 13, Folder 5, JHMC; "The Negro Crisis," Box 13, Folder 5, JHMC.

18. James Meredith, interview by author; James Meredith to Martin Luther King, 25 August 1964, Series 1, Box 15, Folder 47, MLKP.

19. *The Philadelphia Tribune*, 29 June 1963; *The Clarion-Ledger* (Jackson), 3 May 1964; *New York Amsterdam News*, 7 September 1963; *The New York Times*, 28 December 1963, 30 December 1963, 19 August 1964; James Meredith, interview by author; James Meredith, interview by John H. Britton, 12 October 1967, Box 15, Folder 2, JHMC.

20. June Meredith Trip Diary, Box 12, Folder 5, JHMC; *New York Amsterdam News*, 17 October 1964, 3 July 1965, 18 September 1965.

21. "Statement on the Walk to Jackson, Mississippi," Box 14, Folder 3, JHMC; *The New York Times*, 5 January 1965; *The Baltimore Afro-American*, 16 January 1965; FBI File No. 157-2584 (Reported Possible March from Memphis); *The Clarion-Ledger* (Jackson), 8 May 1965.

22. Mary Stanton, *Freedom Walk: Mississippi or Bust* (Jackson: University Press of Mississippi).

23. On Columbia enrollment, see *The New York Times*, 8 September 1965, 14 September 1965; *The Chicago Defender*, 15 September 1965; *The Baltimore Afro-American*, 25 September 1965. On student clubs, see Notes of Washington, D.C., trip, 27 January 1966, Box 13, Folder 4, JHMC; Meredith's notes on various resolutions, 24 February 1966, Box 13, Folder 3, JHMC. On constitutional convention candidacy, see press statement, 31 May 1966, Box 13, Folder 11, JHMC. On speaking engagements, see Annual Men's Day Program, Oak Grove Baptist Church, 17 April 1966, Box 13, Folder 18, JHMC; James Meredith to Charles Hall, 5 January 1966, Box 14, Folder 1, JHMC.

24. Meredith, *Three Years in Mississippi*, 21. For reviews see "The Proud Man," *Newsweek*, 18 April 1966, 112; Barbaralee D. Diamonstein, "Historic Return to College," *Saturday Review*, 28 May 1966, 31–32; *Book Week*, 24 April 1966; *The Mississippi Enterprise*, 2 July 1966; *Muhammad Speaks*, 22 July 1966; *The Chicago Defender*, 10 September 1966; James W. Silver, "Three Years in Mississippi," *The Journal of Negro Education*, winter 1967, 71–72. For correspondence regarding the book see Russell Barrett to James Meredith, 2 May 1966, Box 2, Folder 5, JHMC; Vi Franklin to James Meredith, 10 May 1966, Box 14, Folder 22, JHMC.

25. James Meredith to Tedd, 12 January 1965, Box 12, Folder 9, JHMC; Al Morgan to James Meredith, 29 March 1966, Box 14, Folder 22, JHMC; James Meredith to John Hunt, 18 September 1965, Box 12, Folder 10, JHMC; John Hunt to James Meredith, 3 January 1966, Box 14, Folder 22, JHMC; John Hunt to James Meredith, 22 February 1966, Box 13, Folder 21, JHMC; James Meredith to *The New York Times*, 25 November 1965, Box 12, Folder 12, JHMC; *The New York Times* to James Meredith, Box 12, Folder 13, JHMC.

26. James Meredith to R.L.T. Smith, 24 January 1966, Box 14, Folder 22, JHMC; James Meredith, interview by author. See also "Mississippi Registration by County, Race and Congressional District," Reel 144, SRC.

27. James Meredith to Paul Johnson, 30 January 1966, Box 14, Folder 14, JHMC; James Meredith to Sheriff of DeSoto County, 8 March 1966, Box 14, Folder 13, JHMC; Sovereignty Commission memo, 15 March 1966, SCR ID# 2-54-2-29-1-1-1, MSSC; Jack Cauthen to James Meredith, 16 March 1966, Box 14, Folder 19, JHMC.

28. James Meredith to Paul Johnson, 30 January 1966, Box 14, Folder 14, JHMC; "Walk to Jackson, Mississippi," Box 14, Folder 3, JHMC. The quotation from the second document has been edited for grammar and punctuation.

29. "Statement—My Walk from Memphis to Jackson," 31 May 1966, Box 14, Folder 2, JHMC; Robert Weeks, interview by author; Robert Weeks to James Meredith, Box 14, Folder 25, JHMC; *The Washington Star*, 7 June 1966.

30. Sherwood Ross, interview by author.

31. Sherwood Ross, interview by author; *Los Angeles Times*, 7 June 1966; *The Chicago Defender*, 2 June 1966; Harold Middlebrook, interview by author, telephone, 31 March 2010; *The Southern Courier*, 11–12 June 1966.

32. Sherwood Ross, interview by author; *Memphis World*, 11 June 1966; Joseph Crit-

tenden, interview by author, Memphis, 13 February 2010; *The Washington Post*, 7 June 1966.

33. *New York Amsterdam News*, 3 September 1966.

34. James H. Meredith, "Big Changes Are Coming," *The Saturday Evening Post*, 13 August 1966, 24; Meredith, *A Mission from God*, 7; James Meredith, interview by author.

35. *Memphis Press-Scimitar*, 7 June 1966; Meredith, *Three Years in Mississippi*, 3–7, 184–85.

36. *The Washington Star*, 7 June 1966; *The Washington Post*, 7 June 1966; *The Meridian Star*, 6 June 1966.

37. *Memphis Press-Scimitar*, 6 June 1966, 7 June 1966; *The Record* (Bergen County, N.J.), 8 June 1966; *The Christian Science Monitor*, 15 June 1966.

38. Sherwood Ross, interview by author; *The Washington Star*, 7 June 1966; Joseph Crittenden, interview by author; *DeSoto Times-Promoter*, 10 June 1966; *The New York Times*, 7 June 1966; *Memphis Press-Scimitar*, 7 June 1966.

39. Meredith, "Big Changes Are Coming," 23–24; *Memphis Press-Scimitar*, 7 June 1966.

40. Meredith, "Big Changes Are Coming," 24; *The Washington Star*, 7 June 1966.

41. James Meredith, interview by author; Meredith, "Big Changes Are Coming," 24; Sherwood Ross, interview by author.

42. "The March Meredith Began," *Newsweek*, 20 June 1966, 28; *Memphis Press-Scimitar*, 7 June 1966.

43. *Los Angeles Times*, 7 June 1966.

44. Sherwood Ross, interview by author; *New York Amsterdam News*, 11 June 1966; *The Nashville Tennessean*, 7 June 1966; Meredith, "Big Changes Are Coming," 24; "A Walk in the South to Conquer Old Fears," *Life*, 17 June 1966, 31.

45. *The Tri-State Defender*, 11 June 1966; Joseph Crittenden, interview by author.

46. *New Journal and Guide* (Norfolk, Va.), 10 June 1967; Meredith, "Big Changes Are Coming," 24; Robert Weeks, interview by author; *Memphis Press-Scimitar*, 7 June 1966.

47. *The Nashville Tennessean*, 7 June 1966; *The Washington Daily News*, 7 June 1966.

48. Meredith, *A Mission from God*, 1–2; *The Washington Post*, 7 June 1966; *The Washington Star*, 7 June 1966; "Heat on Highway 51," *Time*, 17 June 1966, 26–27; Sherwood Ross, interview by author; *Los Angeles Times*, 7 June 1966.

49. *The Washington Daily News*, 7 June 1966; *Memphis Press-Scimitar*, 7 June 1966; *The Washington Star*, 7 June 1966; *The Enterprise-Tocsin* (Indianola, Miss.), 16 June 1966; Meredith, "Big Changes Are Coming," 24.

2. Leaving Egypt

1. *The Washington Daily News*, 7 June 1966; *The Tri-State Defender*, 11 June 1966; Sherwood Ross, interview by author.

2. *The Washington Daily News*, 7 June 1966; *The Tri-State Defender*, 11 June 1966; Sherwood Ross, interview by author; *The Atlanta Constitution*, 7 June 1966; *Memphis Press-Scimitar*, 7 June 1966; *Los Angeles Times*, 7 June 1966.

3. *The New York Times*, 8 June 1966; "The 'Death' Blunder," *Time*, 17 June 1966, 62.

4. *The Atlanta Constitution*, 7 June 1966; Curtis Wilkie, *Dixie: A Personal Odyssey Through Events That Shaped the Modern South* (New York: Scribner, 2001), 163–64.

5. *The Nashville Tennessean*, 7 June 1966; Meredith, "Big Changes Are Coming," 25.

6. *Newsday*, 7 June 1966; *Daily News* (New York), 7 June 1966; *The New York Times*, 7 June 1966; *Los Angeles Times*, 7 June 1966; *New York Amsterdam News*, 11 June 1966; *The Baltimore Afro-American*, 18 June 1966; Meredith, "Big Changes Are Coming," 25.

7. *New York Post*, 7 June 1966; *Newsday*, 7 June 1966.

8. "Pontius" to Mr. Jacobson, 6 June 1966, Box 27, Folder HU 2/ST 24, WHCF-HU; *The Washington Post*, 7 June 1966, 8 June 1966; *Chicago Tribune*, 8 June 1966.

9. *Los Angeles Sentinel*, 9 June 1966; Long Beach NAACP to Paul Johnson, Box 142, Folder 3, PBJFP; *The Washington Star*, 7 June 1966.

10. *The New York Times*, 22 October 1968.

11. Meredith, "Big Changes Are Coming," 25; *Chicago's American*, 7 June 1966.

12. Dick Gregory, interview by author, telephone, 6 April 2010; Dick Gregory with James R. McGraw, *Up From Nigger* (New York: Stein and Day, 1976), 130–31; Dick Gregory to Lyndon Johnson, 7 June 1966, Box 40, Folder HU 2/ST 24, WHCF-HU; *Chicago's American*, 7 June 1966; Dick Gregory, *Callus on My Soul: A Memoir* (Atlanta: Longstreet Press, 2000), 113–14.

13. Mel Watkins, *On the Real Side: Laughing, Lying, and Signifying—The Underground Tradition of African-American Humor that Transformed American Culture, from Slavery to Richard Pryor* (New York: Simon and Schuster, 1994), 495–503.

14. Dick Gregory with Robert Lipsyte, *Nigger* (New York: Dutton, 1964), 168–224; Dick Gregory, *The Shadow That Scares Me* (New York: Doubleday, 1968); Gregory, *Up From Nigger*, 53–116; Mark Stansbury, interview by author, Memphis, 17 February 2010.

15. Dick Gregory, interview by author; Meredith, *Three Years in Mississippi*, 236–37, 266–67; Gregory, *Up From Nigger*, 131; Gregory, *Nigger*, 175; *Chicago's American*, 7 June 1966; Gregory, *Callus on My Soul*, 114–15; *Memphis Press-Scimitar*, 7 June 1966; *Newsday*, 7 June 1966.

16. Gregory, *Up From Nigger*, 132.

17. Charles Snodgrass to T. B. Birdsong and A. D. Morgan, 7 June 1966, Box 147, Folder 4, PBJFP; *The Commercial Appeal* (Memphis), 8 June 1966; *Memphis Press-Scimitar*, 7 June 1966; Howell Raines, *My Soul Is Rested: Movement Days in the Deep South Remembered* (New York: Putnam, 1977), 292; Dick Gregory, interview by author.

18. Snodgrass to Birdsong and Morgan, 7 June 1966, Box 147, Folder 4, PBJFP; *The Southern Courier*, 11–12 June 1966; *The Washington Daily News*, 8 June 1966; *Memphis Press-Scimitar*, 7 June 1966.

19. Gregory, *Up From Nigger*, 133; *Memphis Press-Scimitar*, 7 June 1966.

20. *Memphis Press-Scimitar*, 8 June 1966.

21. Floyd McKissick interview, 21 October 1988, EPI; Floyd McKissick, Jr., interview by author, telephone, 22 December 2010; *The Philadelphia Inquirer*, 7 June

1966; *Detroit Free Press*, 7 June 1966; CORE News Release, 7 June 1966, Reel 13, CORE-A.

22. Harold Woodard, "Floyd McKissick: Portrait of a Leader" (M.A. thesis, University of North Carolina, 1981), 2–30; *The New York Times*, 4 January 1966; Fred Powledge, *Free At Last?: The Civil Rights Movement and the People Who Made It* (Boston: Little, Brown, 1991), 34–40; "Biographical Sketch—Floyd B. McKissick," April 1967, Reel 15, CORE-A; August Meier and Elliott Rudwick, *CORE: A Study in the Civil Rights Movement, 1942–1968* (New York: Oxford University Press, 1973), 103, 170–72, 217–18; James Haskins, *Profiles in Black Power* (Garden City, N.Y.: Doubleday, 1972), 75–83.

23. Meier and Rudwick, *CORE*; Raymond Arsenault, *Freedom Riders: 1961 and the Struggle for Racial Justice* (New York: Oxford University Press, 2006); Inge Powell Bell, *CORE and the Strategy of Nonviolence* (New York: Random House, 1968), 92–93, 105–106, 115–19, 160–74, 178–81; James Farmer, *Lay Bare the Heart: An Autobiography of the Civil Rights Movement* (New York: Arbor House, 1985), 254–303; "CORE's Policy of New Direction," February 1966, Reel 5, CORE-A; "What is CORE Doing Now?," April 1966, Reel 5, CORE-A.

24. *The Courier-Journal* (Louisville), 12 June 1966.

25. Meier and Rudwick, *CORE*, 411; "N.A.C. Steering Committee Meeting," 4 June 1966, Reel 9, CORE-A; *Newsday*, 9 June 1966.

26. Martin Luther King, Jr., *Where Do We Go from Here: Chaos or Community?* (Boston: Beacon, 1968; original 1967), 23; Andrew Young, *An Easy Burden: The Civil Rights Movement and the Transformation of America* (Waco, Tex.: Baylor University Press, 2008; original 1996), 393–94.

27. FBI Chicago to Director, 7 June 1966, Part 1, Reel 10, MLK-FBI; James R. Ralph, *Northern Protest: Martin Luther King, Jr., Chicago, and the Civil Rights Movement* (Cambridge, Mass.: Harvard University Press, 1993), 2–96.

28. Fairclough, *To Redeem the Soul of America*, 1–8, 165–68; "Hosea's Book Tape #3," 10 December 1973, Series 2, Box 1, Folder 14, HWC; Bob Fitch, interview by author, telephone, 8 March 2010; Branch, *At Canaan's Edge*, 45, 365–67, 422; Young, *An Easy Burden*, 185, 284–88, 334, 393–94; Andrew Young interview, 27 October 1988, EPI.

29. King, *Where Do We Go from Here*, 24; "The March Meredith Began," *Newsweek*, 20 June 1966, 29.

30. "Guidelines for a Constructive Church," 5 June 1966, Series 3, Box 11, MLKP.

31. David J. Garrow, *Protest at Selma: Martin Luther King, Jr., and the Voting Rights Act of 1965* (New Haven: Yale University Press, 1978).

32. James Lawson interview, 21 July 1969, Container 22, Folder 135, SSC; Charles Morgan, Jr., *One Man, One Voice* (New York: Holt, Rinehart and Winston, 1979), 71–72; James Lawson, "The Meredith March . . . and Tomorrow," *Concern*, 15 July 1966, 4. Lawson article reprinted as James M. Lawson, "Black Power and the Meredith March," *Fellowship*, September 1966, 18–19.

33. *The Nashville Tennessean*, 8 June 1966; "Statement on the Walk to Jackson, Mississippi," Box 14, Folder 3, JHMC. Statement reprinted in *New York Post*, 7 June 1966; *Chicago Tribune*, 8 June 1966; *The Washington Post*, 8 June 1966.

34. Morgan, *One Man, One Voice*, 72; *The Commercial Appeal* (Memphis), 8 June 1966; Harold Middlebrook interview, 21 July 1968, Container 23, Series 2, Folder 1, SSC; *The Washington Daily News*, 7 June 1966; *The Washington Post*, 7 June 1966; King, *Where Do We Go from Here*, 24.

35. Meredith, "Big Changes Are Coming," 25.

36. *The New York Times*, 8 June 1966; *The Boston Globe*, 7 June 1966 (evening edition); John Doar, interview by author, telephone, 17 March 2010; J. Edgar Hoover to Marvin Watson, Box 71B, Folder 3, LBJ-MS; Meredith, "Big Changes Are Coming," 25.

37. *The New York Times*, 8 June 1966; *The Nashville Tennessean*, 8 June 1966.

38. King, *Where Do We Go from Here*, 24–25.

39. Carmichael, *Ready for Revolution*, 486–88; Cleveland Sellers with Robert Terrell, *The River of No Return: The Autobiography of a Black Militant and the Life and Death of SNCC* (Jackson: University Press of Mississippi, 1990; original 1973), 159–60.

40. "SNCC Statement on the Shooting of James Meredith," 6 June 1966, Box 3, Folder 2, DLC; Stokely Carmichael to Meredith Family, Box 3, Folder 2, DLC.

41. William Hansen, interview by author, telephone, 16 December 2010; Carmichael, *Ready for Revolution*, 488–89; Sellers, *The River of No Return*, 160–61.

42. Cleveland Sellers, interview by author, telephone, 27 July 2011; Carmichael, *Ready for Revolution*, 489–90.

43. Lawson, "The Meredith March . . . and Tomorrow," 5; Morgan, *One Man, One Voice*, 72–73; Martin Luther King and Hosea Williams to "Freedom Fighters," Box 19, Folder 1, NSM.

44. Meredith, "Big Changes Are Coming," 25; Cleveland Sellers, interview by author; *The Nashville Tennessean*, 8 June 1966; Joseph Crittenden, interview by author, 13 February 2010; *The Christian Science Monitor*, 9 June 1966; *Memphis Press-Scimitar*, 8 June 1966.

45. *The Nashville Tennessean*, 8 June 1966; *Memphis Press-Scimitar*, 8 June 1966.

46. *Los Angeles Times*, 8 June 1966.

47. Carmichael, *Ready for Revolution*, 503; *Los Angeles Times*, 8 June 1966; James Lawson interview, 21 July 1969, Container 22, Folder 135, SSC; Chester Higgins, "Meredith's Threat to Arm Not Answer, Says Dr. King," *Jet*, 23 June 1966, 20.

48. *New York Post*, 8 June 1966; *The Commercial Appeal* (Memphis), 8 June 1966; King, *Where Do We Go from Here*, 25–26.

49. *The Southern Courier*, 11–12 June 1966; *Chicago Daily News*, 8 June 1966.

50. *Newsday*, 8 June 1966; *Memphis Press-Scimitar*, 8 June 1966.

51. *Newsday*, 8 June 1966.

52. King, *Where Do We Go from Here*, 25–26; Gerold Frank, *An American Death: The True Story of the Assassination of Dr. Martin Luther King, Jr., and the Greatest Manhunt of Our Time* (Garden City, N.Y.: Doubleday, 1972), 17; *The Nashville Tennessean*, 8 June 1966.

53. *The Boston Globe*, 8 June 1966 (evening edition); *Newsday*, 8 June 1966.

54. Samuel "Billy" Kyles, interview by author, Memphis, 23 March 2010; Joseph Crittenden, interview by author; *Memphis Press-Scimitar*, 8 June 1966; *The Nashville Tennessean*, 8 June 1966.

55. "The March Meredith Began," 29; *The Commercial Appeal* (Memphis), 8 June 1966; *The Christian Science Monitor*, 9 June 1966.

56. "Meredith's Threat to Arm Not Answer, Says Dr. King," 16; *The Commercial Appeal* (Memphis), 8 June 1966; *The Christian Science Monitor*, 9 June 1966; "The March Meredith Began," 29–30.

57. "The March Meredith Began," 30; *The Boston Globe*, 8 June 1966; Speech at Meredith Rally, 7 June 1966, Series 3, Box 11, MLKP.

3. Bargains in Blood

1. Morgan, *One Man, One Voice*, 73; Jesse Harris, interview by author, telephone, 5 February 2010; Ed King, interview by author, telephone, 27 August 2011; Cleveland Sellers, interview by author.

2. Morgan, *One Man, One Voice*, 73; Lance Hill, *The Deacons for Defense: Armed Resistance and the Civil Rights Movement* (Chapel Hill: University of North Carolina Press, 2004), 246–47.

3. Hill, *The Deacons for Defense*, 247.

4. Floyd McKissick interview, 21 October 1988, EPI; Cleveland Sellers interview, 21 October 1988, EPI. On CORE and Deacons in Louisiana, see also Meier and Rudwick, *CORE*, 397–99; *The Minnesota Daily*, 28 October 1965, 2 December 1965; Memorandum by Richard Haley on "CORE Deacon Relationship," Reel 10, CORE-A.

5. King, *Where Do We Go from Here*, 26–27; Andrew Young interview, 27 October 1988, EPI; Carmichael, *Ready for Revolution*, 497.

6. Cleveland Sellers, interview by author; Henry Hampton and Steve Fayer, *Voices of Freedom: An Oral History of the Civil Rights Movement from the 1950s through the 1980s* (New York: Bantam, 1991), 288.

7. King, *Where Do We Go from Here*, 27–29.

8. See "The High Spots of Proposed Civil Rights Act of 1966," Part 1, Reel 11, CRJA.

9. On Young, see Dennis C. Dickerson, *Militant Mediator: Whitney M. Young, Jr.* (Lexington: University Press of Kentucky, 1998), 1–7, 135–83; Nancy J. Weiss, *Whitney M. Young, Jr., and the Struggle for Civil Rights* (Princeton: Princeton University Press, 1989), xi–xii, 97–124; *Urban League Newsletter*, Summer 1966, Part III, Box 44, Folder 3, NULP; Whitney Young, "To Be Equal" Column Draft, 22 March 1965, Part III, Box 441, Folder 9, NULP. On Wilkins, see Patricia Sullivan, *Lift Every Voice: The NAACP and the Making of the Civil Rights Movement* (New York: New Press, 2009), 258–59, 321–22, 373–74; Gilbert Jonas, *Freedom's Sword: The NAACP and the Struggle Against Racism in America, 1909–1969* (New York: Routledge, 2005), 172–345; Roy Wilkins with Tom Mathews, *Standing Fast: The Autobiography of Roy Wilkins* (New York: Da Capo Press, 1994; original 1982), 221–307; Manfred Berg, *"The Ticket to Freedom": The NAACP and the Struggle for Black*

Political Integration (Gainesville: University Press of Florida, 2005), 166–90; Deke DeLoach to M. A. Jones, 16 March 1965, Box 24, FBI File B(1), RWP.

10. *Nashville Banner*, 6 June 1966.

11. Ed King, interview by author; Carmichael, *Ready for Revolution*, 494–96; "The March Meredith Began," 30.

12. "Ideas for Proposed Statement," Reel 38, SNCC; Cleveland Sellers interview, 21 October 1988, EPI; Higgins, "Meredith's Threat to Arm Not Answer, Says Dr. King," 18.

13. Stokely Carmichael interview, 7 November 1988, EPI; Milton Viorst, *Fire in the Streets: America in the 1960s* (New York: Simon and Schuster, 1979), 371–72; Clayborne Carson, *In Struggle: SNCC and the Black Awakening of the 1960s* (Cambridge, Mass.: Harvard University Press, 1981), 207; Harold Middlebrook interview, 18 July 1968, Container 23, Series 1, Folder 2, SSC.

14. Garrow, *Bearing the Cross*, 477; Carmichael, *Ready for Revolution*, 496; Ed King, interview by author.

15. Cleveland Sellers, interview by author; Stokely Carmichael interview, 7 November 1988, EPI; "Tape #11 H.P.," Series 2, Box 1, Folder 18, HWC; Roy Wilkins Itinerary, June 1966, Box 25, Folder "Itineraries," RWP; *The Courier-Journal* (Louisville), 9 June 1966; "The March Meredith Began," 30.

16. "Mississippi and the NAACP," *Crisis*, June–July 1966, 315–16; Wilkins, *Standing Fast*, 316; "The March Meredith Began," 30.

17. "Manifesto of the Meredith Mississippi Freedom March," 9 June 1966, SCR ID# 1-67-4-130-1-1-1, MSSC. Copies also available at Reel 13, CORE-A; Part 3, Reel 4, SCLC.

18. Jervis Anderson, *Bayard Rustin: Troubles I've Seen* (Berkeley: University of California Press, 1998), 3–310; Bayard Rustin, "From Protest to Politics: The Future of the Civil Rights Movement," *Commentary*, February 1965, 25–31; "The March Meredith Began," 30; *The Village Voice*, 30 June 1966.

19. *Jackson Daily News*, 7 June 1966.

20. Martin A. Berger, *Seeing Through Race: A Reinterpretation of Civil Rights Photography* (Berkeley: University of California Press, 2011), 1–57; Leigh Raiford, *Imprisoned in a Luminous Glare: Photography and the African American Freedom Struggle* (Chapel Hill: University of North Carolina Press, 2011), 1–9; Martin Katz to James Meredith, 8 June 1966, Box 14, Folder 8, JHMC; Janet J. Moore to James Meredith, Box 14, Folder 24, JHMC; Bert A. Kessler to James Meredith, 11 August 1966, Box 14, Folder 24, JHMC; Mrs. I. Levin to James Meredith, 9 June 1966, Box 14, Folder 9, JHMC; David E. Spiess to James Meredith, 14 June 1966, Box 14, Folder 10, JHMC; Mrs. Jan Hoffman to James Meredith, 9 June 1966, Box 14, Folder 9, JHMC.

21. Harry Apfel to James Meredith, 7 June 1966, Box 14, Folder 7, JHMC; Mrs. William Schneider to James Meredith, Box 14, Folder 10, JHMC; Anne Wyne to James Meredith, 7 June 1966, Box 14, Folder 7, JHMC.

22. *The Philadelphia Inquirer*, 8 June 1966; *The West Palm Beach Times*, 11 June 1966; *Chicago Tribune*, 10 June 1966. For more profiles and columns, see *The Philadelphia Inquirer*, 7 June 1966; *The Courier-Journal* (Louisville), 7 June 1966; *Chicago Daily News*, 7 June 1966; *New York Post*, 7 June 1966; *Newsday*, 7 June 1966; *Arkan-*

sas Gazette, 8 June 1966; *Los Angeles Times*, 8 June 1966; *The Chicago Defender*, 8 June 1966; *The Boston Globe*, 7 June 1966, 11 June 1966. For more letters to the editor, see *New York Post*, 10 June 1966; *The Philadelphia Inquirer*, 11 June 1966; *The Washington Post*, 11 June 1966; *Chicago Daily News*, 15 June 1966; *Newsday*, 18 June 1966. For more editorials, see *San Francisco Chronicle*, 8 June 1966; *Nashville Banner*, 7 June 1966; *The Plain Dealer* (Cleveland), 7 June 1966; *Los Angeles Times*, 8 June 1966; *Boston Herald*, 8 June 1966; *The Washington Star*, 8 June 1966; *The Sun* (Baltimore), 8 June 1966.

23. *The New York Times*, 8 June 1966; *The Chicago Defender*, 18 June 1966; *New York Amsterdam News*, 11 June 1966; *The Philadelphia Inquirer*, 7 June 1966; *Congressional Record—House*, 8 June 1966, 12006.

24. *Montgomery Advertiser*, 8 June 1966; *The Philadelphia Inquirer*, 8 June 1966; *The New York Times*, 11 June 1966; *The Baltimore Afro-American*, 18 June 1966; *Arkansas Gazette*, 8 June 1966.

25. Brian Dooley, *Robert Kennedy: The Final Years* (New York: St. Martin's, 1996), 95–96; *The Boston Globe*, 7 June 1966, 8 June 1966. See also *The Times* (London), 8 June 1966; *The Guardian* (Manchester, U.K.), 8 June 1966; *The Christian Science Monitor*, 9 June 1966.

26. Carter, *The Music Has Gone Out of the Movement*, 145–47; Steven F. Lawson, *In Pursuit of Power: Southern Blacks and Electoral Politics, 1965–1982* (New York: Columbia University Press, 1985), 68–71; Statement by Attorney General Nicholas deB. Katzenbach Before the Subcommittee on Constitutional Rights, Senate Judiciary Committee, Part 1, Reel 11, CRJA; *The Philadelphia Inquirer*, 7 June 1966; *Los Angeles Times*, 7 June 1966.

27. *Arkansas Democrat*, 7 June 1966; *The Niles* (Ohio) *Times*, 7 June 1966; *The New York Times*, 8 June 1966, 11 June 1966; *The Washington Post*, 8 June 1966, 9 June 1966; *The Sun* (Baltimore), 8 June 1966; *Los Angeles Times*, 8 June 1966, 9 June 1966; "Race Issue Inflamed Again: Aftermath of a Shooting," *U.S. News and World Report*, 20 June 1966, 35–38; Ragni Lantz, "Ambush Shooting Puts the Heat on LBJ's Anti-Terror Bill," *Jet*, 23 June 1966, 22–25; *Chicago Daily News*, 7 June 1966; *Chicago Tribune*, 8 June 1966; *Jackson Daily News*, 10 June 1966; *Jackson Daily News*, 13 June 1966; *The Wall Street Journal*, 8 June 1966.

28. *The Chicago Defender*, 7 June 1966; Diary entry, 6 June 1966, DDPJ; *The Washington Post*, 7 June 1966; Letters to Lyndon Johnson, Box 40, Folder HU 2/ST 24, WHCF-HU; *Chicago Tribune*, 9 June 1966.

29. *The Chicago Defender*, 18 June 1966.

30. Meredith, "Big Changes Are Coming," 25–26; *Memphis Press-Scimitar*, 8 June 1966.

31. *Memphis Press-Scimitar*, 8 June 1966; Meredith, "Big Changes Are Coming," 25–26; *The New York Times*, 9 June 1966; *New York Post*, 11 June 1966.

32. *Chicago Daily News*, 8 June 1966; *Memphis Press-Scimitar*, 8 June 1966; Meredith, "Big Changes Are Coming," 26; *Los Angeles Times*, 9 June 1966.

33. *The Washington Post*, 9 June 1966; Owen Brooks, interview by author, Jackson, 25 May 2010; *The Commercial Appeal* (Memphis), 9 June 1966; *New York Post*, 8 June 1966; *Memphis Press-Scimitar*, 9 June 1966; *The Tri-State Defender*, 18 June 1966.

34. *Chicago Daily News*, 8 June 1966; *Los Angeles Times*, 9 June 1966; *The Washington Post*, 9 June 1966.

35. *Chicago Daily News*, 8 June 1966; *The Commercial Appeal* (Memphis), 9 June 1966; Meredith, "Big Changes Are Coming," 26.

36. *The Clarksdale* (Miss.) *Press Register*, 7 June 1966; *Memphis Press-Scimitar*, 7 June 1966; *The Washington Daily News*, 7 June 1966; *The Atlanta Constitution*, 7 June 1966.

37. *The Commercial Appeal* (Memphis), 7 June 1966; *Delta Democrat Times*, 7 June 1966; *The Greenwood Commonwealth*, 7 June 1966; *Memphis Press-Scimitar*, 7 June 1966; *The Meridian Star*, 7 June 1966.

38. *The Baltimore Afro-American*, 25 June 1966; *Call and Post* (Cleveland), 2 July 1966; *Miami Herald*, 7 June 1966; *Chicago Daily News*, 8 June 1966; *New York Post*, 8 June 1966; *The Atlanta Constitution*, 8 June 1966, 10 June 1966; *The Chicago Defender*, 9 June 1966.

39. Highway Patrol memorandum, 7 June 1966, Box 147, Folder 4, PBJFP; *Memphis Press-Scimitar*, 7 June 1966; *The Commercial Appeal* (Memphis), 7 June 1966, 8 June 1966.

40. *Newsday*, 8 June 1966; *The Commercial Appeal* (Memphis), 7 June 1966, 8 June 1966; *Los Angeles Times*, 7 June 1966; *New York Post*, 8 June 1966; *Memphis Press-Scimitar*, 7 June 1966.

41. *The Commercial Appeal* (Memphis), 8 June 1966; *New York Post*, 7 June 1966; Highway Patrol memorandum, 7 June 1966, Box 147, Folder 4, PBJFP; *The Washington Post*, 7 June 1966.

42. *The Record* (Bergen Co., N.J.), 8 June 1966; *The Washington Star*, 7 June 1966; *The Tri-State Defender*, 11 June 1966; *New York Amsterdam News*, 11 June 1966; *The Nashville Tennessean*, 7 June 1966; *The Baltimore Afro-American*, 18 June 1966.

43. *The New York Amsterdam News*, 11 June 1966; *The Baltimore Afro-American*, 18 June 1966; *Call and Post* (Cleveland), 18 June 1966; *Congressional Record—Appendix*, 13 June 1966, A3165-A3166; *Delta Democrat Times*, 7 June 1966.

44. *The Washington Post*, 12 June 1966; *The Boston Globe*, 11 June 1966. See also *New York Post*, 7 June 1966; *The New York Times*, 7 June 1966; *Newsday*, 8 June 1966; *Detroit Free Press*, 8 June 1966; *The Philadelphia Inquirer*, 9 June 1966; *Memphis World*, 11 June 1966; *New York Amsterdam News*, 11 June 1966; *The Baltimore Afro-American*, 18 June 1966; *Call and Post* (Cleveland), 18 June 1966; "The Meredith Ambush," *The Nation*, 20 June 1966, 731–32; "Blind Bigotry on U.S. 51," *The Christian Century*, 22 June 1966, 793.

45. Charles Snodgrass to T. B. Birdsong and A. D. Morgan, 8 June 1966, Box 147, Folder 4, PBJFP; *Delta Democrat Times*, 8 June 1966, 9 June 1966; Coldwater press conference, 8 June 1966, SRTR; *The Chicago Defender*, 9 June 1966.

46. *The Courier-Journal* (Louisville), 9 June 1966; "The March Meredith Began," 31; *Newsday*, 9 June 1966.

47. *The Boston Globe*, 9 June 1966; *The Philadelphia Tribune*, 11 June 1966.

48. *The Boston Globe*, 9 June 1966; *The Nashville Tennessean*, 9 June 1966; *The Christian Science Monitor*, 10 June 1966.

49. *The Nashville Tennessean*, 9 June 1966; *The Chicago Defender*, 10 June 1966; Highway Patrol memorandum, 9 June 1966, Box 147, Folder 4, PBJFP; FBI memorandum, 9 June 1966, Box 71B, Folder 3, LBJ-MS.

50. Highway Patrol memorandum, 9 June 1966, Box 147, Folder 4, PBJFP; Senatobia recording, 8 June 1966, SRTR; *The Commercial Appeal* (Memphis), 9 June 1966; *San Francisco Chronicle*, 9 June 1966.

51. *Newsday*, 9 June 1966; *Daily News* (New York), 9 June 1966; *The Baltimore Afro-American*, 18 June 1966. On June Meredith see *Daily News* (New York), 8 June 1966; *The Chicago Defender*, 11 June 1966; Letters to June Meredith, Box 14, Folder 27, JHMC.

52. *New York Post*, 9 June 1966.

4. Daylight Breaking

1. *The Boston Globe*, 9 June 1966, 10 June 1966; *Newsday*, 10 June 1966.

2. *Newsday*, 10 June 1966; *Detroit Free Press*, 10 June 1966.

3. *Newsday*, 10 June 1966.

4. *The Commercial Appeal* (Memphis), 10 June 1966; Chester Higgins, "Meredith's Threat to Arm Not Answer, Says Dr. King," *Jet*, 23 June 1966, 20.

5. *Newsday*, 10 June 1966; *The Nashville Tennessean*, 10 June 1966; *The Courier-Journal* (Louisville), 10 June 1966; *Delta Democrat Times*, 10 June 1966; *The Philadelphia Inquirer*, 10 June 1966; Highway Patrol memorandum, 9 June 1966, Box 147, Folder 4, PBJFP.

6. *The Boston Globe*, 10 June 1966; *New York Post*, 10 June 1966; *Newsday*, 10 June 1966; John Dittmer, *The Good Doctors: The Medical Committee for Human Rights and the Struggle for Social Justice in Health Care* (New York: Bloomsbury, 2009), 150; Alvin Poussaint, interview by author, telephone, 29 April 2010.

7. Dittmer, *The Good Doctors*, 150–51; *The Washington Post*, 10 June 1966; *Los Angeles Times*, 10 June 1966; Alvin Poussaint, interview by author.

8. *The Boston Globe*, 10 June 1966.

9. Melvyn R. Leventhal, "The Civil Rights Movement Comes to an End," unpublished article in author's possession; Walter Bailey interview, 10 July 1968, Container 20, Folder 11, SSC.

10. On race and politics in Memphis, see Laurie B. Green, *Battling the Plantation Mentality: Memphis and the Black Freedom Struggle* (Chapel Hill: University of North Carolina Press, 2007); Michael K. Honey, *Going Down Jericho Road: The Memphis Strike, Martin Luther King's Last Campaign* (New York: Norton, 2007); Wayne Dowdy, *Crusades for Freedom: Memphis and the Political Transformation of the American South* (Jackson: University Press of Mississippi, 2010).

11. Mark Stansbury, interview by author; Harold Middlebrook interview, 18 July 1968, Container 23, Series 1, Folder 2, SSC; Samuel "Billy" Kyles, interview by author; Roy Wilkins interview, 18 April 1973, Container 24, Folder 250, SSC; Maxine Smith, interview by author; Sherry L. Hoppe and Bruce W. Speck, *Maxine Smith's Unwilling Pupils: Lessons Learned in Memphis's Civil Rights Classroom* (Knoxville:

University of Tennessee Press, 2007), 15–91; Bobby L. Lovett, *The Civil Rights Movement in Tennessee: A Narrative History* (Knoxville: University of Tennessee Press, 2005), 192–200; Sharon D. Wright, *Race, Power, and Political Emergence in Memphis* (New York: Garland, 2000), 55–60, 78–81; Membership Report, 31 May 1966, Box 4, Folder 11, MS-NAACP; Report of Executive Secretary, Box 1, Folder 6, MS-NAACP; Executive Board Minutes, 9 June 1966, Box 3, Folder 6, MS-NAACP; Membership Report, 31 May 1966, Box 4, Folder 11, MS-NAACP; Report of Executive Secretary, Box 1, Folder 6, MS-NAACP; Executive Board Minutes, 9 June 1966, Box 3, Folder 6, MS-NAACP. Memphis had a CORE branch led by NAACP dissident O. Z. Evers, but it had little influence and few members. See O. Z. Evers to CORE, 1 July 1961, Reel 42, CORE; Mary Hamilton to James McCain, 27 April 1963, Reel 42, CORE.

12. Samuel "Billy" Kyles, interview by author; Jesse Turner interview, 29 May 1968, Container 24, Folder 238, SSC.

13. Meredith, *Three Years in Mississippi*, 175–76; Miriam DeCosta-Willis, *Notable Black Memphians* (Amherst, N.Y.: Cambria Press, 2008), 346–49; Dowdy, *Crusades for Freedom*, 109–10; Miriam DeCosta-Willis (Laurie Sugarmon), interview by author, Memphis, 5 March 2010; Archie Willis, interview by author, Memphis, 1 April 2010.

14. FBI memorandum, 9 June 1966, Box 71B, Folder 3, LBJ-MS; *The Boston Globe*, 9 June 1966 (evening edition).

15. David Halberstam, *The Children* (New York: Random House, 1998), 3–234; James Lawson interview, 21 July 1969, Container 22, Folder 134, SSC.

16. David M. Tucker, *Black Pastors and Leaders: Memphis, 1819–1972* (Memphis: Memphis State University Press, 1975), 113–28; Halberstam, *The Children*, 471–76; *The Tri-State Defender*, 18 June 1966; James Lawson interview, 21 July 1969, Container 22, Folder 134, SSC; Lawson, "The Meredith March . . . and Tomorrow," 5; Joel Bernard to Jacqueline Bernard, 13 June 1966, Box 1, Folder 1, JBP; *Memphis Press-Scimitar*, 8 June 1966; *Memphis World*, 18 June 1966.

17. David Acey, interview by author, Memphis, Tennessee, 23 March 2011; *Memphis World*, 18 June 1966; *The Baltimore Afro-American*, 18 June 1966; Joel Bernard to Jacqueline Bernard, 13 June 1966, Box 1, Folder 1, JBP; Jack Sisson memorandum, 30 June 1966, Series 18, Box 4, Folder 1, NCCIJ; Harold Middlebrook, interview by author.

18. *Memphis World*, 18 June 1966; Coldwater press conference, 8 June 1966, SRTR; *Memphis Press-Scimitar*, 16 June 1966; Press releases and advertisements, Reel 13, CORE-A.

19. *The Commercial Appeal* (Memphis), 12 June 1966; Sovereignty Commission memorandum, 9 June 1966, SCR ID# 1-103-0-6-2-1-1, MSSC; Melvyn Leventhal, interview by author, telephone, 10 March 2010.

20. *Chicago Tribune*, 10 June 1966; *Memphis Press-Scimitar*, 10 June 1966.

21. *Detroit Free Press*, 10 June 1966.

22. *The Boston Globe*, 10 June 1966.

23. *Newsday*, 25 June 1966.

24. *New York Post*, 10 June 1966.
25. Highway Patrol memorandum, 9 June 1966, Box 147, Folder 4, PBJFP; *Jackson Daily News*, 10 June 1966; FBI memorandum, 9 June 1966, Part 1, Reel 10, MLK-FBI; Report from Chicago District Commander Edward Egan, Series 4, Box 62, Folder 432, TBP; "The March Meredith Began," *Newsweek*, 20 June 1966, 31.
26. *New York Post*, 9 June 1966.
27. Senatobia speeches, 9 June 1966, SRTR.
28. *New York Post*, 9 June 1966.
29. Mary King, *Freedom Song: A Personal Story of the 1960s Civil Rights Movement* (New York: Morrow, 1987), 451; Len Holt, *The Summer That Didn't End: The Story of the Mississippi Civil Rights Project of 1964 and Its Challenge to the Future of America* (New York: Morrow, 1965), 44; Howard Zinn, *SNCC: The New Abolitionists* (Boston: Beacon, 1965), 40; Jack Newfield, *A Prophetic Minority* (New York: New American Library, 1966), 108–109; Bob Zellner with Constance Curry, *The Wrong Side of Murder Creek: A White Southerner in the Freedom Movement* (Montgomery, Ala.: NewSouth Books, 2008), 262–63; John Lewis with Michael D'Orso, *Walking with the Wind: A Memoir of the Movement* (New York: Simon and Schuster, 1998), 178–79.
30. Carmichael, *Ready for Revolution*, 136–215; Viorst, *Fire in the Streets*, 347–53; Courtland Cox, interview by the author, Jackson, 26 March 2010.
31. Elizabeth Sutherland, ed., *Letters from Mississippi* (New York: McGraw-Hill, 1965), 29–30, 170–75; Sally Belfrage, *Freedom Summer* (London: Andre Deutsch, 1966), 64–65, 134–36; "What Is Good English: A Class by Stokely Carmichael," Reel 63, SNCC.
32. Carson, *In Struggle*, 123–29; Carmichael, *Ready for Revolution*, 410. For documents on DNC Challenge see also Box 1, Folder 1, MFDP.
33. Carmichael, *Ready for Revolution*, 414–17; Stokely Carmichael to Lorna Smith, Box 4, Folder 1, SC-LDS; Hasan Kwame Jeffries, *Bloody Lowndes: Civil Rights and Black Power in Alabama's Black Belt* (New York: New York University Press, 2009), 39–180; Chester Higgins, "SNCC-Backed Candidates Set for November General Elections," *Jet*, 16 June 1966, 8–11. See also Peniel Joseph, *Dark Days, Bright Nights: From Black Power to Barack Obama* (New York: BasicCivitas Books, 2010), 107–18.
34. Stokely Carmichael, "Who Is Qualified?," *The New Republic*, 8 January 1966, 20–22.
35. Notes from SNCC Staff Meeting, 25 November 1965, Box 8, Folder 1, DLC; Cheryl Lynn Greenberg, ed., *A Circle of Trust: Remembering SNCC* (New Brunswick, N.J., 1998), 155–57; King, *Freedom Song*, 518–25; Carson, *In Struggle*, 141–48.
36. "Statement by the Student Nonviolent Coordinating Committee on the War in Vietnam," 6 January 1966, Part 3, Reel 6, SCLC; *The Birmingham News*, 8 January 1966; Herbert Graham III, *The Brothers' Vietnam War: Black Power, Manhood, and the Military Experience* (Gainesville: University Press of Florida, 2003), 15–29; Carson, *In Struggle*, 175–90.
37. Carson, *In Struggle*, 192–99; *The New York Times*, 5 August 1966.
38. Halberstam, *The Children*, 506–509, 522–24; Lewis, *Walking with the Wind*, 362–68.

39. *The Southern Patriot*, May 1966; "Suggestions for Direction of SNCC," 11 May 1966, Box 2, Folder 11, SNCC-AR; "Assumptions Made by SNCC," 11 May 1966, Series 4, Box 62, Folder 430, TBP.

40. Senatobia speeches, 9 June 1966, SRTR.

41. Howard Himmelbaum, interview by author, telephone, 18 January 2011; William Hansen, interview by author; *The New York Times*, 27 May 1966. See also Brent Riffel, "In the Storm: William Hansen and the Student Nonviolent Coordinating Committee in Arkansas," *The Arkansas Historical Quarterly* 63, no. 4 (Winter 2004): 404–419; Randy Finley, "Crossing the White Line: SNCC in Three Delta Towns, 1963–1967," *The Arkansas Historical Quarterly* 65, no. 2 (summer 2006): 117–37; Jennifer Jensen Wallach, "Replicating History in a Bad Way? White Activists and Black Power in SNCC's Arkansas Project," *The Arkansas Historical Quarterly* 67, no. 3 (Autumn 2008): 268–87.

42. Arkansas Staff Meeting Notes, 9 June 1966, Box 1, Folder 7, SNCC-AR; William Hansen, interview by author; Howard Himmelbaum, interview by author; Myrtle Glascoe, interview by author, telephone, 16 March 2011; Mitchell Zimmerman, interview by author, telephone, 15 December 2010.

43. Arkansas Staff Meeting Notes, 9 June 1966, Box 1, Folder 7, SNCC-AR; William Hansen, interview by author; Vincent O'Connor Diary, Box 6, Folder 1, SNCC-AR. See also Bill Hansen, "Arkansas Daze," in Jennifer Jensen Wallach and John A. Kirk, eds., *Arsnick: The Student Nonviolent Coordinating Committee in Arkansas* (Fayetteville: University of Arkansas Press, 2011), 87–100.

44. "Recommendations and Mandates of the SNCC Central Committee," May 1966, Reel 3, SNCC; Central Committee Minutes, 10–12 June 1966, Reel 3, SNCC.

45. Central Committee Minutes, 10–12 June 1966, Reel 3, SNCC; Carmichael, *Ready for Revolution*, 490–91; Sellers, *The River of No Return*, 161–62.

46. Courtland Cox, interview by the author; Central Committee Minutes, 10–12 June 1966, Reel 3, SNCC.

47. Central Committee Minutes, 10–12 June 1966, Reel 3, SNCC.

5. Registering Is All Right

1. *Newsday*, 11 June 1966; Jonathan Steinberg, "Mississippi Election—1966," *Liberation*, May/June 1966, 50–51.

2. Frank R. Parker, *Black Votes Count: Political Empowerment in Mississippi After 1965* (Chapel Hill: University of North Carolina Press, 1990), 31.

3. "A Brief Report on the Panola Project," 16 February 1965, Reel 7, SNCC; Frederick M. Wirt, *Politics of Southern Equality: Law and Social Change in a Mississippi County* (Chicago: Aldine Publishing, 1970), 45–47, 143–48; Frederick M. Wirt, *"We Ain't What We Was": Civil Rights in the New South* (Durham, N.C.: Duke University Press, 1997), 36–52; Sutherland, *Letters From Mississippi*, 86–89; Penny Patch, "The Mississippi Cotton Vote," in Faith Holsaert et al., eds., *Hands on the Freedom Plow: Personal Accounts by Women in SNCC* (Urbana: University of Illinois Press, 2010), 403–409.

4. "Mississippi Registration by County, Race and Congressional District," Reel 144, SRC; Memorandum by Nicholas Katzenbach, 1 June 1966, Box 139, Folder 1, PBJFP; Steven F. Lawson, *Black Ballots: Voting Rights in the South, 1944–1969* (New York: Columbia University Press, 1976), 329–31; Steven F. Lawson, *In Pursuit of Power: Southern Blacks and Electoral Politics, 1965–1982* (New York: Columbia University Press, 1985), 29, 40–41; Letter to Attorney General, 2 February 1966, Part 1, Reel 9, CRJA; William Leon Higgs, "LBJ and the Negro Vote: Case of the Missing Registrars," *The Nation*, 13 December 1965, 460–62; *The New York Times*, 12 June 1966.

5. *The New York Times*, 10 June 1966; Parker, *Black Votes Count*, 34–63.

6. Percy Bruce, interview by the author, telephone, 7 April 2010; Cathryn Hyde, interview by the author, telephone, 7 April 2010; Earl Tucker, interview by the author, 7 April 2010.

7. *The Philadelphia Tribune*, 11 June 1966.

8. "Benton County Freedom Train," 11 June 1966, Box 6, Folder 8, BGRC.

9. Sovereignty Commission memorandum, 9 June 1966, SCR ID# 1-103-0-6-1-1-1, MSSC; Jack Sisson memorandum, 30 June 1966, Series 18, Box 4, Folder 1, NCCIJ; *The Courier-Journal* (Louisville), 11 June 1966; Highway Patrol memorandum, 10 June 1966, Box 147, Folder 4, PBJFP; *Jackson Daily News*, 10 June 1966; Sovereignty Commission memorandum, 10 June 1966, SCR ID# 9-31-5-36-1-1-1, MSSC.

10. FBI memorandum, 11 June 1966, Box 71B, Folder 3, LBJ-MS; *The Washington Post*, 11 June 1966; *The Courier-Journal* (Louisville), 11 June 1966; *The Nashville Tennessean*, 11 June 1966.

11. Press release, 10 June 1966, Reel 13, CORE-A; *Memphis Press-Scimitar*, 10 June 1966; *The Meridian* (Miss.) *Star*, 11 June 1966; *Chicago Daily News*, 10 June 1966, 11 June 1966; *Los Angeles Times*, 11 June 1966.

12. *The Commercial Appeal* (Memphis), 11 June 1966.

13. *The Panolian* (Batesville, Miss.), 16 June 1966; *The Baltimore Afro-American*, 18 June 1966; *New York Post*, 11 June 1966.

14. *The Sun* (Baltimore), 11 June 1966; *Chicago Daily News*, 11 June 1966; *New York Post*, 11 June 1966.

15. *New York Post*, 11 June 1966.

16. Floyd McKissick interview, 21 October 1988, EPI; *Newsday*, 11 June 1966; *New York Post*, 11 June 1966; Press release, 10 June 1966, Reel 13, CORE-A; *The Boston Globe*, 10 June 1966 (evening edition), 11 June 1966; *The Baltimore Afro-American*, 18 June 1966.

17. Sovereignty Commission memorandum, 4 June 1966, SCR ID# 9-31-5-31-1-1-1, MSSC; Lawrence Guyot, interview by the author, telephone, 31 March 2010.

18. John Dittmer, *Local People: The Struggle for Civil Rights in Mississippi* (Urbana: University of Illinois Press, 1994), 320–23; Lawrence Guyot, interview by the author.

19. Notes from SNCC staff meeting, 26 November 1965, Box 8, Folder 1, DLC; Lawrence Guyot and Mike Thelwell, "Toward Independent Political Power," *Freedomways*, Fall 1966, 246–54; Central Committee Minutes, 10–12 June 1966, Reel 3, SNCC.

20. Clifton Whitley, interview by the author, telephone, 29 September 2011; *The Commercial Appeal* (Memphis), 7 June 1966; Chris Myers-Asch, *The Senator and the Sharecropper: The Freedom Struggles of James O. Eastland and Fannie Lou Hamer* (New York: New Press, 2008), 237–39; *Jackson Daily News*, 6 June 1966. See also *The Clarion-Ledger* (Jackson), 3 June 1966, 7 June 1966; *The Greenwood Commonwealth*, 6 June 1966; *The Enterprise-Tocsin* (Indianola, Miss.), 2 June 1966.

21. Ed King, interview with Taylor Branch, 26 February 1992, Series 4, Box 105, Folder 752, TBP; Ed King, interview by author; "Mississippi Primaries: The Aftermath," Box 2, Folder 16, Ellin (Joseph and Nancy) Freedom Summer Collection, USM-CRM.

22. *The New York Times*, 8 June 1966; Memorandum by Sanford Leigh, 30 June 1966, Reel 16, CORE-A; "Mississippi Primaries: The Aftermath Transcript," USM-CRM.

23. Ruby Davis to Patricia Werner, 12 June 1966, Box 1, Folder 1, Ruby Davis Papers, WHS; "Votes for Freedom Candidates in Official Elections, 1962–1966," Box 5, Folder 5, DMR; Sovereignty Commission memorandum, 13 June 1966, SCR ID# 2-51-0-46-1-1-1, MSSC; Sovereignty Commission memorandum, 17 June 1966, Box 134, Folder 1, PBJFP.

24. Lawrence Guyot, interview by the author; Sovereignty Commission memoranda, both 7 June 1966, SCR ID# 9-31-5-32-1-1-1 and SCR ID# 9-31-5-33-1-1-1, MSSC; Press release, 9 June 1966, Box 139, Folder 1, PBJFP; Owen Brooks, interview by the author; Jesse Harris, interview by the author.

25. FBI memorandum, 11 June 1966, Box 71B, Folder 3, LBJ-MS; Sovereignty Commission memorandum, 9 June 1966, SCR ID# 1-103-0-6-1-1-1, MSSC; Joe Morse, "Meridian Project Report," 5 July 1966, Reel 2, MFDP-LC.

26. "Political Workshop in Sunflower," 7 May 1966, HTD; Joe Morse, "Meridian Project Report," 5 July 1966, Reel 2, MFDP-LC; "How Your Mississippi Congressman Voted Last Year," Reel 16, CORE-A; Sanford Leigh memorandum, Reel 16, CORE-A.

27. Wirt, *Politics of Southern Equality*, 48–49.

28. *The Washington Post*, 12 June 1966; Joel Bernard to Jacqueline Bernard, 13 June 1966, Box 1, Folder 1, JBP; "People of Panola County," Box 1, Folder 6, KKK.

29. *The Washington Post*, 12 June 1966; Sovereignty Commission memorandum, 20 June 1966, SCR ID# 1-67-4-129-1-1-1, MSSC.

30. *The Washington Post*, 12 June 1966; *Memphis Press-Scimitar*, 11 June 1966; *The Guardian* (London), 18 June 1966.

31. *Memphis Press-Scimitar*, 11 June 1966; *The Washington Post*, 12 June 1966; *The Atlanta Journal and Constitution*, 12 June 1966.

32. Press release, 11 June 1966, Reel 13, CORE-A; *The Sun* (Baltimore), 12 June 1966; *The Washington Post*, 12 June 1966.

33. *The Sun* (Baltimore), 12 June 1966.

34. Jim Peppler, interview by the author, telephone, 3 February 2010; Bob Fitch, interview by the author; *The New York Times*, 12 June 1966.

35. *The Philadelphia Inquirer*, 12 June 1966; Wirt, *Politics of Southern Equality*, 148–51.

36. Batesville recording, 11 June 1966, SRTR.

37. Charles Evers, interview by the author, Jackson, 25 May 2010; James Meredith to Charles Evers, 26 December 1965, Box 12, Folder 13, JHMC; Charles Evers to James

Meredith, 30 December 1965, Box 12, Folder 13, JHMC; Charles Evers travel schedule 1966, Part 29, Series A, Reel 6, NAACP-B; *The New York Times*, 7 June 1966.

38. *The New York Times*, 11 June 1966; *The Sun* (Baltimore), 12 June 1966.

39. Charles Evers with Grace Halsell, *Evers* (New York: World Publishing, 1971), 99–107; Dittmer, *Local People*, 177–78; Charles Evers, interview by the author; Roy Wilkins to Charles Evers, 13 September 1965, Part 29, Series A, Reel 6, NAACP-B.

40. Charles Evers with Andrew Szanton, *Have No Fear: The Charles Evers Story* (New York: Wiley, 1997), 200–202; Dittmer, *Local People*, 353–62; Emilye Crosby, "'God's Appointed Savior': Charles Evers's Use of Local Movements for National Stature," in Jeanne Theoharis and Komozi Woodard, eds., *Groundwork: Local Black Freedom Movements in America* (New York: New York University Press, 2005), 165–73; Emilye Crosby, *A Little Taste of Freedom: The Black Freedom Struggle in Claiborne County, Mississippi* (Chapel Hill: University of North Carolina Press, 2005), 189–94; Telegrams to Roy Wilkins, Part 29, Series A, Reel 6, NAACP-B. See also Charles Evers to Lyndon Johnson, 31 August 1965; Clifford Alexander to Lyndon Johnson, 1 October 1965; and Buford Ellington to Lyndon Johnson, all in Folder HU 2/ST 24, Box 27, WHCF-HU.

41. Crosby, *A Little Taste of Freedom*, 139; Charles Evers, interview by the author; Ed King, interview by the author; Claude Ramsey interview, 28 April 1981, USM-COH; Lawrence Guyot, interview by the author.

42. Charles Evers, interview by the author; Evers, *Evers*, 127–29; Charles Evers interview, Part 1, Reel 3, OHJA; Rowland Evans and Robert Novak, "Inside Report: Black-White Politics," April 1965, Box 1, Folder 5, MFDP; Lawson, *Black Ballots*, 96–98.

43. *The New York Times*, 10 June 1966.

44. *Jackson Advocate*, 4 June 1966; *The New York Times*, 10 June 1966; Emmett Burns to Gloster Current, 11 June 1966, Gloster Current to Emmett Burns, 21 June 1966, and Jack Young to Gloster Current, 28 May 1966, all in Part 29, Series A, Reel 6, NAACP-B.

45. Ed King, interview by the author; *Los Angeles Times*, 17 June 1966; *The Washington Post*, 17 June 1966.

46. Roy Wilkins telegram, 7 June 1966, Group IV, Box A56, Folder "Meredith, James, 1966," NAACP.

47. Gloster Current to Roy Wilkins, 10 June 1966, Group IV, Box A56, Folder "Meredith, James, 1966," NAACP; Gloster Current to Henry Lee Moon, 13 June 1966, Group IV, Box A56, Folder "Meredith, James, 1966," NAACP; NAACP Press Release, 11 June 1966, Group IV, Box A56, Folder "Meredith, James, 1966," NAACP; Roy Wilkins to NAACP Branch Officers, 10 June 1966, Group IV, Box A56, Folder "Meredith, James, 1966," NAACP; *The Chicago Defender*, 15 June 1966; *Memphis World*, 18 June 1966.

48. Henry Lee Moon to Gloster Current, 13 June 1966, Henry Lee Moon to Gloster Current, 14 June 1966, and Henry Lee Moon to Gloster Current, 15 June 1966, all in Part 29, Series B, Reel 14, NAACP-B; *The Times-Picayune* (New Orleans), 13

June 1966; *The Southern Courier*, 18–19 June 1966; *Jackson Daily News*, 13 June 1966; *The Clarion-Ledger* (Jackson), 13 June 1966.

49. Dittmer, *Local People*, 29–32, 118–19, 200–207, 274–75, 341–44; "Mississippi and the NAACP," *Crisis*, June–July 1966, 317–18; *The Boston Globe*, 19 June 1966; Aaron Henry with Constance Curry, *Aaron Henry: The Fire Ever Burning* (Jackson: University Press of Mississippi, 2000), 199–203; Payne, *I've Got the Light of Freedom*, 29–66; Françoise N. Hamlin, *Crossroads at Clarksdale: The Black Freedom Struggle in the Mississippi Delta after World War II* (Chapel Hill: University of North Carolina Press, 2012), 1–166; Sovereignty Commission memorandum, 24 April 1966, SCR ID# 9-31-5-9-1-1-1, MSSC.

50. *The Clarksdale* (Miss.) *Press-Register*, 10 June 1966, 13 June 1966; FBI File 157-6296-1 (NAACP March for James H. Meredith, Clarksdale, Mississippi); Coahoma County Branch NAACP "Cryer," 10 June 1966, Part IV, Box J6, Folder "Mississippi, 1966–1969," NAACP; *Chicago Daily News*, 13 June 1966; *The Christian Science Monitor*, 17 June 1966.

6. The World Is Watching

1. Sovereignty Commission memorandum, 20 June 1965, SCR ID# 9-31-3-196-1-1-1, MSSC; Sovereignty Commission memorandum, 24 June 1965, SCR ID# 9-31-4-3-1-1-1, MSSC. For Informant X reports on Meredith March, see sequence beginning with SCR ID# 9-31-5-31-1-1-1 and ending with SCR ID# 9-31-5-52-1-1-1, MSSC.

2. Yasuhiro Katagiri, *The Mississippi State Sovereignty Commission: Civil Rights and States' Rights* (Jackson: University of Mississippi Press, 2001); Jenny Irons, *Reconstituting Whiteness: The Mississippi State Sovereignty Commission* (Nashville: Vanderbilt University Press, 2010); Ken Lawrence, interview by Ashaki M. Binta, "Mississippi Spies," *Southern Exposure*, fall 1981, 82–86.

3. "Report on Mississippi State Sovereignty Commission (1964–1967)," SCR ID# 99-131-0-20-4-1-1, MSSC.

4. Sovereignty Commission memorandum, 9 June 1966, SCR ID# 9-31-5-34-1-1-1, MSSC. The original memo misspells "Rustin" as "Ruston" and "leftist" as "leftest."

5. Jack Rosenthal to Bill Moyers, Box 56, HU 2/FG 216, Folder 5, WHCOF; Paul Johnson interview, 8 September 1970, Part 3, Reel 2, OHJA.

6. Memorandum by Jack Sisson, 30 June 1966, Series 18, Box 4, Folder 1, NCCIJ; Jim Peppler, interview by the author; Jo Freeman, interview by the author, telephone, 10 February 2010; Melvyn R. Leventhal, "The Civil Rights Movement Comes to an End," unpublished essay in author's possession; *Los Angeles Times*, 16 June 1966; "B'rer Fox," *Time*, 24 June 1966, 31; "The Talk of the Town," *The New Yorker*, 16 July 1966, 21.

7. Tim Spofford, *Lynch Street: The May 1970 Slayings at Jackson State College* (Kent, Ohio: Kent State University Press, 1988), 43–44.

8. Nicholas deB. Katzenbach, *Some of It Was Fun: Working with RFK and LBJ* (New York: Norton, 2008), 71–84, 108–29; Lawson, *In Pursuit of Power*, 16–17; Nicholas Katzenbach, interview by the author, telephone, 17 March 2010.

9. *Newsday*, 23 June 1966.
10. John Doar, interview by the author; *Chicago Daily News*, 20 June 1966; *The Washington Post*, 11 June 1966, 20 June 1966.
11. Kenneth O'Reilly, *"Racial Matters": The FBI's Secret File on Black America, 1960–1972* (New York: Free Press, 1989), 1–193.
12. Nicholas Katzenbach, interview by the author.
13. *The Baltimore Afro-American*, 25 June 1966; *The Washington Post*, 21 June 1966; *The Christian Science Monitor*, 15 June 1966. FBI memoranda on Meredith March available in Box 71B, Folders 2 and 3, LBJ-MS.
14. FBI memorandum, 10 June 1966, Part 1, Reel 10, MLK-FBI; Wyn Craig Wade, *The Fiery Cross: The Ku Klux Klan in America* (New York: Oxford University Press, 1987), 303–304; Highway Patrol memorandum, 13 June 1966, Box 147, Folder 4, PBJFP.
15. David J. Garrow, *The FBI and Martin Luther King, Jr.: From "Solo" to Memphis* (New York: Norton, 1981), 21–208.
16. FBI surveillance of Stanley Levison, 7–10 June 1966, Part 2, Reel 5, MLK-FBI.
17. *Chicago Daily News*, 8 June 1966, 9 June 1966, 11 June 1966; *Los Angeles Times*, 9 June 1966.
18. See Jackson, *From Civil Rights to Human Rights*.
19. *The Chicago Defender*, 13 June 1966; FBI memorandum, 14 June 1966, Part 1, Reel 10, MLK-FBI.
20. *The Chicago Defender*, 8 June 1966; *Chicago Daily News*, 7 June 1966, 9 June 1966; *Chicago Tribune*, 10 June 1966; James Coleman to Martin Luther King, 13 June 1966, Part 1, Reel 15, SCLC.
21. *The Chicago Defender*, 13 June 1966; FBI memorandum, 14 June 1966, Part 1, Reel 10, MLK-FBI.
22. FBI memoranda, 12 June 1966 and 14 June 1966, Part 1, Reel 10, MLK-FBI; FBI surveillance of Stanley Levison, 12 June 1966, Part 2, Reel 5, MLK-FBI.
23. Lewis, *Walking with the Wind*, 166–67, 299–300; Halberstam, *The Children*, 331–32.
24. Young, *An Easy Burden*, 333–37; Carson, *In Struggle*, 158–66; Fairclough, *To Redeem the Soul of America*, 212–14, 241–48; Sellers, *The River of No Return*, 115–29; Charles E. Fager, *Selma, 1965* (New York: Scribner, 1974), 111, 138–40; Ralph David Abernathy, *And the Walls Came Tumbling Down: An Autobiography* (New York: Harper and Row, 1989), 301, 345.
25. Ralph Abernathy to John Lewis, 19 August 1965, Part 4, Reel 7, SCLC; Martin Luther King speech in Atlanta, 14 January 1966, Series 4, Box 60, Folder 421, TBP; Evelyn Rowley to Martin Luther King, 18 February 1966, Part 1, Reel 15, SCLC; W. L. Tipton to Martin Luther King, 8 June 1966, Part 1, Reel 15, SCLC; S. Jones to Martin Luther King, 14 June 1966, Part 1, Reel 15, SCLC; Rowland Evans and Robert Novak column, 20 March 1965, Reel 22, SNCC; *The New York Times*, 28 May 1966.
26. On Citizenship Education Program see Box 5, Folder 9, VGA; Citizenship School Reports, Part 4, Reel 13, SCLC. On support for Congressional Challenge see Victoria Gray to Randolph Blackwell, 12 October 1965, Series 1, Box 16, Folder 7, MLKP; Victoria Gray to Martin Luther King, 26 May 1966, Series 1, Box 16, Folder 8,

MLKP. On King visit to Mississippi see Belfrage, *Freedom Summer*, 164–66. On SCLC staff in Mississippi see memorandum dated 13 October 1965, Part 4, Reel 8, SCLC; Interview with R. B. Cottonreader, SRTR.

27. David Acey, interview by the author, Memphis, 23 March 2011.

28. Cleveland Sellers, interview by the author; Beulah Powers to Martin Luther King, 24 June 1966, Part 1, Reel 15, SCLC; *The Washington Post*, 10 June 1966.

29. Carmichael, *Ready for Revolution*, 511–13; Stokely Carmichael interview, 7 November 1988, EPI; "Tape #11 H.P.," Series 2, Box 1, Folder 18, HWC.

30. *The Clarion-Ledger* (Jackson), 25 August 1966; Marian Wright Edelman interview, 21 December 1968, EPI; FBI memorandum, Box 71B, Folder 2, LBJ-MS; Sellers, *The River of No Return*, 168–69; Cleveland Sellers interview, 21 October 1968, EPI; Carmichael, *Ready for Revolution*, 511–12.

31. "The Time Has Come," *Eyes on the Prize II: America at the Crossroads*, vol. 1 (Blackside Productions, 1990).

32. FBI memorandum, 12 June 1966, Part 1, Reel 10, MLK-FBI; *The Philadelphia Inquirer*, 13 June 1966; FBI memorandum, 13 June 1966, Box 71B, Folder 2, LBJ-MS; *Chicago Tribune*, 13 June 1966.

33. *Newsday*, 13 June 1966; *The Clarion-Ledger* (Jackson), 13 June 1966.

34. Charles McLaurin, interview by the author, telephone, 14 April 2010; Sovereignty Commission memorandum, 13 June 1966, SCR ID# 9-31-5-37-1-1-1, MSSC; *The New York Times*, 13 June 1966.

35. *The New York Times*, 19 June 1966.

36. Highway Patrol memorandum, 13 June 1966, Box 147, Folder 4, PBJFP; *The New York Times*, 13 June 1966.

37. Ray Goldstein, interview by the author, telephone, 2 March 2010; Jim Peppler, interview by the author; Payne, *I've Got the Light of Freedom*, 265–83; Belinda Robnett, *How Long? How Long?: African-American Women in the Struggle for Civil Rights* (New York: Oxford University Press, 1997), 19–21; Lynne Olson, *Freedom's Daughters: The Unsung Heroines of the Civil Rights Movement from 1830 to 1970* (New York: Touchstone, 2001), 248–63, 313–30. See also Winson Hudson with Constance Curry, *Mississippi Harmony: Memoirs of a Freedom Fighter* (New York: Palgrave Macmillan, 2002).

38. On Hamer see Chana Kai Lee, *For Freedom's Sake: The Life of Fannie Lou Hamer* (Urbana: University of Illinois Press, 1999); Kay Mills, *This Little Light of Mine: The Life of Fannie Lou Hamer* (New York: Dutton, 1993); Danielle McGuire, *At the Dark End of the Street: Black Women, Rape, and Resistance—a New History of the Civil Rights Movement from Rosa Parks to the Rise of Black Power* (New York: Knopf, 2010), 191–95; Myers-Asch, *The Senator and the Sharecropper*; Fannie Lou Hamer, *To Praise Our Bridges: An Autobiography* (Jackson, Miss.: KIPCO, 1967).

39. Roy Goldstein field recording, 12 June 1966, copy in author's possession; Steven Kasher, *The Civil Rights Movement: A Photographic History, 1954–68* (New York: Abbeville, 1996), 210.

40. Roy Goldstein field recording, 12 June 1966, copy in author's possession.
41. Highway Patrol memorandum, 13 June 1966, Box 147, Folder 4, PBJFP; Raines, *My Soul Is Rested*, 422; Martin Luther King sermon, 12 June 1966, Series 3, Box 11, MLKP.
42. FBI memorandum, 14 June 1966, Part 1, Reel 10, MLK-FBI; FBI memorandum, 13 June 1966, Box 71B, Folder 2, LBJ-MS; *The Philadelphia Inquirer*, 13 June 1966; *The Washington Post*, 13 June 1966.
43. *The New York Times*, 12 June 1966; *The Philadelphia Inquirer*, 12 June 1966; New York *Daily News*, 12 June 1966; *Los Angeles Times*, 12 June 1966.
44. *The Wall Street Journal*, 8 June 1966; *The Jackson Times*, 9 June 1966.
45. *The Commercial Appeal* (Memphis), 8 June 1966, 9 June 1966; *Los Angeles Times*, 13 June 1966.
46. Laura Lawson to Martin Luther King, 16 June 1966, Part 1, Reel 15, SCLC; Charles Fisher to Lyndon Johnson, 20 June 1966, Box 40, Folder HU 2/ST 24, WHCF-HU; *The Joplin* (Mo.) *Globe*, 17 June 1966.
47. *Houston Chronicle*, 10 June 1966; *The New York Times*, 12 June 1966; *The Beaumont* (Texas) *Enterprise*, 9 June 1966; *Arkansas Democrat*, 11 June 1966; *The Clarion-Ledger* (Jackson), 30 June 1966; *The Washington Daily News*, 14 June 1966; *St. Louis Globe-Democrat*, 16 June 1966; *St. Louis Watchman Advocate*, 12 June 1966; *The Courier-Journal* (Louisville), 19 June 1966; *The Modesto Bee*, 16 June 1966; *Winona* (Minn.) *Daily News*, 15 June 1966.
48. *The Washington Daily News*, 9 June 1966; *The Washington Star*, 12 June 1966; *The Washington Post*, 13 June 1966.
49. *The Times-Picayune* (New Orleans), 12 June 1966; *The Clarion-Ledger* (Jackson), 12 June 1966; *The Washington Post*, 13 June 1966.

7. Everybody Should Have Their March

1. *The New York Times*, 14 June 1966; *The Southern Courier*, 18–19 June 1966.
2. See Hill, *The Deacons for Defense*.
3. *Delta Democrat Times*, 26 June 1966; Ray Goldstein, interview by author; Carmichael, *Ready for Revolution*, 504; *Los Angeles Times*, 12 June 1966; Sovereignty Commission memorandum, 9 June 1966, Box 139, Folder 1, PBJFP; *The New York Times*, 14 June 1966.
4. *New York Amsterdam News*, 18 June 1966; Akinyele Umoja, "Eye for an Eye: The Role of Armed Resistance in the Mississippi Freedom Movement" (Ph.D. dissertation, Emory University, 1996), 131–37, 166–69; Simon Wendt, *The Spirit and the Shotgun: Armed Resistance and the Struggle for Civil Rights* (Gainesville: University of Florida Press, 2007), 100–128; Stokely Carmichael interview, 7 November 1988, EPI. On armed self-defense see also Christopher B. Strain, *Pure Fire: Self-Defense as Activism in the Civil Rights Era* (Athens: University of Georgia Press, 2005); Timothy B. Tyson, *Radio Free Dixie: Robert F. Williams and the Roots of Black Power* (Chapel Hill: University of North Carolina Press, 1999).

5. Cleveland Sellers interview, 21 October 1988, EPI; Steve Estes, *I Am a Man!: Race, Manhood, and the Civil Rights Movement* (Chapel Hill: University of North Carolina Press, 2005), 39–86; *The New York Times*, 13 June 1966.

6. *The New York Times*, 13 June 1966.

7. Alvin F. Poussaint, "A Negro Psychiatrist Explains the Negro Psyche," *The New York Times Magazine*, 20 August 1967, 53; Juan Williams, *My Soul Looks Back in Wonder: Voices of the Civil Rights Experience* (New York: AARP Books, 2004), 129–31.

8. Interview with Alvin Poussaint, SRTR; Dittmer, *The Good Doctors*, 135–40; Johnny Parham, "A Proposal for the Participation of Students in the Health Fields to Work with the Medical Committee for Human Rights During the Summer of 1966," Box 1, Folder "Exc Com—Proposal, 1966," MCHR.

9. Alvin Poussaint, interview by author; MCHR Volunteer Manual, June 1966, CRM-VET; "Medical Committee for Human Rights—Summer Program (1966) in the South for MCHR Volunteers," Box 2, Folder "Membership, 1964–66," MCHR.

10. Alvin Poussaint, interview by author; Joyce Ladner, interview by author, telephone, 19 May 2010; Phyllis Cunningham, interview by author, telephone, 25 March 2011; Rosalie Ross to Edward Grant, 16 June 1966, Box 1, Folder "Exec. Director Parham, John, 1965–66," MCHR; Fund-raising letter by David French, 17 June 1966, Box 1, Folder "David French, National Chairman, 1966," MCHR; "MCHR Chapters," Box 2, Folder "Other Reports," MCHR; Dittmer, *The Good Doctors*, 149–50.

11. *The Commercial Appeal* (Memphis), 10 June 1966; Alvin Poussaint, interview by author.

12. "Criteria for Screening Applicants for Work with COFO in Mississippi," Box 3, Folder 4, DLC; Dittmer, *The Good Doctors*, 52–53; J. W. Kirkman, "Report on Mississippi," 1 March 1966, Box 6, Folder 8, RBP.

13. Alvin Poussaint, interview by author; "Some Aspects of Black-White Problems As Seen By Field Staff," Box 2, Folder "Jackson, Miss. Field Office, 1966," MCHR.

14. Alvin F. Poussaint, "The Stresses of the White Female Worker in the Civil Rights Movement in the South," Box 3, Folder "Other Papers," MCHR, and later reprinted in *The American Journal of Psychiatry* 123, no. 4 (October 1966): 401–407; Alvin F. Poussaint, "Problems of White Civil Rights Workers in the South," *Psychiatric Opinion* 3 (1966): 18–24.

15. "'African Queen' Complex," *Newsweek*, 23 May 1966, 94–95; "When White Girls Go South as Civil Rights Workers," *US News and World Report*, 30 May 1966, 10; Francis Ward, "'White Queen' Complex Angers Negro Women; Rivalry Revealed," *Jet*, 9 June 1966, 14–21; Alvin Poussaint, interview by author; Jo Freeman, interview by author; Matthew Rinaldi, interview by author, telephone, 4 March 2010; Phyllis Cunningham, interview by author.

16. Alvin F. Poussaint, "The Negro American: His Self-Image and Integration," paper presented to National Medical Association, 8 August 1966, Reel 2, SNCC; Poussaint, "A Negro Psychiatrist Explains the Negro Psyche," 52–57, 73–80; Alvin F. Poussaint and Joyce Ladner, "Black Power," *Archives of General Psychiatry* 18, no. 4 (April 1968): 385–91.

17. *The New York Times*, 12 June 1966.

18. Ray Goldstein, interview by author.
19. *Ames* (Iowa) *Tribune*, 14 June 1966; *The Baltimore Afro-American*, 18 June 1966; *Newsday*, 18 June 1966; *Detroit Free Press*, 11 June 1966; *The New York Times*, 26 June 1966.
20. *The Washington Post*, 10 June 1966.
21. David Dawley interview, 6 July 1989, EPI.
22. Melvyn Leventhal, interview by author; Melvyn Leventhal, "The Civil Rights Movement Comes to an End," unpublished essay in author's possession; *Newsday*, 10 June 1966; *The Washington Post*, 11 June 1966.
23. Jo Freeman, interview by author; Jo Freeman, "On the Origins of the Women's Liberation Movement from a Strictly Personal Perspective," in Rachel Blau DuPlessis and Ann Snitow, eds., *The Feminist Memoir Project: Voices from Women's Liberation* (New York: Three Rivers Press, 1998), 171–75.
24. Jo Freeman, interview by author; Jo Freeman to Mother, 29 June 1966, JFPP; "Miscellaneous Meanderings II," JFPP.
25. Jo Freeman, interview by author; Cathy Deppe, interview by author, telephone, 9 November 2010.
26. Jo Freeman, interview by author; Freeman, "On the Origins of the Women's Liberation Movement," 176–77; Sara Evans, *Personal Politics: The Roots of Women's Liberation, in the Civil Rights Movement and the New Left* (New York: Knopf, 1979), 76–80, 100–101.
27. *Des Moines Tribune*, 13 June 1966. On marching clergymen see also *The Boston Globe* (evening edition), 7 June 1966; *Hattiesburg American*, 16 June 1966; *Detroit Free Press*, 11 June 1966.
28. Memorandum by Benjamin Patton, Box 56, Folder 8, Will Campbell Papers, USM; *The Amarillo Daily News*, 16 June 1966; Matt Ahmann to Council Presidents and Chairmen and Chaplains, 14 June 1966, Series 18, Box 4, Folder 1, NCCIJ.
29. Jack Sisson, interview by the author, telephone, 2 August 2010; Jack Sisson to Matt Ahmann, 30 June 1966, Series 18, Box 4, Folder 1, NCCIJ; Matt Ahmann to Board of Directors, 30 June 1966, Series 18, Box 4, Folder 1, NCCIJ; *The Philadelphia Inquirer*, 11 June 1966; *The Washington Post*, 11 June 1966, 14 June 1966; *Los Angeles Times*, 15 June 1966; Homer A. Jack, "Black Power and the Meredith March," *Gandhi Marg*, October 1966, 295–302.
30. *The Washington Post*, 14 June 1966; *Newsday*, 18 June 1966; Sovereignty Commission memorandum, 1 July 1966, SCR ID# 1-91-0-11-1-1-1, MSSC.
31. *Detroit Free Press*, 14 June 1966; *New York Post*, 9 June 1966; Doug McAdam, *Freedom Summer* (New York: Oxford University Press, 1988), 127–32; *The New York Times*, 12 June 1966.
32. *The Clarion-Ledger* (Jackson), 14 June 1966; "The Talk of the Town," 21–22. The *New Yorker* article was reprinted in Renata Adler, *Toward a Radical Middle: Fourteen Pieces of Reporting and Criticism* (New York: Random House, 1970), 151–63.
33. "The Talk of the Town," 22; *The New York Times*, 18 June 1966.
34. David Doggett, interview by author, telephone, 20 January 2010; Ira Grupper, interview by author, telephone, 15 January 2010; Dick Reavis, interview by author,

telephone, 17 February 2010; Becky Brenner, interview by author, telephone, 6 March 2010.

35. Dick Reavis, interview by author.

36. *The Courier-Journal* (Louisville), 10 June 1966.

37. *The Baltimore Afro-American*, 18 June 1966.

38. *Memphis Press-Scimitar*, 11 June 1966; *The Tri-State Defender*, 18 June 1966; *Detroit Free Press*, 14 June 1966.

39. Coby Smith, unpublished memoir in author's possession.

40. Coby Smith, interview by author, Memphis, Tennessee, 9 February 2010.

41. Coby Smith, interview by author.

42. Coby Smith, unpublished memoir in author's possession; Coby Smith, interview by author.

43. *Newsday*, 18 June 1966; *The New York Times*, 18 June 1966; *New York Post*, 11 June 1966, 28 June 1966.

44. Paul Good, "The Meredith March," *New South*, summer 1966, 5; Young, *An Easy Burden*, 395.

45. Barbara Emerson (Barbara Jean Williams), interview by author, telephone, 16 September 2010.

46. Barbara W. Emerson, "Coming of Age: Civil Rights and Feminism," in DuPlessis and Snitow, *The Feminist Memoir Project*, 54–70; Barbara Emerson, interview by author.

47. MacArthur Cotton, interview by author, Jackson, 27 March 2010; George Greene, interview by author, telephone, 23 April 2010; Hollis Watkins, interview by author, telephone, 12 April 2010.

48. Hollis Watkins, interview by author.

49. Myrtle Glascoe, interview by author; Carrie Young (Carrie Lamar), interview by author, telephone, 19 March 2011; Charlie Cobb, interview by author, telephone, 19 March 2010; Courtland Cox, interview by author.

50. *The Boston Globe* (evening edition), 10 June 1966.

51. Good, "The Meredith March," 4.

52. Courtland Cox interview, 17 April 1996, Box 7, Folder 10, WCBUT; William L. Van Deburg, *New Day in Babylon: The Black Power Movement and American Culture* (Chicago: University of Chicago Press, 1992), 29–62; Jeffrey O.G. Ogbar, *Black Power: Radical Politics and African American Identity* (Baltimore: Johns Hopkins University Press, 2004), 2–4, 156–58, 191–92.

53. *The New York Times*, 12 June 1966.

54. *Newsday*, 13 June 1966; *The Sun* (Baltimore), 13 June 1966; *The New York Times*, 13 June 1966; *New York Amsterdam News*, 18 June 1966; *The Meridian* (Miss.) *Star*, 14 June 1966; *Chicago Tribune*, 14 June 1966.

55. Charmaine McKissick-Melton (Charmaine McKissick), interview by author, telephone, 21 January 2011; Ira Grupper, interview by author; Floyd McKissick interview, 21 October 1988, EPI; "The Talk of the Town," 24.

56. Floyd McKissick, Jr., interview by author; Charmaine McKissick-Melton (Charmaine McKissick), interview by author.

57. *The Commercial Appeal* (Memphis), 14 June 1966; *The Washington Daily News*, 14 June 1966; FBI memorandum, 14 June 1966, Box 71B, Folder 2, LBJ-MS; Highway Patrol memorandum, 13 June 1966, Box 147, Folder 4, PBJFP.

58. *Newsday*, 14 June 1966.

59. Matthew Countryman, *Up South: Civil Rights and Black Power in Philadelphia* (Philadelphia: University of Pennsylvania Press, 2006), 120–79; Thomas J. Sugrue, *Sweet Land of Liberty: The Forgotten Struggle for Civil Rights in the North* (New York: Random House, 2008), 292–94.

60. Countryman, *Up South*, 230–31; *The Philadelphia Tribune*, 7 June 1966.

61. *The Philadelphia Tribune*, 18 June 1966; *Memphis Press-Scimitar*, 13 June 1966; *The Guardian* (London), 18 June 1966; Branch Minutes, 26 June 1966, Box 3, Folder 35, MS-NAACP; *The Washington Post*, 14 June 1966; *The Philadelphia Inquirer*, 14 June 1966.

62. *The Christian Science Monitor*, 23 June 1966; *The Clarion-Ledger* (Jackson), 28 June 1966; *Jackson Daily News*, 14 June 1966.

63. *Chicago Daily News*, 14 June 1966; *The Washington Post*, 15 June 1966.

8. Standing Tall

1. *The Clarion-Ledger* (Jackson), 23 February 2003; James Jones statement, 14 June 1966, Box 147, Folder 4, PBJFP.

2. *Newsday*, 15 June 1966; Mississippi Bureau of Identification Case Report, 13 June 1966, Box 147, Folder 4, PBJFP; *The Washington Post*, 18 June 1966.

3. *Newsday*, 15 June 1966; Chester Higgins, "Bury Victim of Mississippi Klansmen's," *Jet*, 7 July 1966; *The Clarion-Ledger* (Jackson), 23 February 2003; *The Worker*, 16 April 1967.

4. *Detroit Free Press*, 14 June 1966.

5. James W. Silver, *Mississippi: The Closed Society*, new ed. (New York: Harcourt, Brace and World, 1966; original 1963). See also Lambert, *Battle of Ole Miss*, 31–48, 65–82.

6. "The March Through Mississippi," *The World Today* radio program, Series 4, Box 62, Folder 434, TBP; *The Clarion-Ledger* (Jackson), 17 June 1966; *The Commercial Appeal* (Memphis), 26 June 1966; Ozella Day to Paul Johnson, 25 June 1966, Box 61, Folder 5, PBJFP; Ozella Day to James Eastland, 11 August 1966, File Series 3, Subseries 1, Box 43, Folder "Civil Rights—1966," JOEC.

7. Jason Sokol, *There Goes My Everything: White Southerners in the Age of Civil Rights, 1945–1975* (New York: Vintage, 2006), 213–37; David L. Chappell, *A Stone of Hope: Prophetic Religion and the Death of Jim Crow* (Chapel Hill: University of North Carolina Press, 2004), 105–78; Charles Marsh, *God's Long Summer: Stories of Faith and Civil Rights* (Princeton: Princeton University Press, 1997), 82–115; Carolyn Renee Dupont, "Mississippi Praying: White Religion and Black Equality, 1954–1966" (Ph.D. dissertation, University of Kentucky, 2003), 83–138; Charles C. Bolton, *The Hardest Deal of All: The Battle Over School Integration in Mississippi, 1870–1980* (Jackson: University Press of Mississippi, 2005), 117–40; Joseph Crespino,

In Search of Another Country: Mississippi and the Conservative Counterrevolution (Princeton: Princeton University Press, 2007), 144–266.

8. *Newsday*, 10 June 1966; Interview with T. L. Alexander, 10 June 1966, SRTR; *The Times-Picayune* (New Orleans), 15 June 1966; *The Meridian* (Miss.) *Star*, 13 June 1966, 28 June 1966, 29 June 1966; "Attention: Mississippians," SCR ID# 1-67-4-113-1-1-1, MSSC; *The Commercial Appeal* (Memphis), 19 June 1966, 29 June 1966; *The Clarion-Ledger* (Jackson), 14 June 1966, 29 June 1966, 4 July 1966.

9. *The Clarion-Ledger* (Jackson), 15 June 1966, 8 July 1966; *Detroit Free Press*, 12 June 1966; *The Christian Science Monitor*, 11 June 1966; *Detroit Free Press*, 14 June 1966.

10. Willie Morris, *North Toward Home* (Boston: Houghton Mifflin, 1967), 77–90; *Detroit Free Press*, 13 June 1966.

11. *Chicago Daily News*, 10 June 1966; *Los Angeles Times*, 10 June 1966; *New York Post*, 10 June 1966; Arlie Schardt interview, 14 November 1988, EPI.

12. *New York Post*, 13 June 1966.

13. John A. Whalen, *Maverick Among the Magnolias: The Hazel Brannon Smith Story* (Bloomington, Ind.: XLibris, 2000), 108–243; Arthur J. Kaul, "Hazel Brannon Smith and the *Lexington Advertiser*," in David R. Davies, ed., *The Press and Race: Mississippi Journalists Confront the Movement* (Jackson: University Press of Mississippi, 2001), 233–62; Jeffrey Brian Howell, "The Undiscovered Country: The Civil Rights Movement in Holmes County, Mississippi, 1965–1968" (M.A. thesis, Mississippi State University, 2005), 72–107; Jan Whitt, *Burning Crosses and Activist Journalism: Hazel Brannon Smith and the Mississippi Civil Rights Movement* (Lanham, Md.: University Press of America), 23–46; *The Lexington* (Miss.) *Advertiser*, 17 February 1966, 24 February 1966, 10 March 1966, 24 March 1966, 31 March 1966, 14 April 1966, 21 April 1966, 28 April 1966, 9 June 1966, 21 July 1966. See also Box 1, Folder 28, Hazel Brannon Smith Papers, MSU.

14. *The Lexington* (Miss.) *Advertiser*, 9 June 1966, 23 June 1966.

15. Ginger Rudeseal Carter, "Hodding Carter, Jr., and the *Delta Democrat-Times*," in Davies, ed., *The Press and Race*, 265–93; Gene Roberts and Hank Klibanoff, *The Race Beat: The Press, the Civil Rights Struggle, and the Awakening of a Nation* (New York: Vintage, 2006), 43–46, 64–66, 73–74, 203–204; James C. Cobb, *The Most Southern Place on Earth: The Mississippi Delta and the Roots of Regional Identity* (New York: Oxford University Press, 1992), 320–22; Crespino, *In Search of Another Country*, 30–33.

16. Ann Waldron, *Hodding Carter: The Reconstruction of a Racist* (Chapel Hill, N.C.: Algonquin Books of Chapel Hill, 1993), 306–10; *Delta Democrat Times*, 14 June 1966.

17. *Delta Democrat Times*, 20 June 1966; *The Northside Reporter*, 23 June 1966; Hodding Carter to Don and Pat Underwood, 22 June 1966, Box 25, Folder "Hodding Carter: Correspondence: 1966: U," HBWCP.

18. *The Greenwood Commonwealth*, 22 June 1966; *The Coffeeville* (Miss.) *Courier*, 23 June 1966; *Hattiesburg American*, 8 June 1966, 13 June 1966, 22 June 1966, 24 June 1966; *The Meridian* (Miss.) *Star*, 26 June 1966. See also Susan Weill, *In a Mad-*

house's Din: Civil Rights Coverage by Mississippi's Daily Press, 1948–1968 (Westport, Conn.: Praeger, 2002).

19. Roberts and Klibanoff, *The Race Beat*, 82–84; David R. Davies, "Jimmy Ward and the Jackson *Daily News*," in Davies, ed., *The Press and Race*, 87–109; *The Clarion-Ledger* (Jackson), 14 June 1966, 6 July 1966, 17 July 1966; *Jackson Daily News*, 10 June 1966, 17 June 1966.

20. *Jackson Daily News*, 8 June 1966–9 June 1966, 15 June 1966–17 June 1966, 21 June 1966, 25 June 1966, 28 June 1966, 4 July 1966, 16 July 1966.

21. Typed notes by Bill Minor, Box 9, Folder "Meredith, James—University of Mississippi (2/3)," WFMP.

22. Eagles, *The Price of Defiance*, 321–23, 326–28; Erle Johnston, *Mississippi's Defiant Years, 1953–1973* (Forest, Miss.: Lake Harbor Publishers, 1990), 222–27.

23. Crespino, *In Search of Another Country*, 115–19; Reid Stoner Durr, "The Triumph of Progressivism: Governor Paul B. Johnson, Jr., and Mississippi in the 1960s" (Ph.D. dissertation, University of Southern Mississippi, 1994), 196–492; Robert E. Luckett, "Yapping Dogs: Joe T. Patterson and the Limits of Massive Resistance" (Ph.D. dissertation, University of Georgia, 2009), 261–64; Paul Johnson Speech at State Democratic Convention, July 1964, Box 2, Folder 14, DLC.

24. Press release, 7 June 1966, Box 104, Folder 15, PBJFP; Jack Rosenthal to Bill Moyers, Box 56, HU 2/FG 216, Folder 5, WHCOF.

25. Press release, 7 June 1966, Box 104, Folder 15, PBJFP; *The Lexington* (Miss.) *Advertiser*, 9 June 1966; *The Southern Courier*, 11–12 June 1966; John Stennis to Lyndon Johnson, 7 June 1966, Box 27, Folder HU 2/ST 24, WHCF-HU.

26. Sokol, *There Goes My Everything*, 38–39, 85–86; Prentiss Walker to James Eastland, 25 June 1966, File Series 1, Subseries 18, Box 10, Folder 21, JOEC; *Congressional Record—Senate*, 21 July 1966, 15795.

27. *Congressional Record—Senate*, 16 June 1966, 12928; *The Clarion-Ledger* (Jackson), 15 June 1966, 17 June 1966, 22 June 1966.

28. *Congressional Record—House*, 20 July 1966, 15609. See also Joseph Crespino, "Mississippi as Metaphor: Civil Rights, the South, and the Nation in the Historical Imagination," in Lassiter and Crespino, *The Myth of Southern Exceptionalism*, 108–15.

29. Raines, *My Soul Is Rested*, 297–303; Neil R. McMillen, *The Citizens' Council: Organized Resistance and the Second Reconstruction, 1954–65* (Urbana: University of Illinois Press, 1971); *The Citizen*, May 1966, Box 2, CCC.

30. Robert B. Patterson, "The Truth Cries Out," 8 January 1966, Box 1, Folder 25, CCC; *The Citizen*, April 1966, June 1966, September 1966, Box 2, CCC.

31. Crespino, *In Search of Another Country*, 110–11; Jackson chapter sheet opposing compulsory school integration, Box 1, Folder 4, APWR; *Memphis Press-Scimitar*, 12 August 1964; Minutes from meetings, 21 June 1966 and 5 July 1966, Box 1, Folder 6, APWR.

32. Crespino, *In Search of Another Country*, 111–12; Wade, *The Fiery Cross*, 333–35.

33. O'Reilly, "*Racial Matters,*" 195–227; Don Whitehead, *Attack on Terror: The FBI Against the Ku Klux Klan in Mississippi* (New York: Funk and Wagnalls, 1970), 257–59.

34. Patricia Michelle Buzard, "Worth Dying For: The Trials of Vernon F. Dahmer" (M.A. thesis, University of Southern Mississippi, 2002); Carol Ann Estes, "The Death of Vernon Dahmer: Klan Violence and Mississippi Justice in the 1960s" (M.A. thesis, University of Southern Mississippi, 1988); Whitehead, *Attack on Terror*, 233–57, 302–303; Oral History with Ellie Dahmer, USM-CRM; "Malice Toward Some," *Newsweek*, 11 April 1966, 39–40; *The Washington Post*, 24 June 1966.

35. Press release, 14 June 1966, Reel 13, CORE-A; *The New York Times*, 14 June 1966.

36. Clive Webb, *Rabble Rousers: The American Far Right in the Civil Rights Era* (Athens: University of Georgia Press, 2010), 1–11.

37. Bruce Hartford, interview by author, telephone, 8 March 2010; Lewis Johnson, interview with the author, Grenada, Mississippi, 22 March 2010; Jo Freeman, interview by author; Andrew Jaffe, "Grenada, Mississippi: Perspective on the Backlash," *New South*, Fall 1966, 17; Carole Anne Mathison to Vincent O'Connor, March 1966, Box 6, Folder 9, SNCC-AR.

38. Jaffe, "Grenada, Mississippi," 16–17; Good, "The Meredith March," 3–4.

39. Highway Patrol memorandum, Box 147, Folder 4, PBJFP; Good, "The Meredith March," 6; Harriet Tanzman interview; "Tape #11 H.P.," Series 2, Box 1, Folder 18, HWC.

40. *The New York Times*, 15 June 1966; *Los Angeles Times*, 19 June 1966; Jo Freeman to Al and Cynthia, 25 July 1966, JFPP.

41. Charles Reagan Wilson, *Baptized in Blood: The Religion of the Lost Cause, 1865–1920* (Athens: University of Georgia Press, 1980), 18–19, 37–57; David Goldfield, *Still Fighting the Civil War: The American South and Southern History* (Baton Rouge: Louisiana State University Press, 2002), 1–42.

42. David Blight, *Race and Reunion: The Civil War in American Memory* (Cambridge, Mass.: Harvard University Press, 2001), 258–72, 282–92; Wilson, *Baptized in Blood*, 99–118; *Newsday*, 10 June 1966.

43. Blight, *Race and Reunion*, 300–337.

44. *The New York Times*, 15 June 1966.

45. *Los Angeles Times*, 15 June 1966; Jaffe, "Grenada, Mississippi," 18–19; *Congressional Record—Senate*, 16 June 1966, 12928; *The Clarion-Ledger* (Jackson), 23 June 1966.

46. *Newsday*, 15 June 1966; *Chicago Daily News*, 14 June 1966; *The Washington Post*, 15 June 1966; *The Denver Post*, 15 June 1966.

47. Lewis Johnson, interview by author.

9. Politics and Poverty

1. *Los Angeles Times*, 19 June 1966.

2. Good, "The Meredith March," 6–7; Jaffe, "Grenada, Mississippi," 18–19.

3. *The Washington Post*, 15 June 1966; "The Strange March Through Mississippi," *U.S. News and World Report*, 27 June 1966, 48; *Newsday*, 15 June 1966.

4. *The Philadelphia Inquirer*, 15 June 1966; FBI memorandum, 14 June 1966, Part 1, Reel 10, MLK-FBI.

5. *The Commercial Appeal* (Memphis), 15 June 1966; FBI memoranda, 14 June 1966 and 15 June 1966, Part 1, Reel 10, MLK-FBI; Jo Freeman to Al and Cynthia, 25 July 1966, JFPP.

6. *Newsday*, 16 June 1966, 21 June 1966.

7. Press release, 15 June 1966, Reel 13, CORE-A; *Newsday*, 16 June 1966.

8. *The Washington Post*, 15 June 1966; *Newsday*, 16 June 1966, 21 June 1966; Good, "The Meredith March," 7; Jaffe, "Grenada, Mississippi," 20; *The New York Times*, 15 June 1966, 26 June 1966.

9. *Newsday*, 16 June 1966; *The Boston Globe* (evening edition), 16 June 1966; "Mississippi Primaries: The Aftermath," Box 1, Folder 5, MFDP.

10. *Los Angeles Times*, 16 June 1966; *The Chicago Defender*, 16 June 1966; *The New York Times*, 16 June 1966; *Chicago Tribune*, 16 June 1966; *The Boston Globe*, 16 June 1966.

11. *The New York Times*, 10 June 1966, 12 June 1966; James Meredith announcement, Box 13, Folder 8, JHMC; *New York Amsterdam News*, 18 June 1966.

12. *The Washington Daily News*, 15 June 1966; *The Clarion-Ledger* (Jackson), 13 June 1966.

13. Karl Fleming, *Son of the Rough South: An Uncivil Memoir* (New York: Public-Affairs, 2005), 287–89; Karl Fleming, "He Shot Me Like . . . A Goddam Rabbit," *Newsweek*, 20 June 1966, 30.

14. Fleming, "He Shot Me Like . . . A Goddam Rabbit," 30.

15. *Congressional Record—Appendix*, 13 June 1966, A3177; *Chicago Daily News*, 11 June 1966; *The Courier Journal* (Louisville), 9 June 1966, 17 June 1966; "Is Meredith Right?," *The Nation*, 27 June 1966, 9; Jake Friesen to Edgar Stoesz, 12 June 1966, Box 1, Folder 3, JFP; FBI surveillance of Stanley Levison, 16 June 1966, Part 2, Reel 5, MLK-FBI.

16. *New York Post*, 11 June 1966; *The Pittsburgh Courier*, 25 June 1966; *New York Amsterdam News*, 18 June 1966; *Book Week*, 24 April 1966; *The Village Voice*, 16 June 1966; *The Washington Daily News*, 23 June 1966. The *Book Week* and *Village Voice* articles were reprinted in Martin Duberman, *The Uncompleted Past* (New York: Random House, 1969), 129–39.

17. *Memphis Press-Scimitar*, 24 June 1966.

18. *The Commercial Appeal* (Memphis), 15 June 1966; *Hattiesburg American*, 15 June 1966.

19. *The Clarion-Ledger* (Jackson), 7 June 1966, 23 June 1966, 25 June 1966; *Jackson Daily News*, 9 June 1966, 13 June 1966; *Hattiesburg American*, 13 June 1966; *The Southern Reporter*, 23 June 1966; *The Vicksburg Evening Post*, 7 June 1966; Irene Doran to June Meredith, 7 June 1966, Box 10, Folder 2, JHMC; Letter to James Meredith, 10 June 1966, Box 10, Folder 12, JHMC; "A Postscript on Civil Rights," WBT-WBTV editorial, 14 June 1966, Part 1, Reel 15, SCLC; *Congressional Record*, 21 June 1966, 13171; *Memphis Press-Scimitar*, 7 June 1966, 8 June 1966; *Delta Democrat Times*, 7 June 1966.

20. *Jackson Daily News*, 7 June 1966; *The Meridian* (Miss.) *Star*, 14 June 1966; *The Clarion-Ledger* (Jackson), 16 June 1966, 24 June 1966.

21. *The Clarion-Ledger* (Jackson), 10 June 1966, 13 June 1966; *The Vicksburg Evening Post*, 12 June 1966; *The Meridian* (Miss.) *Star*, 26 June 1966; *Memphis Press-Scimitar*, 7 June 1966; *Los Angeles Times*, 8 June 1966.
22. *The Clarion-Ledger* (Jackson), 10 June 1966; Frank Boykin to James Eastland, 10 June 1966, File Series 1, Subseries 18, Box 1, Folder 52, JOEC; Press release, 7 June 1966, Box 104, Folder 15, PBJFP; *The Daily World* (Opelousas, La.), 9 June 1966; *Jackson Daily News*, 10 June 1966; Thornton Hardie to Lyndon Johnson, 13 June 1966, Box 40, Folder HU 2/ST 24, WHCF-HU; *The Enterprise-Tocsin* (Indianola, Miss.), 16 June 1966; *The Meridian* (Miss.) *Star*, 29 June 1966; Mrs. R. L. Cox to James Eastland, 22 August 1966, File Series 3, Subseries 1, Box 43, Folder "Civil Rights—1966," JOEC.
23. *Congressional Record*, 8 June 1966, 11999.
24. Erle Johnston to Herman Glazier, 14 June 1966, Box 139, Folder 1, PBJFP. On Scarbrough's negative opinion of the march, see Sovereignty Commission memorandum, 8 June 1966, SCR ID# 2-38-1-102-1-1-1, MSSC.
25. Erle Johnston to Herman Glazier, 14 June 1966, Box 139, Folder 1, PBJFP.
26. Sovereignty Commission memorandum, 20 June 1966, SCR ID# 1-67-4-145-1-1-1, MSSC.
27. Sovereignty Commission memorandum, 20 June 1966, SCR ID# 1-67-4-145-1-1-1, MSSC; Sovereignty Commission memorandum, 27 June 1966, SCR ID# 1-67-4-146-1-1-1, MSSC.
28. *Memphis Press-Scimitar*, 17 June 1966; *The Boston Globe* (evening edition), 18 June 1966.
29. Paul Good, "The Thorntons of Mississippi: Peonage on the Plantation," *The Atlantic Monthly*, September 1966, 95–100.
30. "Notes on the Condition of the Mississippi Negro—1966," Box 1, Folder 4, WWP; Myers-Asch, *The Senator and the Sharecropper*, 129–31, 224–30; Foster Davis, "The Delta: Rich Land and Poor People," *The Reporter*, 24 March 1966, 41–43; Amzie Moore statement before National Advisory Commission on Rural Poverty, Box 2, Folder 4, AMP.
31. Report on hunger and poverty in the Delta, Box 4, Folder 28, DMR; "The Delta: A Problematic Situation in Need of a Remedial Alternative," Reel 45, CORE; Tony Dunbar, *Our Land Too* (New York: Pantheon, 1971), 30–57; *Newsday*, 20 June 1966. See also Cobb, *The Most Southern Place on Earth*, 253–76.
32. Memorandum by Victoria Gray, 10 February 1966, Reel 16, CORE; Delta Ministry newsletter, February 1966, Box 3, Folder 16, DMR; "DP's in the Delta," *Newsweek*, 14 February 1966, 28–29; *The New York Times*, 7 February 1966; Nicholas Katzenbach to Lyndon Johnson, 14 February 1966, Folder HU 2/ST 24, Box 27, WHCF-HU.
33. "A Negro Campout on White House 'Doorstep,'" *U.S. News and World Report*, 18 April 1966, 12; "White House Camp-In," *Newsweek*, 18 April 1966, 38. See also John Stennis to Lyndon Johnson, 7 April 1966, Box 27, Folder HU 2/ST 24, WHCF-HU.

34. Dittmer, *Local People*, 363, 368–70; Myers-Asch, *The Senator and the Sharecropper*, 243–44; January 1966 newsletter, Box 1, Folder 3, CDGM; Sovereignty Commission memorandum, 25 April 1966, SCR ID# 9-31-5-10-1-1-1, MSSC.

35. Dittmer, *Local People*, 370–71; Unita Blackwell with JoAnne Pritchard Morris, *Barefootin': Life Lessons from the Road to Freedom* (New York: Crown, 2006), 149–50; *Jackson Daily News*, 7 April 1966.

36. Dittmer, *Local People*, 371–75; Harry McPherson, *A Political Education* (Boston: Little, Brown, 1972), 353–54; Christopher Jencks, "Accommodating Whites: A New Look at Mississippi," *The New Republic*, 16 April 1966, 18–21. For the 1966 proposal and grant, see Box 1, Folders 4–5, CDGM. See also David C. Carter, "Romper Lobbies and Coloring Lessons: Grassroots Visions and Political Realities in the Battle for Head Start in Mississippi, 1965–1967," in Paul A. Cimbala and Barton C. Shaw, eds., *Making a New South: Race, Leadership, and Community after the Civil War* (Gainesville: University Press of Florida, 2007), 191–208.

37. Jencks, "Accommodating Whites," 21–22; Polly Greenberg, *The Devil Has Slippery Shoes: A Biased Biography of the Child Development Group in Mississippi* (London: Macmillan, 2009), 298–300, 461–63, 509–29.

38. *The Washington Post*, 16 June 1966; Good, "The Meredith March," 11; *The Clarksdale Press Register*, 15 June 1966; *The New York Times*, 16 June 1966; *Chicago Daily News*, 15 June 1966.

39. FBI memorandum, 16 June 1966, Box 71B, Folder 2, LBJ-MS; *The Chicago Defender*, 18 June 1966; *The Nashville Tennessean*, 16 June 1966; *The Clarion-Ledger* (Jackson), 16 June 1966.

40. *The Chicago Defender*, 18 June 1966; *The Clarion-Ledger* (Jackson), 16 June 1966; Press release, 16 June 1966, Reel 13, CORE-A; FBI memorandum, 16 June 1966, Box 71B, Folder 2, LBJ-MS; *The New York Times*, 16 June 1966.

41. Press release, 11 June 1966, Reel 13, CORE-A; *The Baltimore Afro-American*, 18 June 1966, 25 June 1966.

42. *The Baltimore Afro-American*, 2 July 1966; *The Guardian*, 2 July 1966.

43. *The Guardian*, 2 July 1966.

44. *The Washington Post*, 14 June 1966.

45. *The Southern Courier*, 18–19 June 1966; Kasher, *The Civil Rights Movement*, 211.

46. *The Philadelphia Tribune*, 18 June 1966.

47. FBI memorandum, 16 June 1966, Box 71B, Folder 2, LBJ-MS; *The Southern Courier*, 18–19 June 1966; *The Clarksdale Press-Register*, 16 June 1966.

48. *The Wall Street Journal*, 22 June 1966; John Doar, interview by the author.

49. *The Wall Street Journal*, 22 June 1966; Willie Blue, interview by author, telephone, 5 April 2010.

50. FBI memorandum, 16 June 1966, Box 71B, Folder 2, LBJ-MS; Martin Luther King telegram via Junius Griffin, 14 June 1966, Series 3, Box 11, MLKP; *The Washington Post*, 16 June 1966; *Chicago Daily News*, 16 June 1966; *The Clarksdale Press-Register*, 16 June 1966; "The Talk of the Town," 25.

51. "The Talk of the Town," 25.

10. Down to the Crossroads

1. *The Guardian* (London), 25 June 1966; *The New York Times*, 17 June 1966.
2. Highway Patrol memorandum, 17 June 1966, Box 147, Folder 4, PBJFP; *The Clarion-Ledger* (Jackson), 17 June 1966; *The Greenwood Commonwealth*, 16 June 1966; *The Guardian* (London), 25 June 1966.
3. Highway Patrol memorandum, 17 June 1966, Box 147, Folder 4, PBJFP; *The Clarion-Ledger* (Jackson), 17 June 1966; *The Guardian* (London), 25 June 1966; *The Greenwood Commonwealth*, 16 June 1966; *Los Angeles Times*, 17 June 1966.
4. *The Greenwood Commonwealth*, 17 June 1966; Highway Patrol memorandum, 17 June 1966, Box 147, Folder 4, PBJFP.
5. *The Washington Post*, 17 June 1966; *The Clarion-Ledger* (Jackson), 17 June 1966.
6. Stokely Carmichael to Stanley Wise, 15 June 1966, Reel 2, SNCC; Stokely Carmichael to Cado Lee, 14 June 1966, Reel 2, SNCC; Stokely Carmichael to Eloise Smith, 15 June 1966, Reel 2, SNCC; Beverly to Stokely Carmichael, 12 June 1966, Reel 2, SNCC; Stokely Carmichael to Beverly, 15 June 1966, Reel 2, SNCC; Stokely Carmichael to Len Chandler, 15 June 1966, Reel 2, SNCC; Stokely Carmichael to Edward Vaughn, 15 June 1966, Reel 2, SNCC; Stokely Carmichael to Tim Hall, 15 June 1966, Reel 2, SNCC; Ike Coleman and John Buffington to Stokely Carmichael, 9 June 1966, Reel 2, SNCC; Stokely Carmichael to Isaac Coleman, 14 June 1966, Reel 2, SNCC.
7. Herman Kitchens to SNCC Central Committee, 28 May 1966, Reel 2, SNCC; Stokely Carmichael to Herman Kitchens, 15 June 1966, Reel 2, SNCC; Loretta Gueye to SNCC, 6 June 1966, Reel 2, SNCC; Stokely Carmichael to Loretta Gueye, 15 June 1966, Reel 2, SNCC.
8. Stokely Carmichael to Lorna Smith, 15 June 1966, Box 4, Folder 1, SC-LDS.
9. Stokely Carmichael to George Besch, 15 June 1966, Reel 2, SNCC; Stokely Carmichael to John Tillson, 15 June 1966, Reel 2, SNCC; Stokely Carmichael to Laura Hippensteel, 15 June 1966, Reel 2, SNCC; Stokely Carmichael to Rose Saltzman, 15 June 1966, Reel 2, SNCC.
10. Elizabeth Sunderland to Stokely Carmichael, 10 June 1966, Reel 2, SNCC; Stokely Carmichael to Elizabeth Sunderland, 15 June 1966, Reel 2, SNCC.
11. Sovereignty Commission memorandum, 15 June 1966, SCR ID# 9-31-5-39-1-1-1, MSSC.
12. Payne, *I've Got the Light of Freedom*, 225–29; Steven George Salzman, "Beyond Freedom Songs: The Life Story of a Mississippi Civil Rights Worker" (M.A. thesis, University of Virginia, 1990), 17–29; Carmichael, *Ready for Revolution*, 279–80, 387, 506.
13. *Mississippi Black Paper*, 22–24; Carmichael, *Ready for Revolution*, 506.
14. *The Clarion-Ledger* (Jackson), 17 June 1966; *The Commercial Appeal* (Memphis), 17 June 1966.
15. *The Greenwood Commonwealth*, 17 June 1966; Highway Patrol memorandum, 17 June 1966, Box 147, Folder 4, PBJFP.
16. FBI memorandum, 17 June 1966, Box 71B, Folder 2, LBJ-MS; Highway Patrol memorandum, 17 June 1966, Box 147, Folder 4, PBJFP.

17. Nan Elizabeth Woodruff, *American Congo: The African American Freedom Struggle in the Delta* (Cambridge, Mass.: Harvard University Press, 2003); Cobb, *The Most Southern Place on Earth*, 277–305; Palmer, *Deep Blues*, 124–27.

18. Joe Sinsheimer, "Never Turn Back: An Interview with Sam Block," *Southern Exposure*, Summer 1987, 41–43.

19. Dittmer, *Local People*, 128–50; Payne, *I've Got the Light of Freedom*, 132–58.

20. Hogan, *Many Minds, One Heart*, 85–88; Payne, *I've Got the Light of Freedom*, 180–264; Dittmer, *Local People*, 150–57; Endesha Ida Mae Holland, *From the Mississippi Delta: A Memoir* (New York: Simon and Schuster, 1997).

21. See Bruce Watson, *Freedom Summer: The Savage Season That Made Mississippi Burn and Made America a Democracy* (New York: Viking, 2010); McAdam, *Freedom Summer*; Belfrage, *Freedom Summer*; Sutherland, ed., *Letters from Mississippi*; Tracy Sugarman, *A Stranger at the Gates: A Summer in Mississippi* (New York: Hill and Wang, 1966); Holt, *The Summer That Didn't End*.

22. Ed King, interview by author.

23. Carson, *In Struggle*, 149–50, 172–73; Notes from SNCC staff meeting, 26 November 1965, Box 8, Folder 1, DLC; Notes from 1966, Box 1, Folder 4, MFDP—Quitman County Records, WHS; Mary Lane interview with Robert Wright, 12 July 1969, Series 4, Box 104, Folder 748, TBP; Stokely Carmichael to Lorna Smith, 29 March 1966, Box 4, Folder 1, SC-LDS; SNCC Staff List, Box 1, Folder 2, Roberta Yancy Collection, SCRBC; Notes from 11 April 1966 and "Why Are We Boycotting?," both in Box 1, Folder 1, James Moore Papers, WHS; Jim Colbert to Kathleen Kahn, 29 October 1966, Box 1, Folder 1, Kathleen Kahn Papers, WHS.

24. Sovereignty Commission memorandum, 7 May 1966, SCR ID# 9-31-5-20-1-1-1, MSSC; Jesse Harris, interview by author.

25. MacArthur Cotton, interview by author.

26. Wiley Mallett, interview by author, telephone, 9 March 2010; Jean Morton (Jean Mallett), interview by author, telephone, 30 March 2010; Luther Mallett, interview by author, telephone, 9 March 2010.

27. *The Washington Post*, 17 June 1966; Cobb, *The Most Southern Place on Earth*, 236–37.

28. "A Delta Discussion—IV of A Series," 19 November 1965, and "A Delta Discussion—Issue V of a Series," both in Box 3, Folder 2, RRC.

29. Charles Sampson to Paul Johnson, 16 June 1966, Box 142, Folder 3, PBJFP; Charles Sampson to Paul Johnson, 17 June 1966, Box 147, Folder 4, PBJFP; *The Washington Post*, 17 June 1966.

30. *The Greenwood Commonwealth*, 16 June 1966.

31. FBI surveillance notes, 16 June 1966, Part 2, Reel 5, MLK-FBI; Press release, 16 June 1966, Reel 13, CORE-A.

32. *The Greenwood Commonwealth*, 17 June 1966; Jack Sisson to Matt Ahmann, 30 June 1966, Series 18, Box 4, Folder 1, NCCIJ.

33. *The Guardian* (London), 25 June 1966; Cobb, *On the Road to Freedom*, 299.

34. *The Greenwood Commonwealth*, 17 June 1966; *The Guardian* (London), 25 June 1966.

35. *The Clarion-Ledger* (Jackson), 17 June 1966; *The Greenwood Commonwealth*, 17 June 1966; *The Guardian* (London), 25 June 1966.

36. *The Clarion-Ledger* (Jackson), 17 June 1966; *The Greenwood Commonwealth*, 17 June 1966; *The Guardian* (London), 25 June 1966.

37. *The Greenwood Commonwealth*, 17 June 1966; Charles McLaurin, interview by author; *The Guardian* (London), 25 June 1966.

38. Carson, *In Struggle*, 208–209; Willie Blue, interview by author.

39. Coby Smith, interview by author; Courtland Cox interview, 17 April 1996, Box 7, Folder 10, WCBUT; "Agenda—Tuesday—17th of May," Reel 3, SNCC.

40. James Forman, *The Making of Black Revolutionaries* (Washington, D.C.: Open Hand Publishing, 1985; original 1972), 456–57; Carson, *In Struggle*, 209; Central Committee Minutes, 10–12 June 1966, Reel 3, SNCC; *New York Post*, 9 June 1966; *Los Angeles Times*, 12 June 1966.

41. Carson, *In Struggle*, 209; Stokely Carmichael interview, 7 November 1988, EPI.

42. Carmichael, *Ready for Revolution*, 507; Stokely Carmichael interview, 7 November 1988, EPI.

43. "'Black Power!,'" *Newsweek*, 27 June 1966, 36; *The New York Times*, 17 June 1966; *The Guardian* (London), 25 June 1966; *Los Angeles Times*, 17 June 1966.

44. "'Black Power!,'" 36; Sellers, *The River of No Return*, 166–67.

45. Bob Fitch, interview by author.

46. *The Washington Post*, 17 June 1966; "'Black Power!,'" 36.

47. David Doggett, interview by author; David Dawley interview, 6 July 1989, EPI.

48. Lewis Zuchman, interview by author, telephone, 9 July 2010; Art Spielman, interview by author, telephone, 9 April 2010.

49. Lewis Zuchman, interview by author; Art Spielman, interview by author; Charles Sampson to Paul Johnson, 17 June 1966, Box 147, Folder 4, PBJFP; Highway Patrol memorandum, 17 June 1966, Box 147, Folder 4, PBJFP.

50. Yahya Shabazz (John Summerall), interview by author, telephone, 31 October 2010; *The New York Times*, 19 June 1966; *The Guardian* (London), 25 June 1966.

11. The Crow and the Blackbird

1. *The New York Times*, 18 June 1966. On Medgar Evers see Michael Vinson Williams, *Medgar Evers: Mississippi Martyr* (Fayetteville: University of Arkansas Press, 2011).

2. Highway Patrol memorandum, 17 June 1966, Box 147, Folder 4, PBJFP; Sovereignty Commission memorandum, 14 June 1966, SCR ID# 9-31-5-38-1-1-1, MSSC; Sovereignty Commission memorandum, 15 June 1966, SCR ID# 9-31-5-40-1-1-1, MSSC; *The New York Times*, 17 June 1966, 18 June 1966.

3. Highway Patrol memorandum, 20 June 1966, Box 147, Folder 4, PBJFP; Maryann Vollers, *Ghosts of Mississippi: The Murder of Medgar Evers, the Trials of Byron de la Beckwith, and the Haunting of the New South* (Boston: Little, Brown, 1995), 3–4, 19–30, 160–84, 203–208; Belfrage, *Freedom Summer*, 121; *The Lexington* (Miss.) *Advertiser*, 23 June 1966.

4. Highway Patrol memorandum, 20 June 1966, Box 147, Folder 4, PBJFP; *Chicago*

Daily News, 17 June 1966; *The Greenwood Commonwealth*, 17 June 1966; *The Boston Globe* (evening edition), 17 June 1966.

5. Highway Patrol memoranda, 17 June 1966 and 20 June 1966, Box 147, Folder 4, PBJFP; Press release, 17 June 1966, Reel 13, CORE-A; *The Greenwood Commonwealth*, 17 June 1966.

6. Highway Patrol memorandum, 20 June 1966, Box 147, Folder 4, PBJFP; *Chicago Daily News*, 17 June 1966.

7. *Chicago Daily News*, 18 June 1966.

8. *The Washington Post*, 18 June 1966.

9. *The Washington Post*, 19 June 1966; *Los Angeles Times*, 18 June 1966.

10. *Chicago Daily News*, 18 June 1966.

11. *Chicago Daily News*, 18 June 1966; *The Washington Post*, 18 June 1966.

12. *The Washington Post*, 18 June 1966.

13. *The Washington Post*, 18 June 1966; *The New York Times*, 18 June 1966.

14. FBI memorandum, 18 June 1966, Box 71B, Folder 2, LBJ-MS; *The Atlanta Constitution*, 18 June 1966; *The Baltimore Afro-American*, 25 June 1966.

15. *The New York Times*, 18 June 1966; *The Philadelphia Tribune*, 21 June 1966; *The Meridian* (Miss.) *Star*, 18 June 1966.

16. *The Meridian* (Miss.) *Star*, 18 June 1966; *The Commercial Appeal* (Memphis), 18 June 1966; Highway Patrol memorandum, 20 June 1966, Box 147, Folder 4, PBJFP; *Chicago Daily News*, 18 June 1966.

17. *Chicago Daily News*, 18 June 1966; *Newsday*, 17 June 1966; *The Greenwood Commonwealth*, 20 June 1966.

18. "A Delta Discussion—Issue V of a Series," Box 3, Folder 2, RRC; *The Washington Post*, 18 June 1966.

19. Sherwood Ross, interview by author; *The Washington Post*, 18 June 1966; Interview with Ted Alexander, SRTR.

20. *The Washington Post*, 20 June 1966.

21. *Los Angeles Times*, 23 June 1966.

22. Roberts and Klibanoff, *The Race Beat*, 400; *Newsday*, 18 June 1966; *The Washington Post*, 18 June 1966.

23. Roberts and Klibanoff, *The Race Beat*, 86–394; Robert J. Donovan and Ray Scherer, *Unsilent Revolution: Television News and American Public Life* (New York: Cambridge University Press, 1992), 3–22; Sasha Torres, *Black, White, and In Color: Television and Black Civil Rights* (Princeton: Princeton University Press, 2003), 13–35; Pat Watters, *Down to Now: Reflections on the Black Civil Rights Movement* (New York: Pantheon, 1971), 69–81.

24. *The Philadelphia Tribune*, 24 May 1966; *The Plain Dealer* (Cleveland), 19 June 1966; *Call and Post* (Cleveland), 25 June 1966.

25. Ed King, interview by author; Ed King interview, 26 June 1992, Series 4, Box 105, Folder 752, TBP.

26. Arlie Schardt interview, 14 November 1988, EPI; Cleveland Sellers, interview by author; "The Talk of the Town," 22–23; *The Clarksdale Press Register*, 15 June 1966.

27. *The Times-Picayune* (New Orleans), 20 June 1966; *The Clarion-Ledger* (Jackson), 20 June 1966; *The Tri-State Defender*, 25 June 1966.

28. Good, "The Meredith March," 2–16; "The Talk of the Town," 21–25; Paul Good, *The Trouble I've Seen: White Journalist/Black Movement* (Washington, D.C.: Howard University Press, 1975), 254–57.

29. Matt Herron, interview by author, telephone, 20 April 2010; Jim Peppler, interview by author; Bob Fitch, interview by author. See also Raiford, *Imprisoned in a Luminous Glare*, 67–128.

30. Good, "The Meredith March," 3; Arlie Schardt interview, 14 November 1988, EPI.

31. *The Clarion-Ledger* (Jackson), 19 June 1966; Charles McLaurin, interview by author.

32. On Schuyler see *The Meridian* (Miss.) *Star*, 13 June 1966; *The Santa Ana* (Calif.) *Evening Register*, 14 June 1966; *The Times* (Shreveport, La.), 16 June 1966; *The Philadelphia Tribune*, 21 June 1966; George S. Schuyler, *Black and Conservative: The Autobiography of George S. Schuyler* (New Rochelle, N.Y.: Arlington House, 1966), 1–3, 341–52. On Greene see *Jackson Advocate*, 25 June 1966; Julius Eric Thompson, *Percy Greene and the "Jackson Advocate": The Life and Times of a Radical Conservative Black Newspaperman, 1897–1977* (Jefferson, N.C.: McFarland, 1994), 43–47, 79–80; Caryl A. Cooper, "Percy Greene and the *Jackson Advocate*," in Davies, *The Press and Race*, 56–83.

33. Joy Ann Williamson, *Radicalizing the Ebony Tower: Black Colleges and the Black Freedom Struggle in Mississippi* (New York: Teachers College Press, 2008), 28–29, 118–23; Sammy Jay Tinsley, "A History of Mississippi Valley State College" (Ph.D. dissertation, University of Mississippi, 1972), 252–54; J. H. White, *Up from a Cotton Patch: J. H. White and the Development of Mississippi Valley State College* (Itta Bena, Miss.: J. H. White, 1979); Wilhelm Joseph, interview by author, telephone, 18 March 2011.

34. *The Meridian* (Miss.) *Star*, 19 June 1966; *The Boston Globe* (evening edition), 18 June 1966; *The Washington Post*, 19 June 1966.

35. Highway Patrol memorandum, 20 June 1966, Box 147, Folder 4, PBJFP; *The Clarion-Ledger* (Jackson), 19 June 1966; *Chicago Tribune*, 19 June 1966.

36. *The Washington Post*, 19 June 1966.

37. *The Washington Post*, 19 June 1966.

38. FBI memorandum, 18 June 1966, Box 71B, Folder 2, LBJ-MS.

39. Sovereignty Commission memorandum, 18 June 1966, SCR ID# 9-31-5-42-1-1-1, MSSC; *The Meridian* (Miss.) *Star*, 19 June 1966.

40. *The Washington Post*, 19 June 1966; *Chicago Daily News*, 20 June 1966.

41. *The Washington Post*, 19 June 1966, 20 June 1966; *Chicago Daily News*, 20 June 1966.

42. FBI memorandum, 18 June 1966, Box 71B, Folder 2, LBJ-MS; *The Meridian* (Miss.) *Star*, 19 June 1966; *Chicago Tribune*, 19 June 1966.

43. Julius Lester, *Look Out, Whitey!: Black Power's Gon' Get Your Mama!* (New York: Dial Press, 1968), 101.

44. *The Philadelphia Inquirer*, 25 June 1966; "Black Power," *The New Republic*, 18 June 1966, 5–6; *The Washington Post*, 22 June 1966; *Detroit Free Press*, 22 June 1966; *The Courier-Journal* (Louisville), 23 June 1966; *Los Angeles Times*, 24 June 1966; *The Atlanta Constitution*, 18 June 1966, 25 June 1966; *The Tri-State Defender*, 18 June 1966, 25 June 1966; *Memphis World*, 25 June 1966; *The Philadelphia Tribune*, 28 June 1966; *The Baltimore Afro-American*, 2 July 1966; *The New York Times*, 23 June 1966.

45. "The Talk of the Town," 24.

46. *The Guardian* (London), 25 June 1966; Good, "The Meredith March," 8.

47. "The Talk of the Town," 24; Paul Good, "A White Look at Black Power," *The Nation*, 8 August 1966, 113–14; Carmichael, *Ready for Revolution*, 499–502; Arlie Schardt interview, 14 November 1988, EPI.

48. Good, "The Meredith March," 8–9; Harold Middlebrook interview, 18 July 1968, Container 23, Series 1, Folder 2, SSC; *The Washington Star*, 23 June 1966.

49. "Face the Nation" transcript, 19 June 1966, Reel 2, SNCC.

50. Good, "A White Look at Black Power," 114.

12. Delta Blues

1. Interview with Mississippi Mau Mau, SRTR; Sherwood Ross, interview by author.

2. *The Village Voice*, 16 June 1966.

3. "Civil Rights Forecast: Maybe a Bit Cooler," *Business Week*, 4 June 1966, 31–32; *Miami Herald*, 22 June 1966, 23 June 1966; *The Plain Dealer* (Cleveland), 25 June 1966; *Chicago Tribune*, 24 June 1966; *Call and Post* (Cleveland), 2 July 1966.

4. Sugrue, *Sweet Land of Liberty*, 324–34.

5. FBI memorandum, 20 June 1966, Box 71B, Folder 2, LBJ-MS; *The Times-Picayune* (New Orleans), 18 June 1966, 19 June 1966.

6. *The Boston Globe*, 17 June 1966, 20 June 1966; *The Bay State Banner*, 25 June 1966; *The Christian Science Monitor*, 22 June 1966.

7. William Strickland, interview by author; Samuel Leiken to John Holloman, 6 May 1964, Box 17, Folder 3, NSM; Dena Maloney to Carlene Warren, 8 August 1966, Box 14, Folder 5, NSM; Bill Strickland to Victoria Gray, 13 April 1966, Box 17, Folder 7, NSM; Bill Strickland to Cliff Vaugh, 20 June 1966, Box 19, Folder 8, NSM; William Strickland to Robert Moses, 24 June 1966, Box 2, Folder 3, AMP.

8. William Strickland, interview by author; Manning Marable, *Malcolm X: A Life of Reinvention* (New York: Viking, 2011); Joseph, *Waiting 'Til the Midnight Hour*, 1–131; Ogbar, *Black Power*, 11–60; Malcolm X as told to Alex Haley, *The Autobiography of Malcolm X* (New York: Ballantine, 1992; original 1964); Joseph, *Dark Days, Bright Nights*, 35–105.

9. Judson L. Jeffries, "A Retrospective Look at the Black Power Movement," in Judson L. Jeffries, ed., *Black Power in the Belly of the Beast* (Urbana: University of Illinois Press), 1–11; Jeanne Theoharis, "Introduction," in Jeanne Theoharis and Komozi Woodard, eds., *Freedom North: Black Freedom Struggles Outside the South, 1940–1980* (New York: Palgrave Macmillan, 2003), 1–15; Sugrue, *Sweet Land of Liberty*,

313–41; Joseph, *Waiting 'Til the Midnight Hour*, 45–50, 54–62, 88–89, 118–21. On historiography of the Black Power movement, see Peniel E. Joseph, "The Black Power Movement: A State of the Field," *The Journal of American History* 96, no. 3 (December 2009): 751–76; Peniel E. Joseph, "The Black Power Movement, Democracy, and America in the King Years," *The American Historical Review* 114, no. 4 (October 2009): 1009–16; Peniel E. Joseph, "Rethinking the Black Power Era," *The Journal of Southern History* 75, no. 3 (August 2009): 707–16.

10. *The Boston Globe*, 20 June 1966; *The Times-Picayune* (New Orleans), 20 June 1966; *Jackson Daily News*, 20 June 1966.

11. Highway Patrol memoranda, 19 June 1966 and 20 June 1966, Box 147, Folder 4, PBJFP; *The Times-Picayune* (New Orleans), 20 June 1966.

12. *The New York Times*, 20 June 1966; *The Washington Post*, 20 June 1966; *The Chicago Defender*, 20 June 1966.

13. *The Chicago Defender*, 21 June 1966; *The Washington Post*, 20 June 1966; Highway Patrol memoranda, 19 June 1966 and 20 June 1966, Box 147, Folder 4, PBJFP.

14. *The Times-Picayune* (New Orleans), 20 June 1966.

15. *The Times-Picayune* (New Orleans), 20 June 1966; *The Boston Globe*, 20 June 1966; *The Philadelphia Inquirer*, 20 June 1966.

16. Art Spielman, interview by author; *The New York Times*, 19 June 1966.

17. Joseph Morse, interview by author, telephone, 12 February 2010.

18. "The Time Has Come," *Eyes on the Prize II: America at the Crossroads*, vol. 1 (Blackside Productions, 1990); Matt Herron, interview by author; *The New York Times*, 19 June 1966, 30 July 1966; Homer Jack to *Boston Herald*, 30 June 1966, Series 3, Box 21, HJP.

19. Shelton Stromquist interview, October 1980, MDAH; "The Talk of the Town," 21; Don Jelinek interview, CRM-VET; *Memphis Press-Scimitar*, 20 June 1966.

20. *The Washington Post*, 20 June 1966.

21. Dunbar, *Our Land Too*, 58–63; Alan Lomax, *The Land Where the Blues Began* (New York: Delta Books, 1993), 70, 81, 104; William Ferris, *Give My Poor Heart Ease: Voices of the Mississippi Blues* (Chapel Hill: University of North Carolina Press, 2009); Michael Thelwell, "Fish Are Jumping an' the Cotton Is High," *The Massachusetts Review* 7, no. 2 (1966): 362–74.

22. Joyce Ladner, interview by author.

23. Joyce Ladner, "What 'Black Power' Means to Negroes in Mississippi," *Trans-action* 5 (November 1967): 7–11; Andrew Kopkind, "The Birth of Black Power," *Ramparts*, October 1966, 4–8.

24. Joyce Ladner, interview by author; Ladner, "What 'Black Power' Means to Negroes in Mississippi," 11–15. See also Ruby Magee interview, USM-COH.

25. Bruce Hilton, *The Delta Ministry* (London: Macmillan, 1969), 13–18; Mark Newman, *Divine Agitators: The Delta Ministry and Civil Rights in Mississippi* (Athens: University of Georgia Press, 2004), 1–106; James F. Findlay, *Church People in the Struggle: The National Council of Churches and the Black Freedom Movement, 1950–1970* (New York: Oxford University Press, 1993), 1–139.

26. Subcommittee Reports to the Evaluation Committee of the Delta Ministry Commission, 6 May 1966, Part 2, Reel 8, SCLC.

27. Owen Brooks, interview by author; Richard Tuttle to Paul Moore, 17 May 1966, Box 20, Folder 5, DMR; Peggy Billings, "A White Mississippian Looks at the Delta Ministry," Box 2, Folder 2, Catherine Clarke Collection, SCRBC; "Showdown in the Delta," *Newsweek*, 6 June 1966, 67; Stanley Bohn, "Findings of Mississippi Trip February 1966," 8 March 1966, Box 1, Folder 7, JFP; "Delta Ministry reports . . . ," SCR ID# 2-157-2-2-1-1-1, MSSC; Leon Howell, *Freedom City: The Substance of Things Hoped For* (Richmond, Va.: John Knox Press, 1969), 46; "Northern Mississippi on $3 a Day," Reel 23, CORE-A; Bob Beech to Marshal Scott, 17 June 1966, Box 1, Folder 5, RBP; Press release from 1966, Box 3, Folder 18, DMR.

28. Holly Springs MFDP fund-raising letter, 21 June 1966, Box 1, Folder 1, EHP; FBI memoranda, 18 June 1966 and 20 June 1966, Box 71B, Folder 2, LBJ-MS.

29. Jean Morton (Jean Mallett), interview by author.

30. "The Talk of the Town," 24; *The Washington Post*, 29 June 1966; FBI memorandum, 21 June 1966, Box 71B, Folder 2, LBJ-MS.

31. *The New York Times*, 21 June 1966; Highway Patrol memoranda, 20 June 1966 and 21 June 1966, Box 147, Folder 4, PBJFP; *The Commercial Appeal* (Memphis), 21 June 1966; *The Sun* (Baltimore), 21 June 1966.

32. FBI memorandum, 21 June 1966, Box 71B, Folder 2, LBJ-MS; *The Sun* (Baltimore), 21 June 1966; *The Commercial Appeal* (Memphis), 21 June 1966.

33. *The Greenwood Commonwealth*, 21 June 1966; *Los Angeles Times*, 21 June 1966; Dunbar, *Our Land Too*, 4, 66–67.

34. Howell, "The Undiscovered Country," 33–71; FBI memorandum, 21 June 1966, Box 71B, Folder 2, LBJ-MS; *The Lexington* (Miss.) *Advertiser*, 23 June 1966. On Holmes County see also Rural Organizing and Cultural Center, *Minds Stayed on Freedom: The Civil Rights Struggle in the Rural South, an Oral History* (Boulder, Colo.: Westview Press, 1991); Kenneth T. Andrews, *Freedom Is a Constant Struggle: The Mississippi Civil Rights Movement and Its Legacy* (Chicago: University of Chicago Press, 2004).

35. *The Denver Post*, 21 June 1966; *The Courier-Journal* (Louisville), 21 June 1966; Highway Patrol memorandum, 21 June 1966, Box 147, Folder 4, PBJFP.

36. Dunbar, *Our Land Too*, 3–29; *Memphis Press-Scimitar*, 21 June 1966; *The Greenwood Commonwealth*, 21 June 1966.

37. "The Talk of the Town," 24; *The Clarion-Ledger* (Jackson), 21 June 1966.

38. Sovereignty Commission memorandum, 20 June 1966, SCR ID# 9-31-5-43-1-1-1, MSSC.

39. Sovereignty Commission memorandum, 20 June 1966, SCR ID# 9-31-5-43-1-1-1, MSSC.

40. Robert Lewis Shayon, "The Real Stokely Carmichael," *Saturday Review*, 9 July 1966, 42; "Tape #11 H.P.," Series 2, Box 1, Folder 18, HWC; Good, "A White Look at Black Power," 115; Young, *An Easy Burden*, 397–99, 404–405.

41. FBI surveillance of Stanley Levison, 15 June 1966, 18 June 1966, 21 June 1966, 22 June 1966, Part 2, Reel 5, MLK-FBI; Halberstam, *The Children*, 528.

42. *Detroit Free Press*, 20 June 1966.

43. *The New York Times*, 20 June 1966; *Detroit Free Press*, 20 June 1966.

44. King, *Where Do We Go from Here*, 29–30; *The New York Times*, 21 June 1966; *The Atlanta Constitution*, 22 June 1966, 24 June 1966; Good, "A White Look at Black Power," 116.

13. Brotherly Love

1. *Meridian Star*, 21 June 1966.

2. Joseph Morse, interview by author; Paul Murray, interview by author, telephone, 1 February 2010.

3. *Jackson Daily News*, 21 June 1966; Matthew Rinaldi, interview by author.

4. Highway Patrol memoranda, 21 June 1966 and 22 June 1966, Box 147, Folder 4, PBJFP; *The Clarion-Ledger* (Jackson), 22 June 1966.

5. Highway Patrol memorandum, 21 June 1966, Box 147, Folder 4, PBJFP; Crosby, *A Little Taste of Freedom*, 178–83; *The New York Times*, 22 June 1966.

6. Highway Patrol memoranda, 22 June 1966, Box 147, Folder 4, PBJFP; *The Clarion-Ledger* (Jackson), 22 June 1966; *Newsday*, 23 June 1966.

7. *The Clarion-Ledger* (Jackson), 22 June 1966; Morris, *North Toward Home*, 3–8; Willie Morris, *Yazoo: Integration in a Deep-Southern Town* (New York: Harper's Magazine Press, 1971), 14–16; *Newsday*, 23 June 1966; *Yazoo City Herald*, 23 June 1966.

8. *The Times-Picayune* (New Orleans), 22 June 1966; *Yazoo City Herald*, 23 June 1966.

9. Seth Cagin and Philip Dray, *We Are Not Afraid: The Story of Goodman, Schwerner, and Chaney and the Civil Rights Campaign for Mississippi* (New York: Macmillan, 1988), 8–15, 36–46, 273–301.

10. Cagin and Dray, *We Are Not Afraid*, 324–45, 369–75, 435–38; John Drabble, "The FBI, COINTELPRO-WHITE HATE, and the Decline of the Ku Klux Klan in Mississippi," *The Journal of Mississippi History* 66, no. 4 (Winter 2004): 367–78; "Toward Outlawing Murder," *Time*, 8 April 1966, 28–29; "Solid Prospect," *Newsweek*, 11 April 1966, 38–39; *The Meridian* (Miss.) *Star*, 18 June 1966.

11. Cagin and Dray, *We Are Not Afraid*, 376–77.

12. Turner Catledge to Rita Cooper, 9 February 1966, Series II.C, Box 29, Folder "Philadelphia, Mississippi, 1955–1969," Turner Catledge Papers, MSU; Florence Mars, *Witness in Philadelphia* (Baton Rouge: Louisiana State University Press, 1977), 189–93, 203–204.

13. George Smith, interview by author, telephone, 15 February 2010; Mars, *Witness in Philadelphia*, 117–19, 194–200.

14. George Smith, interview by author; Clinton Collier interview, 28 July 1981, USM-COH; George Raymond and Annie Devine to Lyndon Johnson, 2 May 1966, Box 40, Folder HU 2/ST 24, WHCF-HU; "Congressional Candidates," Box 1, Folder 3, MFDP; "MFDP Key List Mailing," 2 May 1966, Box 1, Folder 4, MFDP; Nina Boal, interview by author, telephone, 26 January 2010.

15. "Mark Mississippi Martyrdom With 12-Mile March," *Jet*, 8 July 1965, 8; Mars, *Witness in Philadelphia*, 183–84; George Smith, interview by author; Press release, 17 June 1966, Reel 13, CORE-A; John Steele, interview by author, telephone, 17 September 2010; FBI memoranda, 20 June 1966 and 21 June 1966, Box 71B, Folder 2, LBJ-MS; Margaret Long, "Black Power in the Black Belt," *The Progressive*, October 1966, 20.

16. Hill, *The Deacons for Defense*, 248–49; Highway Patrol memorandum, 21 June 1966, Box 139, Folder 1, PBJFP.

17. *Los Angeles Times*, 22 June 1966; *The New York Times*, 22 June 1966.

18. *The New York Times*, 22 June 1966; Mars, *Witness in Philadelphia*, 207; "The New Racism," *Time*, 1 July 1966, 12.

19. David Doggett, interview by author; Owen Brooks, interview by author; Alvin Poussaint, interview by author.

20. *Chicago Daily News*, 21 June 1966; *The Meridian* (Miss.) *Star*, 22 June 1966; *The Times-Picayune* (New Orleans), 22 June 1966; Highway Patrol memorandum, 21 June 1966, Box 139, Folder 1, PBJFP.

21. Long, "Black Power in the Black Belt," 21; Mars, *Witness in Philadelphia*, 207.

22. *The Philadelphia Inquirer*, 22 June 1966; "The New Racism," 12; *New York Post*, 21 June 1966.

23. *Arkansas Times*, 29 August 2012.

24. *The New York Times*, 22 June 1966.

25. *The Washington Post*, 22 June 1966.

26. Jose Yglesias, "Dr. King's March on Washington, Part II," *The New York Times Magazine*, 31 March 1968, 70; Luther Mallett, interview by author; Matthew Rinaldi, interview by author.

27. *The New York Times*, 22 June 1966; *The Washington Post*, 22 June 1966; George Smith, interview by author; *The Tri-State Defender*, 25 June 1966.

28. *Chicago Daily News*, 21 June 1966.

29. "The New Racism," 12; Highway Patrol memorandum, 21 June 1966, Box 147, Folder 4, PBJFP; *The Washington Post*, 22 June 1966; Good, "The Meredith March," 11; *New York Post*, 22 June 1966; *The New York Times*, 22 June 1966.

30. "The March—In Step and Out," *Newsweek*, 4 July 1966, 15; *The New York Times*, 22 June 1966; *The Washington Post*, 22 June 1966; *Los Angeles Times*, 22 June 1966.

31. *The New York Times*, 22 June 1966; Arlie Schardt interview, 14 November 1988, EPI.

32. Sovereignty Commission memorandum, 21 June 1966, Box 139, Folder 1, PBJFP; *The Washington Post*, 22 June 1966.

33. Highway Patrol memoranda, 21 June 1966 and 22 June 1966, Box 147, Folder 4, PBJFP; Sovereignty Commission memorandum, 25 June 1966, Box 139, Folder 1, PBJFP; Notes from telephone conversations with John Doar and Roy Moore, 21 June 1966, Box 139, Folder 1, PBJFP.

34. Press releases, 22 June 1966, Reel 13, CORE-A; *Arkansas Gazette*, 24 June 1966; *New York Post*, 22 June 1966; *The New York Times*, 23 June 1966.

35. Long, "Black Power in the Black Belt," 21; Joe Morse, "Meridian Project Report," 5 July 1966, Reel 2, MFDP-LC.

36. Matthew Rinaldi, interview by author; Luther Mallett, interview by author; *The Washington Post*, 22 June 1966.

37. Nina Boal, interview by author; *The Washington Post*, 22 June 1966; Highway Patrol memorandum, 21 June 1966, Box 147, Folder 4, PBJFP; *The New York Times*, 23 June 1966.

38. *Arkansas Times*, 29 August 2012; *The Washington Post*, 22 June 1966.

39. *The Washington Post*, 22 June 1966, 23 June 1966; *Newsday*, 22 June 1966; Highway Patrol memorandum, 21 June 1966, Box 147, Folder 4, PBJFP.

40. *The Washington Post*, 23 June 1966; *The New York Times*, 23 June 1966; Highway Patrol memorandum, 21 June 1966, Box 147, Folder 4, PBJFP.

41. *The Atlanta Constitution*, 22 June 1966; Nina Boal, interview by author.

42. *The Washington Post*, 23 June 1966; *The New York Times*, 23 June 1966.

43. Ibid.

44. David M. Oshinsky, *"Worse Than Slavery": Parchman Farm and the Ordeal of Jim Crow Justice* (New York: Free Press, 1996), 223–39; Myers-Asch, *The Senator and the Sharecropper*, 99–166; *The Carrollton Conservative*, 19 May 1966; Joanne Grant, "Mississippi and 'The Establishment,'" *Freedomways* 5, no. 2 (1965): 294–300.

45. J. Todd Moye, *Let the People Decide: Black Freedom and White Resistance Movements in Sunflower County, Mississippi, 1945–1986* (Chapel Hill: University of North Carolina Press, 2004), 87–170; Charles McLaurin, interview by author; "News of the Week #4," 16 March 1966, Box 5, Folder 7, BGRC; "The Case Against Sunflower County Progress, Inc.," Box 6, Folder 5, BGRC; "Sunflower County: A Call to Action," Box 1, Folder 5, MFDP; Joseph Skinner to William Kuntsler, 11 May 1966, Reel 2, FLHP; Harry Belafonte et al. to Stokely Carmichael, 17 June 1966, Reel 2, SNCC. See also Constance Curry, *Silver Rights* (San Diego: Harcourt Brace, 1995), 3–72, 107–57.

46. *Delta Democrat Times*, 21 June 1966, 22 June 1966; Charles McLaurin, interview by author; *The Enterprise-Tocsin* (Indianola, Miss.), 23 June 1966, 30 June 1966.

47. Charles McLaurin, interview by author; Highway Patrol memorandum, 21 June 1966, Box 147, Folder 4, PBJFP; *The Clarion-Ledger* (Jackson), 22 June 1966.

48. "The New Racism," *Time*, 1 July 1966, 13; *Delta Democrat Times*, 21 June 1966.

49. *Memphis Press-Scimitar*, 22 June 1966.

50. Gene Roberts, "From 'Freedom High' to 'Black Power': The Story of Snick," *The New York Times Magazine*, 25 September 1966, 27; Long, "Black Power in the Black Belt," 21.

51. Highway Patrol memorandum, 22 June 1966, Box 147, Folder 4, PBJFP; FBI memorandum, 22 June 1966, Part 1, Reel 10, MLK-FBI; Long, "Black Power in the Black Belt," 21.

52. Roberts, "From 'Freedom High' to 'Black Power,'" 27.

53. Long, "Black Power in the Black Belt," 21; Speech at Yazoo City Rally, 21 June 1966, Series 3, Box 11, MLKP.

54. Roberts, "From 'Freedom High' to 'Black Power,'" 27–28.

55. Speech at Yazoo City Rally, 21 June 1966, Series 3, Box 11, MLKP.

14. The Prize Bull

1. Melvyn R. Leventhal, "The Civil Rights Movement Comes to an End," unpublished essay in author's possession; Jack Sisson to Matt Ahmann, 30 June 1966, Series 18, Box 4, Folder 1, NCCIJ; King, *Where Do We Go from Here*, 30.
2. Owen Brooks, interview by author.
3. King, *Where Do We Go from Here*, 30–32.
4. Highway Patrol memoranda, 22 June 1966 and 23 June 1966, Box 147, Folder 4, PBJFP; FBI memorandum, 23 June 1966, Box 71B, Folder 2, LBJ-MS; *Yazoo City Herald*, 23 June 1966.
5. *Yazoo City Herald*, 23 June 1966, 7 July 1966.
6. Robert C.O. Chinn, Jr., interview by author, Canton, 26 May 2010.
7. Jesse Clear, interview by author, telephone, 3 March 2010.
8. Sovereignty Commission memorandum, 23 June 1966, SCR ID# 9-31-5-45-1-1-1, MSSC; Sovereignty Commission memorandum, 23 June 1966, Box 5, Folder 4, LFCRC; Branch, *At Canaan's Edge*, 491.
9. *The Commercial Appeal* (Memphis), 21 June 1966.
10. Joseph A. Califano, Jr., *The Triumph and Tragedy of Lyndon Johnson: The White House Years* (College Station: Texas A&M University Press, 2000), 58–59.
11. Robert Dallek, *Lone Star Rising: Lyndon Johnson and His Times, 1906–1960* (New York: Oxford University Press, 1991); Robert Dallek, *Flawed Giant: Lyndon Johnson and His Times, 1961–1973* (New York: Oxford University Press, 1998), 1–237; James Farmer interview, Part 3, Reel 1, OHJA; Roy Wilkins interview, Part 3, Reel 3, OHJA; Wilkins, *Standing Fast*, 295–307.
12. Lyndon Johnson speech at Howard University, 4 June 1965, Office Files of Richard N. Goodwin, Box 18, Folder "White House Conference on the Negro," LBJ; Carter, *The Music Has Gone Out of the Movement*, 1–29.
13. President Johnson's Notes on Conversation with Roy Wilkins, 5 January 1966, Box 8, Folder "January 1966," LBJ-RT.
14. Nick Kotz, *Judgment Days: Lyndon Baines Johnson, Martin Luther King Jr., and the Laws That Changed America* (Boston: Mariner Books, 2005), xi–xix, 91–94, 250–53, 298–314; President Johnson's Notes on Conversation with Martin Luther King, 20 August 1965, Box 7, Folder "August 1965," LBJ-RT.
15. President Johnson's Notes on Conversation with Martin Luther King, 20 August 1965, Box 7, Folder "August 1965," LBJ-RT; James S. Olson and Randy Roberts, *Where the Domino Fell: America and Vietnam, 1945–1965*, 3rd ed. (St. James, N.Y.: Brandywine Press, 1999), 129–53.
16. Martin Luther King Sermon at Ebenezer Baptist Church, 16 January 1966, Series 4, Box 60, Folder 421, TBP; *Memphis Press-Scimitar*, 30 May 1966; FBI memorandum, 2 June 1966, Box 32, Folder "King, Martin Luther, 1966–67 [2 of 2]," LBJ-MS.
17. FBI memorandum, 1 February 1966, Series 4, Box 61, Folder 424, TBP; FBI memorandum, 3 February 1966, Box 32, Folder "Martin Luther King, 1966–67 [2 of 2],"

LBJ-MS; Clifford Alexander to Lyndon Johnson, 7 January 1966, Series 4, Box 60, Folder 422, TBP; Martin Luther King to Lyndon Johnson, Series 1, Box 13, Folder 8, MLKP.

18. Mail Summaries from WH 5-1, Box 8, Folder "Mail Summaries, January 1966–June 1966," LBJ; *The Clarion-Ledger* (Jackson), 5 June 1966; G. Calvin Mackenzie and Robert Weisbrot, *The Liberal Hour: Washington and the Politics of Change in the 1960s* (New York: Penguin Press, 2008), 317–19, 328–32; *Chicago Tribune*, 5 June 1966; *The Greenwood Commonwealth*, 6 June 1966; *Cleveland Plain Dealer*, 9 June 1966; *St. Louis Globe-Democrat*, 10 June 1966; *The Meridian* (Miss.) *Star*, 15 June 1966.

19. Carter, *The Music Has Gone Out of the Movement*, 56–61, 172–78; Doris Kearns, *Lyndon Johnson and the American Dream* (New York: Harper and Row, 1976), 304–307; Joseph Califano to Lyndon Johnson, 18 June 1966, Box 56 [2 of 2], Folder HU 2/FG 216 #2, WHCOF.

20. Lee Rainwater and William L. Yancey, *The Moynihan Report and the Politics of Controversy* (Cambridge, Mass.: MIT Press, 1967); James T. Patterson, *Freedom Is Not Enough: The Moynihan Report and America's Struggle Over Black Family Life—from LBJ to Obama* (New York: Basic Books, 2010), 47–86.

21. Rick Perlstein, *Nixonland: The Rise of a President and the Fracturing of America* (New York: Scribner, 2008), 70–95; Matthew Dallek, *The Right Moment: Ronald Reagan's First Victory and the Decisive Turning Point in American Politics* (New York: Free Press, 2000), 128–211.

22. *The Washington Post*, 11 June 1966, 13 June 1966, 17 June 1966; *The Clarion-Ledger* (Jackson), 5 June 1966; *Jackson Daily News*, 29 June 1966; *The Atlanta Constitution*, 18 June 1966; *The Times-Picayune* (New Orleans), 20 June 1966; *New York Post*, 21 June 1966; *The Sun* (Baltimore), 20 June 1966.

23. Kevin L. Yuill, "The 1966 White House Conference on Civil Rights," *The Historical Journal* 41, no. 1 (1998): 259–82; Carter, *The Music Has Gone Out of the Movement*, 75–101; Jesse Gray, "The All-Black March on the White House Conference June 1st and 2nd: A Statement," FBI File No. 157-5943 (New York Committee to Coordinate the Black March Against the White House Conference on Civil Rights, June 1–2, 1966, Washington, D.C.).

24. Ragni Lantz, "'Righteous Anger' Need Not Be Silenced: LBJ at Rights Confab," *Jet*, 16 June 1966, 16–21; "Council's Report and Recommendations to the Conference," Part 1, Reel 6, CRJA; "No Miracles," *Time*, 10 June 1966, 35–36; "Moderate vs. Militant," *Newsweek*, 13 June 1966, 38; Rovere, "Letter from Washington," 118–43; *The Washington Post*, 3 June 1966, 7 June 1966; *Los Angeles Times*, 7 June 1966, 9 June 1966; *The Philadelphia Inquirer*, 5 June 1966; Ben Heineman interview, Part 3, Reel 2, CRJA.

25. Robert Kintner to Lyndon Johnson, 1 June 1966, Box 56 [2 of 2], Folder HU 2/FG 216 #6, WHCOF; McPherson, *A Political Education*, 348–49; Lyndon Johnson speech at White House Conference on Civil Rights, 1 June 1966, Office Files of Frederick Panzer, Box 331, Folder "Civil Rights [Civil Rights Releases (WH)],"

LBJ; Harry McPherson summary of White House Conference on Civil Rights, 2 June 1966, DDPJ; Cliff Carter to Lyndon Johnson, 3 June 1966, Part 1, Reel 12, CRJA.

26. *The Guardian* (London), 18 June 1966; *The Washington Post*, 7 June 1966.

27. Branch, *At Canaan's Edge*, 495–97; *The Boston Globe* (evening edition), 8 June 1966; *The Washington Star*, 26 June 1966.

28. Floyd McKissick to Lyndon Johnson, 20 June 1966, Box 40, Folder HU 2/ST 24, WHCF-HU.

29. Martin Luther King to Lyndon Johnson, 22 June 1966, Part 1, Reel 11, CRJA; Benjamin Payton to Lyndon Johnson, 22 June 1966, Box 40, Folder HU 2/ST 24, WHCF-HU; *The New York Times*, 23 June 1966; FBI memorandum, 23 June 1966, Part 1, Reel 10, MLK-FBI; *The Clarion-Ledger* (Jackson), 24 June 1966.

30. Harry McPherson to Lyndon Johnson, 23 June 1966, Part 1, Reel 11, CRJA.

31. Lyndon Johnson to Martin Luther King, 23 June 1966, Series 1, Box 13, Folder 8, MLKP.

32. *The Washington Star*, 23 June 1966; *The Sun* (Baltimore), 24 June 1966.

33. *The Washington Star*, 26 June 1966; *The Courier-Journal* (Louisville), 27 June 1966; *The New York Times*, 27 June 1966; *The Washington Post*, 27 June 1966.

34. "Possible Questions at a Press Conference," Part 1, Reel 12, CRJA.

35. Clifford Alexander to Martin Luther King, 22 June 1966, Series 1, Box 13, Folder 8, MLKP; Clifford Alexander to A. Philip Randolph, 22 June 1966, Reel 2, APRP; *The Sun* (Baltimore), 24 June 1966.

36. Flonzie Brown Wright, *Looking Back to Move Ahead: An Experience of History and Hope* (Germantown, Ohio: FBW & Associates, 1994), 89; *The Washington Post*, 24 June 1966; Good, "The Meredith March," 12.

15. The Shadow of Death

1. Anne Moody, *Coming of Age in Mississippi* (New York: Laurel Books, 1976; original 1968), 286–305; Robert C.O. Chinn, Jr., interview by author; Umoja, "Eye for an Eye," 68, 117–122; Bill Winfield, interview by author, telephone, 17 February 2010; C. O. Chinn, Sr., arrest record, *Chinn v. Mississippi*, Reel 13, SCRLR; Documents from *C. O. Chinn v. Canton*, Reel 13, SCRLR.

2. Attorney notes with C. O. Chinn, 23 June 1966 and 6 October 1966, *Chinn v. Mississippi*, Reel 13, SCRLR.

3. Attorney notes with C. O. Chinn, 23 June 1966, *Chinn v. Mississippi*, Reel 13, SCRLR; *The Denver Post*, 23 June 1966; *Jackson Daily News*, 23 June 1966.

4. Attorney notes with C. O. Chinn, 23 June 1966 and 6 October 1966, *Chinn v. Mississippi*, Reel 13, SCRLR.

5. "The Evidence at Trial" and "In the Supreme Court of Mississippi, No. 44, 496," *Chinn v. Mississippi*, Reel 13, SCRLR; *Jackson Daily News*, 11 October 1966.

6. "In the Supreme Court of Mississippi, No. 44, 496," *Chinn v. Mississippi*, Reel 13, SCRLR; *Jackson Daily News*, 23 June 1966.

7. SNCC research on Madison County, 25 October 1965, Box 1, Folder 3, WWP; Dittmer, *Local People*, 187–88.

8. Debbie Bernstein, "Canton Project History," 28 February 1965, Reel 10, CORE-A; Dittmer, *Local People*, 185–90, 221–23.

9. Annie Devine interview, November 1966, ARC; Tom Dent, "Annie Devine Remembers," *Freedomways* 22, no. 2 (1982): 81–92; Tom Dent, *Southern Journey: A Return to the Civil Rights Movement* (New York: Morrow, 1997), 346–47; Robert E. Luckett, Jr., "Annie Devine: A Mother in and of the Civil Rights Movement," *The Journal of Mississippi History* 70, no. 3 (fall 2008): 265–88. On Congressional Challenge see Box 1, Folder 5 and Box 1, Folder 7, MFDP.

10. Hollis Watkins, interview by author; Richard Jewett, "Mississippi Field Report," 19 January 1965, Reel 45, CORE; Matteo Suarez interview, 11 August 1969, Series 4, Box 104, Folder 748, TBP; Field report by George Raymond, January 1965, Part 3, Folder 6868, FBMP; George Raymond to Mrs. Newman Levy, 29 January 1965, Reel 22, CORE; "School Integration 1965," "Madison County School Desegregation Project '66," and "Welfare Project," all in Box 1, Folder 1, Michael Grossman Papers, WHS.

11. James McRee, interview by author, telephone, 22 September 2011; Shirley Simmons, interview by author, Canton, Mississippi, 26 May 2010; Robert C. O. Chinn, Jr., interview by author; "File Madison County Project," Reel 7, SNCC; Greenberg, *The Devil Has Slippery Shoes*, 31, 500–501; Flonzie Brown Wright (Flonzie Goodloe), interview by author, telephone, 25 January 2011; *Newsday*, 25 June 1966.

12. Mark Newman, "The Catholic Church in Mississippi and Desegregation, 1963–1973," *The Journal of Mississippi History* 67, no. 4 (winter 2005): 331–55; Jake Friesen, interview by author, telephone, 1 February 2010; Jake Friesen to Edgar Stoesz, 8 June 1966 and 12 June 1966, both in Box 1, Folder 3, JFP; "Valley View Weekly News," 14 June 1966, Box 1, Folder 2, WWP.

13. James McRee, interview by author; Flonzie Brown Wright (Flonzie Goodloe), interview by author; Luke Mikschl, "Holy Child Jesus Mission and 'The March,'" Series 20, Box 2, Folder 10, NCCIJ; Luke Mikschl interview, 26 September 1978, OHC-MC; *The New York Times*, 25 June 1966.

14. "Black Out Downtown Canton," Box 9, Folder 25, RRC; "Facts on Canton Arrests, 6-23-66," *C. O. Chinn v. Canton*, Reel 13, SCRLR; *The Baltimore Afro-American*, 2 July 1966.

15. "Facts on Canton Arrests, 6-23-66," *C. O. Chinn v. Canton*, Reel 13, SCRLR; *The New York Times*, 24 June 1966.

16. "Facts on Canton Arrests, 6-23-66," *C. O. Chinn v. Canton*, Reel 13, SCRLR; *Chicago Daily News*, 23 June 1966; *The New York Times*, 23 June 1966.

17. "Facts on Canton Arrests, 6-23-66," *C. O. Chinn v. Canton*, Reel 13, SCRLR; Press release, 23 June 1966, Reel 13, CORE-A; *Chicago Daily News*, 23 June 1966; *The New York Times*, 23 June 1966.

18. *Chicago Daily News*, 23 June 1966; George Greene, interview by author; "Facts on Canton Arrests, 6-23-66," *C. O. Chinn v. Canton*, Reel 13, SCRLR; Highway Patrol memorandum, 24 June 1966, Box 147, Folder 4, PBJFP.

19. "Facts on Canton Arrests, 6-23-66," *C. O. Chinn v. Canton*, Reel 13, SCRLR; Press release, 23 June 1966, Reel 13, CORE-A; *The Washington Post*, 24 June 1966.
20. Paul Johnson interview, 8 September 1970, Part 3, Reel 2, OHJA.
21. Gloster Current to Roy Wilkins et al., 23 June 1966, Group IV, Box A56, Folder "Meredith, James, 1966," NAACP.
22. Ruby Hurley, Annual Report for Southeast Regional Office, Part 29, Series A, Reel 17, NAACP-B; Press release, 23 June 1966, Reel 13, CORE-A.
23. *The Washington Post*, 24 June 1966; FBI memorandum, 24 June 1966, Box 71B, Folder 2, LBJ-MS.
24. FBI memorandum, 24 June 1966, Box 71B, Folder 2, LBJ-MS; Good, "The Meredith March," 12; *The Boston Globe*, 24 June 1966.
25. *Jackson Daily News*, 24 June 1966; Recording from Canton, 23 June 1966, SRTR; Flonzie Brown Wright (Flonzie Goodloe), interview by author; Jesse McCullough, interview by author, telephone, 24 September 2010.
26. Good, "The Meredith March," 12; *The Boston Globe*, 24 June 1966; Recording from Canton, 23 June 1966, SRTR.
27. *The Boston Globe*, 24 June 1966.
28. *Jackson Daily News*, 24 June 1966; *San Francisco Chronicle*, 24 June 1966; *New York Post*, 24 June 1966.
29. *The Boston Globe*, 24 June 1966.
30. *Jackson Daily News*, 24 June 1966; *The New York Times*, 24 June 1966; *New York Post*, 24 June 1966; *The Boston Globe*, 24 June 1966.
31. Sherwood Ross, interview by author.
32. *The New York Times*, 24 June 1966; Report from Canton, 23 June 1966, SRTR.
33. *San Francisco Chronicle*, 24 June 1966; "The Time Has Come," *Eyes on the Prize II: America at the Crossroads*, vol. 1 (Blackside Productions, 1990).
34. "The March—In Step and Out," *Newsweek*, 4 July 1966, 15.
35. Good, "The Meredith March," 12.
36. *Chicago Tribune*, 24 June 1966; *The New York Times*, 24 June 1966.
37. *New York Post*, 24 June 1966; Canton report, 23 June 1966, SRTR; *San Francisco Chronicle*, 24 June 1966; *The Boston Globe*, 24 June 1966.
38. *The Washington Post*, 24 June 1966; "The New Racism," 12.
39. *The New York Times*, 24 June 1966; *Jackson Daily News*, 24 June 1966; Wiley Mallett, interview by author; *New York Post*, 24 June 1966; *The Philadelphia Tribune*, 9 July 1966.
40. Jacob Russell (Russ Johnson), interview by author, telephone, 25 September 2012; Wiley Mallett, interview by author; David Doggett, interview by author; Bruce Hartford, interview by author.
41. *The Washington Post*, 24 June 1966; *The Philadelphia Tribune*, 24 June 1966.
42. David Doggett, interview by author; *San Francisco Chronicle*, 24 June 1966; *Los Angeles Times*, 24 June 1966.
43. *New York Post*, 24 June 1966; "The New Racism," 12; "Canton, Mississippi," 23 June 1966, Reel 38, SNCC.
44. Good, "The Meredith March," 12.

45. Arlie Schardt interview, 14 November 1988, EPI; Jean Morton, interview by author; Barbara Emerson, interview by author; "The New Racism," 12.

46. *The New York Times*, 24 June 1966.

47. Jo Freeman to Al and Cynthia, 25 July 1966, JFPP.

48. Jo Freeman to Mother, 29 June 1966, JFPP; Connemara Wadsworth interview; Jo Freeman to Al and Cynthia, 25 July 1966, JFPP.

49. Clarice Coney, interview by author, Canton, Mississippi, 26 May 2010; Greenberg, *The Devil Has Slippery Shoes*, 401–404, 650–51.

50. Luke Mikschl, "Holy Child Jesus Mission and 'The March,'" Series 20, Box 2, Folder 10, NCCIJ; Dittmer, *The Good Doctors*, 153–54; Alvin Poussaint, interview by author. On Harvey see Tiyi Morris, "Local Women and the Civil Rights Movement in Mississippi: Re-visioning Womanpower Unlimited," in Theoharis and Woodward, *Groundwork*, 193–214; Suzanne E. Smith, *To Serve the Living: Funeral Directors and the African American Way of Death* (Cambridge, Mass.: Belknap Press of Harvard University Press, 2010), 133–140.

51. Young, *An Easy Burden*, 402–403.

52. Andrew Young interview, 27 October 1988, EPI; Andrew Young interview, *Playboy*, July 1977, 74.

53. Young, *An Easy Burden*, 403; Andrew Young interview, 27 October 1988, EPI.

54. Floyd McKissick interview, 21 October 1988, EPI; "The Talk of the Town," 24.

55. Carmichael, *Ready for Revolution*, 508; Jake Friesen, interview by author; "The Talk of the Town," 24; Good, "The Meredith March," 13; Dittmer, *The Good Doctors*, 153.

56. Charles Evers, interview by author; Evers, *Evers*, 145–46; Alvin Poussaint, interview by author.

57. Charles McLaurin, interview by author.

58. CBS News Special Report, *The March in Mississippi*, 26 June 1966, PCM; Canton report, 23 June 1966, SRTR.

59. Robert C.O. Chinn, Jr., interview by author; *Chicago Daily News*, 24 June 1966; FBI memorandum, 24 June 1966, Box 71B, Folder 2, LBJ-MS.

60. *Chicago Daily News*, 24 June 1966; Victoria Gray Adams, "They Didn't Know the Power of Women," in Holsaert et al., *Hands on the Freedom Plow*, 239; *Newsday*, 24 June 1966.

61. *Newsday*, 24 June 1966; *Los Angeles Times*, 24 June 1966.

62. *The Times-Picayune* (New Orleans), 24 June 1966; Bruce Hartford, interview by author; Connemara Wadsworth, interview by author; *The New York Times*, 24 June 1966; "The Time Has Come," *Eyes on the Prize II*.

63. *The Alamo Messenger*, 1 July 1966; Luke Mikschl, "Holy Child Jesus Mission and 'The March,'" Series 20, Box 2, Folder 10, NCCIJ.

64. Shirley Simmons, interview by author; Connemara Wadsworth, interview by author.

65. *The New York Times*, 24 June 1966; *Los Angeles Times*, 25 June 1966; *Newsday*, 25 June 1966; *The Baltimore Afro-American*, 2 July 1966; Gloster Current to Roy Wilkins et al., 24 June 1966, Group IV, Box A56, Folder "Meredith, James, 1966," NAACP.

66. *Los Angeles Times*, 25 June 1966; Sovereignty Commission memorandum, 25 June 1966, SCR ID# 2-24-4-35-1-1-1, MSSC; Jack Cauthen to Paul Johnson, 1 July 1966, Box 142, Folder 3, PBJFP.

67. *The Madison County Herald*, 30 June 1966; Mitchell Wells interview, 25 August 1982, OHC-MC; O. D. Crawford interview, 29 January 1982, OHC-MC.

68. For letters to King, see Virginia Lee Grimes to Martin Luther King, 24 June 1966, Part 1, Reel 15, SCLC; Peter Gray et al. to Martin Luther King, 26 June 1966, Part 1, Reel 16, SCLC. For telegrams to Paul Johnson see LC Dorosz to Paul Johnson, 24 June 1966, Don Goodwin to Paul Johnson, 24 June 1966, Helen Exner to Paul Johnson, 25 June 1966, Marie Loameyer to Paul Johnson, 26 June 1966, and Marian Manley to Paul Johnson, 26 June 1966, all in Box 61, Folder 5, PBJFP. For pleas to Lyndon Johnson, see Roy Wilkins to Lyndon Johnson, 24 June 1966, Group IV, Box A56, Folder "Meredith, James, 1966," NAACP; Telegrams from Carl Moultrie, William Ryan, John Conyers, Don Edwards, Ben Rosenthal, Emanuel Mauravchik, Robert Stone, Matthew Ahmann, Barbara Moffett, Paul Moore, and David French, all 24 June 1966, Box 40, Folder HU 2/ST 24, WHCF-HU. For editorials, see *Miami Herald*, 25 June 1966; *New York Post*, 25 June 1966; *The Washington Post*, 25 June 1966.

69. Bob Fitch, interview by author; Matt Herron, interview by author; Harry Benson, interview by author.

70. *The New York Times*, 25 June 1966.

71. *The Washington Post*, 25 June 1966; *The New York Times*, 25 June 1966; *Detroit Free Press*, 26 June 1966; *Chicago Daily News*, 25 June 1966; *Los Angeles Times*, 25 June 1966.

72. Sovereignty Commission memoranda, 24 June 1966 and 25 June 1966, SCR ID# 9-31-5-47-1-1-1 and 9-31-5-49-1-1-1, MSSC; Good, *Troubles I've Seen*, 261.

16. Uninvited Guests

1. FBI memorandum, 25 June 1966, Box 71B, Folder 2, LBJ-MS; *The Sun* (Baltimore), 26 June 1966.

2. *The Denver Post*, 23 June 1966; FBI memorandum, 24 June 1966, Box 71B, Folder 2, LBJ-MS; Highway Patrol memorandum, 23 June 1966, Box 147, Folder 4, PBJFP; *The Nashville Tennessean*, 23 June 1966; *Jackson Daily News*, 23 June 1966; *The Philadelphia Inquirer*, 23 June 1966.

3. *The New York Times*, 23 June 1966; Sovereignty Commission memorandum, 23 June 1966, SCR ID# 9-31-5-45-1-1-1, MSSC; Sovereignty Commission memorandum, 23 June 1966, Box 5, Folder 4, LFCRC.

4. Press release, 22 June 1966, Reel 13, CORE-A; Bill Simpson, "Telephone Conversation with Assistant U.S. Attorney General John Doar," Box 139, Folder 1, PBJFP; FBI memorandum, 24 June 1966, Box 71B, Folder 2, LBJ-MS.

5. *The Meridian* (Miss.) *Star*, 23 June 1966; *The Guardian* (Manchester, U.K.), 25 June 1966; Mars, *Witness to Philadelphia*, 211.

6. FBI memorandum, 24 June 1966, Box 71B, Folder 2, LBJ-MS; Matt Ahmann to Program and Clerical Staff Members, 23 June 1966, Series 18, Box 4, Folder 1, NCCIJ; *Los Angeles Times*, 24 June 1966.

7. John Steele, interview by author; FBI memorandum, 25 June 1966, Box 71B, Folder 2, LBJ-MS; *The Washington Post*, 25 June 1966; *The Sun* (Baltimore), 25 June 1966; *New York Post*, 25 June 1966; Jim Peppler, interview by author.

8. *The New York Times*, 25 June 1966; *The Boston Globe*, 25 June 1966; *Newsday*, 25 June 1966.

9. *The Washington Post*, 25 June 1966; Matthew Rinaldi, interview by author.

10. *The Washington Post*, 25 June 1966; *New York Post*, 25 June 1966; Philadelphia demonstration, 24 June 1966, D46, WLBT.

11. *New York Post*, 25 June 1966; Mars, *Witness to Philadelphia*, 211–12.

12. *The Boston Globe*, 25 June 1966; *New York Post*, 25 June 1966.

13. *New York Post*, 25 June 1966.

14. *The New York Times*, 25 June 1966; *Memphis Press-Scimitar*, 24 June 1966; Philadelphia demonstration, 24 June 1966, D46, WLBT; *The Sun* (Baltimore), 25 June 1966; *The Boston Globe*, 25 June 1966.

15. James Lawson interview, 21 July 1969, Container 22, Folder 135, SSC; Jo Freeman to Al and Cynthia, 25 July 1966, JFPP; Matt Herron, interview by author; FBI memorandum, 25 June 1966, Box 71B, Folder 2, LBJ-MS.

16. James Lawson interview, 21 July 1969, Container 22, Folder 135, SSC; Joe Morse, "Meridian Project Report," 5 July 1966, Reel 2, MFDP-LC.

17. *The Sun* (Baltimore), 25 June 1966; *New York Post*, 24 June 1966; Mars, *Witness in Philadelphia*, 212.

18. *The Washington Star*, 25 June 1966; FBI memorandum, 24 June 1966, Box 71B, Folder 2, LBJ-MS; *The Clarion-Ledger* (Jackson), 25 June 1966.

19. *The Washington Star*, 25 June 1966; Luke Mikschl, "Holy Child Jesus Mission and 'The March,'" Series 20, Box 2, Folder 10, NCCIJ.

20. Sovereignty Commission memorandum, 24 June 1966, SCR ID# 9-31-5-46-1-1-1; Highway Patrol memorandum, 27 June 1966, Box 147, Folder 4, PBJFP; Jim McGuire to Matt Ahmann, 9 September 1966, Series 18, Box 4, Folder 1, NCCIJ; Luke Mikschl, "Holy Child Jesus Mission and 'The March,'" Series 20, Box 2, Folder 10, NCCIJ.

21. Madison County Movement Flyer, personal collection of Joan Mulholland, copy in author's possession; "Black Out Downtown Canton," Box 9, Folder 25, RRC; *The Meridian* (Miss.) *Star*, 24 June 1966; Sovereignty Commission memorandum, 25 June 1966, SCR ID# 2-24-4-35-1-1-1, MSSC; *The Militant*, 11 July 1966.

22. *Los Angeles Times*, 25 June 1966; *Jackson Daily News*, 24 June 1966; FBI memorandum, 25 June 1966, Box 71B, Folder 2, LBJ-MS.

23. Highway Patrol memorandum, 24 June 1966, Box 147, Folder 4, PBJFP; *The Philadelphia Inquirer*, 25 June 1966.

24. Memoranda from Jim McGuire to Matt Ahmann, 29 June 1966 and 30 June 1966, Series 18, Box 4, Folder 1, NCCIJ; *Detroit Free Press*, 25 June 1966.

25. *Chicago Daily News*, 25 June 1966.

26. *The Washington Star*, 25 June 1966.

27. Sovereignty Commission memorandum, 24 June 1966, SCR ID# 9-31-5-46-1-1-1, MSSC; Flonzie Brown Wright (Flonzie Goodloe), interview by author; *The Washington Star*, 25 June 1966.

28. Jim McGuire to Matt Ahmann, 30 June 1966, Series 18, Box 4, Folder 1, NCCIJ; *Detroit Free Press*, 25 June 1966; Sovereignty Commission memorandum, 24 June 1966, SCR ID# 9-31-5-46-1-1-1, MSSC; Paul Murray, interview by author; Flonzie Brown Wright (Flonzie Goodloe), interview by author; *The Washington Star*, 25 June 1966; James Lawson interview, 21 July 1969, Container 22, Folder 135, SSC.

29. Fund-raising letter, Box 13, Folder 8, JHMC; *The Baltimore Afro-American*, 11 June 1966; *New York Post*, 17 June 1966.

30. MacKenzie and Weisbrot, *The Liberal Hour*, 35, 53.

31. *Meet the Press* transcript, 19 June 1966, Box 14, Folder 4, JHMC.

32. *The Boston Globe*, 20 June 1966; *Memphis Press-Scimitar*, 20 June 1966; *The New York Times*, 20 June 1966; *The Philadelphia Tribune*, 25 June 1966.

33. *The Sun* (Baltimore), 23 June 1966; *Chicago Tribune*, 23 June 1966; *The Chicago Defender*, 25 June 1966, 27 June 1966.

34. *New York Post*, 23 June 1966; *The New York Times*, 22 June 1966, 24 June 1966; *The Commercial Appeal* (Memphis), 24 June 1966; *Memphis Press-Scimitar*, 24 June 1966.

35. *The Commercial Appeal* (Memphis), 24 June 1966; *Chicago Daily News*, 10 June 1966; *Call and Post* (Cleveland), 25 June 1966.

36. *The Commercial Appeal* (Memphis), 24 June 1966; *The Atlanta Constitution*, 25 June 1966; *The Sun* (Baltimore), 26 June 1966.

37. *The Washington Star*, 25 June 1966; *Chicago Tribune*, 25 June 1966.

38. *Jackson Daily News*, 25 June 1966; "Walk to Jackson, Mississippi," Box 14, Folder 3, JHMC; *The Sun* (Baltimore), 26 June 1966; Sellers, *The River of No Return*, 168.

39. Paul Murray, "We Picked a Great Time to Go to Canton," unpublished memoir in author's possession.

40. Paul Murray, interview by author; *New York Post*, 28 June 1966.

41. *The Nashville Tennessean*, 25 June 1966; *New York Post*, 28 June 1966; Paul Murray, interview by author; Sovereignty Commission memorandum, SCR ID# 1-91-0-4-1-1-1, MSSC.

42. *Chicago Daily News*, 25 June 1966; Jim McGuire to Matt Ahmann, Series 18, Box 4, Folder 1, NCCIJ; *Los Angeles Times*, 25 June 1966; Flonzie Brown Wright (Flonzie Goodloe), interview by author.

43. *The Nashville Tennessean*, 25 June 1966; *The Washington Post*, 25 June 1966, 26 June 1966; "The March—In Step and Out," *Newsweek*, 4 July 1966, 16; *Newsday*, 25 June 1966.

44. *The Nashville Tennessean*, 25 June 1966; Lewis, *Walking with the Wind*, 369–73; John Lewis interview, 5 December 1988, EPI; "Black Power in the Red," *Time*, 1 July 1966, 68; *The New York Times*, 1 July 1966.

45. Paul Good, "Odyssey of a Man—and a Movement," *The New York Times Magazine*, 25 June 1967, 5, 44–48.

46. Undated column in *New York Post*, Box 1, Clippings Scrapbook, Volume 1, SC-LDS; *Memphis Press-Scimitar*, 25 June 1966.

47. James Lawson interview, 21 July 1969, Container 22, Folder 135, SSC; "The Talk of the Town," 24.

48. Luke Mikschl, "Holy Child Jesus Mission and 'The March,'" Series 20, Box 2, Folder 10, NCCIJ; Paul Murray, interview by author. See also Paul Thom Murray, "Negro Leadership in a Southern Town" (M.A. thesis, Ohio State University, 1967), 29–31.

17. We're the Greatest

1. Wendell Paris, interview by author, Jackson, 27 March 2010.

2. Wendell Paris, interview by author; James Forman, *Sammy Younge, Jr.: The First Black College Student to Die in the Black Liberation Movement* (New York: Grove Press, 1968), 61–62, 137–38, 158–59, 176, 192–94; Robert J. Norrell, *Reaping the Whirlwind: The Civil Rights Movement in Tuskegee* (New York: Knopf, 1985), 173–82.

3. Forman, *Sammy Younge, Jr.*, 197–261; Norrell, *Reaping the Whirlwind*, 182–93; Wendell Paris, interview by author.

4. Wendell Paris, interview by author.

5. Harold Middlebrook interview, 18 July 1968, Container 23, Series 1, Folder 2, SSC.

6. "To Be Equal" Radio Script, 15 June 1966, Box 195, WYP; *The Philadelphia Tribune*, 21 June 1966; Press statement, 14 June 1966, Box 209, WYP; *Los Angeles Times*, 15 June 1966; *The Clarion-Ledger* (Jackson), 19 June 1966.

7. Speech in Jackson, 26 June 1966, Box 143, WYP; "To Be Equal" Radio Script, 29 June 1966, Box 195, WYP; *The Philadelphia Tribune*, 25 June 1966; FBI memorandum, 24 June 1966, Box 71B, Folder 2, LBJ-MS; Weiss, *Whitney M. Young, Jr., and the Struggle for Civil Rights*, 112; Whitney Young to Hosea Williams, 12 August 1966, Part III, Box 406, Folder 7, NULP.

8. *The Washington Post*, 22 June 1966; "To Be Equal" Radio Script, 6 July 1966, Box 195, WYP.

9. Jack Cauthen to James Meredith, 16 March 1966, Box 14, Folder 19, JHMC.

10. Meredith, "Big Changes Are Coming," 27. See also Edgar Stoesz, "Mississippi-Mexico Trip Diary," 6–16 September 1966, Box 1, Folder 7, JFP.

11. Jack Cauthen interview, 29 June 1982, OHC-MC.

12. *The Boston Globe* (evening edition), 25 June 1966; *New York Post*, 25 June 1966; Highway Patrol memorandum, 25 June 1966, Box 147, Folder 4, PBJFP.

13. *New York Post*, 25 June 1966; *San Francisco Chronicle*, 26 June 1966; *Los Angeles Times*, 26 June 1966.

14. *The Washington Post*, 26 June 1966; *The Nashville Tennessean*, 26 June 1966.

15. *The Nashville Tennessean*, 26 June 1966; Gregory, *Up from Nigger*, 134–35; Sovereignty Commission memorandum, 18 June 1966, SCR ID# 9-31-5-42-1-1-1, MSSC; FBI memorandum, 29 June 1966, Reel 10, FBI-MLK; *The Times-Picayune* (New Orleans), 26 June 1966.

16. *Chicago Tribune*, 26 June 1966; FBI memorandum, 27 June 1966, Box 71B, Folder 2, LBJ-MS; *Memphis Press-Scimitar*, 25 June 1966.

17. FBI memorandum, 27 June 1966, Box 71B, Folder 2, LBJ-MS; *The Nashville Tennessean*, 26 June 1966.

18. Joyce Ladner, interview by author; Joanne Gavin, interview by author, telephone, 26 January 2010; Williamson, *Radicalizing the Ebony Tower*, 16–17; Katagiri, *The Mississippi State Sovereignty Commission*, 153.

19. Moody, *Coming of Age in Mississippi*, 261–85; Arsenault, *Freedom Riders*, 332–33; Williamson, *Radicalizing the Ebony Tower*, 54–58, 64–69, 97–105; Clarice T. Campbell and Oscar Allan Rodgers, Jr., *Mississippi: The View from Tougaloo* (Jackson: University Press of Mississippi, 1979), 196–219; Joyce Ladner, interview by author.

20. George Owens interview, 8 April 1980, MDAH.

21. *The New York Times*, 26 June 1966; Joyce Ladner, interview by author; James C. Coleman oral history, 12 April 2000, TCSC.

22. *Los Angeles Times*, 26 June 1966.

23. Jill Wakeman (Goodman) to friends, 27 June 1966, Box 1, Folder 1, JWCRC; *The Washington Post*, 26 June 1966.

24. Meredith March and Rally, 26 June 1966, D49, WLBT; *The Philadelphia Tribune*, 28 June 1966; Coby Smith, interview by author; Rafer Johnson with Philip Goldberg, *The Best That I Can Be: An Autobiography* (Boston: G. K. Hall, 1999), 191.

25. Wil Haygood, *In Black and White: The Life of Sammy Davis, Jr.* (New York: Knopf, 2003), 3–5, 180–81, 353–56; *The New York Times*, 22 June 1966; Sammy Davis, Jr., and Jane and Burt Boyar, *Why Me?: The Sammy Davis, Jr. Story* (New York: Farrar, Straus and Giroux, 1989), 186–89; *The Meridian* (Miss.) *Star*, 26 June 1966; *The Times-Picayune* (New Orleans), 26 June 1966.

26. Peter Manso, *Brando: The Biography* (New York: Hyperion, 1994), 649–63; Joan Mulholland, interview by author, telephone, 20 April 2010; Harry Benson, interview by author; *The Philadelphia Tribune*, 28 June 1966; Rally for Meredith March, 25 June 1966, D47, WLBT.

27. Owen Brooks, interview by author; Barbara Emerson (Barbara Jean Williams), interview by author; Tougaloo Rally flyer, TCSC; FBI surveillance, 11 June 1966 and 20 June 1966, Part 2, Reel 5, MLK-FBI; Brian Ward, *Radio and the Struggle for Civil Rights in the South* (Gainesville: University Press of Florida, 2004), 249–77. See also Brian Ward, *Just My Soul Responding: Rhythm and Blues, Black Consciousness, and Race Relations* (Berkeley: University of California Press, 1998), 1–336.

28. *Jackson Daily News*, 26 June 1966; *The Times-Picayune* (New Orleans), 26 June 1966; "The Talk of the Town," 24–25.

29. Rally for Meredith March, 25 June 1966, D47, WLBT; *The Village Voice*, 30 June 1966; *The Washington Post*, 26 June 1966.

30. James Sullivan, *The Hardest Working Man: How James Brown Saved the Soul of America* (New York: Gotham, 2008), 3–6; Ward, *Just My Soul Responding*, 201–202; James Brown, *I Feel Good: A Memoir of a Life in Soul* (New York: New American Library, 2005), 132–33.

31. Cleveland Sellers, interview by author; Sullivan, *Hardest Working Man*, 110–11.

32. Chester Higgins, "Divided on Tactics, Leaders Agree March a Success," *Jet*, 14 July 1966, 26; Rally for Meredith March, 25 June 1966, D47, WLBT.

33. Herbert Callendar to George Raymond, 13 July 1966, Reel 16, CORE-A; RJ Smith, *The One: The Life and Music of James Brown* (New York: Gotham, 2012), 178–81, 188–214. See also Van Deburg, *New Day in Babylon*, 204–16.

34. *Los Angeles Times*, 13 June 1966; *The Washington Star*, 26 June 1966; Sovereignty Commission memorandum, 15 June 1966, SCR ID# 9-31-5-41-2-1-1, MSSC; *The Meridian* (Miss.) *Star*, 14 June 1966.

35. Press release, Reel 13, CORE-A.

36. Halberstam, *The Children*, 528; *Los Angeles Times*, 23 June 1966.

37. Charles Marx to T. B. Birdsong and A. D. Morgan, 20 June 1966, Box 147, Folder 4, PBJFP; *The Washington Star*, 26 June 1966; Grady Poulard, interview by author, telephone, 15 August 2011.

38. Freedom March News Conference, 22 June 1966, D45, WLBT; Press release, Reel 13, CORE-A; *The Washington Star*, 26 June 1966; *Vicksburg Citizen's Appeal*, 20 July 1966; MFDP Flyer, Box 5, Folder 3, AMP.

39. Dorothy Stewart, interview by author, telephone, 18 November 2010; Ruby Magee interview, 18 May 1972, USM-COH; Fred Clark interview, 10 June 1994, USM-COH; Aaron Henry interview, Part 3, Reel 2, OHJA; Joyce Ladner, interview by author.

40. Jefferson Rogers, "Meredith Mississippi Freedom March," Group IV, Box A56, Folder "Meredith, James, 1966," NAACP; Walter Fauntroy to Local Pilgrimage Coordinators, Group IV, Box A56, Folder "Meredith, James, 1966," NAACP; *The Washington Star*, 18 June 1966, 26 June 1966; Highway Patrol memorandum, 21 June 1966, Box 147, Folder 4, PBJFP; FBI memoranda, 23 June 1966 and 25 June 1966, Box 71B, Folder 2, LBJ-MS; *The Chicago Defender*, 21 June 1966.

41. *The Atlanta Constitution*, 25 June 1966.

42. "The Talk of the Town," 23.

43. *Jackson Daily News*, 23 June 1966; *The Meridian* (Miss.) *Star*, 24 June 1966; *The Guardian* (Manchester, U.K.), 27 June 1966.

44. Press Conference with Jackson Mayor, 23 June 1966, D45, WLBT; Press releases by Paul Johnson, 24 June 1966 and 25 June 1966, Box 104, Folder 15, PBJFP; *Jackson Daily News*, 23 June 1966, 25 June 1966; *The Clarion-Ledger* (Jackson), 24 June 1966, 25 June 1966; *The Meridian* (Miss.) *Star*, 24 June 1966.

45. *The Meridian* (Miss.) *Star*, 30 June 1966; *Los Angeles Times*, 23 June 1966; FBI memorandum, 23 June 1966, Box 71B, Folder 2, LBJ-MS.

46. Three memoranda from A. D. Morgan to Jack Hutchison, all 22 June 1966, Box 147, Folder 4, PBJFP; Sovereignty Commission memorandum, undated, SCR ID# 9-31-5-51-1-1-1, MSSC; Sovereignty Commission memorandum, 25 June 1966, SCR ID# 2-24-4-35-1-1-1, MSSC.

47. Dittmer, *Local People*, 344–46.

48. *The Times-Picayune* (New Orleans), 23 June 1966; *The Meridian* (Miss.) *Star*, 25 June 1966; Melvyn R. Leventhal, "The Civil Rights Movement Comes to an End," unpublished essay in author's possession; C. A. Smith to Paul Johnson, 25 June 1966, Box 61, Folder 5, PBJFP; Memorandum to Herman Glazier, 22 June 1966, Box 139, Folder 1, PBJFP; Erle Johnston to Herman Glazier, 20 June 1966, Box 139,

Folder 1, PBJFP; Sovereignty Commission memorandum, 15 June 1966, SCR ID# 9-31-5-41-2-1-1, MSSC.

49. *The Commercial Appeal* (Memphis), 25 June 1966; CBS News Special Report, *The March in Mississippi*, 26 June 1966, PCM; *Los Angeles Times*, 26 June 1966; Interview with Herman Glazier, 10 September 1993, USM-COH.

50. Ed King, interview by author; Ed King interview, 26 February 1992, Series 4, Box 105, Folder 752, TBP.

51. Ed King, interview by author.

52. Dorothy Stewart, interview by author; Voter Registration for Hinds County, Mississippi, through 8 July 1966, Box 1, Folder 1, Frederick Heinze Papers, WHS.

53. Dittmer, *Local People*, 86–90, 157–69; John R. Salter, Jr., *Jackson, Mississippi: An American Chronicle of Struggle and Schism* (Malabar, Fla.: Robert E. Krieger, 1987); Joyce Ladner, interview by author.

54. Meeting of the Executive Committee, Jackson Branch, 1 September 1965, Part 29, Series A, Reel 6, NAACP-B; Doris Allison to Gloster Current, 18 December 1965, Part IV, Box C18, Folder "Jackson, 1966–69," NAACP.

55. Gloster Current to Samuel Bailey, 19 January 1966, Part IV, Box C18, Folder "Jackson, 1966–69," NAACP; Gloster Current to John Frazier, 13 June 1966, and John Frazier to Gloster Current, 21 June 1966, both in Part IV, Box C18, Folder "Jackson, 1966–69," NAACP; Jackson Branch Newsletter, 16 June 1966, Part IV, Box J6, Folder "Mississippi, 1966–69," NAACP; Press release, 2 July 1966, Group IV, Box A56, Folder "Meredith, James, 1966," NAACP.

56. Roy Wilkins, Testimony Before Constitutional Rights Subcommittee of Senate Judiciary Committee, 16 June 1966, Box 58, Folder "Speeches and Writings, 1966 April–June," RWP; Press release, St. Louis Branch, 21 June 1966, Part 29, Series B, Reel 4, NAACP-B; *The Pittsburgh Courier*, 2 July 1966; *Memphis World*, 25 June 1966; *New York Post*, 18 June 1966.

57. *The Philadelphia Inquirer*, 25 June 1966; *The Philadelphia Tribune*, 28 June 1966.

58. Wilkins, *Standing Fast*, 316–17.

59. Sovereignty Commission memorandum, 26 June 1966, Box 5, Folder 4, LFCRC.

60. Gloster Current to Roy Wilkins et al., 23 June 1966 and 24 June 1966, Group IV, Box A56, Folder "Meredith, James, 1966," NAACP; Charles Marx to T. B. Birdsong and A. D. Morgan, 20 June 1966, Box 147, Folder 4, PBJFP; Roy Wilkins to Delegates of the 57th Annual NAACP Convention, 5 July 1966, Group IV, Box A56, Folder "Meredith, James, 1966," NAACP; Charles Evers to Ruby Hurley, 1 July 1966, Part 29, Series A, Reel 6, NAACP-B; Press release, 2 July 1966, Group IV, Box A56, Folder "Meredith, James, 1966," NAACP.

61. *The Philadelphia Tribune*, 28 June 1966; Alvin Poussaint, interview by author.

62. Roy Wilkins to Delegates of the 57th Annual NAACP Convention, 5 July 1966, Group IV, Box A56, Folder "Meredith, James, 1966," NAACP; *The Washington Post*, 28 June 1966; *Memphis Press-Scimitar*, 29 June 1966; *The Meridian* (Miss.) *Star*, 29 June 1966; *The Clarion-Ledger* (Jackson), 13 July 1966; *The New York Times*, 17 July 1966; *New York Amsterdam News*, 9 July 1966.

18. Dreams and Nightmares

1. Frank Figgers, interview by the author, telephone, 14 April 2010.
2. Elizabeth French, "One Tourist's Impressions of the Meaning of the Meredith March," July 1966, Box 6, Folder 8, RBP.
3. See Sarah Patton Boyle, *The Desegregated Heart: A Virginian's Stand in Time of Transition* (New York: Morrow, 1962).
4. French, "One Tourist's Impressions of the Meaning of the Meredith March."
5. Jill Wakeman (Goodman) to friends, 27 June 1966, Box 1, Folder 1, JWCRC; *The Village Voice*, 30 June 1966. On Moses see Eric Burner, *And Gently He Shall Lead Them: Robert Parris Moses and Civil Rights in Mississippi* (New York: New York University Press, 1994).
6. French, "One Tourist's Impressions of the Meaning of the Meredith March."
7. FBI memorandum, 27 June 1966, Box 71B, Folder 2, LBJ-MS; Coretta Scott King, *My Life with Martin Luther King Jr.* (New York: Holt, Rinehart and Winston, 1969), 277–79; Dexter King, *Growing Up King: An Intimate Memoir* (New York: Warner Books, 2003), 43–44.
8. FBI memorandum, 27 June 1966, Box 71B, Folder 2, LBJ-MS; "Route of March— June 26," Reel 13, CORE-A; *The Washington Post*, 27 June 1966; *The Catholic Herald Citizen*, 2 July 1966; *The Village Voice*, 14 July 1966.
9. *Jackson Daily News*, 27 June 1966; *The Clarion-Ledger* (Jackson), 27 June 1966; *Detroit Free Press*, 27 June 1966; Bruce Hartford, interview by author.
10. *The Clarion-Ledger* (Jackson), 27 June 1966.
11. *Jackson Daily News*, 27 June 1966.
12. *Detroit Free Press*, 27 June 1966; Ed King, interview by author; Nelson Lichtenstein, *Walter Reuther: The Most Dangerous Man in Detroit* (Urbana: University of Illinois Press, 1995), 370–413.
13. *The Philadelphia Tribune*, 28 June 1966; *The Clarion-Ledger* (Jackson), 27 June 1966; *The Philadelphia Inquirer*, 26 June 1966; *Pittsburgh Press*, 25 June 1966, 27 June 1966, 29 June 1966, 3 July 1966, 5 July 1966; *Pittsburgh Post-Gazette*, 27 June 1966–29 June 1966, 30 June 1966, 1 July 1966, 6 July 1966; *The Pittsburgh Courier*, 16 July 1966; *The Jackson Times*, 14 July 1966.
14. *The Militant*, 11 July 1966; *The New York Times*, 27 June 1966.
15. *Los Angeles Times*, 27 June 1966; *The Washington Post*, 27 June 1966; *The New York Times*, 27 June 1966; *The Tri-State Defender*, 2 July 1966.
16. *The Washington Post*, 27 June 1966; *The New York Times*, 27 June 1966; Jim Peppler, interview by author; Watters, *Down to Now*, 351–52; *Detroit Free Press*, 27 June 1966.
17. *The Chicago Defender*, 27 June 1966; *The Washington Post*, 27 June 1966, 25 November 2010; William Hohri interview, 27 September 1997, DVHC.
18. *The Washington Post*, 27 June 1966; *The Times-Picayune* (New Orleans), 27 June 1966; *The New York Times*, 27 June 1966; *Los Angeles Times*, 27 June 1966.
19. *Newsday*, 27 June 1966; *Detroit Free Press*, 27 June 1966; "Black Power: Politics of Frustration," *Newsweek*, 11 July 1966, 31.

20. *Newsday*, 27 June 1966; *The New York Times*, 27 June 1966; *The Village Voice*, 30 June 1966; *The Washington Post*, 27 June 1966.

21. Wiley Mallett, interview by author; Coby Smith, unpublished memoir in author's possession; Coby Smith, interview by author.

22. Joyce Ladner, interview by author; Good, "The Meredith March," 15; "Route of March—June 26," Reel 13, CORE-A; FBI surveillance, 28 June 1966, Part 2, Reel 5, MLK-FBI; *Jackson Daily News*, 27 June 1966; *The Chicago Defender*, 27 June 1966.

23. *The Village Voice*, 30 June 1966.

24. Denver Washington, interview by author, telephone, 18 March 2010; Martin Kinney, interview by author, telephone, 24 March 2010; *The New York Times*, 27 June 1966; James C. Coleman oral history, 12 April 2000, TCSC.

25. Frankye Adams-Johnson (Frankye Adams), interview by author, telephone, 26 April 2010; Cathy Deppe, interview by author; *The New York Times*, 27 June 1966, 28 June 1966.

26. French, "One Tourist's Impressions of the Meaning of the Meredith March."

27. *The Chicago Defender*, 27 June 1966; *Detroit Free Press*, 27 June 1966; FBI memorandum, 27 June 1966, Box 71B, Folder 2, LBJ-MS; CBS News Special Report, *The March in Mississippi*, 26 June 1966, PCM.

28. *The Clarion-Ledger* (Jackson), 27 June 1966; *The Washington Post*, 27 June 1966.

29. *The Village Voice*, 30 June 1966; Henry Bucher and Lovett Elango, "Mississippi Trip," Box 6, Folder 8, RBP; CBS News Special Report, *The March in Mississippi*, 26 June 1966, PCM; Jill Wakeman (Goodman) to friends, 27 June 1966, Box 1, Folder 1, JWCRC; French, "One Tourist's Impressions of the Meaning of the Meredith March."

30. French, "One Tourist's Impressions of the Meaning of the Meredith March"; Henry Bucher and Lovett Elango, "Mississippi Trip," Box 6, Folder 8, RBP.

31. Meredith March, 26 June 1966, D50, WLBT; *The Washington Post*, 27 June 1966; C. J. Jones, interview by author, telephone, 1 April 2010.

32. *Chicago Tribune*, 27 June 1966; CBS News Special Report, *The March in Mississippi*, 26 June 1966, PCM; William McAndrew to Paul Johnson, 27 June 1966, Box 142, Folder 3, PBJFP; Elmer Lower to Paul Johnson, 30 June 1966, Box 61, Folder 5, PBJFP; Frank Stanton to Paul Johnson, 28 June 1966, Box 61, Folder 5, PBJFP.

33. Program for Meredith Mississippi Freedom March, Correspondence Files, Folder 1603, MMP; *The Meridian* (Miss.) *Star*, 27 June 1966; Speech in Jackson, 26 June 1966, Box 143, WYP; Meredith March, 26 June 1966, D51, WLBT; Branch, *At Canaan's Edge*, 493–94.

34. Meredith March, 26 June 1966, D51, WLBT; *The Boston Globe*, 9 July 1966; *The Baltimore Afro-American*, 9 July 1966; *The New York Times*, 27 June 1966.

35. Meredith March, 26 June 1966, D51, WLBT; Dittmer, *The Good Doctors*, 156; Alvin Poussaint, interview by author.

36. Program for Meredith Mississippi Freedom March, Correspondence Files, Folder 1603, MMP; Meredith March and Rally, 26 June 1966, D49, WLBT.

37. *The Boston Globe*, 27 June 1966; Floyd McKissick interview, 21 October 1988, EPI; *New York Post*, 27 June 1966.

38. Sundquist, *King's Dream*, 105–69; Meredith March and Rally, 26 June 1966, D49, WLBT; Meredith March, 26 June 1966, D51, WLBT.

39. Meredith March, 26 June 1966, D51, WLBT.

40. *Chicago Tribune*, 27 June 1966; French, "One Tourist's Impressions of the Meaning of the Meredith March."

41. Mel Leventhal, interview by author; Melvyn R. Leventhal, "The Civil Rights Movement Comes to an End," unpublished essay in author's possession.

42. *The Guardian* (Manchester, U.K.), 28 June 1966; *The Times* (London), 28 June 1966; *The Christian Science Monitor*, 29 June 1966; *Los Angeles Times*, 28 June 1966; *The New York Times*, 26 June 1966, 28 June 1966; *The Philadelphia Inquirer*, 28 June 1966; "Which Way Now?," *Commonweal*, 8 July 1966, 430–31; *The Washington Post*, 28 June 1966.

43. *The New York Times*, 28 June 1966, 30 June 1966; *The Clarion-Ledger* (Jackson), 30 June 1966; Press release, 29 June 1966, Box 104, Folder 15, PBJFP; Speech for Mayor Allen Thompson, 28 June 1966, Box 97, Folder 4, PBJFP; Speech at Neshoba County Fair, 4 August 1966, Box 97, Folder 7, PBJFP.

44. *Jackson Daily News*, 28 June 1966, 21 July 1966, 6 September 1966; *The Clarion-Ledger* (Jackson), 28 June 1966, 29 June 1966; *The Southern Review*, 1 July 1966, 15 July 1966; *The Jackson Times*, 14 July 1966, 21 July 1966; *The Commercial Appeal* (Memphis), 28 June 1966; *Delta Democrat Times*, 27 June 1966; *The Lexington* (Miss.) *Advertiser*, 30 June 1966.

45. "Marching Where?," *The Reporter*, 14 July 1966, 12–16; "Too Many Cooks, Too Much Spice," *The Christian Century*, 13 July 1966, 880–81; Higgins, "Divided on Tactics, Leaders Agree March a Success," 14–18; Bob Fitch, interview by author; Jo Freeman to Al and Cynthia, 25 July 1966, JFPP; *The Washington Post*, 28 June 1966.

46. Charlie Cobb, interview by author.

47. Bruce Hartford, interview by author; *The Washington Post*, 28 June 1966.

48. *The Washington Post*, 28 June 1966; *The Southern Courier*, 2–3 July 1966; *The Lexington* (Miss.) *Advertiser*, 30 June 1966; *The Wall Street Journal*, 27 June 1966; Whitney Young to Hosea Williams, 12 August 1966, Part III, Box 406, Folder 7, NULP; Hosea Williams to Whitney Young, 21 August 1966, Part III, Box 406, Folder 7, NULP; Sovereignty Commission memorandum, 27 June 1966, SCR ID# 9-31-5-50-1-1-1, MSSC. FBI surveillance, 28 June 1966, Part 1, Reel 10, MLK-FBI.

49. Sovereignty Commission memorandum, 27 June 1966, SCR ID# 9-31-5-52-1-1-1, MSSC.

50. *The New York Times*, 29 June 1966; *The Chicago Defender*, 30 June 1966; Jo Freeman to Al and Cynthia, 25 July 1966, JFPP. For scholarship on the Meredith March, see Branch, *At Canaan's Edge*, 475–95; Garrow, *Bearing the Cross*, 473–89; Payne, *I've Got the Light of Freedom*, 376–78; Dittmer, *Local People*, 389–402; Carter, *The Music Has Gone Out of the Movement*, 103–31; Carson, *In Struggle*, 206–11; Joseph, *Waiting 'Til the Midnight Hour*, 132–46; Ogbar, *Black Power*, 60–63; Aram Goudsouzian, "Three Weeks in Mississippi: James Meredith, Aubrey Norvell, and the Politics of Bird Shot," *The Journal of the Historical Society* 11, no. 1 (March 2011): 23–58.

51. *Memphis World*, 2 July 1966; *Call and Post* (Cleveland), 9 July 1966; *The Chicago Defender*, 2 July 1966, 9 July 1966; *The Baltimore Afro-American*, 9 July 1966.

52. *The Washington Post*, 27 June 1966; *The Lexington* (Miss.) *Advertiser*, 30 June 1966; *The New York Times*, 26 June 1966; *Los Angeles Times*, 28 June 1966; *The Times-Picayune* (New Orleans), 28 June 1966; Henry Bucher and Lovett Elango, "Mississippi Trip," Box 6, Folder 8, RBP.

53. *The Guardian* (London), 2 July 1966; Owen Brooks, interview by author; Jesse Harris, interview by author; Hollis Watkins, interview by author. For historiographical discussions on both local movements and the "long civil rights movement," see Payne, *I've Got the Light of Freedom*, 413–41; J. Todd Moye, "Focusing Our Eyes on the Prize: How Community Studies Are Reframing and Rewriting the History of the Civil Rights Movement," in Emilye Crosby, ed., *Civil Rights History from the Ground Up: Local Struggles, A National Movement* (Athens: University of Georgia Press, 2011), 147–71; Jacquelyn Dowd Hall, "The Long Civil Rights Movement and the Political Uses of the Past," *The Journal of American History* 91, no. 4 (March 2005): 1233–63; Sundiata Cha-Jua and Clarence Lang, "The 'Long Movement' as Vampire: Temporal and Spatial Fallacies in Recent Black Freedom Studies," *The Journal of African American History* 92 (Spring 2007): 265–88; Charles Eagles, "Toward New Histories of the Civil Rights Era," *The Journal of Southern History* 66, no. 4 (November 2000): 815–48; Steven F. Lawson, "Long Origins of the Short Civil Rights Movement, 1954–1968," in Danielle L. McGuire and John Dittmer, eds., *Freedom Rights: New Perspectives on the Civil Rights Movement* (Lexington: University Press of Kentucky), 9–37; Matthew D. Lassiter and Joseph Crespino, "Introduction: The End of Southern History," in Matthew D. Lassiter and Joseph Crespino, eds., *The Myth of Southern Exceptionalism* (New York: Oxford University Press, 2010), 3–22.

54. L. C. Dorsey, interview by author, Jackson, 24 May 2010; Kim Lacy Rogers, *Life and Death in the Delta: African American Narratives of Violence, Resilience, and Social Change* (New York: Palgrave Macmillan, 2006), 56–57; L. C. Dorsey, "Harder Times Than These," in Dorothy Abbott, ed., *Mississippi Writers: Reflections on Childhood and Youth*, vol. 2 (Jackson: University Press of Mississippi, 1986), 165–74.

55. L. C. Dorsey, interview by author.

Epilogue: Highway 51 Revisited

1. *The New York Times*, 16 June 1967, 25 June 1967; *New Journal and Guide* (Norfolk, Va.), 1 July 1967; Meredith, *"Me and My Kind,"* 52; *The Baltimore Afro-American*, 1 July 1967.

2. *The New York Times*, 25 June 1967, 26 June 1967, 30 June 1967, 1 July 1967; Sovereignty Commission memorandum, 27 June 1967, SCR ID# 9-31-7-2-1-1-1, MSSC; *The Baltimore Afro-American*, 1 July 1967, 8 July 1967; *The Chicago Defender*, 20 June 1967.

3. Sovereignty Commission memorandum, 19 June 1967, SCR ID# 1-108-0-6-1-1-1,

MSSC; Sovereignty Commission memorandum, 30 June 1967, SCR ID# 1-67-4-156-1-1-1, MSSC; *The Clarion-Ledger* (Jackson), 30 June 1967, 3 July 1967.

4. *The Chicago Defender*, 22 November 1966; *The Commercial Appeal* (Memphis), 22 November 1966, 3 December 1966; "Surprise Package," *Newsweek*, 5 December 1966, 32; WATS Report, 29 November 1966, Box 19, Folder 9, NSM.

5. *The Commercial Appeal* (Memphis), 3 December 1966; *The New York Times*, 30 June 1968. Aubrey Norvell has twice declined interview requests from the author.

6. *The New York Times*, 27 June 1967, 28 June 1967; *The Chicago Defender*, 27 June 1967.

7. *The Chicago Defender*, 5 July 1967; *The New York Times*, 5 July 1967.

8. *The Chicago Defender*, 5 July 1967.

9. Roy Wilkins at 5th Annual Convention of NAACP, 5 July 1966, Box 58, Folder "Speeches and Writings, 1966 July–December," RWP; *The New York Times*, 6 June 1966, 8 June 1966, 10 June 1966; Roy Wilkins to Alpha Kappa Alpha, 17 August 1966, Box 58, Folder "Speeches and Writings, 1966 July–December," RWP; Roy Wilkins to National Insurance Association, 21 July 1966, Box 58, Folder "Speeches and Writings, 1966 July–December," RWP; Roy Wilkins and Gloster Current, 24 October 1966, Group IV, Box A14, Folder "Young Turks," NAACP; Roy Wilkins to Della Brown, 13 December 1966, Group IV, Box A18, Folder "Black Power, 1966–69," NAACP.

10. Press release, 11 July 1966, Box 209, WYP; Press release, 24 July 1966, Part II, Box 45, Folder 9, NULP; Whitney Young interview on WINS, 31 July 1966, Box 192, WYP; "Leading the League," *Newsweek*, 22 August 1966, 23; Press release, 24 July 1966, Part III, Box 45, Folder 9, NULP; "To Be Equal" Radio Script, 20 December 1966, Box 195, WYP; *The New York Times*, 12 July 1966, 24 July 1966, 5 August 1966. See also Whitney M. Young, *Beyond Racism: Building an Open Society* (New York: McGraw-Hill, 1969), 236–43; Weiss, *Whitney M. Young, Jr., and the Struggle for Civil Rights*, 175–90; Robert L. Allen, *Black Awakening in Capitalist America: An Analytic History* (Trenton, N.J.: Africa World Press, 1970), 70–77.

11. *Call and Post* (Cleveland), 16 July 1966; Samuel DuBois Cook, "The Tragic Myth of Black Power," *New South*, Summer 1966, 58–64; *Chicago Tribune*, 4 July 1966; Carl T. Rowan, "Crisis in Civil Rights Leadership," *Ebony*, November 1966, 27–37; *The New York Times*, 17 August 1966, 14 October 1966, 16 October 1966.

12. Bayard Rustin to Robert Hill, 12 July 1966, Reel 21, BRP; *New York Amsterdam News*, 25 June 1966; Elijah Muhammad to Whitney Young, 6 July 1966, Part 3, Box 406, Folder 7, NULP; Whitney Young to Elijah Muhammad, 20 July 1966, Part 3, Box 406, Folder 7, NULP.

13. "Negro Leaders Dividing—The Effect," *U.S. News and World Report*, 18 July 1966, 31–34; "Black Power for Whom?," *The Christian Century*, 20 July 1966, 903–904; "The Pseudo-Power of 'Black Power,'" *America*, 23 July 1966, 89; Raymond Moley, "Pattern of Revolution," *Newsweek*, 8 August 1966, 84; *The National Observer*, 11 July 1966, 10 October 1966; "Black Power: Politics of Frustration," *Newsweek*, 11 July 1966, 26–32; *The New York Times*, 7 July 1966, 10 July 1966, 12 July 1966, 24 July 1966, 5 August 1966, 7 August 1966.

14. *The New York Times*, 7 July 1966, 25 July 1966, 19 September 1966, 27 September 1966, 24 October 1966; "What's Ahead for the Negro," *Newsweek*, 28 November 1966, 30–31; C. Vann Woodward, "What Happened to the Civil Rights Movement?," *Harper's*, January 1967, 29–37.

15. Louis Harris survey, 15 August 1966, Part 1, Reel 11, CRJA; *The New York Times*, 7 September 1966, 22 September 1966, 28 September 1966, 30 September 1966; "The Longest, Hottest Summer," *Newsweek*, 22 August 1966, 57; "Backlash," *The Christian Century*, 12 October 1966, 1232–33; "A New White Backlash?," *The Saturday Evening Post*, 10 September 1966, 88; "Backlash and Fear," *America*, 1 October 1966, 376–77; "Backlash Jitters," *The New Republic*, 22 October 1966, 5–6; "Riots, Battles, Power Marches—It's Still a Hot Summer," *U.S. News and World Report*, 15 August 1966, 36–37; "Apartheid for America?," *National Review*, 26 July 1966, 716–17; William F. Buckley, Jr., "Time for a Hiatus?," *National Review*, 18 October 1966, 1035; "Here Lies Integration," *National Review*, 27 December 1966, 1305–306; Dan T. Carter, *From George Wallace to Newt Gingrich: Race in the Conservative Counterrevolution, 1963–1994* (Baton Rouge: Louisiana State University Press, 1996), 9–10, 14–15; Richard M. Nixon, "If Mob Rule Takes Hold in U.S.—A Warning from Richard Nixon," *U.S. News and World Report*, 15 August 1966, 64–65; Perlstein, *Nixonland*, 86–89, 137–38, 157–63.

16. "The Policing Job Washington Now Is Trying to Get," *U.S. News and World Report*, 22 August 1966, 38–39; "A Symptom of Anger," *Newsweek*, 22 August 1966, 59–60; "Changed Climate," *Time*, 16 September 1966, 30–31; "The Issue Is Conduct," *Newsweek*, 26 September 1966, 32; "Ahead of Its Time," *Time*, 30 September 1966, 20–21; Carter, *The Music Has Gone Out of the Movement*, 147–50; Perlstein, *Nixonland*, 121–27, 130–31, 163–66; *The New York Times*, 9 November 1966–11 November 1966; "The Atlantic Report: Washington," *The Atlantic Monthly*, November 1966, 4–12.

17. *The New York Times*, 21 July 1966, 21 August 1966; Clifford Alexander to Lyndon Johnson, 27 July 1966, Part 1, Reel 11, CRJA; Carter, *The Music Has Gone Out of the Movement*, 154–250.

18. *The New York Times*, 2 July 1966–5 July 1966; CORE to Martin Luther King, 27 June 1966, Series 1, Box 6, Folder 33, MLKP.

19. "At the Breaking Point," *Time*, 15 July 1966, 15–16; *The New York Times*, 6 July 1966; *Chicago Tribune*, 6 July 1966; *Wilmington News*, 7 July 1966; "Line in the Dust," *Newsweek*, 18 July 1966, 23–24.

20. Floyd McKissick to American Society of Newspaper Editors, 20 April 1967, Part 3, Folder 6994, FBMP; Press release, 7 July 1966, Part 3, Folder 6775a, FBMP; *The New York Times*, 8 July 1966; Floyd McKissick, "Programs for Black Power," Reel 6, CORE-A; Floyd McKissick, "The Civil Rights Movement Is Dead," Reel 5, CORE-A; Floyd McKissick, "Constructive Militancy," Senate Hearings Presentation, 8 December 1966, Reel 5, CORE-A; Floyd McKissick, "Is Integration Necessary?," *The New Republic*, 3 December 1966, 33–36.

21. *New York Amsterdam News*, 3 September 1966, 12 November 1966; *The Tri-State Defender*, 9 July 1966, 16 July 1966, 23 July 1966, 20 August 1966; *Memphis World*,

13 August 1966; *The New York Times*, 15 July 1966, 17 July 1966, 22 July 1966–24 July 1966, 31 July 1966, 7 August 1966, 14 August 1966, 27 September 1966; Vincent Harding, "Black Power and the American Christ," *The Christian Century*, 4 January 1967, 10–13; "Power Black or White and Christian Conscience," 1 August 1966, Part 1, Reel 2, SCLC; *The New York Times*, 31 July 1966; Roger Wilkins, *A Man's Life: An Autobiography* (Woodbridge, Conn.: Ox Bow Press, 1991; original 1982), 155, 184–87, 230–36; C. T. Vivian, *Black Power and the American Myth* (Philadelphia: Fortress Press, 1970), 60–67, 82–86; Simon Hall, "The NAACP, Black Power, and the African American Freedom Struggle, 1966–69," *The Historian* 69, no. 1 (22 March 2007): 49–82; Dan Robertson to Roy Wilkins, 5 December 1966, Group IV, Box A18, Folder "Black Power, 1966–69," NAACP. See also many other letters to Roy Wilkins in Group IV, Box A18, Folder "Black Power, 1966–69," NAACP.

22. See Van Deburg, *New Day in Babylon*; Jeffries, ed., *Black Power in the Belly of the Beast*; Ogbar, *Black Power*; Joseph, *Waitin' Til the Midnight Hour*.

23. Young, *Beyond Racism*; Weiss, *Whitney M. Young, Jr., and the Struggle for Civil Rights*, 175–90.

24. Floyd B. McKissick, "Black Business Development with Social Commitment to Black Communities," in John H. Bracey, Jr., August Meier, and Elliott Rudwick, eds., *Black Nationalism in America* (Indianapolis: Bobbs-Merrill, 1970), 492–503; "Floyd McKissick: Making Black Capitalism Work," in Jeffrey M. Elliott, ed., *Black Voices in American Politics* (San Diego: Harcourt Brace Jovanovich, 1986), 281–95; Timothy J. Minchin, "'A Brand New Shining City': Floyd B. McKissick Sr. and the Struggle to Build Soul City, North Carolina," *The North Carolina Historical Review* 82, no. 2 (April 2005): 125–55; Devin Fergus, *Liberalism, Black Power, and the Making of American Politics* (Athens: University of Georgia Press, 2009), 196–231.

25. Lerone Bennett, Jr., "Stokely Carmichael: Architect of Black Power," *Ebony*, July 1966, 25–32; Eldridge Cleaver, "My Father & Stokely Carmichael," *Ramparts*, February 1967, 10–14; Gordon Parks, *Born Black* (Philadelphia: J. P. Lippincott, 1971), 92–108.

26. Bernard Weinraub, "The Brilliancy of Black," *Esquire*, January 1967, 130–35; "Who's Carmichael?," *The Christian Century*, 17 August 1966, 1000–1001; Robert L. Scott and Wayne Brockriede, *The Rhetoric of Black Power* (New York: Harper and Row, 1969), 84–131.

27. "SNCC: Comments by Stokely Carmichael," Miller (Michael J.) Civil Rights Collection, USM-CRM; "Stokely Carmichael Responds to Vital Questions America Asks," Reel 63, SNCC; Stokely Carmichael statement on Civil Rights Bill of 1966, 1 July 1966, Reel 3, SNCC; Stokely Carmichael, "What We Want," *The New York Review of Books*, 22 September 1966, 5–6; Stokely Carmichael, "Toward Black Liberation," *The Massachusetts Review*, Autumn 1966, 639–51; "Black Power: The Widening Dialogue," *New South*, Summer 1966, 65–80; Kwame Ture and Charles V. Hamilton, *Black Power* (New York: Vintage, 1992; original 1967); Stokely Carmichael (Kwame Ture), *Stokely Speaks: From Black Power to Pan-Africanism* (Chicago: Lawrence Hill Books, 2007); Roberts, "From 'Freedom High' to 'Black Power,'" 128.

28. Paul Good, "A Tale of Two Cities," *The Nation*, 21 November 1966, 534–38; Stokely Carmichael statement on Atlanta riot, 8 September 1966, Reel 3, SNCC; *San Francisco Examiner*, 10 September 1966, 11 September 1966; *The Clarion Ledger* (Jackson), 12 September 1966; *New York Post*, 19 August 1967; *Congressional Record—Senate*, 18 April 1967, 5404–10; FBI Files on Stokely Carmichael, Box 73B, Folder "Student Nonviolent Coordinating Committee (Stokely Carmichael) Aug.–Dec. 1966," LBJ-MS; Stokely Carmichael File, FBI-RR; Reel 1, FBI-SNCC. See also "Black Power: War Cry of Insurrectionists," 1966 pamphlet produced by *The Independent American* (New Orleans), MDAH.

29. Carson, *In Struggle*, 229–42; Francesca Athene Polletta, "Strategy and Identity in 1960's Black Protest: The Activism of the Student Nonviolent Coordinating Committee, 1960–1967" (Ph.D. dissertation, Yale University, 1994), 345–54; Fay Bellamy, "A Little Old Report," Box 8, Folder 1, DLC; Alice Moore to Stokely Carmichael, 10 August 1966, Reel 2, SNCC; Forman, *The Making of Black Revolutionaries*, 519–22; FBI memorandum, 26 August 1966, Box 73B, Folder "Student Nonviolent Coordinating Committee (Stokely Carmichael), Aug.–Dec. 1966," LBJ-MS; "The Black-Power Brokers," *Newsweek*, 21 December 1966, 21–22; Andrew Kopkind, "The Future of 'Black Power,'" *The New Republic*, 7 January 1967, 16–18; "Report of the Communication Section of the Atlanta Office," Reel 3, SNCC; Bill Ware to Stokely Carmichael and Cleveland Sellers, 20 February 1967, Reel 3, SNCC; Letters to SNCC and Stokely Carmichael, Reel 2, SNCC.

30. Viorst, *Fire in the Streets*, 376–77.

31. Carmichael, *Ready for Revolution*, 607–781; Peniel E. Joseph, "Revolution in Babylon: Stokely Carmichael and America in the 1960s," *Souls* 9, no. 4 (December 2007): 291–98; Joseph, *Dark Days, Bright Nights*, 148–60; Clayborne Carson, "Stokely Carmichael/Kwame Ture: Courageous Warrior in an On-Going Struggle," *The Black Scholar* 27, no. 3/4 (Fall 1997/Winter 1998): 44–45; Ekwueme Michael Thelwell, "Stokely Carmichael to Kwame Ture (1941–1998): 'Infinitely political, infinitely human,'" *The Massachusetts Review* 40, no. 3 (Autumn 1999): 325–41.

32. *Chicago Tribune*, 2 July 1966; *The New York Times*, 6 July 1966, 7 July 1966, 9 July 1966, 17 July 1966, 4 August 1966; SCLC fund-raising letter, October 1966, Box 19, Folder 1, NSM; King, *Where Do We Go from Here*, 1–66; King, "Nonviolence: The Only Road to Freedom," 27–34.

33. *The New York Times*, 11 July 1966, 30 July 1966, 10 October 1966, 15 October 1966, 17 October 1966; SNCC Central Committee to Martin Luther King, 3 August 1966, Series 1, Box 23, Folder 18, MLKP; Robert Green to Martin Luther King, 12 September 1966, Series 1, Box 23, Folder 18, MLKP; Kendall Smith to Martin Luther King, 17 September 1966, Series 1, Box 23, Folder 18, MLKP; FBI memoranda, 4 October 1966 and 17 October 1966, Box 32, Folder "King, Martin Luther, 1966–67 [2 of 2]," LBJ-MS; FBI surveillance, 9 September 1966, 29 September 1966, 1 October 1966, Part 2, Reel 6, MLK-FBI.

34. Ralph, *Northern Protest*, 105–80; Branch, *At Canaan's Edge*, 501–506; "Open City," *The New Republic*, 17 September 1966, 9–10.

35. Mrs. Charles Jacobs to Martin Luther King, 8 August 1966; A Citizen of Chicago

to Martin Luther King, 15 August 1966; Anonymous to Martin Luther King, 15 August 1966; J. A. Slegailis to Martin Luther King, 19 August 1966; James Langere to Martin Luther King, 3 August 1966; George Hamilton to Martin Luther King, 15 August 1966; all in Part 1, Reel 16, SCLC. See also "Too Much Integration?," *Newsweek*, 19 September 1966, 31–32.

36. "The Touchiest Target," *Time*, 15 August 1966, 29; "We Have Got to Deliver Non-violent Results," *Newsweek*, 22 August 1966, 58–59; Yglesias, "Dr. King's March on Washington, Part II," 60; "Crossing the Red Sea," *Time*, 2 September 1966, 19; "Pharaoh's Lesson," *Time*, 9 September 1966, 22.

37. Martin Luther King speech at Frogmore, 14 November 1966, Part 1, Reel 20, SCLC.

38. King, *Where Do We Go from Here*, 67–191; David Halberstam, "The Second Coming of Martin Luther King," *Harper's*, August 1967, 39–51.

39. Branch, *At Canaan's Edge*, 683–766; Abernathy, *And the Walls Came Tumbling Down*, 412–13; Frank, *An American Death*, 17; Honey, *Going Down Jericho Road*.

40. Amy Nathan Wright, "The 1968 Poor People's Campaign, Marks, Mississippi, and the Mule Train," in Crosby, *Civil Rights History from the Ground Up*, 109–43; Jaffe, "Grenada, Mississippi," 15–27; *The New York Times*, 11 July 1966, 9 August 1966, 10 August 1966; Dittmer, *Local People*, 402–407; Crespino, *In Search of Another Country*, 136–41.

41. Bolton, *The Hardest Deal of All*, xi–xii; Carter, *The Music Has Gone Out of the Movement*, 149.

42. Paul Murray, interview by author; Jake Friesen to Edgar Stoesz, 21 July 1966, Box 1, Folder 3, JFP; Jake Friesen to Stanley Bohn, 17 August 1966, Box 1, Folder 3, JFP; "People in Search of Identity," Box 1, Folder 4, James McRee Papers, MDAH; Sovereignty Commission memorandum, 6 July 1967, SCR ID# 1-67-4-153-1-1-1, MSSC.

43. Lawrence Guyot letter, 14 November 1966, Box 1, Folder 3, MFDP; MFDP Flyer, Box 5, Folder 3, AMP; "Mississippians United to Elect Black Candidates," 1967 pamphlet, Box 1, Folder 15, VGA; Crandall, "Black Power in the Deep South," 119–26; Lawrence Guyot, interview by author; MacArthur Cotton, interview by author.

44. Bruce Detwiler, "A Time To Be Black," *The New Republic*, 17 September 1966, 19–22; Frank Millspaugh, "Black Power," *Commonweal*, 5 August 1966, 500–503; Sid Walker letter, 14 August 1966, Box 1, Folder 1, EHP; Susan Sadoff Lorenzini letter, 12 February 1967, Box 1, Folder 1, HTD; Joel Bernard to Jacqueline Bernard, 24 July 1966, Box 1, Folder 1, JBP; Shelton Stromquist interview, October 1980, MDAH; David Doggett, interview by author; Ira Grupper, interview by author; Joseph Morse, interview by author; Nina Boal, interview by author.

45. Dittmer, *Local People*, 408–23; Crosby, "'God's Appointed Savior,'" 182–83; Crosby, *A Little Taste of Freedom*, 207–23.

46. Dittmer, *Local People*, 377–88; Carter, *The Music Has Gone Out of the Movement*, 119–31; *The Clarion-Ledger* (Jackson), 24 August 1966.

47. Crespino, *In Search of Another Country*, 237–78; Chris Danielson, "'Lily White and Hard Right': The Mississippi Republican Party and Black Voting, 1965–1980,"

The Journal of Southern History 75, no. 1 (February 2009): 83–118; Chris Daniel-son, *After Freedom Summer: How Race Realigned Mississippi Politics, 1965–1986* (Gainesville: University Press of Florida, 2011), 124–54; Earl Black and Merle Black, *The Rise of the Southern Republicans* (Cambridge, Mass.: Harvard University Press, 2002), 117–19; Dittmer, *Local People*, 423–30.

48. Meredith, "Big Changes Are Coming," 23–27; Agreement with Charles Lewis, 1 September 1966, Box 13, Folder 2, JHMC; Sovereignty Commission memoran-dum, 7 December 1966, SCR ID# 1-114-0-5-1-1-1, MSSC; *New York Amsterdam News*, 20 August 1966; Frederick Wyngarden letter, 23 October 1966, Box 14, Folder 24, JHMC; *The Baltimore Afro-American*, 29 October 1966; *Chicago Tri-bune*, 11 July 1966; *The Philadelphia Tribune*, 18 October 1966; *Los Angeles Senti-nel*, 11 August 1966; Speech at Los Angeles Sports Arena, 14 August 1966, Box 14, Folder 5, JHMC.

49. *Meet the Press* transcript, 21 August 1966, Box 58, Speeches and Statements, Folder "1966 July-December," RWP; Charles E. Fager, *White Reflections on Black Power* (Grand Rapids, Mich.: William B. Eerdmans, 1967), 34–37; WDSU editorial tran-script, 22 August 1966, Box 13, Folder 11, JHMC; *The Chicago Defender*, 23 August 1966; *The Baltimore Afro-American*, 3 September 1966. *Meet the Press* transcript also available in Box 192, WYP.

50. *National Review*, 13 December 1966.

51. *The New York Times*, 8 March 1967–10 March 1967, 12 March 1967; *New York Amsterdam News*, 11 March 1967; Motley, *Equal Justice Under Law*, 185–87; "The Loner & the Shaman," *Time*, 17 March 1967, 23–24; "Blacklash in Harlem," *News-week*, 20 March 1967, 27–28. On Powell in the 1960s see Wil Haygood, *King of the Cats: The Life and Times of Adam Clayton Powell, Jr.* (Boston: Houghton Mifflin, 1993), 237–71.

52. Andrew Kopkind, "The Ambiguous Heroes of Harlem," *Life*, 24 March 1967, 32–32A; "The Loner," *The Reporter*, 23 March 1967, 17; *The New York Times*, 13 March 1967; 14 March 1967; "Why Meredith Quit the Race with Powell," *U.S. News and World Report*, 27 March 1967, 16; "Hometown Advice," *Newsweek*, 27 March 1967, 39–40; Floyd McKissick to James Meredith, 13 March 1967, Part 3, Folder 6818, FBMP.

53. *Jackson Daily News*, 22 July 1967; "The New Black Entrepreneur," *Newsweek*, 23 December 1968, 10; *The New York Times*, 20 May 1969; *The Commercial Appeal* (Memphis), 14 May 1969; *New York Amsterdam News*, 17 May 1969, 24 May 1969, 21 June 1969; *The Chicago Defender*, 14 September 1974; *The New York Times*, 28 June 1971; *The Times-Picayune* (New Orleans), 11 October 1971, 9 June 1974, 10 June 1974; *The Clarion-Ledger* (Jackson), 5 November 1971; *The Chicago Defender*, 29 March 1972, 7 October 1989; *The Baltimore Afro-American*, 9 November 1974.

54. James Meredith, interview by author; James Meredith, "Black Leaders and the Wish to Die," *Ebony*, May 1973, 154–59; William A. Link, *Righteous Warrior: Jesse Helms and the Rise of Modern Conservatism* (New York: St. Martin's, 2008), 371–72, 409–10; John Ed Bradley, "The Man Who Would Be King," *Esquire*, De-cember 1992, 101–10; Meredith, *A Mission from God*, 230–32.

55. *The Chicago Defender,* 12 July 1966, 20 August 1966, 24 June 1968, 24 July 1969; *Call and Post* (Cleveland), 9 August 1969, 13 September 1969; FBI File No. 157-15433-1 (March of James Howard Meredith); *The Florence Times,* 22 September 1974; *The Commercial Appeal* (Memphis), 23 March 1991, 4 June 1996; *Los Angeles Sentinel,* 4 July 1996.
56. Paul Hendrickson, "The Dilemmas and Demons of James Meredith," *The Journal of Blacks in Higher Education* 40 (summer 2003): 91–94; Hendrickson, *Sons of Mississippi,* 117–24, 279–83; Bradley, "The Man Who Would Be King," 110.

ACKNOWLEDGMENTS

Sometimes I felt like I was haunted by ghosts. They drifted by when I spotted a sign for a short stretch of "Old Hwy 51," along the original path set by Meredith, or when I was driving through the Delta and I zipped past strip malls and fast-food joints and then caught a glimpse of an old road, or an old face—in that moment, I could imagine King or Carmichael leading a mass of people through town in 1966. During most of the time spent researching and writing this book, my wife and I lived in downtown Memphis, in an apartment overlooking the National Civil Rights Museum, which is built into the former Lorraine Motel. Famous as the site of King's assassination in 1968, the Lorraine also hosted the early, contentious meetings about the path and strategy of the Meredith March. The burdens of the past were right outside our window.

But telling this story was a rewarding journey, and along the way I had many able guides, including many dedicated archivists in Memphis and Mississippi. My profound thanks to John Wall and Jennifer Ford at the University of Mississippi Archives and Special Collections, Mattie Sink at Mississippi State University Special Collections, the McCain Library and Archives at the University of Southern Mississippi, Minnie Watson at Tougaloo College Special Collections, Ed Frank at the University of Memphis Special Collections, the Memphis and Shelby County Room at the Memphis Public Library, the Madison County–Canton Public Library, and the Mississippi Department of Archives and History. Interlibrary Loan Services at the University of Memphis made much of my basic research possible, and whenever I picked up another stack of books or reel of microfilm, Frankie Perry made me smile.

Thanks in part to generous support from the Department of History at the University of Memphis, I researched in collections around the country. My gratitude to Allen Fisher at the Lyndon Baines Johnson Library and Museum, Cynthia Lewis and Elaine Hall at the King Library and Archives at the Martin Luther King, Jr. Center for Nonviolent Change, the Manuscript Division at the Library of Congress, Special Collections at Stanford University, the Southern Historical Collection at the University of

North Carolina at Chapel Hill, the Wisconsin Historical Society, the Schomburg Center for Research in Black Culture, Special Collections at the University of California–Los Angeles, the Rare Book and Manuscript Library at Columbia University, the Paley Center for the Media, the Auburn Avenue Research Library, and the Manuscript, Archives, and Rare Book Library at Emory University. I also obtained materials from Swarthmore College Special Collections, thanks to Wendy Chmielewski; from Duquesne University Special Collections, thanks to Tom White; and from Raynor Memorial Library at Marquette University, thanks to Philip Runkel.

The most challenging and rewarding aspect of the research was conducting one hundred interviews, almost all with participants in the March Against Fear. Their voices lent me constant reminders of the demonstration's human dimensions. I have deep gratitude for their generosity of time and spirit, and I only wish I could have included more of their compelling stories. My thanks to David Acey, Frankye Adams-Johnson, Harry Benson, Willie Blue, Nina Boal, Becky Brenner, Owen Brooks, Percy Bruce, Robert C.O. Chinn, Jr., Jesse Clear, Charlie Cobb, Clarice Coney, MacArthur Cotton, Courtland Cox, Joseph Crittenden, Phyllis Cunningham, Miriam DeCosta-Willis, Cathy Deppe, John Doar, David Doggett, L. C. Dorsey, Barbara Emerson, Charles Evers, Frank Figgers, Bob Fitch, Dianna Freelon-Foster, Jo Freeman, Jake Friesen, Joanne Gavin, Myrtle Glascoe, Ray Goldstein, George Greene, Dick Gregory, Ira Grupper, Lawrence Guyot, William Hansen, Jerry Harris, Jesse Harris, Bruce Hartford, Matt Herron, Howard Himmelbaum, Cathryn Hyde, Lewis Johnson, C. J. Jones, Wilhelm Joseph, Nicholas Katzenbach, Ed King, Martin Kinney, Samuel "Billy" Kyles, Joyce Ladner, Mel Leventhal, Luther Mallett, Wiley Mallett, Jesse McCullough, Floyd McKissick, Jr., Charmaine McKissick-Melton, Charles McLaurin, James McRee, James Meredith, Harold Middlebrook, Joseph Morse, Jean Morton, Joan Mulholland, Paul Murray, Wendell Paris, Jim Peppler, Grady Poulard, Alvin Poussaint, Dick Reavis, Matthew Rinaldi, Sherwood Ross, Jacob Russell, Otis Sanford, Cleveland Sellers, Yahya Shabazz, Shirley Simmons, John Sisson, Coby Smith, George Smith, Maxine Smith, Art Spielman, Mark Stansbury, John Steele, Dorothy Stewart, William Strickland, Harriet Tanzman, Earl Tucker, Sterling Tucker, Connemara Wadsworth, Denver Washington, Hollis Watkins, Dorothy Weathers, Robert Weeks, Clifton Whitley, Archie Willis, Bill Winfield, Flonzie Brown Wright, Carrie Young, Mitchell Zimmerman, and Lewis Zuchman.

A number of interviewees shared more than their memories: I got tapes of radio dispatches from Sherwood Ross, field recordings from Ray Goldstein, newspaper clippings from Joanne Gavin, and documents from Joan Mulholland. Mel Leventhal, Paul Murray, and Coby Smith all shared drafts of unpublished autobiographical reflections. Jo Freeman not only allowed me to use documents from her personal collection, but also put me in touch with a host of Meredith Marchers.

Cynthia Palmer of the Veterans of the Mississippi Civil Rights Movement deserves my outsize thanks for help in contacting a number of the state's activists. Bruce Hartford, a Meredith Marcher himself, maintains the website www.crmvet.org, which was indispensable for finding march participants. Further thanks to Eric Etheridge, Lance Hill, John Howell, Jim Kates, Betty Garman Robinson, and Jayme Stone for helping me locate potential interviewees.

It was exceptionally satisfying to exchange ideas with a community of scholars. I sharpened some early work on a panel with Anne Choi, Zanice Bond de Perez, and George Sanchez at a meeting of the American Historical Association, as well as through conversations with two different filmmakers, Phil Bertelsen and Clay Haskell. An article on James Meredith and Aubrey Norvell for *The Journal of the Historical Society* depended on close early readings from Scott Marler, Chuck McKinney, Sarah Potter, Johnny Smith, and Dave Welky. My friends at Rhodes College invited me to their "Historians at Work" series, allowing me to discuss chapter drafts with Tim Huebner, Jeff Jackson, Chuck McKinney, and Gail Murray. My colleague Susan O'Donovan dissected a chapter with enthusiasm and intelligence, as did my graduate students Michael Blum, James Conway, Shawn Fisher, and Malcolm Frierson. When it comes to historical narrative, I rely heavily on Randy Roberts and Dave Welky, and both read chapters with typically sharp eyes. I am further thankful for the professional support of Janann Sherman and Beverly Bond.

To my gratitude, historians of Mississippi and the movement welcomed me into their club. Emilye Crosby, Jenny Irons, Todd Moye, and Robby Luckett all read chapters and offered important insights. I also participated on an outstanding panel at a meeting of the Oral History Association with Daphne Chamberlain, Emilye Crosby, Wesley Hogan, and Robby Luckett, which offered the further opportunity to discuss the march with Vincent Harding.

My agent, Matt McGowan, lent his support, intelligence, and calmness. At Farrar, Straus and Giroux, I had the initial fortune of close readings from Paul Elie and Mark Krotov, both of whom delivered feedback that challenged me as a writer and historian. I am especially lucky that the manuscript ended up in the hands of Alex Star. His editorial guidance sharpened this book, to my great appreciation.

As always, I am deeply grateful for my parents, Nishan and Mary Goudsouzian, for everything they do for our family. Further thanks to my brothers, Steve and Haig, my sisters-in-law, Lara and Jarka, my in-laws, Bill and Cherie Dykes, and my extended clan of aunts, uncles, cousins, and rug rats. My wife, Chrystal, to whom this book is dedicated, read every chapter and offered great suggestions. More important, she makes me smile and keeps my life interesting. With the arrival of our two little ones, Leo and Oscar, our journey just keeps getting better.

INDEX

A Note About the Author

Aram Goudsouzian is Chair of the History Department at the University of Memphis. He grew up in Winchester, Massachusetts, and earned his B.A. from Colby College and his Ph.D. from Purdue University. He is the author of *King of the Court: Bill Russell and the Basketball Revolution*, *The Hurricane of 1938*, and *Sidney Poitier: Man, Actor, Icon*. He lives in Memphis, Tennessee.